The Supreme Court:

Law

and Discretion

THE AMERICAN HERITAGE SERIES

THE

American Heritage

Series

UNDER THE GENERAL EDITORSHIP OF

LEONARD W. LEVY AND ALFRED YOUNG

The Supreme Court:

Law

and Discretion

EDITED BY

WALLACE MENDELSON

The University of Texas

THE BOBBS-MERRILL COMPANY, INC.

INDIANAPOLIS *and* NEW YORK

Copyright © 1967 by The Bobbs-Merrill Company, Inc.
Printed in the United States of America
Library of Congress Catalog Card Number: 66-16756
Designed by Stefan Salter Associates

First Printing

For
David Fellman

Not only wise himself,
he brings out wisdom in others.

Democracy is a device that insures
we shall be governed no better than we deserve.

George Bernard Shaw

FOREWORD

The past three decades of the Supreme Court's history have been the most constructive since the time of Marshall. American constitutional law has been modernized, while outworn and reprehensible precedents have fallen like cold clinkers through an open grate. Economic due process and doctrines constricting government powers have been junked, as has a general propensity to void legislation that the justices personally dislike. Plenitude of power, both national and state, and a concept of cooperative federalism now characterize our highest public law. The authority of the government to control the economy is virtually undisputed; from New Deal to Great Society the welfare state has been sustained. At the same time that the Court emancipated government, it vitalized the constitutional law of human rights. Cases involving free speech, the claims of the criminally accused, and equality for racial minorities now bulk largest on the Court's docket. The supreme tribunal has at last caught up with the folklore: it has become the protector of civil liberties and civil rights, sometimes anticipating rather than following the election returns.

The Court itself is almost always in a state of tension. The constructive work of the past three decades has been accompanied by an intramural controversy between an activist wing, led by Justices Black and Douglas, and an anti-activist wing led by Justices Frankfurter and Harlan. Professor Wallace Mendelson describes that controversy and its great importance with a wealth of insight and no little partisanship. Despite a brief genuflection in the direction of Justice Black, Mendelson's spirited advocacy of Frankfurter's position flavors his introduction and headnotes. Readers will have a target worthy of their mettle if they disagree with Mendelson.

But Mendelson has made a rich and judicious selection of the relevant opinions of the Court, thereby opening the evidence for all to evaluate for themselves. And his sampling of the pre-1937 opinions places the controversy within its historical context. Though he cares about technical aspects of the judicial process, he is mainly preoccupied with the piercing questions of a political theorist, for the functions of the Supreme Court cut to the heart of our political democracy. Mendelson, who is an outstanding and prolific constitutional scholar, brings to this study a lawyer's training, experience, and sense of advocacy. But he is also a gifted political scientist with a good sense of history. In his book, *Justices Black and Frankfurter,* he wisely quotes Lincoln's comment that two men may honestly differ about a question and both be right. Readers, unlike judges, do not have to choose one side or another. They may conclude that whether there is, or is not, a right side to the controversy between the activists and anti-activists, it is in the best interests of the nation, as well as of the Court, if both positions are strongly represented and neither long dominates the other.

This book is one of a series of which the aim is to provide the essential primary sources of the American experience, especially of American thought. The series, when completed, will constitute a documentary library of American history, filling a need long felt among scholars, students, librarians, and general readers for authoritative collections of original materials. Some volumes will illuminate the thought of significant individuals, such as James Madison or Louis Brandeis; some will deal with movements, such as those of the Antifederalists or the Populists; others will be organized around special themes, such as Puritan political thought, or American Catholic thought on social questions. Many volumes will take up the large number of subjects traditionally studied in American history for which, surprisingly, there are no documentary anthologies; others will pioneer in introducing contemporary subjects of increasing importance to scholars. The series aspires to maintain the high standards demanded of contemporary editing, providing authentic texts, intelligently and unobtrusively edited. It will also have the distinction of presenting pieces of substantial length which give the full character and flavor of the original. The series will be the most comprehensive and authoritative of its kind.

Leonard W. Levy
Alfred Young

CONTENTS

PART THREE

OFF-THE-BENCH VIEWS   469

EPILOGUE

PROLOGUE

The question that the present times [1955] put into the minds of thoughtful people is to what extent Supreme Court interpretations will or can preserve the free government of which the Court is a part. A cult of libertarian judicial activists now assails the Court almost as bitterly for renouncing power as the earlier "liberals" once did for assuming too much power.

Mr. Justice Robert H. Jackson

It is not new to have controversy centered upon the Court, but the particular point of concern is new. The great controversies in the past—for instance, in 1937, when President Roosevelt tried to alter the personnel on the Court— arose because the Court was *resisting* change in our political system. At the present time [1965], the controversy arises largely because the Court's decisions have been *forcing* change in our general governmental system.

Charles S. Hyneman

PART ONE

INTRODUCTION:

LAW

AND JUDICIAL DISCRETION

Plato's ancient problem still taunts us. Is it "more advantageous to be subject to the best man or the best laws?"[1] We have long since chosen the Rule of Law, but that catchphrase hardly meets the difficulty. As Plato observed, laws are by definition *general* rules. This is their essence and their weakness. Generality deals with averages—the stuff of books. It falters before the complexities of life. In Plato's words, law

> . . . is like an obstinate and ignorant tyrant who will not allow any-
> thing to be done contrary to his appointment or any question to be
> asked—not even in sudden changes of circumstances when some-
> thing happens to be better than what he commanded. . . . The law
> cannot comprehend exactly what is noblest, or more just, or at
> once ordain what is best, for all. The differences of men and ac-
> tions, and the endless irregular movements of human things, do
> not admit of any universal and simple rule. . . . A perfectly simple
> principle can never be applied to a state of things which is the re-
> verse of simple.[2]

---

[1] See Aristotle, *Politics* III.14, 1286a8–9. Cf. Plato, *Statesman* 294A–295C.

[2] *Ibid.*

1

In this view the law's generality and rigidity are at best a rough makeshift, far inferior to the discretion of the philosopher-king, whose pure wisdom would render real justice by giving each man *his* due—not the due of some imaginary average man.[3]

Aristotle anticipated our choice by repudiating the all-wise ruler: "He who bids man rule adds an element of the beast; for desire is a wild beast, and passion perverts the minds of rulers, even when they are the best of men. The law is reason unaffected by desire." It is "intelligence without passion"—the accumulated wisdom of the ages. Yet Aristotle knew, with Plato, that law cannot anticipate the endless combinations and permutations of circumstance.

> . . . All law is universal but about some things it is not possible to make a universal statement which shall be correct. In those cases then in which it is necessary to speak universally but not possible to do so correctly, the law takes the usual [or average] case, though it is not ignorant of the possibility of error.[4]

And so, having rejected the philosopher-king in favor of the Rule of Law, we call him back to limited service—and name him judge. In this capacity he fills the gap between the generalities of law and the specifics of life. Holmes put it neatly: "General propositions do not decide concrete cases"—thus judges must. In short, we have synthesized the wisdom of Plato and the wisdom of Aristotle. We expect judges to enforce the law, but we know they must exercise discretion in applying it to the intractable facts of life. How much law and how much discretion (or Justice) are appropriate in the decision of a concrete case? What are the proper proportions in each of the myriad contexts in which a court must resolve the discrepancy

---

[3] I have drawn heavily here and in the following paragraph upon Charles Howard McIlwain, *The Growth of Political Thought in the West* (New York: The Macmillan Company, 1932), chaps. 2, 3.

[4] See *Nicomachean Ethics*, V.10, 1137b10–15.

between the generic directives of the law and the unanticipated, or imperfectly foreseen, controversies that demand adjudication? This is a basic problem in the judicial process. A tendency one way rather than the other is the difference between our "activist" and our more self-restraining judges.

The written Constitution, of course, does not avoid the basic difficulty. It comes to us, after all, out of the eighteenth century. It was written by men wise enough to know they could not prescribe the details of policy for an "undefined and expanding future." Nor were they in complete accord among themselves on vital issues—just as we are not. And so for the most part they wrote not only in generalities but often in calculated evasion of crucial issues. In short, the Founding Fathers, and the amenders as well, avoided strait-jacketing precision. Their forte was the suggestive, open-ended hint. That is why the Constitution has survived when other works of its age—in medicine, engineering, physics, and what not— have long since passed away.

The Constitution lives on in a changing world because it grows not only by formal amendment but also by "interpretation"—a process in which the judiciary plays a large, yet by no means an exclusive, role. Lawmaking, then, is an inherent and inevitable part of the judicial process. Judges must be more than mimics. Greatness on the bench—as elsewhere— lies in creativity. "We shall know," Cardozo said, "that the process of judging is a phase of a never ending movement, and that something more is expected of those who play their part in it than imitative reproduction, the lifeless repetition of a mechanical routine."[5] *The great problem is this: How shall judges contribute their bit to the law's growth without encroaching upon the legislative function?* Lord Bryce spoke of the need to reconcile tradition and convenience. Dean Pound

---

[5] Benjamin N. Cardozo, *The Growth of the Law* (New Haven, Conn.: Yale University Press, 1924), p. 142.

stressed the competing claims of stability and change. Sir Frederick Pollock wrote brilliantly on judicial valor and caution.

> . . . Obviously, the most abstruse and delicate piercings of modern mathematics or of chemistry could not achieve a formula for an appropriate apportionment of the relevant components of valor and caution, stability and change, tradition and convenience, in the myriad instances that solicit judicial judgment.[6]

The English have avoided part of this problem. Long ago they limited the judge's job by rejecting judicial, in favor of parliamentary, supremacy. Either way, some human agency will have the "last" word.[7] We give it to a Supreme Court; the English give it to a supreme legislature.[8] Assuming that we retain our system, the question is: *How far, and with what materials, shall judges build constitutional law?* For build it they must, in the process called "interpretation."

Two great traditions—the Platonic and the Aristotelian— reveal two quite different responses to these problems. As Mr. Justice Frankfurter put it, with somewhat less than strict neutrality:

> . . . The decisions in the cases that really give trouble rest on judgment, and judgment derives from the totality of a man's nature and experience. Such judgment will be exercised by two

---

[6] Felix Frankfurter, "Judge Henry W. Edgerton," *Cornell Law Quarterly,* 43 (1957), 161.

[7] "That the Courts are especially fitted to be the ultimate arbiters of policy is an intelligent and tenable doctrine. But let them and us face the fact that five judges of the Supreme Court *are* conscious molders of policy instead of impersonal vehicles of revealed truth." Felix Frankfurter, *Law and Politics,* ed. E. F. Prichard, Jr., and A. MacLeish (New York: Harcourt Brace and Company, 1939), p. xiii. The context of this bitter remark was what is now widely considered the laissez-faire abuse of the judicial function by activist judges in the 1920's and 1930's.

[8] Under both systems, of course, the people have the *final* word— through constitutional amendment in this country, and via parliamentary elections in England.

types of men, broadly speaking, but, of course, with varying emphasis—those who express their private views or revelations, deeming them, if not *vox dei,* at least *vox populi;* or those who feel strongly that they have no authority to promulgate law by their merely personal view and whose whole training and proved performance substantially insure that their conclusions reflect understanding of, and due regard for, law as the expression of the views and feelings that may fairly be deemed representative of the community as a continuing society.[9]

It will be noted that here even a convinced anti-activist recognizes the problem is not whether judges shall make or merely find the law, *but whether the judges' creativity shall be guided by their own standards or by those of the community.* Mr. Justice Stone expressed the same thought in less provocative language:

. . . [T]he great constitutional guarantees and immunities of personal liberty and of property, which give rise to the most perplexing questions of constitutional law and government, are but statements of standards to be applied by courts according to the circumstances and conditions which call for their application. The chief and ultimate standard which they exact is reasonableness of official action. . . . They are not statements of specific commands. They do not prescribe formulas as to which governmental action must conform. . . .

Whether the constitutional standard of reasonableness of official action is subjective, that of the judge who must decide, or objective in terms of a considered judgment of what the community may regard as within the limits of the reasonable, are questions which the cases have not specifically decided. Often these standards do not differ. When they do not, it is a happy augury for the development of law which is socially adequate. But the judge whose decision may control government action, as well as in deciding questions of private law, must ever be alert

---

[9] Felix Frankfurter, "Some Observations on the Nature of the Judicial Process of Supreme Court Litigation," *Proceedings of the American Philosophical Society,* 98 (1954), 233.

to discover whether they do differ and, differing, whether his own or the objective standard will represent the sober second thought of the community, which is the firm base on which all law must ultimately rest.[10]

THE ORTHODOX, OR ANTI-ACTIVIST, VIEW

—MR. JUSTICE FRANKFURTER

Judicial review has been a storm center in American history because it involves political choice without commensurate political responsibility. Oliver Wendell Holmes said:

> . . . I think it most important to remember whenever a doubtful case arises with certain analogies on one side and other analogies on the other, that what really is before us is a conflict between two social desires, each of which seeks to extend its dominion over the case, and which cannot both have their way. . . . Where there is doubt the simple tool of logic does not suffice, and even if it is disguised and unconscious, the judges are called on to exercise the sovereign prerogative of choice.[11]

The "great generalities" of the Due Process and the Commerce clauses, for example, can be judicially interpreted in the light of laissez-faire or the opposite. Either way, the people have no direct recourse, for federal judges are not answerable at the polls. As though recognizing this tension between judicial review and popular government, the Supreme Court has long since developed a series of self-restraining principles. Justice Louis Brandeis expressed their essence when he said, "The

---

[10] Harlan F. Stone, "The Common Law in the United States," *Harvard Law Review*, 50 (1936), 23–25.

[11] Oliver Wendell Holmes, *Collected Legal Papers* (New York: Harcourt, Brace and Company, 1920), p. 239. Generally, easy cases are settled in the lower courts; those reaching the Supreme Court do so almost inevitably because they are, as Holmes put it, doubtful.

most important thing we do is not doing."[12] What he meant, of course, is that the more the Court restrains itself, the greater are the freedom and responsibility of the people to govern themselves. He did not suggest that judicial review should be abandoned; after all, it is an established part of our constitutional system. But he recognized that standards for judgment are often vague; that the judiciary has very limited capacity to find and assess all of the data necessary for an informed judgment on the broad social issues behind the immediate claims of litigants; that judicial intervention in such matters is necessarily sporadic, indeed largely haphazard; that judges have no unique immunity from error; and that error in upholding a statute can be corrected by the people far more readily than error raised to the status of a constitutional limitation. And so it is that Brandeis—like Justice Felix Frankfurter—was "forever disposing of issues by assigning [i.e., leaving] their disposition to some other [more politically responsible] sphere of competence."[13] For ultra-activists this, of course, is nothing less than abdication of judicial duty.

Perhaps the most basic of the Court's self-restraining principles is avoidance of unnecessary constitutional commitments. After all, there is fatal "finality" in a decision on the meaning of the Constitution. The only legal way the people can change it is the cumbersome, minority-controlled process of formal amendment. And so, as Mr. Justice Brandeis summarized the ancient tradition:

> "Considerations of propriety, as well as long-established practice, demand that we refrain from passing upon the constitutionality of an act of Congress unless obliged to do so in the proper performance of our judicial function, when the question is raised

---

[12] See Alexander M. Bickel, *The Unpublished Opinions of Mr. Justice Brandeis* (Cambridge, Mass.: The Belknap Press of Harvard University Press, 1957), chap. 1.

[13] Louis L. Jaffe, "The Judicial Universe of Mr. Justice Frankfurter," *Harvard Law Review*, 62 (1949), 359.

by a party whose interests entitle him to raise it." *Blair v. United States*, 250 U.S. 273, 279. . . .

The Court has frequently called attention to the "great gravity and delicacy" of its function in passing upon the validity of an act of Congress; and has restricted exercise of this function by rigid insistence that the jurisdiction of federal courts is limited to actual cases and controversies; and that they have no power to give advisory opinions. On this ground it has in recent years ordered the dismissal of several suits challenging the constitutionality of important acts of Congress. . . .

The Court developed, for its own governance in the cases confessedly within its jurisdiction, a series of rules under which it has avoided passing upon a large part of all the constitutional questions pressed upon it for decision. They are:

1. The Court will not pass upon the constitutionality of legislation in a friendly, nonadversary, proceeding, declining because to decide such questions "is legitimate only in the last resort, and as a necessity in the determination of real, earnest, and vital controversy between individuals. It never was the thought that, by means of a friendly suit, a party beaten in the legislature could transfer to the courts an inquiry as to the constitutionality of the legislative act." . . .

2. The Court will not "anticipate a question of constitutional law in advance of the necessity of deciding it." . . . "It is not the habit of the court to decide questions of a constitutional nature unless absolutely necessary to a decision of the case." . . .

3. The Court will not "formulate a rule of constitutional law broader than is required by the precise facts to which it is to be applied." . . .

4. The Court will not pass upon a constitutional question although properly presented by the record, if there is also present some other ground upon which the case may be disposed of. This rule has found most varied application. Thus, if a case can be decided on either of two grounds, one involving a constitutional question, the other a question of statutory construction or general law, the Court will decide only the latter. . . . Appeals from the highest court of a state challenging its decision of a question under the federal Constitution are frequently dismissed because

the judgment can be sustained on an independent state ground. . . .

5. The Court will not pass upon the validity of a statute upon complaint of one who fails to show that he is injured by its operation. . . . Among the many applications of this rule, none is more striking than the denial of the right of challenge to one who lacks a personal or property right. Thus, the challenge by a public official interested only in the performance of his official duty will not be entertained. . . . In *Fairchild v. Hughes*, 258 U.S. 126, the Court affirmed the dismissal of a suit brought by a citizen who sought to have the Nineteenth Amendment declared unconstitutional. In *Massachusetts v. Mellon*, 262 U.S. 447, the challenge of the federal Maternity Act was not entertained although made by the commonwealth on behalf of all its citizens.

6. The Court will not pass upon the constitutionality of a statute at the instance of one who has availed himself of its benefits. . . .

7. "When the validity of an act of Congress is drawn in question, and even if a serious doubt of constitutionality is raised, it is a cardinal principle that this Court will first ascertain whether a construction of the statute is fairly possible by which the question may be avoided." . . .[14]

A related principle finds expression in the doctrine of political questions. It holds that courts should avoid involvement in matters traditionally left to legislative policy-making; in matters as to which there are no adequate constitutional standards to guide judicial judgment; or in matters as to which there are no adequate modes of judicial relief. In *Coleman* v. *Miller*,[15] for example, the Court was asked to decide whether a proposed constitutional amendment had expired simply because it had not been ratified by three-fourths of the states in a "reasonable" period of time. Refusing decision, the Court said:

. . . Where are to be found the criteria for such a judicial determination? None are to be found in the Constitution or statute. . . .

[14] Concurring opinion in *Ashwander* v. *TVA*, 297 U.S. 288 (1936).
[15] 307 U.S. 433 (1939).

When a proposed amendment springs from a conception of economic needs, it would be necessary, in determining whether a reasonable time had elapsed since its submission, to consider [among other things] the economic conditions prevailing in the country, whether these had so far changed since the submission as to make the proposal no longer responsive to the conception which inspired it or whether conditions were such as to intensify the feeling of need and the appropriateness of the proposed remedial action. In short, the question of a reasonable time . . . would involve . . . appraisal of a great variety of relevant conditions, political, social, and economic which can hardly be said to be within the appropriate range of evidence receivable in a court of justice. . . . On the other hand, these conditions are appropriate for the consideration of the political departments of the government.

Another principle of judicial restraint recognizes, as Chief Justice John Marshall said, that "The question, whether a law be void for repugnancy to the Constitution, is, at all times, a question of much delicacy, which ought seldom, if ever, to be decided in the affirmative in a doubtful case."[16] As Mr. Justice Washington put it a few years later:

. . . the [constitutional] question which I have been examining is involved in difficulty and doubt. But if I could rest my opinion in favor of the constitutionality of the law . . . on no other ground than this doubt . . . that alone would . . . be a satisfactory vindication of it. It is but a decent respect due to the wisdom, the integrity, and the patriotism of the legislative body, by which any law is passed, to presume in favor of its validity, until its violation of the Constitution is proved beyond all reasonable doubt. This has always been the language of this Court . . . and I know it expresses the honest sentiments of each and every member of the bench.[17]

---

[16] *Fletcher* v. *Peck*, 6 Cranch 87 (1810), reproduced below. To what extent Marshall practiced this principle of judicial restraint is another matter.
[17] *Ogden* v. *Saunders*, 12 Wheaton 213 (1827).

In this view, a legislative act may be held invalid only when the Court is prepared to say that no reasonable mind could uphold the legislative view. For doubt entails choice, and in a democracy choice is the province of the people. This rule of doubt is related to the common-law guide—the reasonable man. Who is this creature? Like jury and legislature, he symbolizes all of us. He is an "external standard," an American Everyman, whereby the troubled judge seeks to guard against his own personal bias in favor of the "views and feelings that may fairly be deemed representative of the community as a continuing society."[18]

Behind all these self-denying ordinances of the orthodox tradition lies a common principle: Government by the judiciary is a poor substitute for government by the people. With this and its supporting doctrines there has been all but universal agreement, on and off the bench. Thus it may be fairly called the orthodox view, though in practice it is not equally respected by all judges. The anti-activist is perhaps a bit more concerned, and a bit more successful, than others in distinguishing between "law" and his own heart's desire. In this no one can hope to be completely successful, yet we know as a matter of experience that some men—on or off the bench— achieve much more objectivity than others. Mr. Justice Frankfurter's opinion in the second *Flag Salute* case[19] is no doubt the classic modern expression of the anti-activist approach.

When Professor Frankfurter left Harvard for the bench in 1939, he was generally considered a liberal—in some quarters even a radical. More recently, he has been accused of conservatism. Yet it seems clear that his basic outlook did not change. In private life he was one of the great liberals of our

---

[18] See note 9, above; and Benjamin N. Cardozo, *The Nature of the Judicial Process* (New Haven, Conn.: Yale University Press, 1921), pp. 88–90.

[19] Reproduced below (*West Virginia State Board of Education* v. *Barnette*).

day. But it is crucial in his philosophy that a judge's private convictions are one thing, his duty on the bench quite another. This was the teaching of Holmes. By failing to heed it, the proprietarians among the "nine old men" destroyed the old Court—just as the libertarians might have destroyed the new one, if they had had enough votes to do so. As both professor and judge, with respect to both liberty and property, Felix Frankfurter was skeptical of government by the judiciary. The judge's job, as he understood it, is to decide "cases" and "controversies," not to create a brave new world—for the legislative function has been given to others:

> . . . As society becomes more and more complicated and individual experience correspondingly narrower, tolerance and humility in passing judgment on the experience and beliefs expressed by those entrusted with the duty of legislating emerge as the decisive factors in . . . adjudication.

He found strange indeed the neo-activist conception of democracy which holds that the people may be trusted with relatively unimportant things but not with those deemed crucial; i.e., with economic problems but not with those of civil liberty.

It is not that the Justice loved liberty less, but rather that he loved democracy—*in all its aspects*—more. The difficulty is that both individual freedom and majority rule are indispensable in the democratic dream. Yet neither can fully prevail without destroying the other. To reconcile them is the basic problem of free government. Chief Justice Stone put it briefly:

> . . . There must be reasonable accommodation between the competing demands of freedom of speech and religion on the one hand, and other interests of society which have some claims upon legislative protection. To maintain the balance between them is essential to the well-ordered functioning of government under a constitution. Neither is absolute, and neither can constitutionally be made the implement for the destruction of the other. That is where the judicial function comes in.

Mr. Justice Frankfurter could not believe or pretend that re-conciliation is achieved via word-play with cliché like "liberty of contract" or "freedom of speech." The single-value, condi-tioned reflex gave him no respite from the painful process of judgment. For he knew, with Holmes, that his own "certitude was not the test of certainty"—that when legislatures disagreed with him they might be right. It followed that judicial intru-sion upon the extrajudicial processes of government was per-missible only in accordance with that ancient tradition of re-straint which all American judges have professed—when their particular "preferred place" values were not at stake.

Obviously Mr. Justice Frankfurter found the crux of the democratic process not so much in its immediate legislative product as in the educative and tension-relieving role of the process itself. A generation ago he wrote:

> . . . In a democracy, politics is a process of popular education—the task of adjusting the conflicting interests of diverse groups, . . . and bending the hostility and suspicion and ignorance en-gendered by group interests . . . toward mutual understanding.

To frustrate these pragmatic political accommodations by judi-cial absolutes is to frustrate our chief device for maintaining peace among men who are deeply divided—sometimes even in their conceptions of right and wrong. Moreover, "holding de-mocracy in judicial tutelage is not the most promising way to foster disciplined responsibility in a free people."

It is ironical that Mr. Justice Frankfurter is now condemned by some for the very quality that won him a seat on the bench —respect for the political processes. It is even more ironical that, for essentially the same approach that earned the con-servative Holmes a liberal reputation, the liberal Frankfurter is now deemed by some a conservative. What has changed, of course, is the relative liberalism of Court and legislatures. But in Felix Frankfurter's view the people's representatives are due equal deference, be they liberal or conservative. He saw as an abiding democratic principle what some find merely a gambit in the great game of power politics.

One need not insist that the Justice never fell short of his own goal. But surely his defections were few, and it may be that he left more choices to the people than has any other great modern judge (except, perhaps, Learned Hand). If this is abdication—as some insist when their "preferred place" values are at stake—it is abdication in favor of "the exhilarating adventure of a free people determining its own destiny."

Plainly Felix Frankfurter was always uneasy with judicial supremacy—whether with respect to personal interests called property, or those called liberty. Of course, the people may go wrong (whatever that means ultimately). Yet, in his view, "to fail and learn by failure is one of the sacred rights of a democracy."

Here, no doubt, is the heart of the matter. Behind all the subtle complexity of his jurisprudence lay a patient confidence in the people. He completely rejected what Professor Berman calls the "underlying assumptions" of Soviet law—that "the citizen is not a mature, independent adult . . . but an immature, dependent child or youth. . . ." And so, from first to last, Felix Frankfurter was wary of judicial efforts to impose Justice on the people—to force upon them "better" government than they were able at the moment to give themselves. It was his deepest conviction that no five men, or nine, are wise enough or good enough to wield such power over an entire nation. Morris R. Cohen put it bluntly: If judges are to govern, they ought to be elected.

JUDICIAL ACTIVISM

There is no official definition of the activist view, because no judge has ever openly professed it. Sympathetic observers, however, suggest that it rejects the orthodox approach as a delusion, if not an outright fraud. They insist that "political choice is inevitable and inherent in judging, and that judges should

make no false pretense of objectivity. Rather . . . they should recognize that they are making policy, and . . . should consciously exercise their judicial power to achieve social justice" —*as they see it.*[20] This, it would seem, is precisely what activist judges do. A judicial activist, for example, does not deny the orthodox duty of respect for community values when the meaning of the Constitution is less than clear. He seems, however, to have a special gift for dissipating doubt. Where others are uncertain, he is apt to find unmistakable guidance in the "plain words" or the "clear intention" of the Founding Fathers, or in history itself, or in some "higher law." So too, when his preferred values are at stake, he is apt to ignore or even reverse the presumption of constitutionality.[21] Since all this is done in the service of Justice (as the activist sees it), he apparently feels no qualms in ignoring "legal technicalities"—i.e., what in other contexts we call the Rule of Law.

In short, professing no explicit overall philosophy, activism is what activism does. And so we turn from theory to the practice of two outstanding activists (and their opponents) in the "interpretation" of the Fourteenth Amendment. No part of the Constitution is better calculated to test a judge's skill and bias, for in some of its major provisions the Fourteenth Amendment is the essence of vagueness. After slavery had been abolished, the Black Codes soon demonstrated that more would be required if Negroes were to enjoy the status of free men. Evidently recognizing the impossibility of itemizing all forms of discrimination—and obviously far from full agreement on precisely what should be outlawed—the framers of the Fourteenth Amendment resorted to broad generalities:

. . . No State shall make or enforce any law which shall abridge the privileges or immunities of citizens of the United States; nor

---

[20] James M. Burns and J. W. Peltason, *Government by the People* (5th ed., Englewood Cliffs, N.J.: Prentice-Hall, Inc., 1963), p. 513.

[21] See Robert G. McCloskey, *The American Supreme Court* (Chicago: The University of Chicago Press, 1960), pp. 191–192; and see *Prince* v. *Massachusetts*, 321 U.S. 158 (1944).

shall any State deprive any person of life, liberty, or property without due process of law; nor deny to any person within its jurisdiction the equal protection of the laws.

In avoiding the straitjacket of precision, they risked the opposite danger of vacuity. What, after all, are the "privileges and immunities" of United States citizenship? What "process" is "due" in what circumstances? And what is "equal protection"? (Plato suggested that the equal treatment of unequals is the ultimate injustice.) Surely none of these terms is self-defining or self-applying.

MR. JUSTICE FIELD—
THE OLD ECONOMIC ACTIVISM

One of the threads in the fabric of American history is the clash between political and economic power. The early struggle between Jeffersonians and Hamiltonians made it clear that victory went to the side that could win judicial support. Or perhaps it is more accurate to say that a growing faith in democracy insured the supremacy of political power unless the judiciary intervened. The industrial revolution following the Civil War posed the old problem in modern terms. Large-scale business provoked social pressures that eventually brought legislation and then litigation. The problem is epitomized in the Granger movement. Prosperity springing from the Civil War and the railroad boom was followed in the seventies by severe agrarian depression. Farmers found that freight charges were often discriminatory, if not extortionate, and that monopolistic practices were destroying the free, open market. For relief, they turned to government and got the famous Granger legislation. This "hayseed socialism" raised in modern form the ancient problem of how far the community may interfere with private property in the interest of public well-being. More specifically, could the states regulate rates charged by

railroads and grain elevators? To Chief Justice Waite and his Court, this was essentially a political, not a legal, issue: "We know that this [regulatory] power may be abused; but that is no argument against its existence. For protection against abuses by legislatures the people must resort to the polls, not to the courts."[22] This, of course, is a classic expression of the orthodox, or anti-activist, position.

Justice Stephan J. Field had a different view: "If this [the majority position] be sound law, if there be no protection, either in the principles upon which our republican government is founded or in the prohibitions of the Constitutions against such invasion of private rights, all property and all business in the State are held at the mercy of a majority of its legislators. . . ."[23]

Field's "ifs" raised weighty questions. Was there in fact anything in the federal Constitution (or in "republican principles") limiting or forbidding state regulation of *local* economic affairs? Business lawyers found no hope in the original document. For want of better authority, they turned to the vague generalities of the Fourteenth Amendment, though the Supreme Court—speaking of all three Civil War Amendments —had recently said:

> . . . no one can fail to be impressed with the one pervading purpose found in them all, lying at the foundation of each, and without which none of them would have been even suggested; we mean the freedom of the slave race, the security and firm establishment of that freedom, and the protection of the newly made freeman. . . .[24]

Could a constitutional amendment devised in broad generalities for settlement of the slavery problem somehow be converted into a shield for businessmen against the wrath of

---

[22] *Munn* v. *Illinois*, 94 U.S. 113, 126ff. (1877). This was the leading "Granger case."
[23] *Ibid.* 136ff.
[24] *Slaughter-House Cases*, 16 Wallace 36 (1873).

outraged consumers? In a dissenting opinion, Mr. Justice Field found the nexus between free private enterprise and the Fourteenth Amendment. The latter, he said, had been adopted to give legal effect to the "declaration of 1776 of inalienable rights."[25] As he put it more fully in a later case:

> . . . Among these . . . rights, as proclaimed in that great document, is the right of men to pursue their happiness, by which is meant the right to pursue any lawful business or vocation, in any manner not inconsistent with the equal rights of others, which may increase their prosperity or develop their faculties, so as to give them their highest enjoyment.[26]

In short, as Field saw it, the Fourteenth Amendment incorporated the Declaration of Independence, which in turn embraced laissez-faire as indispensable to the pursuit of happiness. Today, of course, all this seems fantastic, if not desecratory. Field obviously saw "economic liberty" in a light that has long since dimmed. He saw it as William Graham Summer saw it.[27] According to this view, material progress is the basic moral norm. The man who contributes greatly to the community's economic wealth is the good man; he who hampers it is bad. Such an ethic inevitably exalts property, profits, and the great business leaders who prove their Darwinian fitness in the struggle of business life. These tested captains of industry alone know what is best for society in the crucial area of worldly progress. Here the democratic dogma of popular rule is not merely nonsense, it is pernicious. Economic freedom is the ultimate freedom, to which generally all other liberty must be subordinated. Equality means equality to acquire and hold property. Departures from laissez-faire are "undemo-

---

25 *Ibid.*

26 *Butchers' Union Co.* v. *Crescent City Co.*, 111 U.S. 746, 757 (1884).

27 I am much indebted here to Robert G. McCloskey, *American Conservatism in the Age of Enterprise* (Cambridge, Mass.: Harvard University Press, 1951), chap. 4.

cratic." All this to the end that mankind may rise above starvation standards. In the words of Daniel Webster, property is the "fund out of which the means of protecting life and liberty are usually furnished. We have no experience . . . that any other rights are safe where property is not safe."[28] In this view, the acquisitive instinct is not raw selfishness but a blessing in disguise. Along with property, it is the foundation of social morality, the mainstay of civilization itself, man's chief hope for security in a harsh and turbulent world. So viewed, of course, property and free private enterprise deserve a "preferred place" among the values protected by the Constitution.

Yet even on this premise Field's position is difficult to comprehend. He did not entirely repudiate state police power to protect the public morals, health, safety, and welfare. His concern, it would seem, was merely to fix "appropriate" (that is, Field-approved) limits. Thus, he alone protested when Pennsylvania intruded upon the oleomargarine industry to protect "the public health and to prevent adulteration of dairy products and fraud in the sale thereof."[29] For Field, the regulation "rested simply upon the fact that it had pleased the legislature. . . . This was not enough. The lawmakers should have been happy that science had discovered a new food! The liberty of the Due Process Clause means "something more than freedom from physical restraint or imprisonment"; it includes the right to "pursue one's happiness." Yet, whereas it was improper legislative whim to regulate grain elevators and oleomargarine, it was permissible to control alcoholic beverages[30] and to require railroads to erect cattle guards along their rights of way.[31] Those who fail to see the distinctions that seemed so crucial to Field in these cases need not despair. The

[28] *Journal of Debates and Proceedings in the Convention of Delegates Chosen to Revise the Constitution of Massachusetts, 1820* (1853), p. 312.

[29] *Powell v. Pennsylvania,* 127 U.S. 678 (1888).

[30] *Crowley v. Christensen,* 137 U.S. 86 (1890).

[31] *Missouri Pacific Ry. v. Humes,* 115 U.S. 512 (1885).

Supreme Court also failed to see them, and upheld the legislature in each instance. Similarly—over Field's bitter dissents
—it upheld Congress on the crucial issues of legal tender,[32]
the sinking funds,[33] and the telegraph lines.[34]

America was undergoing the *sturm und drang* of a great
socio-economic revolution that transformed it in a few decades
from a simple agrarian fledgling to an urban-industrial giant.
New needs clashed with old values; ideals that we had cherished were in danger. Accommodation and adjustment were
inevitable. How could this be accomplished without legislation? Conditions being new, we would have to experiment.
Legislatures then ought to be free of dogmatic, frontier-
inspired, conceptual limitations—or so the Court believed.

While Chief Justice Waite presided on the bench (1874–
1888) judicial restraint prevailed. As a recent biographer put it,
Waite "held to a simple—but never disproven—faith that the
people, acting through legislatures, know their own best interest. Because of this and because he trusted the legislative
process to provide its own self-correctives, Waite believed that
judges ought to be chary about upsetting legislative decisions.
Moreover, [he] displayed a receptivity for realities dictated
by facts, a fact consciousness, that in the hands of articulate
judicial craftsmen such as . . . Holmes and Brandeis has become a characteristic of the best in the modern Supreme
Court's decisions."[35]

It comes, perhaps, to this: When Waite faced a constitutional
challenge to legislation, he tried to understand the real-life
problem as it was thrust upon the legislature, and to appraise
the legislative solution in that light. Field, on the other hand,

---

[32] *Legal Tender Cases*, 12 Wallace 457 (1871).

[33] See *The Sinking Fund Cases*, 99 U.S. 700 (1879), reproduced
on following pages.

[34] *Pensacola Telegraph Co.* v. *Western Union*, 96 U.S. 1 (1877).

[35] Peter C. Magrath, *Morrison R. Waite* (New York: The Macmillan
Company, 1963), p. 320.

seemed to see a statute as an abstraction completely divorced from its earthly setting. Thus, almost inevitably its earthbound pragmatic balance of rival social interests would violate Field's ideal universe. And so, year after year, he persisted with an avalanche of Platonic dissents, repeating endlessly in one form or another: "I do not give any weight to *Munn* v. *Illinois*"—i.e., the Granger cases.[36] Fortified by the righteousness of Truth itself—*and the rising forces of the business community*—Field ultimately prevailed. By the time of his retirement in 1897 his views were largely the law of the land. Judicial respect for the pragmatic processes of the legislative way of life had dimmed.

Mr. Justice Field was a classic judicial activist. Tailoring history to his purpose, he found that the Declaration of Independence was incorporated in the Fourteenth Amendment. This protected the businessman's "pursuit of happiness," but it did not shield Negroes from discrimination—despite their having been created equal.[37] For Field, right and wrong were clear and obvious absolutes; there were no shadings in between. It must never have occurred to him, as it did to Holmes, that "certitude is not the test of certainty." He did not merely believe that he was right, he "knew" it. His forte was the organ-toned, Platonic abstraction unchecked by the rude realities of life. In Field's opinions there is little evidence that he ever appreciated the practical problems reflected in the legislation he so rhetorically dispatched, or that he ever saw more than one side of a controversy. Unaffected by reality, and garbed in Truth, his opinions had an air of conviction and righteousness. Beside them, the Court's conscientious self-restraint was like a candle in the sun. He could thus take and tenaciously hold extreme positions that were simply untenable in terms of history, precedent, or the purposes of those who

---

[36] See *Ruggles* v. *Illinois,* 108 U.S. 526, 541 (1883).

[37] See Field's position in *Ex parte Virginia,* 100 U.S. 339 (1880), reproduced on following pages.

gave us the Fourteenth Amendment. In large part his views (as to both property and Negro liberty) ultimately prevailed—for a time—because for a time America's business was business.

MR. JUSTICE BLACK—

LIBERTARIAN ACTIVISM

The Great Depression and the Court fight in the mid-1930's destroyed all that Field had stood for on the bench. Thanks principally to Justices Holmes, Brandeis, Stone, and Cardozo, property (or more broadly, private enterprise) had been dislodged from its "preferred position" in the Fourteenth Amendment before Hugo Black became a Justice in 1937.[38] Yet it was (and is) still sufficiently there to provide what little comfort may be found in the old principle that the Court will veto economic regulations that no reasonable mind could support.[39] Even this, however, was too much for Mr. Justice Black. Apparently determined to read all substantive economic protection out of the Fourteenth Amendment, and to give "personal liberty" special protection, he early insisted that the corporation was not a "person," as that term is used in the Due Process Clause.[40] Because corporations conduct most American business, this would go far to achieve the apparent goal; but it would not do so completely. A few months later the Justice had a more comprehensive solution. Shifting from Due Process (which protects "property"), he resorted to the Privileges and Immunities of Citizenship Clause (in which the word "property" does not appear).[41] Both of these apparent efforts to

---

[38] See, for example, *Nebbia* v. *New York*, 291 U.S. 502 (1934); *West Coast Hotel Co.* v. *Parrish*, 300 U.S. 379 (1937).

[39] No legislative act has been held invalid on "substantive due process" (laissez-faire) grounds since 1936.

[40] *Connecticut General Life Insurance Co.* v. *Johnson*, 303 U.S. 85 (1938).

[41] *Hague* v. *CIO*, 307 U.S. 496, 500 (1939).

protect only "personal" freedom from state intrusion collapsed in the *Bridges* and *Times-Mirror* cases involving free speech and press.[42] The difficulty was that the claimants were respectively an *alien* and a *corporation*—and both of these Black had already in effect excluded from Fourteenth Amendment protection. A few years later, in *Adamson*,[43] the Justice tried another tack. "Separately and as a whole" the three general clauses of the Fourteenth Amendment incorporate not the Declaration of Independence but the Bill of Rights—no more and no less.[44] This was not whim or heart's desire, but historic fact as Black saw it. For Mr. Justice Frankfurter and the Court it was improvised history,[45] made to order to accommodate a libertarian conception of what the Constitution ought to mean. In any event, the effect of Black's new position was that the great "personal" freedoms would be protected against state (as well as federal) interference, and laissez-faire be damned. For surely no one now could dream that the Bill of Rights stooped so low as to encompass "economic liberty" (whatever Field may have thought of the Declaration of Independence).

Only one judge—Douglas—has joined Black in these views; and no one has followed them consistently. Both Justices ignored their corporation gambit in order to protect freedom of the press in the *Times-Mirror* case (though later they revived it when only "material" interests were at stake).[46] So, too, on occasion they have found protection in the Fourteenth Amendment for interests not covered in the old Bill of Rights—equal

---

[42] 314 U.S. 252 (1941). These cases are reproduced on following pages.

[43] 332 U.S. 46, 71 (1947). This case is reproduced on following pages.

[44] *Barron* v. *Baltimore,* 7 Peters 243 (1833), had long since recognized that the Bill of Rights in the federal Constitution applies only to the national government.

[45] See particularly Frankfurter's concurring opinion in *Adamson;* and Charles Fairman, "Does the Fourteenth Amendment Incorporate the Bill of Rights?", *Stanford Law Review,* 2 (1949), 5.

[46] *Wheeling Steel Corp.* v. *Glander,* 337 U.S. 562, 576 (1949).

legislative apportionment, for example.[47] The Court's more viable and more flexible *Palko* theory of the Fourteenth Amendment avoids these embarrassments. It recognizes that all *basic* freedoms (whether or not expressly mentioned in the Bill of Rights) are included in the broad generalities of the Civil War Amendment. But it has allowed the states some leeway to meet new problems and develop new conceptions of fair play in areas where the Bill of Rights reflects not basic principles of freedom but the peculiarities of the time and place from which it sprang.[48] In short, the Court's approach accepts the great generalities of the Fourteenth Amendment as embodying a dynamic conception of basic fairness—not the limited views of the eighteenth century.[49]

The Bill of Rights, for example, requires indictment by grand jury, and jury trials in *all* criminal cases and in civil cases involving more than twenty dollars. The grand jury is an expensive and cumbersome device, inspired by social conditions that no longer exist. Even when the Fourteenth Amendment was adopted, almost half of the ratifying states had largely abandoned the grand jury. For minor offenses at the state and local level the petit jury has become all but obsolete. It is not to be forgotten that the right to jury trials in *all* federal prosecutions was adopted in 1791 on the accurate assumption that there would be relatively few categories of federal crime, and that those few would be weighty. To insist upon a right to trial by jury for *all* petty state and local offenses would be as great a perversion as to insist upon it in all state and local civil cases involving more than twenty dollars. The significance of

---

[47] *Reynolds* v. *Sims*, 377 U.S. 533 (1964). This case is reproduced on following page.

[48] See *Palko* v. *Connecticut*, 302 U.S. 319 (1937); and Frankfurter's concurring opinion in *Adamson* v. *California*, 332 U.S. 46 (1947), reproduced below.

[49] It is also calculated to leave local government to the states in matters in which something less than basic human freedom is involved.

that sum was one thing in 1791; it is something quite different now! Just as Judge Black sometimes finds more in the Fourteenth Amendment than his *Adamson* rule permits, so (one suspects) he would feel compelled to find less should these jury problems arise in litigation.

Disturbed, no doubt, by Field's perversion of the Fourteenth Amendment, Mr. Justice Black apparently wants to forestall future perversions by tying that amendment to the "specific" provisions of the Bill of Rights. This procedure would seem to be not only a perversion of history[50] but an effort to find certainty where none exists. Consider, for example, the First Amendment's guarantee of freedom of speech and press. For years all members of the Court have recognized that this is a basic liberty protected by the Fourteenth Amendment. But even Justices Black and Douglas—the two great activist, libertarian leaders of the modern Court—are not in full agreement on the meaning and application of this basic concept.[51] Ironically, Black resorts to "history" to get the First Amendment into the Fourteenth; then he completely ignores the historic meaning—or nonmeaning—of the First Amendment. As a great modern libertarian scholar ultimately admitted:

> . . . The truth is, I think, that the framers had no very clear idea as to what they meant by "the freedom of speech or of the press," but we can say . . . with reasonable assurance . . . [that] the freedom which Congress was forbidden to abridge was not, for them, some absolute concept which had never existed on earth.[52]

---

[50] See Page 23, note 45. Charles Fairman, "Does the Fourteenth Amendment Incorporate the Bill of Rights?"

[51] See, for example, *Communist Party* v. *SACB*, 367 U.S. 1 (1961); *Barr* v. *Mateo*, 360 U.S. 564 (1959); *Tenney* v. *Brandhove*, 341 U.S. 367 (1951). And for a brief note on the disagreements *among famous libertarians*, beginning with Milton and Mill, as to the meaning of free utterance, see Wallace Mendelson, "On the Meaning of the First Amendment: Absolutes in the Balance," *California Law Review*, 50 (1962), 821.

[52] Zechariah Chafee, book review, *Harvard Law Review*, 62 (1949), 891. See also Leonard W. Levy, *Legacy of Suppression* (Cambridge, Mass.: The Belknap Press of Harvard University Press, 1960).

Indeed, there is probably no more equivocal word in the En-lish language than "freedom." To borrow from Lincoln, the world has never had a good definition of it; what is freedom for the lion is death for the lamb. Even so stout a libertarian as Alexander Meiklejohn has chided those who insist that the words "abridging freedom of speech or of press" are "plain words, easily understood."[53] Surely the Framers would have communicated more clearly if they had omitted the ambiguous word and stated simply: "Congress shall pass no law abridging speech or press." This suggests, of course, that they used the word "freedom" as a limiting, not an enlarging, term—one that referred to the Blackstonian conception of free utterance, which prevailed in the late eighteenth century.[54]

Deviled by the ambiguous generalizing of the First Amend-ment, the Court (inspired quite plainly by Frankfurter) weighs the competing interests of each concrete case in their real-life setting[55]—remembering that in a democracy "personal freedom" must enjoy a special respect, yet not forgetting the presumption in favor of legislative settlements. Thus, in *Beau-harnais*,[56] the Court upheld an Illinois group-libel law as ap-plied to a fanatic vilification of the Negro people. Considering the states' long and bloody experience with race riots (just as Waite explored real-life problems in *Munn* v. *Illinois*), the Court observed, through Mr. Justice Frankfurter:

> No one will gainsay that it is libelous falsely to charge another with being a rapist, robber, carrier of knives and guns, user of marijuana. The precise question before us, then, is whether the protection of "liberty" in the Due Process Clause of the Four-

---

[53] Alexander Meiklejohn, "The First Amendment Is an Absolute," in *1961 Supreme Court Review*, ed. Philip Kurland (Chicago: The Univer-sity of Chicago Press, 1961), p. 247.

[54] See Leonard W. Levy, *Legacy of Suppression.*

[55] More accurately, it applies the "reasonable man" test to the balance struck by the political branches.

[56] *Beauharnais* v. *Illinois,* 343 U.S. 250 (1952).

teenth Amendment prevents a State from punishing such libels—
as criminal libel has been defined, limited and constitutionally
recognized time out of mind—directed at designated collectivities
and flagrantly disseminated. There is even authority, however
dubious, that such utterances were also crimes at common law.
It is certainly clear that some American jurisdictions have sanctioned their punishment under ordinary criminal libel statutes.
We cannot say, however, that the question is concluded by history and practice. But if an utterance directed at an individual
may be the object of criminal sanctions, we cannot deny to a
State power to punish the same utterance directed at a defined
group, unless we can say that this is a wilful and purposeless
restriction unrelated to the peace and well-being of the State.

Illinois did not have to look beyond her own borders or await
the tragic experience of the last three decades to conclude that
wilful purveyors of falsehood concerning racial and religious
groups promote strife and tend powerfully to obstruct the mani-
fold adjustments required for free, ordered life in a metropolitan,
polyglot community. From the murder of the abolitionist Love-
joy in 1837 to the Cicero riots of 1951, Illinois has been the
scene of exacerbated tension between races, often flaring into
violence and destruction. In many of these outbreaks, utterances
of the character here in question, so the Illinois legislature could
conclude, played a significant part. The law was passed on June
29, 1917, at a time when the State was struggling to assimilate
vast numbers of new inhabitants, as yet concentrated in discrete
racial or national or religious groups—foreign-born brought to
it by the crest of the great wave of immigration, and Negroes
attracted by jobs in war plants and the allurements of northern
claims. Nine years earlier, in the very city where the legislature
sat, what is said to be the first northern race riot had cost the
lives of six people, left hundreds of Negroes homeless and
shocked citizens into action far beyond the borders of the State.
Less than a month before the bill was enacted, East St. Louis
had seen a day's rioting, prelude to an outbreak, only four days
after the bill became law, so bloody that it led to Congressional
investigation. A series of bombings had begun which was to cul-
minate two years later in the awful race riot which held Chicago

in its grip for seven days in the summer of 1919. Nor have tension and violence between the groups defined in the statute been limited in Illinois to clashes between whites and Negroes.

In the face of this history and its frequent obligato of extreme racial and religious propaganda, we would deny experience to say that the Illinois legislature was without reason in seeking ways to curb false or malicious defamation of racial and religious groups, made in public places and by means calculated to have a powerful emotional impact on those to whom it was presented. . . .

It may be argued, and weightily, that this legislation will not help matters; that tension and on occasion violence between racial and religious groups must be traced to causes more deeply embedded in our society than the rantings of modern Knownothings. Only those lacking responsible humility will have a confident solution for problems as intractable as the frictions attributable to differences of race, color or religion. This being so, it would be out of bounds for the judiciary to deny the legislature a choice of policy, provided it is not unrelated to the problem and not forbidden by some explicit limitation on the State's power. That the legislative remedy might not in practice mitigate the evil, or might itself raise new problems, would only manifest once more the paradox of reform. It is the price to be paid for the trial-and-error inherent in legislative efforts to deal with obstinate social issues. . . .

Long ago this Court recognized that the economic rights of an individual may depend for the effectiveness of their enforcement on rights in the group, even though not formally corporate, to which he belongs. American Steel Foundries v. Tri-City Central Trades Council, 257 U.S. 184, 189. Such group-protection on behalf of the individual may, for all we know, be a need not confined to the part that a trade union plays in effectuating rights abstractly recognized as belonging to its members. It is not within our competence to confirm or deny claims of social scientists as to the dependence of the individual on the position of his racial or religious group in the community. It would, however, be arrant dogmatism, quite outside the scope of our authority in passing on the powers of a State, for us to deny that the

Illinois Legislature may warrantably believe that a man's job and his educational opportunities and the dignity accorded him may depend as much on the reputation of the racial and religious group to which he willy-nilly belongs, as it does on his own merits. This being so, we are precluded from saying that speech concededly punishable when immediately directed at individuals cannot be outlawed if directed at groups with whose position and esteem in society the affiliated individual may be inextricably involved.

We are warned that the choice we permit the Illinois legislature here may be abused, that the law may be discriminatorily enforced; prohibiting libel of a creed or of a racial group, we are told, is but a step from prohibiting libel of a political party. Every power may be abused, but the possibility of abuse is a poor reason for denying Illinois the power to adopt measures against criminal libels sanctioned by centuries of Anglo-American law. "While this Court sits" it retains and exercises authority to nullify action which encroaches on freedom of utterance under the guise of punishing libel. Of course discussion cannot be denied and the right, as well as the duty, of criticism must not be stifled.

Earlier, in the first *Flag Salute* case,[57] Mr. Justice Black had endorsed this humilitarian approach toward doubtful legislation. He was not far from it in a 1946 case involving an effort by a company town to outlaw religious proselytizing on its streets:

> . . . When we balance the constitutional rights of owners of property against those of the people to enjoy freedom of press and religion, as we must here, we remain mindful of the fact that the latter occupy a preferred position. . . .[58]

Thereafter—beginning perhaps with the *Douds* case[59] in 1950 —the First Amendment seems to have acquired a fresh clarity for Mr. Justice Black. Another crisis was upon us. In Field's

---

[57] *Minersville School District* v. *Gobitis,* 310 U.S. 586 (1940).

[58] *Marsh* v. *Alabama,* 326 U.S. 501 (1946).

[59] *American Communication Assn.* v. *Douds,* 339 U.S. 382 (1950).

day the problem had been industrial revolution. Now it was the cold war with Communism. Each presented a strange new challenge to old democratic values. Each, as the Court saw it, required adjustments and revaluations that were best left to the political processes. Mr. Justice Black, of course, thought otherwise, as had Field in the earlier crisis. After a laborious series of experiments—not unlike his search for meaning in the Fourteenth Amendment—Black rejected the balancing of interests, and resorted to Platonic absolutes: The "Bill of Rights means what it says"; "'no law abridging' mean[s] *no law abridging"*; the balancing of interests violates "the genius of our *written* Constitution"; the First Amendment's "unequivocal command that there shall be no abridgment of free speech and assembly shows that the men who drafted our Bill of Rights did all the balancing that was to be done in this field"; government cannot punish people for talking about public affairs "whether or not such discussion incites to action, legal or illegal." In short, "the First Amendment with the Fourteenth, 'absolutely' forbids [laws punishing public discussion—here race libel] without any 'ifs' or 'buts' or 'whereases.'"[60] In this view, even the universally traditional laws against libel, slander, and obscenity are unconstitutional—and so, apparently, are the customary powers of courts to protect judicial trials from the perversion of trial-by-newspaper. Repudiating the "sophisticated" view that "you cannot have any absolute 'thou shalt nots,'" Mr. Justice Black concludes: "I have an idea there are some absolutes. I do not think I am far in that respect from the Holy Scriptures."[61]

---

[60] The language quoted in this and the preceding sentence is from Mr. Justice Black in *Konigsberg* v. *California,* 366 U.S. 36 (1961); *Smith* v. *California,* 361 U.S. 147 (1959); *Barenblat* v. *United States,* 360 U.S. 109 (1959); *Yates* v. *United States,* 354 U.S. 298 (1957); *Beauharnais* v. *Illinois,* 343 U.S. 250 (1952).

[61] See the *Bridges* and *Times-Mirror* cases reproduced on following pages; and Edmond Cahn, "Mr. Justice Black and First Amendment 'Absolutes': A Public Interview," *New York University Law Review,* 37 (1962), 549.

Few generous souls can contemplate Mr. Justice Black's rhetoric in favor of "unrestricted" utterance without a thrilling rededication to the cause of freedom.[62] But one suspects that his words acquire their power as Field's did—by their platonic avoidance of the rude stuff of mundane life. Mr. Justice Jackson's comment on an activist opinion in which Black joined is relevent here:

> [It] . . . reverses this conviction by reiterating generalized approbations of freedom of speech with which, in the abstract, no one will disagree. Doubts as to their applicability are lulled by avoidance of more than passing reference to the circumstances of Terminiello's speech and judging it as if he had spoken to persons as dispassionate as empty benches, or like modern Demosthenes practicing his Philippics on a lonely seashore.
>
> But the local court that tried Terminiello was not indulging in theory. It was dealing with a riot and with a speech that provoked a hostile mob and incited a friendly one, and threatened violence between the two.[63]

Plainly Justices Black and Field were spared the doubts that troubled most of their early colleagues. Each had a noble vision of the betterment of mankind—and though their "absolutes"

---

[62] Some insist that Mr. Justice Black is a great judge because his words teach respect for "personal freedom." Others find that his deeds—like Field's—teach disdain for law, and for the capacity of the people to govern themselves in crucial matters.

[63] *Terminiello* v. *Chicago*, 337 U.S. 1, 13 (1949). The accused (a suspended priest) spoke in an auditorium to about eight hundred persons under the sponsorship of the Christian Veterans of America. His remarks, according to Mr. Justice Jackson (just returned from the Nürnberg trials), "followed, with fidelity that is more than conincidental, the pattern of European fascist leaders." Linking New Dealers, Jews, and Communists together as common "conspirators," his talk was rife with racial and religious provocation. Outside, a hostile crowd (Communist-led, according to Terminiello) tried to force the doors. The police prevented an open clash, but there was substantial violence, including the smashing of doors and windows. Mr. Justice Jackson saw in this episode a struggle between "totalitarian groups" for what Hitler called "the conquest of the streets."

were incompatible, each found his (and his alone) embedded in the Fourteenth Amendment. Each no doubt had truth by the tail: property and personal liberty *are* basic in the American way of life, yet inevitably they collide with one another and with other basic values.[64]

Both judges spoke with a moral fervor that paled the Court's initial sober self-restraint. Each necessarily relied upon "right" rather than precedent, and upon his own imaginative version of history. Each saw the vexing new problems of his day in terms that defied reality as others saw it. Each, confident that he knew the Truth, could dispense with the reasonable man, the balancing of interests, and the presumption of validity. These are tools for men who, like Waite and Frankfurter, are apt to see crucial values on both sides of a case; who seldom find plain answers to modern problems in the broad generalities of the old Constitution; who question the propriety of intrusion upon the political processes in doubtful cases; who are not satisfied that judges have better access to Truth, or more immunity from error, than the people themselves.

Surely the old Constitution speaks more ambiguously and requires more outside help than Justices Field and Black admit. What human beings wrote in the eighteenth century, or even in 1868, does not and could not give plain (or absolute) answers to Atomic Age problems without contemporary assistance.

What, then, is the Rule of Law in the judicial process? For anti-activists, it entails avoidance of pretense that the Constitution lays down unmistakable rules of decision for difficult cases. It means that, in the adaptive process by which the old document survives in a changing world, courts must play a second-

---

[64] Note, for example, the clash between freedom of the press and the right to a fair trial, as seen in *Bridges* and *Times-Mirror,* reproduced below. Consider also the problem of free utterance vis-à-vis a reputation destroyed by libel or slander. The story of a famous libel case is told in Louis Nizer, *My Life in Court* (Garden City, N.Y.: Doubleday & Company, Inc., 1961).

ary role—lest society be confined by the limited wisdom of a few independent judges. It means that when judges do intervene, their decisions should turn on fully disclosed, rational grounds within the accepted legal tradition—not on unavowed sympathy for this or that class of litigants. It means that successive decisions should be rationally coherent, that judges should respect their own precedents. But coherence and respect for past commitments do not require blindness to changing social needs. We know now that law must be stable; yet it cannot stand still. To reconcile these opposing claims, antiactivist judges make changes in the law—but (save the rare case) only within accepted presuppositions and only to vitalize existing rules. They do not invoke new major premises. Rather, they build inductively with existing materials, to provide continuity without rigidity and to preserve for the people alone the power to make major shifts in social policy. They do not worship the past, but they know that without respect for precedent, judicial law is lawless—i.e., *ad hoc* and retrospective, providing no standards by which men can order their affairs. Continuity, after all, is to judicial law what prospectivity is to legislative law: the means by which men learn what is required of them before they act. For a healthy society, both stability and change are indispensable. Our separation of governmental functions imposes major responsibility upon courts for stability, upon legislatures for change. Such was the teaching of Waite, Holmes, Brandeis, Learned Hand, Stone, Cardozo, and Frankfurter.

MR. JUSTICE BLACK—

THE NEW ECONOMIC ACTIVISM

Some of Mr. Justice Black's many admirers have insisted that whereas judicial activism is undemocratic in the economic realm, it is justified as a bulwark for personal freedom in civil-liberty cases. No doubt much may be said for this double standard, but Mr. Justice Black seems as thoroughly activist in economic cases as in those pertaining to civil liberty. If Judge Field gave business a "preferred position" vis-à-vis labor and the consumer, neo-activism apparently reverses the preference. This seems particularly clear in cases involving the interpretation of congressional legislation.

The antitrust laws, for example, are calculated to protect consumers from business "monopolies" and "monopolistic" practices. In some ten years (1949-1959) the Supreme Court reached a business "monopoly" issue in nineteen Sherman Act cases. Only Mr. Justice Black found a violation of the law in every instance; the Court found otherwise in twenty-six percent of the cases.[65]

During the same period, the Justice displayed a similarly rigorous attitude toward business by voting "pro-labor" in every Fair Labor Standards Act case.[66] Indeed, in the entire eighteen-year history of this act, through April 20, 1959, he voted consistently pro-labor—except in four cases noncontroversial enough to be decided unanimously. The Court voted "pro-business" in one-fourth of the fifty-nine cases in question.

The Federal Employers' Liability Act evidence cases present another facet of what seems to be the "preferred position" that modern judicial activism gives to selected economic interests. FELA contemplates "compensation" for workers' injuries resulting from employer negligence. The cases in question turn upon the adequacy of the evidence offered by the worker to prove the negligence of his employer. Each case, of course, is *sui generis* in that it requires evaluation of the unique circumstances of a particular accident. Surely litigation turning upon

---

[65] For a more extensive study of this and related material discussed briefly here, see Milton Handler, "Recent Antitrust Developments," in *The Record of the Association of the Bar of the City of New York*, 13 (1958), 417–464; and Wallace Mendelson, *Justices Black and Frankfurter: Conflict in the Court* (Chicago: The University of Chicago Press, 1961), chap. 2.

[66] *Ibid.* Cases disposed of summarily are not considered here.

unique fact situations can have small claim upon the time and energy of the nation's highest court—a court whose special function is to expound the *law* in matters of *national* significance. Speaking for a unanimous bench, Mr. Justice Holmes put it simply: "We do not grant a certiorari to review evidence and discuss specific facts."[67] At most, these are matters for state supreme courts or the United States Courts of Appeals. Indeed, this seems to be recognized by all members of the post-1937 Court when *employers* apply for certiorari review in these FELA negligence cases. In short, there are not four judges (four votes control for certiorari purposes) who are willing to impose the alien task of negligence litigation upon the Supreme Court at the request of employees. There have been four however, who frequently have done so at the instance of workers (over sustained dissent). The net result is that employers do not get the added chance to win their cases, but workers often do.[68] Mr. Justice Black has been a leader of the activist four in the FELA cases. His brother Frankfurter has been the chief opponent.[69]

---

[67] *United States* v. *Johnston*, 268 U.S. 220, 227 (1924).

[68] These cases come up to the Supreme Court on the charge that the courts below erred in taking them from juries. Some effort has been made to justify Supreme Court intervention on right-to-jury grounds. *Dice* v. *Akron, C. & Y. Ry.*, 342 U.S. 359, 363 (1952). But no one questions that right in these cases. Conversely, no member of the Supreme Court has questioned the judicial duty to take an FELA case from a jury when the evidence plainly points in one direction. See, for example, *Herdman* v. *Pennsylvania Rd. Co.*, 352 U.S. 518 (1957). Accordingly, we are back to the basic problem—evaluation of the peculiar evidence of each unique industrial accident. (Of course, a different problem is presented when the charge is abuse of judicial discretion by the lower courts.)

If the crux of these FELA cases really is the right to trial by jury, why is it that the same principle, similarly invoked in other types of litigation, does not bring scores of cases to the Supreme Court?

[69] For the classic dissents, see *Wilkerson* v. *McCarthy*, 336 U.S. 53 (1949), and *Rogers* v. *Missouri Pacific Rd. Co.*, 352 U.S. 518 (1957). See also "Certiorari Policy in FELA Cases," *Harvard Law Review*, 69, (1956), 1441.

What happens when these issues come before the Court is revealing. In more than sixty cases, during more than twenty years (1939–1959), Mr. Justice Black never voted against a workman—except once, when the plaintiff on the witness stand had all but repudiated his own claim.[70] The uniformity of Mr. Justice Black's position here—as in the antitrust, FLSA and, indeed, the free utterance cases—suggests that for him (as for Field) the particular facts of a controversy are much less decisive than is the nature of the claim (as a platonic abstraction).

The FELA evidence cases are particularly interesting— and revealing—because they repeat *in reverse* the tendency of pre-1937 judicial activism. For example, during the 1923–1932 terms, certiorari was granted largely at the request of employers, and twenty-nine of the thirty-five decisions were anti-labor.[71] In that era, Mr. Justice Brandeis objected on anti-activist grounds to what he considered an abuse of certiorari, just as Mr. Justice Frankfurter did later. What Professor Freund said of the one is equally relevant to the other: "Despite the human appeal of these cases, Brandeis never allowed himself to regard them as the proper business of the appellate jurisdiction of the Supreme Court."[72]

Present-day activists, who so often find potential negligence on the part of employers, surely give that concept an expanded meaning. Doubtless they do so in response to the modern emphasis on security. The customary concept of negligence (in whose image FELA was adopted) reflects the frontier ideal of individualism. Under it, every man is responsible for his own welfare, and is answerable to no one except for clear, direct, and personal fault. As Mr. Justice Frankfurter has suggested frequently, this may be cruel and outdated—but it is

---

[70] See Wallace Mendelson, *Justices Black and Frankfurter,* page 22.
[71] See Frankfurter and Landis, "Business of the Supreme Court at October Term, 1931," *Harvard Law Review,* 46 (1933), 240–253.
[72] Quoted in *Rogers* v. *Missouri Pacific Rd. Co.,* 353 U.S. 500 (1957).

the basis of FELA. The more modern trend, emphasizing the interdependence of men in industrial society, expects some operations to insure their own risks regardless of fault. Should courts recognize this trend and "interpret" (i.e., rewrite) congressional law accordingly, or should they leave such matters to Congress?—which, after all, meets every year precisely for the purpose of making such changes in legislative law as the community may desire.[73] And what is the point of free utterance (which the activists so gallantly espouse), if its legislative fruits are to be mangled by judicial "interpretation"? Obviously, activists and their opponents react quite differently to these questions.

It is one thing to question Mr. Justice Black's judicial techniques; it is another to discount his ultimate values. If Field gave a "preferred place" to the captains of industry, Black seemed to favor the underdog. Almost inevitably, his opinions sustained workman or consumer vis-à-vis business; the hard-pressed criminal-case defendant; the oppressed religious fanatic; the purveyor of unpopular views. As John Frank put it, with deep esteem born of close association, Mr. Justice Black

> . . . sees the social point of a case, its implications to the lives of people, in a flash; and he has the energy and the ability to devise ways—new ways if need be—of serving what in his conception is the largest good. He is a representative of that movement in American history which we variously call the Grange, the Populists, the New Freedom, and the New Deal. He is one of the tiny handful of representatives of that movement ever to reach the Supreme Court. . . . His significance as a Justice is that he knows what to do with the power thus given him. . . .
>
> In deciding cases Black is frequently a sentimentalist about

---

[73] It is often argued that activism (read judicial lawmaking) is justifiable in constitutional decisions because of the cumbrous, minority-controlled nature of the formal process of constitutional amendment. Obviously, this view has no relevance as a justification for judicial activism vis-à-vis legislation.

people. A vivid and dramatic imagination fills in details that may or may not exist. If a case involves an injured veteran, for example, Black sees the veteran, and his family, and his children. If it should be an injured railroad worker, the man becames as real to Black on an abstract record as if Black himself were making the address to the jury. In these and in the farmer foreclosure cases, now less frequent than they were, Black's sympathies are so completely and automatically enlisted for the unfortunate that he is very nearly as much of a pleader as a judge.[74]

Be it, or be it not, a judge's function, Mr. Justice Black's struggle for civil liberty challenges the conscience of the crowd. His restless probing at the frontiers of freedom may help us to achieve more enlightened notions of public decency —and thus, inevitably, a more enlightened legal order. His humane sympathy for those to whom the world is less than kind, his courage, creative vigor, and perseverance mark him as a dedicated being in pursuit of noble dreams. But is the bench a proper vehicle to use in pursuing them?

Finally, what of the Rule of Law in Mr. Justice Black's jurisprudence? It has been said that his views are too strong to be "judicial," his votes too predictable in nonlegal terms. "Does [his] concept of a dynamic Constitution square with the accepted notion of law?" Here is the answer of an admiring former law clerk:

> . . . It can well be [said] that no other concept is capable of maintaining the rule of law. When judges act as the self-restrained embodiments of "received traditions" they attempt to follow the rule of law; but instead of ruling, the law eventually withers. In a dynamic society the law passively handed down becomes a relic the words of which no longer mean what they used to mean; the Constitution may then be left "a magnificent structure, indeed, to look at, but totally unfit for use." "Our form of government may remain notwithstanding legislation or

---

[74] John P. Frank, *Mr. Justice Black: The Man and His Opinions* (New York: Alfred A. Knopf, 1948), pp. 134, 139.

decision, but, as long ago observed, it is with governments, as with religions, the form may survive the substance of the faith."

To obey the law, to preserve it in any true sense, surely can mean nothing less than to keep its spirit functioning—to see that it continues to achieve the objectives for which it was originally designed. This takes more than a passive Court. It requires a Court that sees, understands, and creates—and then actively enforces the law in its current setting so that it becomes a reality for the people. Only when given life by such a Court can the law "rule."

The qualities that are required of a judge of constitutional law are rare indeed. He must have not only much learning and skill in the law, but also a profound ability to see the issues of his day in the tangled facts of the cases before him. And he must have the courage to act on the basis of what he sees, no matter how unpopular such action may be. These are the indispensable qualities of a judge which Black brought to the Court.[75]

CONCLUSION

Ultimately, of course, the difference between judicial activism and judicial restraint is a matter of degree or tendency. Cases arise, inevitably, in which the most restrained of judges gives way to the conception of a higher duty; nor can the activist always escape community views or the demands of precedent. Yet occasional clouds before the sun do not obscure the difference between night and day. Mr. Justice Douglas exposed the essence of judicial activism when, reviewing a recent book, he observed: "It makes a mockery of judges who insist that if they were not imprisoned by the law they could do justice." His brother, Jackson, revealed the essence of judicial restraint when he said, "We cannot have equal justice under law except we have some law."

This brings us back to Plato, where we started: Is it better

---

[75] Charles Reich, "Mr. Justice Black and the Living Constitution," *Harvard Law Review*, 76 (1963), 752–753. Copyright © 1963 by The Harvard Law Review Association. See Mr. Justice Black's "response" in *Griswold* v. *Connecticut,* page 373.

to be governed by activist men in judicial office, or should we strive for the Rule of Law—recognizing that it can never be perfectly attained? Shall federal judges, unanswerable at the polls, make the most or the least of their inevitable opportunity for creating public policy? Should they interfere as much as possible, or as little, with government by the people? Shall discretion—which is a vital *part* of the judges' job—swallow up and dominate the judicial process?

As Plato recognized, even the true philosopher-king could not stay in power on his own merits. He would need the support of a "noble fiction"—the pretense, for example, that his decrees spring not from his own will but from some "higher law" (or from the "plain words" of those who gave us the great charter and its amendments). The fiction, of course, is calculated to hide the implacable moral difference between obedience to law and subservience to a fellow man. The ultimate collapse of Field's accomplishment may be another facet of history's hint that no fiction, however noble, can forever cloak the philosopher-king with moral respectability. Soon or late, it seems, his nakedness appears; and then we must begin again the unending struggle for the Rule of Law—for government by something more respectable than the will of those who for the moment hold high office.

PART TWO

VIEWS

FROM THE BENCH

PROEM—TWO KINDS OF JUDGES

Calder v. *Bull*
3 Dallas 386 (1798)

When a state court found a certain will invalid, property of the deceased vested in Calder. The state legislature authorized a new judicial hearing, and the new decision (recognizing the validity of the will) vested the property in Bull. The question in the present case is whether the federal Constitution prohibited the state from disturbing Calder's vested rights by authorizing a retrial. Note Mr. Justice Chase's activist reference to "higher law" that binds the states even in the absence of express constitutional prohibitions. Compare this with Mr. Justice Iredell's more restrained view of the judicial function. Surely here is a classic example of the "two types of men" mentioned by Mr. Justice Frankfurter (see page 4).

[CHASE, Justice.] . . . I cannot subscribe to the omnipotence of a State Legislature, or that it is absolute and without controul; although its authority should not be expressly restrained by the Constitution, or fundamental law, of the State. The people of the United States erected their Constitutions, or forms of government, to establish justice, to promote the general welfare, to secure the blessings of liberty; and to protect their persons and property from violence. The purposes for which men enter into society will determine the nature and terms of the social compact; and as they are the foundation of the legislative power, they will decide what are the proper objects of it: The nature, and ends of legislative power will limit the exercise of it. This fundamental principle flows from the very nature of our free Republican governments, that no man should be compelled to do what the laws do not require; nor to refrain from acts which the laws permit. There are acts which the Federal, or State, Legislature cannot do, without exceeding their authority. There are certain vital principles in our free Republican governments, which will determine and over-rule an apparent and flagrant abuse of legislative power; as to authorize manifest injustice by positive law; or to take away that security for personal liberty, or private property, for the protection whereof the government was established. An *act* of the Legislature (for I cannot call it a law) contrary to the great first principles of the social compact, cannot be considered a rightful exercise of legislative authority. The obligation of a law in governments established on express compact, and on republican principles, must be determined by the nature of the power, on which it is founded. A few instances will suffice to explain what I mean. A law that punished a citizen for an innocent action, or, in other words, for an act, which, when done, was in violation of no existing law; a law that destroys, or impairs, the lawful private contracts of citizens; a law that makes a man a Judge in his own cause; or a law that takes property from A. and gives it to B.: It is against all reason and justice, for a people to entrust a Legislature with *such* powers; and, therefore, it cannot be presumed that they have done it. The genius, the nature, and the spirit, of our State Governments, amount to a prohibition of such acts of legislation; and the general principles of law and reason forbid them. The Legislature may enjoin, permit, forbid, and punish; they may declare new crimes; and establish rules of conduct for all its citizens in future cases; they may command what is right, and prohibit what is wrong; but they cannot change innocence into guilt; or punish innocence as a crime; or violate the right of an antecedent lawful private contract; or the right of private property. To maintain that our Federal, or State, Legislature possesses such powers, if they had not been expressly restrained; would, in my opinion, be a political heresy, altogether inadmissible in our free republican governments. . . .

[*Mr. Justice Chase concluded, however, that the law in question was not invalid.*]

IREDELL, Justice. Though I concur in the general result of the opinions which have been delivered, I cannot entirely adopt the reasons that are assigned upon the occasion.

From the best information to be collected, relative to the Constitution of Connecticut, it appears, that the Legislature of that State has been in the uniform, uninterrupted, habit of exercising a general superintending power over its courts of law, by granting new trials. It may, indeed, appear strange to some of us, that in any form, there should exist a power to grant, with respect to suits depending or adjudged, new rights of trial, new privileges of proceeding, not previously recognized and regulated by positive institutions; but such is the established usage of Connecticut, and it is obviously consistent with the general superintending authority of her Legislature. Nor is it altogether without some sanction for a Legislature to act as a court of justice. In England, we know, that one branch of the Parliament, the house of Lords, not only exercises a judicial power in cases of impeachment, and for the trial of its own members, but as the court of dernier resort, takes cognizance of many suits at law, and in equity: And that in construction of law, the jurisdiction there exercised is by the King in full Parliament; which shews that, in its origin, the causes were probably heard before the whole Parliament. When Connecticut was settled, the right of empowering her Legislature to superintend the Courts of Justice, was, I presume, early assumed; and its expediency, as applied to the local circumstances and municipal policy of the State, is sanctioned by a long and uniform practice. The power, however, is judicial in its nature; and whenever it is exercised, as in the present instance, it is an exercise of judicial, not of legislative, authority.

But, let us, for a moment, suppose, that the resolution, granting a new trial, was a legislative act, it will by no means follow, that it is an act affected by the constitutional prohibition, that "no State shall pass any ex post facto law." I will endeavour to state the general principles, which influence me, on this point, succinctly and clearly, though I have not had an opportunity to reduce my opinion to writing.

If, then, a government, composed of Legislative, Executive and Judicial departments, were established, by a Constitution, which imposed no limits on the legislative power, the consequence would inevitably be, that whatever the legislative power chose to enact, would be lawfully enacted, and the judicial power could never interpose to pronounce it void. It is true, that some speculative jurists have held, that a legislative act against natural justice must, in itself, be void; but I cannot think that, under such a government any Court of Justice would possess a power to declare it so. Sir William Blackstone, having put the strong case of an act of Parliament, which should authorize a man to try his own cause, explicitly adds, that even in that case, "there is no court that has power to defeat the intent of the Legislature, when couched in such evident and express words, as leave no doubt whether it was the intent of the Legislature, or no." 1 Bl. Com. 91.

In order, therefore, to guard against so great an evil, it has been the policy of all the American States, which have, individually, framed their State Constitutions since the revolution, and of the people of the United States, when they framed the Federal Constitution, to define with precision the objects of the legislative power, and to restrain its exercise within marked and settled boundaries. If any act of Congress, or of the Legislature of a State, violates those constitutional provisions, it is unquestionably void; though, I admit, that as the authority to declare it void is of a delicate and awful nature, the Court will never resort to that authority, but in a clear and urgent case. If, on the other hand, the Legislature of the Union, or the Legislature of any member of the Union, shall pass a law, within the general scope of their constitutional power, the Court cannot pronounce it to be void, merely because it is, in their judgment, contrary to the principles of natural justice. The ideas of natural justice are regulated by no fixed standard: the ablest and the purest men have differed upon the subject; and all that the Court could properly say, in such an event, would be, that the Legislature (possessed of an equal right of opinion) had passed an act which, in the opinion of the judges, was inconsistent with the abstract principles of natural justice. There are then but two lights, in which the subject can be viewed: 1st. If the Legislature pursue the authority delegated to them, their acts are valid. 2d. If they transgress the boundaries of that authority, their acts are invalid. In the former case, they exercise the discretion vested in them by the people, to whom alone they are responsible for the faithful discharge of their trust: but in the latter case, they violate a fundamental law, which must be our guide, whenever we are called upon as judges to determine the validity of a legislative act.

Still, however, in the present instance, the act or resolution of the Legislature of Connecticut, cannot be regarded as an ex post facto law; for, the true construction of the prohibition extends to criminal, not to civil, cases. It is only in criminal cases, indeed, in which the danger to be guarded against, is greatly to be apprehended. The history of every country in Europe will furnish flagrant instances of tyranny exercised under the pretext of penal dispensations. Rival factions, in their efforts to crush each other, have superseded all the forms, and suppressed all the sentiments, of justice; while attainders, on the principle of retaliation and proscription, have marked all the vicissitudes of party triumph. The temptation to such abuses of power is unfortunately too alluring for human virtue; and, therefore, the framers of the American Constitutions have wisely denied to the respective Legislatures, Federal as well as State, the possession of the power itself: they shall not pass any ex post facto law; or, in other words, they shall not inflict a punishment for any act, which was innocent at the time it was committed; nor increase the degree of punishment previously denounced for any specific offence.

The policy, the reason and humanity, of the prohibition, do not, I repeat, extend to civil cases, to cases that merely affect the private property of citizens. Some of the most necessary and important acts of Legislation are, on the contrary, founded upon the principle, that private rights must yield to public exigencies. Highways are run through private grounds. Fortifications, Lighthouses, and other public edifices, are necessarily sometimes built upon the soil owned by individuals. In such, and similar cases, if the owners should refuse voluntarily to accommodate the public, they must be constrained, as far as the public necessities require; and justice is done, by allowing them a reasonable equivalent. Without the possession of this power the operations of Government would often be obstructed, and society itself would be endangered. It is not sufficient to urge, that the power may be abused, for such is the nature of all power—such is the tendency of every human institution: and, it might as fairly be said, that the power of taxation, which is only circumscribed by the discretion of the Body, in which it is vested, ought not to be granted, because the Legislature, disregarding its true objects, might, for vision-ary and useless projects, impose a tax to the amount of nineteen shillings in the pound. We must be content to limit power where we can, and where we cannot, consistently with its use, we must be content to repose a salutary confidence. It is our consolation that there never existed a Government, in ancient or modern times, more free from danger in this respect, than the Governments of America.

Upon the whole, though there cannot be a case, in which an ex post facto law in criminal matters is requisite, or justifiable (for Providence never can intend to promote the prosperity of any country by bad means) yet, in the present instance the objection does not arise: Because, 1st. if the act of the Legislature of Connecticut was a judicial act, it is not within the words of the Constitution; and 2d. even if it was a legislative act, it is not within the meaning of the prohibition.

CUSHING, Justice. The case appears to me to be clear of all difficulty, taken either way. If the act is a judicial act, it is not touched by the Federal Constitution: and, if it is a legislative act, it is maintained and justified by the ancient and uniform practice of the State of Connecticut.

JUDGMENT affirmed.

THE CLASSIC ERA—NATURAL LAW
AND VESTED INTERESTS (1789–1865)

The Fourteenth Amendment was not adopted until 1868. The Contract Clause of the Constitution (Art. 1, Sec. 10), however, was a forerunner, as a vessel into which activist judges could pour the wine of their Justice. It had been included in the Constitution in view of the "stay laws" that some states had adopted to stay the foreclosure of mortgages in the depression following the Revolutionary War. Could it somehow be made to serve a very different purpose?

Shortly before the constitutional convention, Blackstone's *Commentaries* had held that "so great is the regard of the law for private property, that it will not authorize the least violation of it; no, not even for the common good of the whole community."[76] This attitude found expression in what Professor Corwin has called the first major doctrine of American constitutional law—the doctrine of vested interests. Its essence was that "the effect of legislation on existing property rights was a primary test of its validity."[77] How Marshall's Court read this doctrine into the Contract Clause, and how Taney's Court diluted it, are seen in the two cases that follow. It is interesting that in the *Dartmouth College* case (a few years after *Fletcher*) Marshall recognized that such a case was "not in the mind of the Convention" when it put the Contract Clause into the Constitution. He could well have said the same thing with respect to *Fletcher*. Later activists seem considerably less candid.

Fletcher v. *Peck*

6 Cranch 87 (1810)

This case grew out of the Yazoo land-fraud scandal after the much-bribed Georgia legislature in 1795 granted about thirty-five million acres of frontier land to a syndicate for an unconscionable half a million dollars. In the following year, a newly elected legislature re-

---

[76] Sir William Blackstone, *Commentaries on the Laws of England,* ed. William C. Jones (San Francisco, Calif.: Bancroft-Whitney Co., 1916), 1, p. 240.

[77] Edward S. Corwin, *Liberty Against Government* (Baton Rouge, La.: Louisiana State University Press, 1948), p. 72.

voked the grant, on the ground that it had been obtained by fraud. Fletcher, allegedly an innocent purchaser from the syndicate, brought this suit under a covenant that the title had not been impaired by any subsequent legislation. (In 1803 Congress paid Georgia $1,250,000 for its interest in the property, and in 1814 appropriated $5,000,000 to buy up all claims under the Georgia act of 1795.) Note the blending of natural law and the Contract Clause in Marshall's opinion, and the reliance upon natural law alone in Johnson's.

MARSHALL, CH. J. delivered the opinion of the Court as follows: . . .

In this case the legislature may have had ample proof that the original grant was obtained by practices which can never be too much reprobated, and which would have justified its abrogation so far as respected those to whom crime was imputable. But the grant, when issued, conveyed an estate in fee-simple to the grantee, clothed with all the solemnities which law can bestow. This estate was transferrable; and those who purchased parts of it were not stained by that guilt which infected the original transaction. Their case is not distinguishable from the ordinary case of purchasers of a legal estate without knowledge of any secret fraud which might have led to the emanation of the original grant. According to the well known course of equity, their rights could not be affected by such fraud. Their situation was the same, their title was the same, with that of every other member of the community who holds land by regular conveyances from the original patentee.

Is the power of the legislature competent to the annihilation of such title, and to a resumption of the property thus held?

The principle asserted is, that one legislature is competent to repeal any act which a former legislature was competent to pass; and that one legislature cannot abridge the powers of a succeeding legislature.

The correctness of this principle, so far as respects general legislation, can never be controverted. But, if an act be done under a law, a succeeding legislature cannot undo it. The past cannot be recalled by the most absolute power. Conveyances have been made, those conveyances have vested legal estates, and, if those estates may be seized by the sovereign authority, still, that they originally vested is a fact, and cannot cease to be a fact.

When, then, a law is in its nature a contract, when absolute rights have vested under that contract, a repeal of the law cannot divest those rights; and the act of annulling them, if legitimate, is rendered so by a power applicable to the case of every individual in the community.

It may well be doubted whether the nature of society and of government does not prescribe some limits to the legislative power; and, if any be prescribed, where are they to be found, if the property of an individual, fairly and honestly acquired may be seized without compensation.

To the legislature all legislative power is granted; but the question, whether the act of transferring the property of an individual to the public, be in the nature of the legislative power, is well worthy of serious reflection.

It is the peculiar province of the legislature to prescribe general rules for the government of society; the application of those rules to individuals in society would seem to be the duty of other departments. How far the power of giving the law may involve every other power, in cases where the constitution is silent, never has been, and perhaps never can be, definitely stated.

The validity of this rescinding act, then, might well be doubted, were Georgia a single sovereign power. But Georgia cannot be viewed as a single, unconnected, sovereign power, on whose legislature no other restrictions are imposed than may be found in its own constitution. She is a part of a large empire; she is a member of the American union; and that union has a constitution of supremacy of which all acknowledge, and which imposes limits to the legislatures of the several states, which none claim a right to pass. The constitution of the United States declares that no state shall pass any bill of attainder, *ex post facto* law, or law impairing the obligation of contracts.

Does the case now under consideration come within this prohibitory section of the constitution?

In considering this very interesting question, we immediately ask ourselves what is a contract? Is a grant a contract?

A contract is a compact between two or more parties, and is either executory or executed. An executory contract is one in which a party binds himself to do, or not to do, a particular thing; such was the law under which the conveyance was made by the governor. A contract executed is one in which the object of contract is performed; and this, says Blackstone, differs in nothing from a grant. The contract between Georgia and the purchasers was executed by the grant. A contract executed, as well as one which is executory, contains obligations binding on the parties. A grant, in its own nature, amounts to an extinguishment of the right of the grantor, and implies a contract not to reassert that right. A party is, therefore, always estopped by his own grant.

Since, then, in fact, a grant is a contract executed, the obligation of which still continues, and since the constitution uses the general term contract, without distinguishing between those which are executory and those which are executed, it must be construed to comprehend the latter as well as the former. A law annulling conveyances between individuals, and declaring that the grantors should stand seised of their former estates, notwithstanding those grants, would be as repugnant to the constitution as a law discharging the vendors of property from the obligation of executing their contracts by conveyances. It would be strange if a contract to convey was secured by the constitution, while an absolute conveyance remained unprotected.

If, under a fair construction of the constitution, grants are comprehended under the term contracts, is a grant from the state excluded from the operation of the provision? Is the clause to be considered as inhibiting the state from impairing the obligation of contracts between two individuals, but as excluding from that inhibition contracts made with itself?

The words themselves contain no such distinction. They are general, and are applicable to contracts of every description. If contracts made with the state are to be exempted from their operation, the exception must arise from the character of the contracting party, not from the words which are employed. . . .

It is, then, the unanimous opinion of the court, that, in this case, the estate having passed into the hands of a purchaser for a valuable consideration, without notice, the state of Georgia was restrained, either by general principles which are common to our free institutions, or by the particular provisions of the constitution of the United States, from passing a law whereby the estate of the plaintiff in the premises so purchased could be constitutionally and legally impaired and rendered null and void.

[Affirmed.]

Mr. Justice JOHNSON. In this case I entertain, on two points, an opinion different from that which has been delivered by the court.

I do not hesitate to declare that a State does not possess the power of revoking its own grants. But I do it on a general principle, on the reason and nature of things: a principle which will impose laws even on the deity.

A contrary opinion can only be maintained upon the ground that no existing legislature can abridge the powers of those which will succeed it. To a certain extent this is certainly correct; but the distinction lies between power and interest, the right of jurisdiction and the right of soil.

The right of jurisdiction is essentially connected to, or rather identified with, the national sovereignty. To part with it is to commit a species of political suicide. In fact, a power to produce its own annihilation is an absurdity in terms. It is a power as utterly incommunicable to a political as to a natural person. But it is not so with the interests or property of a nation. Its possessions nationally are in nowise necessary to its political existence; they are entirely accidental, and may be parted with in every respect similarly to those of the individuals who compose the community. When the legislature have once conveyed their interest or property in any subject to the individual, they have lost all control over it; have nothing to act upon; it has passed from them; is vested in the individual; becomes intimately blended with his existence, as essentially so as the blood that circulates through his system. The government may indeed demand of him the one or the other, not because they are not his, but because whatever is his is his country's.

As to the idea, that the grants of a legislature may be void because the legislature are corrupt, it appears to me to be subject to insuperable difficulties. The acts of the supreme power of a country must be considered pure for the same reason that all sovereign acts must be considered just; because there is no power that can declare them otherwise. The absurdity in this case would have been strikingly perceived, could the party who passed the act of cession have got again into power, and declared themselves pure, and the intermediate legislature corrupt. . . .

I have thrown out these ideas that I may have it distinctly understood that my opinion on this point is not founded on the provision in the Constitution of the United States, relative to laws impairing the obligation of contracts. It is much to be regretted that words of less equivocal signification had not been adopted in that article of the Constitution. There is reason to believe, from the letters of Publius, which are well known to be entitled to the highest respect, that the object of the convention was to afford a general protection to individual rights against the acts of the State legislatures. Whether the words, "acts impairing the obligation of contracts," can be construed to have the same force as must have been given to the words "obligation and *effect* of contracts," is the difficulty in my mind.

There can be no solid objection to adopting the technical definition of the word "contract," given by Blackstone. The etymology, the classical signification, and the civil law idea of the word, will all support it. But the difficulty arises on the word "obligation," which certainly imports an existing moral or physical necessity. Now a grant or conveyance by no means necessarily implies the continuance of an obligation beyond the moment of executing it. It is most generally but the consummation of a contract, is functus officio the moment it is executed, and continues afterwards to be nothing more than the evidence that a certain act was done.

I enter with great hesitation upon this question, because it involves a subject of the greatest delicacy and much difficulty. The States and the United States are continually legislating on the subject of contracts, prescribing the mode of authentication, the time within which suits shall be prosecuted for them, in many cases affecting existing contracts by the laws which they pass, and declaring them to cease or lose their effect for want of compliance, in the parties, with such statutory provisions. All these acts appear to be within the most correct limits of legislative powers, and most beneficially exercised, and certainly could not have been intended to be affected by this constitutional provision; yet where to draw the line, or how to define or limit the words, "obligation of contracts," will be found a subject of extreme difficulty.

To give it the general effect of a restriction of the State powers in favor of private rights, is certainly going very far beyond the obvious and necessary import of the words, and would operate to restrict the States in the exercise of that right which every community must exercise, of possessing itself of the property of the individual, when necessary for public uses; a right which a magnanimous and just government will never exercise without amply indemnifying the individual, and which perhaps amounts to nothing more than a power to oblige him to sell and convey, when the public necessities require it. . . .

I have been very unwilling to proceed to the decision of this cause at all. It appears to me to bear strong evidence, upon the face of it, of being a mere feigned case. It is our duty to decide on the rights, but not on the speculations of parties. My confidence, however, in the respectable gentlemen who have been engaged for the parties, has induced me to abandon my scruples in the belief that they would never consent to impose a mere feigned case upon this court.

Charles River Bridge v. *Warren Bridge*

11 Peters 420 (1837)

In 1785 Massachusetts chartered the Charles River toll bridge between Boston and what is now Cambridge. As the two towns grew, traffic increased and the single bridge became inadequate. In 1828 the state authorized a competing bridge. This case arose when the owners of the original bridge sought injunctive and other relief.

Whereas Mr. Justice Story clung to the old doctrine of vested interests, Chief Justice Taney and the Court (acknowledging the importance of private property) recognized that there were also crucial public interests at stake. They found a way to uphold the legislature's evaluation of these competing claims without altogether destroying the old doctrine of vested interests.

Story observed that Marshall had heard the case shortly before his death, and shared the dissenting view. Marshall, it would seem, was the first great activist on the Supreme Court; his successor, Taney, was the first great anti-activist. Ironically, Taney is remembered chiefly for the *Dred Scott* fiasco, which has obscured his standing as one of our most able judges. (See Wallace Mendelson, *Capitalism, Democracy, and the Supreme Court* [Appleton-Century-Crofts, 1960], chap. 3.)

MR. JUSTICE TANEY delivered the opinion of the Court. . . .

This brings us to the act of the legislature of Massachusetts, of 1785, by which the plaintiffs were incorporated by the name of "The Proprietors of the Charles River Bridge;" and it is here, and in the law of 1792, prolonging their charter, that we must look for the extent and nature of the franchise conferred upon the plaintiffs.

Much has been said in the argument of the principles of construction by which this law is to be expounded, and what undertakings, on the part of the state, may be implied. The court think there can be no serious difficulty on that head. It is the grant of certain franchises by the public to a private corporation, and in a matter where the public interest is concerned. The rule of construction in such cases is well settled, both in England and by the decisions of our own tribunals. In 2 Barn. & Adol., 793, in the case of the *Proprietors of the Stourbridge Canal* v. *Wheeley and others,* the court say, "The canal having been made under an act of parliament, the rights of the plaintiffs are derived entirely from that act. This, like many other cases, is a bargain between a company of adventurers and the public, the terms of which are expressed in the statute; and the rule of construction, in all such cases, is now fully established to be this; that any ambiguity in the terms of the contract must operate against the adventurers, and in favor of the public, and the plaintiffs can claim nothing that is not clearly given them by the act." And the doctrine thus laid down is abundantly sustained by the authorities referred to in this decision.

. . . The argument in favour of the proprietors of the Charles river bridge, is . . . that the power claimed by the state, if it exists, may be so used as to destroy the value of the franchise they have granted to the corporation. . . . The existence of the power does not, and cannot depend upon the circumstances of its having been exercised or not. . . .

. . . The object and end of all government is to promote the happiness and prosperity of the community by which it is established; and it can never be assumed, that the government intended to diminish its power of accomplishing the end for which it was created. And in a country like ours, free, active, and enterprising, continually advancing in numbers and wealth, new channels of communication are daily found necessary, both for travel and trade; and are essential to the comfort, convenience, and prosperity of the people. A state ought never to be presumed to surrender this power, because, like the taxing power, the whole community have an interest in preserving it undiminished. And when a corporation alleges, that a state has surrendered, for seventy years, its power of improvement and public accommodation, in a great and important line of travel, along which a vast number of its citizens must daily pass, the community have a right to insist, in the language of this court above quoted, "that its abandonment ought not to be presumed in a case in which the deliberate purpose of the state to abandon it does not appear." The continued existence of a government would be of no great value, if by implications and presumptions it was disarmed of the powers necessary to accomplish the ends of its creation; and the functions it was designed to perform, transferred to the hands of privileged corporations. The rule of construction announced by the court was not confined to the taxing power; nor is it so limited in the opinion delivered. On the contrary, it was distinctly placed on the ground that the interests of the community were concerned in preserving, undiminished, the power then in question; and whenever any power of the state is said to be surrendered or diminished, whether it be the taxing power or any other affecting the public interest, the same principle applies, and the rule of construction must be the same. No one will question that the interests of the great body of the people of the state would, in this instance, be affected by the surrender of this great line of travel to a single corporation, with the right to exact toll, and exclude competition for seventy years. While the rights of private property are sacredly guarded, we must not forget that the community also have rights, and that the happiness and well-being of every citizen depends on their faithful preservation.

Adopting the rule of construction above stated as the settled one, we proceed to apply it to the charter of 1785, to the proprietors of the Charles river bridge. This act of incorporation is in the usual form, and the privileges such as are commonly given to corporations of that kind. It confers on them the ordinary faculties of a corporation, for the purpose of building the bridge; and establishes certain rates of toll, which the company are authorized to take: this is the whole grant. There is no exclusive privilege given to them over the waters of Charles river, above or below their bridge; no right to erect another bridge themselves, nor to prevent other persons from erecting one, no engagement from the state, that another shall not be erected; and no undertaking not to sanction competition, nor to make improvements that may diminish the amount of its income. Upon all these subjects, the charter is silent; and nothing is said in it about a line of travel, so much insisted on in the argument, in which they are to have exclusive privileges. No words are used from which an intention to grant any of these rights can be inferred; if the plaintiff is entitled to them, it must be implied, simply, from the nature of the grant; and cannot be inferred, from the words by which the grant is made.

The relative position of the Warren bridge has already been described. It does not interrupt the passage over the Charles river bridge, nor make the way to it, or from it, less convenient. None of the faculties or franchises granted to that corporation, have been revoked by the legislature; and its right to take the tolls granted by the charter remains unaltered. In short, all the franchises and rights of property, enumerated in the charter, and there mentioned to have been granted to it, remain unimpaired. But its income is destroyed by the Warren bridge; which, being free, draws off the passengers and property which would have gone over it, and renders their franchise of no value. This is the gist of the complaint. For it is not pretended, that the erection of the Warren bridge would have done them any injury, or in any degree affected their right of property, if it had not diminished the amount of their tolls. In order, then, to entitle themselves to relief, it is necessary to show, that the legislature contracted not to do the act of which they complain; and that they impaired, or in other words, violated, that contract by the erection of the Warren bridge.

The inquiry, then, is, does the charter contain such a contract on the part of the state? Is there any such stipulation to be found in that instrument? It must be admitted on all hands, that there is none; no words that even relate to another bridge, or to the diminution of their tolls, or to the line of travel. If a contract on that subject can be gathered from the charter, it must be by implication; and cannot be found in the words used. Can such an agreement be implied? The rule of construction before stated is an answer to the question; in charters of this description, no rights are taken from the public, or given to the corporation, beyond those which the words of the charter, by their natural and proper construction, purport to convey. There are no words which import such a contract as the plaintiffs in error contend for, and none can be implied. . . .

Indeed, the practice and usage of almost every state in the Union, old enough to have commenced the work of internal improvement, is opposed to the doctrine contended for on the part of the plaintiffs in error. Turnpike roads have been made in succession, on the same line of travel; the later ones interfering materially with the profits of the first. These corporations have, in some instances, been utterly ruined by the introduction of newer and better modes of transportation and travelling. In some cases, railroads have rendered the turnpike roads on the same line of travel so entirely useless, that the franchise of the turnpike corporation is not worth preserving. Yet in none of these cases have the corporations supposed that their privileges were invaded, or any contract violated on the part of the state. Amid the multitude of cases which have occurred, and have been daily occurring for the last forty or fifty years, this is the first instance in which such an implied contract has been contended for, and this court called upon to infer it from an ordinary act of incorporation, containing nothing more than the usual stipulations and provisions to be found in every such law. The absence of any such controversy, when there must have been so many occasions to give rise to it, proves that neither states, nor individuals, nor corporations, ever imagined that such a contract could be implied from such charters. It shows, that the men who voted for these laws never imagined that they were forming such a contract; and if we maintain that they have made it, we must create it by a legal fiction, in opposition to the truth of the fact, and the obvious intention of the party. We cannot deal thus with the rights reserved to the states; and by legal intendments and mere technical reasoning, take away from them any portion of that power over their own internal police and improvement, which is so necessary to their well-being and prosperity.

And what would be the fruits of this doctrine of implied contracts, on the part of the states, and of property in a line of travel by a corporation, if it should now be sanctioned by this court? To what results would it lead us? If it is to be found in the charter to this bridge, the same process of reasoning must discover it, in the various acts which have been passed, within the last forty years, for turnpike companies. And what is to be the extent of the privileges of exclusion on the different sides of the road? The counsel who have so ably argued this case, have not attempted to define it by any certain boundaries. How far must the new improvement be distant from the old one? How near may you approach, without invading its rights in the privileged line? If this court should establish the principles now contended for, what is to become of the numerous railroads established on the same line of travel with turnpike companies; and which have rendered the franchises of the turnpike corporations of no value? Let it once be understood, that such charters carry with them these implied contracts, and give this unknown and undefined property in a line of travelling; and you will soon find the old turnpike corporations awakening from their sleep and calling upon this court to put down the improvements which have taken their place. The millions of property which have been invested in railroads and canals, upon lines of travel which had been before occupied by turnpike corporations, will be put in jeopardy. We shall be thrown back to the improvements of the last century, and obliged to stand still, until the claims of the old turnpike corporations shall be satisfied; and they shall consent to permit these states to avail themselves of the lights of modern science, and to partake of the benefit of those improvements which are now adding to the wealth and prosperity, and the convenience and comfort, of every other part of the civilized world. Nor is this all. This court will find itself compelled to fix, by some arbitrary rule, the width of this new kind of property in a line of travel; for if such a right of property exists, we have no lights to guide us in marking out its extent, unless, indeed, we resort to the old feudal grants, and to the exclusive rights of ferries, by prescription, between towns; and are prepared to decide that when a turnpike road from one town to another, had been made, no railroad or canal, between these two points, could afterwards be established. This court are not prepared to sanction principles which must lead to such results. . . .

The judgment of the supreme judicial court of the commonwealth of Massachusetts, dismissing the plaintiffs' bill, must therefore, be affirmed, with costs.

[Mr. Justice McLean delivered an opinion in which he urged that the bill be dismissed for want of jurisdiction.]

Mr. Justice Story, dissenting. . . .
The present . . . is not the case of a royal grant, but of a

legislative grant, by a public statute. The rules of the common law in relation to royal grants have, therefore, in reality, nothing to do with the case. We are to give this act of incorporation a rational and fair construction, according to the general rules which govern in all cases of the exposition of public statutes. We are to ascertain the legislative intent; and that once ascertained, it is our duty to give it a full and liberal operation. . . .

I admit, that where the terms of a grant are to impose burthens upon the public, or to create a restraint injurious to the public interest, there is sound reason for interpreting the terms, if ambiguous, in favour of the public. But at the same time, I insist, that there is not the slightest reason for saying, even in such a case, that the grant is not to be construed favourably to the grantee, so as to secure him in the enjoyment of what is actually granted. . . .

. . . Our legislatures neither have, nor affect to have any royal prerogatives. There is no provision in the constitution authorizing their grants to be construed differently from the grants of private persons, in regard to the like subject matter. The policy of the common law, which gave the crown so many exclusive privileges, and extraordinary claims, different from those of the subject, was founded in a good measure, if not altogether, upon the divine right of kings, or at least upon a sense of their exalted dignity and pre-eminence over all subjects, and upon the notion, that they are entitled to peculiar favour, for the protection of their kingly privileges. They were always construed according to common sense and common reason, upon their language and their intent. What reason is there, that our legislative acts should not receive a similar interpretation? Is it not at least as important in our free governments, that a citizen should have as much security for his rights and estate derived from the grants of the legislature, as he would have in England? What solid ground is there to say, that the words of a grant in the mouth of a citizen, shall mean one thing, and in the mouth of the legislature shall mean another thing? That in regard to the grant of a citizen, every word shall in case of any question of interpretation or implication be construed against him, and in regard to the grant of the government, every word shall be construed in its favour? That language shall be construed, not according to its natural import and implications from its own proper sense, and the objects of the instrument; but shall change its meaning, as it is spoken by the whole people, or by one of them? There may be very solid grounds to say, that neither grants nor charters ought to be extended beyond the fair reach of their words; and that no implications ought to be made, which are not clearly deducible from the language, and the nature and objects of the grant.

In the case of the legislative grant, there is no ground to impute surprise, imposition or mistake to the same extent as in a mere private grant of the crown. The words are the words of the legislature upon solemn deliberation, and examination, and debate. Their purport is presumed to be well known, and the public interests are watched, and guarded by all the varieties of local, personal and professional jealousy; as well as by the untiring zeal of numbers, devoted to the public service. . . .

But it has been argued, and the argument has been pressed in every form which ingenuity could suggest, that if grants of this nature are to be construed liberally, as conferring any exclusive rights on the grantees, it will interpose an effectual barrier against all general improvements of the country. . . . For my own part, I can conceive of no surer plan to arrest all public improvements, founded on private capital and enterprise, than to make the outlay of that capital uncertain, and questionable both as to security, and as to productiveness. No man will hazard his capital in any enterprise, in which, if there be a loss, it must be borne exclusively by himself; and if there be success, he has not the slightest security of enjoying the rewards of that success for a single moment. . . .

Upon the whole, my judgment is that the act of the legislature of Massachusetts granting the charter of Warren bridge, is an act impairing the obligation of the prior contract and grant to the proprietors of Charles river bridge; and, by the Constitution of the United States, it is, therefore, utterly void. I am for reversing the decree of the state court, (dismissing the bill), and for remanding the cause to the state court for further proceedings. . . .

[*Mr. Justice Thompson concurred in the foregoing opinion.*]

THE BEGINNING OF LAISSEZ-FAIRE ACTIVISM (1865–1888)

If the doctrine of vested interests was the first great proprietarian principle in American constitutional law, it was followed in the Gilded Age by the far more aggressive and comprehensive doctrine of Spencerian laissez-faire. As Professor Corwin observed, "The Country was presented with a new, up-to-date version of natural law."[78] Without neglecting vested interests, the new emphasis was upon economic liberty—i.e., liberty of contract— and, as one of the great captains of industry is said to have put it, "the public be damned." The cases in this section show how the judicial doctrine of laissez-faire began as a dissenting, or minority, view.

Munn v. *Illinois*
94 U.S. 113 (1877)

Here, as in the *Fletcher* and *Charles River Bridge* cases, is another clash between private and public interests. And here again, "two

---

[78] Edward S. Corwin, *Liberty Against Government*, p. 138.

kinds of men" on the bench find opposite answers to the problem. In the post-bellum era, Mr. Justice Field was the great judicial activist; Chief Justice Waite was his foil.

MR. CHIEF JUSTICE WAITE delivered the opinion of the court:

The question to be determined in this case is whether the General Assembly of Illinois can, under the limitations upon the legislative power of the States imposed by the Constitution of the United States, fix by law the maximum of charges for the storage of grain in warehouses at Chicago and other places in the State having not less than one hundred thousand inhabitants, "in which grain is stored in bulk, and in which the grain of different owners is mixed together, or in which grain is stored in such a manner that the identity of different lots or parcels cannot be accurately preserved."

It is claimed that such a law is repugnant: . . .

3. To that part of Amendment XIV. which ordains that no State shall "Deprive any person of life, liberty or property, without due process of law, nor deny to any person within its jurisdiction the equal protection of the laws." . . .

Every statute is presumed to be constitutional. The courts ought not to declare one to be unconstitutional, unless it is clearly so. If there is doubt, the expressed will of the Legislature should be sustained.

The Constitution contains no definition of the word "deprive," as used in the 14th Amendment. To determine its signification, therefore, it is necessary to ascertain the effect which usage has given it, when employed in the same or a like connection.

While this provision of the Amendment is new in the Constitution of the United States as a limitation upon the powers of the States, it is old as a principle of civilized government. It is found in Magna Charta, and, in substance if not in form, in nearly or quite all the constitutions that have been from time to time adopted by the several States of the Union. By the 5th Amendment, it was introduced into the Constitution of the United States as a limitation upon the powers of the National Government, and by the 14th, as a guaranty against any encroachment upon an acknowledged right of citizenship by the Legislatures of the States. . . . With the 5th Amendment in force, Congress, in 1820, conferred power upon the City of Washington "to regulate . . . the rates of wharfage at private wharves, . . . the sweeping of chimneys, and to fix the rates of fees therefor, . . . and the weight and quality of bread," 3 Stat. at L., 587, sec. 7; and in 1848, "to make all necessary regulations respecting hackney carriages and the rates of fare of the same, and the rates of hauling by cartmen, wagoners, carmen and draymen, and the rates of commission of auctioneers," 9 Stat. at L., 224, sec. 2.

From this it is apparent that, down to the time of the adoption of the 14th Amendment, it was not supposed that statutes regulating the use, or even the price of the use, of private property necessarily deprived an owner of his property without due process of law. Under some circumstances they may, but not under all. The Amendment does not change the law in this particular; it simply prevents the States from doing that which will operate as such a deprivation.

This brings us to inquire as to the principles upon which this power of regulation rests, in order that we may determine what is within and what without its operative effect. Looking, then, to the common law, from whence came the right which the Constitution protects, we find that when private property is "affected with a public interest, it ceases to be juris privati only." This was said by Lord Chief Justice Hale more than two hundred years ago, in his treatise De Portibus Maris, 1 Harg. L. Tr., 78, and has been accepted without objection as an essential element in the law of property ever since. Property does become clothed with a public interest when used in a manner to make it of public consequence, and affect the community at large. When, therefore, one devotes his property to a use in which the public has an interest, he, in effect, grants to the public an interest in that use, and must submit to be controlled by the public for the common good, to the extent of the interest he has thus created. He may withdraw his grant by discontinuing the use; but, so long as he maintains the use, he must submit to the control.

Thus, as to ferries, Lord Hale says, in his treatise De Jure Maris, 1 Harg. L. Tr., 6, the King has "A right of franchise or privilege, that no man may set up a common ferry for all passengers, without a prescription time out of mind, or a charter from the King. He may make a ferry for his own use or the use of his family, but not for the common use of all the King's subjects passing that way; because it doth in consequence tend to a common charge, and is become a thing of public interest and use, and every man for his passage pays a toll, which is a common charge, and every ferry ought to be under a public regulation, viz.: that it give attendance at due times, keep a boat in due order, and take but reasonable toll; for if he fail in these he is finable." . . .

And, again, as to wharves and wharfingers, Lord Hale, in his treatise De Portibus Maris, already cited, says:

"A man, for his own private advantage, may, in a port or town, set up a wharf or crane, and may take what rates he and his customers can agree for cranage, wharfage, housellage, pesage, for he doth no more than is lawful for any man to do, viz.: makes the most of his own. . . . If the King or subject have a public wharf, unto which all persons that come to that port must come and unlade or lade their goods as for the purpose, because they are the wharfs only licensed by the Queen, . . . or because there is no other wharf in that port, as it may fall out where a port is newly erected; in that case there cannot be taken arbitrary and excessive duties for cranage, wharfage, pesage, etc., neither can they be enhanced to an immoderate rate; but the duties must be reasonable and moderate, though settled by the King's license or charter. For now the wharf, and

crane and other conveniences are affected with a public interest, and they cease to be juris privati only; as if a man set out
a street in new building on his own land, it is now no longer
bare private interest, but is affected by a public interest." . . .

From the same source comes the power to regulate the
charges of common carriers, which was done in England as
long ago as the third year of the reign of William and Mary,
and continued until within a comparatively recent period. And
in the first statute we find the following suggestive preamble,
to wit:

"And whereas, divers wagoners and other carriers, by combination amongst themselves, have raised the prices of carriage of goods in many places to excessive rates, to the great
injury of the trade: Be it, therefore, enacted," etc. 3 W. & M.
ch. 12, sec. 24; 3 Stat. at L. (Gt. Britain), 481.

Common carriers exercise a sort of public office, and have
duties to perform in which the public is interested. N.J. Nav.
Co. v. Merch. Bk., 6 How., 382.

Their business is, therefore, "affected with a public interest,"
within the meaning of the doctrine which Lord Hale has so
forcibly stated.

But we need not go further. Enough has already been said
to show that, when private property is devoted to a public use,
it is subject to public regulation. It remains only to ascertain
whether the warehouses of these plaintiffs in error, and the
business which is carried on there, come within the operation
of this principle.

For this purpose we accept as true the statements of fact
contained in the elaborate brief of one of the counsel of the
plaintiffs in error. From these it appears that "The great producing region of the West and Northwest sends its grain by
water and rail to Chicago, where the greater part of it is
shipped by vessel for transportation to the sea-board by the
Great Lakes, and some of it is forwarded by railway to the
Eastern ports. . . . Vessels, to some extent, are loaded in the

Chicago harbor, and sailed through the St. Lawrence directly
to Europe. . . . The quantity (of grain) received in Chicago
has made it the greatest grain market in the world. This business has created a demand for means by which the immense
quantity of grain can be handled or stored, and these have
been found in grain warehouses, which are commonly called
elevators, because the grain is elevated from the boat or car,
by machinery operated by steam, into the bins prepared for
its reception, and elevated from the bins, by a like process,
into the vessel or car which is to carry it on. . . . In this way
the largest traffic between the citizens of the country north and
west of Chicago, and the citizens of the country lying on the
Atlantic coast north of Washington is in grain which passes
through the elevators of Chicago. In this way the trade in
grain is carried on by the inhabitants of seven or eight of the
great States of the West with four or five of the States lying
on the seashore, and forms the largest part of interstate commerce in these States. The grain warehouses or elevators in
Chicago are immense structures, holding from 300,000 to
1,000,000 bushels at one time, according to size. They are divided into bins of large capacity and great strength. . . . They
are located with the river harbor on one side and the railway
tracks on the other; and the grain is run through them from
car to vessel, or boat to car, as may be demanded in the course
of business. It has been found impossible to preserve each
owner's grain separate, and this has given rise to a system of
inspection and grading, by which the grain of different owners
is mixed, and receipts issued for the number of bushels which
are negotiable, and redeemable in like kind, upon demand.
This mode of conducting the business was inaugurated more
than twenty years ago, and has grown to immense proportions.
The railways have found it impracticable to own such elevators, and public policy forbids the transaction of such business by the carrier; the ownership has, therefore, been by
private individuals, who have embarked their capital and de-

voted their industry to such business as a private pursuit." . . .

It matters not in this case that these plaintiffs in error had built their warehouses and established their business before the regulations complained of were adopted. What they did was, from the beginning, subject to the power of the body politic to require them to conform to such regulations as might be established by the proper authorities for the common good. They entered upon their business and provided themselves with the means to carry it on subject to this condition. If they did not wish to submit themselves to such interference, they should not have clothed the public with an interest in their concerns. The same principle applies to them that does to the proprietor of a hackney carriage, and as to him it has never been supposed that he was exempt from regulating statutes or ordinances because he had purchased his horses and carriage and established his business before the statute or the ordinance was adopted.

It is insisted, however, that the owner of property is entitled to a reasonable compensation for its use, even though it be clothed with a public interest, and that what is reasonable is a judicial and not a legislative question.

As has already been shown, the practice has been otherwise. In countries where the common law prevails, it has been customary from time immemorial for the Legislature to declare what shall be a reasonable compensation under such circumstances, or, perhaps more properly speaking, to fix a maximum beyond which any charge made would be unreasonable. Undoubtedly, in mere private contracts, relating to matters in which the public has no interest, what is reasonable must be ascertained judicially. But this is because the Legislature has no control over such a contract. So, too, in matters which do affect the public interest, and as to which legislative control may be exercised, if there are no statutory regulations upon the subject, the courts must determine what is reasonable. The controlling fact is the power to regulate at all. If that exists, the right to establish the maximum of charge, as one of the means of regulation, is implied. In fact, the common law rule, which requires the charge to be reasonable, is itself a regulation as to price. Without it the owner could make his rates at will, and compel the public to yield to his terms, or forego the use.

But a mere common law regulation of trade or business may be changed by statute. A person has no property, no vested interest, in any rule of the common law. That is only one of the forms of municipal law, and is no more sacred than any other. Rights of property which have been created by the common law cannot be taken away without due process; but the law itself, as a rule of conduct, may be changed at the will, or even at the whim, of the Legislature, unless prevented by constitutional limitations. Indeed, the great office of statutes is to remedy defects in the common law as they are developed, and to adapt it to the changes of time and circumstances. To limit the rate of charge for services rendered in a public employment, or for the use of property in which the public has an interest, is only changing a regulation which existed before. It establishes no new principle in the law, but only gives a new effect to an old one.

We know that this is a power which may be abused; but that is no argument against its existence. For protection against abuses by Legislatures the people must resort to the polls, not to the courts. . . .

We conclude, therefore, that the statute in question is not repugnant to the Constitution of the United States, and that there is no error in the judgment. In passing upon this case we have not been unmindful of the vast importance of the questions involved. This and cases of a kindred character were argued before us more than a year ago by the most eminent counsel, and in a manner worthy of their well earned reputations. We have kept the cases long under advisement, in order that their decision might be the result of our mature deliberations.

The judgment is affirmed.

Mr. Justice Field, dissenting:

I am compelled to dissent from the decision of the court in this case, and from the reasons upon which that decision is founded. The principle upon which the opinion of the majority proceeds is, in my judgment, subversive of the rights of private property, heretofore believed to be protected by constitutional guaranties against legislative interference, and is in conflict with the authorities cited in its support. . . .

The validity of the legislation was, among other grounds, assailed in the state court as being in conflict with that provision of the State Constitution which declares that no person shall be deprived of life, liberty or property without due process of law, and with that provision of the 14th Amendment of the Federal Constitution which imposes a similar restriction upon the action of the State. The state court held, in substance, that the constitutional provision was not violated so long as the owner was not deprived of the title and possession of his property; and that it did not deny to the Legislature the power to make all needful rules and regulations respecting the use and enjoyment of the property, referring, in support of the position, to instances of its action in prescribing the interest on money, in establishing and regulating public ferries and public mills, and fixing the compensation in the shape of tolls, and in delegating power to municipal bodies to regulate the charges of hackmen and draymen, and the weight and price of bread. In this court the legislation was also assailed on the same ground, our jurisdiction arising upon the clause of the 14th Amendment, ordaining that no State shall deprive any person of life, liberty or property without due process of law. But it would seem from its opinion that the court holds that property loses something of its private character when employed in such a way as to be generally useful. The doctrine declared is that property "Becomes clothed with a public interest when used in a manner to make it of public consequence, and affect the community at large;" and from such clothing the right of the Legislature is deduced to control the use of the property, and to determine the compensation which the owner may receive for it. When Sir Matthew Hale, and the sages of the law in his day, spoke of property as affected by a public interest, and ceasing from that cause to be juris privati solely, that is, ceasing to be held merely in private right, they referred to property dedicated by the owner to public uses, or to property the use of which was granted by the government, or in connection with which special privileges were conferred. Unless the property was thus dedicated, or some right bestowed by the government was held with the property, either by specific grant or by prescription of so long a time as to imply a grant originally, the property was not affected by any public interest so as to be taken out of the category of property held in private right. But it is not in any such sense that the terms "clothing property with a public interest" are used in this case. From the nature of the business under consideration—the storage of grain— which, in any sense in which the words can be used, is a private business, in which the public are interested only as they are interested in the storage of other products of the soil, or in articles of manufacture, it is clear that the court intended to declare that, whenever one devotes his property to a business which is useful to the public, "affects the community at large," the Legislature can regulate the compensation which the owner may receive for its use, and for his own services in connection with it. "When, therefore," says the court, "one devotes his property to a use in which the public has an interest, he, in effect, grants to the public an interest in that use, and must submit to be controlled by the public for the common good, to the extent of the interest he has thus created. He may withdraw his grant by discontinuing the use; but, so long as he maintains the use, he must submit to the control." The building used by the defendants was for the storage of grain; in such storage, says the court, the public has an interest; therefore, the defendants, by devoting the building to that storage, have granted the public an interest in that use, and must submit to have their compensation regulated by the Legislature.

If this be sound law, if there be no protection, either in the principles upon which our republican government is founded, or in the prohibitions of the Constitution against such invasion of private rights, all property and all business in the State are held at the mercy of a majority of its Legislature. The public has no greater interest in the use of buildings for the storage of grain than it has in the use of buildings for the residences of families, nor, indeed, anything like so great an interest; and, according to the doctrine announced, the Legislature may fix the rent of all tenements used for residences, without reference to the cost of their erection. If the owner does not like the rates prescribed, he may cease renting his houses. He has granted to the public, says the court, an interest in the use of the buildings, and "He may withdraw his grant by discontinuing the use; but, so long as he maintains the use, he must submit to the control." The public is interested in the manufacture of cotton, woolen and silken fabrics; in the construction of machinery; in the printing and publication of books and periodicals, and in the making of utensils of every variety, useful and ornamental; indeed, there is hardly an enterprise or business engaging the attention and labor of any considerable portion of the community, in which the public has not an interest in the sense in which that term is used by the court in its opinion; and the doctrine which allows the Legislature to interfere with and regulate the charges which the owners of property thus employed shall make for its use, that is, the rates at which all these different kinds of business shall be carried on, has never before been asserted, so far as I am aware, by any judicial tribunal in the United States.

The doctrine of the state court, that no one is deprived of his property, within the meaning of the constitutional inhibition, so long as he retains its title and possession, and the doctrine of this court, that, whenever one's property is used in such a manner as to affect the community at large, it becomes by that fact clothed with a public interest, and ceases to be juris privati only, appear to me to destroy, for all useful purposes, the efficacy of the constitutional guaranty. All that is beneficial in property arises from its use, and the fruits of that use; and whatever deprives a person of them deprives him of all that is desirable or valuable in the title and possession. If the constitutional guaranty extends no further than to prevent a deprivation of title and possession, and allows a deprivation of use and the fruits of that use, it does not merit the encomiums it has received. Unless I have misread the history of the provision now incorporated into all our State Constitutions, and by the 5th and 14th Amendments into our Federal Constitution, and have misunderstood the interpretation it has received, it is not thus limited in its scope, and thus impotent for good. It has a much more extended operation than either court, State or Federal, has given to it. The provision, it is to be observed, places property under the same protection as life and liberty. Except by due process of law, no State can deprive any person of either. The provision has been supposed to secure to every individual the essential conditions for the pursuit of happiness; and for that reason has not been heretofore, and should never be, construed in any narrow or restricted sense.

No State "shall deprive any person of life, liberty or property without due process of law," says the 14th Amendment to the Constitution. By the term "life," as here used, something more is meant than mere animal existence. The inhibition against its deprivation extends to all those limbs and faculties by which life is enjoyed. The provision equally prohibits the mutilation of the body by the amputation of an arm or leg, or the putting out of an eye, or the destruction of any other organ of the body through which the soul communicates with the outer world. The deprivation not only of life, but of whatever God has given to everyone with life, for its growth and enjoyment is prohibited by the provision in question, if its efficacy be not frittered away by judicial decision.

By the term "liberty," as used in the provision, something more is meant than mere freedom from physical restraint or the bounds of a prison. It means freedom to go where one may choose, and to act in such manner, not inconsistent with the equal rights of others, as his judgment may dictate for the promotion of his happiness; that is, to pursue such callings and avocations as may be most suitable to develop his capacities, and give to them their highest enjoyment.

The same liberal construction which is required for the protection of life and liberty, in all particulars in which life and liberty are of any value, should be applied to the protection of private property. If the Legislature of a State, under pretense of providing for the public good, or for any other reason, can determine, against the consent of the owner, the uses to which private property shall be devoted, or the prices which the owner shall receive for its uses, it can deprive him of the property as completely as by a special Act for its confiscation or destruction. If, for instance, the owner is prohibited from using his building for the purposes for which it was designed, it is of little consequence that he is permitted to retain the title and possession; or, if he is compelled to take as compensation for its use less than the expenses to which he is subjected by its ownership, he is, for all practical purposes, deprived of the property, as effectually as if the Legislature had ordered his forcible dispossession. If it be admitted that the Legislature has any control over the compensation, the extent of that compensation becomes a mere matter of legislative discretion. The amount fixed will operate as a partial destruction of the value of the property, if it fall below the amount which the owner would obtain by contract and, practically, as a complete destruction if it be less than the cost of retaining its possession. There is, indeed, no protection of any value under the constitutional provision which does not extend to the use and income of the property, as well as to its title and possession. . . .

I am of opinion that the judgment of the Supreme Court of Illinois should be reversed.

Mr. Justice Strong, also dissenting:

When the judgment in this case was announced by direction of a majority of the court, it was well known by all my brethren that I did not concur in it. It had been my purpose to prepare a dissenting opinion, but I found no time for the preparation, and I was reluctant to dissent in such a case without stating my reasons. Mr. Justice Field has now stated them as fully as I can, and I concur in what he has said.

Ex Parte Virginia
100 U.S. 339 (1880)

This case is particularly interesting in that it shows the Court's early attitude toward the Fourteenth Amendment in relation to Negroes—an attitude presumably that reflects the general understanding of those who had witnessed the Civil War and the adoption of the Fourteenth Amendment. Compare Field's interpretation of the amendment here with that in *Munn* v. *Illinois* preceding, where economic (rather than civil) liberty was at stake.

Mr. Justice Strong delivered the opinion of the court:

The petitioner, J. D. Coles, was arrested, and he is now held in custody under an indictment found against him in the District Court of the United States for the Western District of Virginia. The indictment charged that the said Coles, being a Judge of the County Court of Pittsylvania County of that

State, and an officer charged by law with the selection of jurors to serve in the Circuit and County Courts of said county in the year 1878, did then and there exclude and fail to select as grand and petit jurors certain citizens of said County of Pittsylvania, of African race and black color, said citizens possessing all other qualifications prescribed by law, and being by him the said J. D. Coles, excluded from the jury lists made out by him as such Judge, on account of their race, color and previous condition of servitude, and for no other reason, against the peace and dignity of the United States, and against the form of the Statute of the United States in such case made and provided.

Being thus in custody, he has presented to us his petition for a writ of habeas corpus and a writ of certiorari, to bring up the record of the district court, in order that he may be discharged; and he avers that the District Court had and has no jurisdiction of the matters charged against him in said indictment; that they constitute no offense punishable in said District Court; and that the finding of said indictment, and his consequent arrest and imprisonment, are unwarranted by the Constitution of the United States, or by any law made in pursuance thereof, and are in violation of his rights and of the rights of the State of Virginia, whose judicial officer he is. . . .

In the present case, the petitioner Coles is in custody under a bench-warrant directed by the District Court, and the averment is that the court had no jurisdiction of the indictment on which the warrant is founded. . . .

The indictment and bench-warrant, in virtue of which the petitioner Coles has been arrested and is held in custody, have their justification if any they have, in the Act of Congress of March 1, 1875, sec. 4, 18 Stat. at L., 336. That section enacts that "No citizen, possessing all other qualifications which are or may be prescribed by law shall be disqualified for service as grand or petit juror in any court of the United States, or of any State, on account of race, color or previous condition of servitude; and any officer or other person charged with any duty in the selection or summoning of jurors who shall exclude or fail to summon any citizen for the cause aforesaid, shall, on conviction thereof, be deemed guilty of a misdemeanor, and be fined not more than $5,000." The defendant has been indicted for the misdemeanor described in this Act, and it is not denied that he is now properly held in custody to answer the indictment, if the Act of Congress was warranted by the Constitution. The whole merits of the case are involved in the question, whether the Act was thus warranted.

The provisions of the Constitution that relate to this subject are found in the 13th and 14th Amendments. . . .

One great purpose of these Amendments was to raise the colored race from that condition of inferiority and servitude in which most of them had previously stood into perfect equality of civil rights with all other persons within the jurisdiction of the States. They were intended to take away all possibility of oppression by law because of race or color. They were intended to be, what they really are, limitations of the power of the States and enlargements of the power of Congress. They are, to some extent, declaratory of rights, and though in form prohibitions, they imply immunities, such as may be protected by congressional legislation. We have occasion in the Slaughter-House Cases, 16 Wall. 36, to express our opinion of their spirit and purpose, and to some extent of their meaning. We have again been called to consider them in the cases of Tenn. v. Davis [100 U.S. 257] and Strauder v. West Va., just decided [100 U.S. 303]. In this latter case we held that the 14th Amendment secures, among other civil rights, to colored men, when charged with criminal offenses against a State, an impartial jury trial by jurors indifferently selected or chosen without discrimination against such jurors because of their color. We held that immunity from any such discrimination is one of the equal rights of all persons, and that any withholding it by a

State is a denial of the equal protection of the laws, within the meaning of the Amendment. We held that such an equal right to an impartial jury trial, and such an immunity from unfriendly discrimination, are placed by the Amendment under the protection of the General Government and guarantied by it. We held, further, that this protection and this guaranty, as the 5th section of the Amendment expressly ordains, may be enforced by Congress by means of appropriate legislation.

All of the Amendments derive much of their force from this latter provision. It is not said the judicial power of the General Government shall extend to enforcing the prohibitions and to protecting the rights and immunities guarantied. It is not said that branch of the government shall be authorized to declare void any action of a State in violation of the prohibitions. It is the power of Congress which has been enlarged. Congress is authorized to enforce the prohibitions by appropriate legislation. Some legislation is contemplated to make the Amendments fully effective. Whatever legislation is appropriate, that is, adapted to carry out the objects the Amendments have in view, whatever tends to enforce submission to the prohibitions they contain, and to secure to all persons the enjoyment of perfect equality of civil rights and the equal protection of the laws against state denial or invasion, if not prohibited, is brought within the domain of congressional power. . . .

We have said the prohibitions of the 14th Amendment are addressed to the States. . . . They have reference to actions of the political body denominated a State, by whatever instruments or in whatever modes that action may be taken. A State acts by its legislative, its executive or its judicial authorities. It can act in no other way. The constitutional provision, therefore, must mean that no agency of the State, or of the officers or agents by whom its powers are exerted, shall deny to any person within its jurisdiction the equal protection of the laws. Whoever, by virtue of public position under a state government, deprives another of property, life or liberty without due process of law, or denies or takes away the equal protection of the laws, violates the constitutional inhibition; and as he acts in the name and for the State, and is clothed with the State's power, his act is that of the State. This must be so, or the constitutional prohibition has no meaning. Then the State has clothed one of its agents with power to annul or to evade it.

But the constitutional Amendment was ordained for a purpose. It was to secure equal rights to all persons, and, to insure to all persons the enjoyment of such rights, power was given to Congress to enforce its provisions by appropriate legislation. Such legislation must act upon persons, not upon the abstract thing denominated a State, but upon the persons who are the agents of the State in the denial of the rights which were intended to be secured. Such is the Act of March 1, 1875, 18 Stat. at L., 336, and we think it was fully authorized by the Constitution.

The argument in support of the petition for a habeas corpus ignores entirely the power conferred upon Congress by the 14th Amendment. Were it not for the 5th section of that Amendment, there might be room for argument that the 1st section is only declaratory of the moral duty of the State, as was said in Ky. v. Dennison, 24 How. 66. The Act under consideration in that case provided no means to compel the execution of the duty required by it, and the Constitution gave none. It was of such an Act Chief Justice Taney said, that a power vested in the United States to inflict any punishment for neglect or refusal to perform the duty required by the Act of Congress "Would place every State under the control and dominion of the General Government, even in the administration of its internal concerns and reserved rights." But the Constitution now expressly gives authority for congressional interference and compulsion in the cases embraced within the 14th Amendment. It is but a limited authority, true, extending only to a single class of cases; but within its limits it is complete. The remarks made in Ky. v. Dennison and in Collector v. Day, 11 Wall. 113, though entirely just as applied to the cases in which they were made, are inapplicable to the case we have now in hand. . . .

It was insisted during the argument on behalf of the petitioner that Congress cannot punish a State Judge for his official acts; and it was assumed that Judge Cole[s], in selecting the jury as he did, was performing a judicial act. This assumption cannot be admitted. Whether the act done by him was judicial or not is to be determined by its character, and not by the character of the agent. Whether he was a county judge or not is of no importance. The duty of selecting jurors might as well have been committed to a private person as to one holding the office of a judge. It often is given to county commissioners, or supervisors or assessors. In former times, the selection was made by the sheriff. In such cases, it surely is not a judicial act, in any such sense as is contended for here. It is merely a ministerial act, as much so as the act of a sheriff holding an execution, in determining upon what piece of property he will make a levy, or the act of a roadmaster in selecting laborers to work upon the roads. That the jurors are selected for a court makes no difference. So are court-criers, tipstaves, sheriffs, etc. Is their election or their appointment a judicial act?

But if the selection of jurors could be considered in any case a judicial act, can the act charged against the petitioner be considered such when he acted outside of his authority and in direct violation of the spirit of the state statute? That statute gave him no authority, when selecting jurors, from whom a panel might be drawn for a Circuit Court, to exclude all colored men merely because they were colored. Such an exclusion was not left within the limits of his discretion. It is idle, therefore, to say that the Act of Congress is unconstitutional because its inflicts penalties upon state judges for their judicial action. It does no such thing.

Upon the whole, as we are of opinion that the Act of Congress upon which the indictment against the petitioner was founded is constitutional, and that he is correctly held to answer it, and as, therefore, no object would be secured by issuing a writ of habeas corpus, the petitions are denied.

MR. JUSTICE FIELD, dissenting:

I dissent from the judgment of the court in this case, and from the reasons by which it is supported; and I will state the grounds of my dissent. . . .

The petitioner, J. D. Coles, is the Judge of the County Court of the County of Pittsylvania, in Virginia, and has held that office for some years. It is not pretended that, in the discharge of his judicial duties, he has ever selected as jurors persons who were not qualified to serve in that character, or who were not of sound judgment, or who were not free from legal exception. It is not even suggested in argument that he has not at all times faithfully obeyed the law of the State; yet he has been indicted in the District Court of the United States for the Western District of Virginia for having, on some undesignated day in the year 1878, excluded and failed to select as grand and petit jurors citizens of the county, on account of race, color and previous condition of servitude. The indictment does not state who those citizens were, or set forth any particulars of the offense, but charges it in the general words of a definition. . . .

It is difficult to understand how an indictment so defective could have been drawn by the public prosecutor, unless we accept, as an explanation of it, the extraordinary statement of counsel, that the District Judge instructed the grand jury to the effect, that, whenever it appeared that a State Judge, in discharging the duty imposed on him by the law of the State to prepare annually a list of such inhabitants of his county as he should "think well qualified to serve as jurors, being persons of sound judgment and free from legal exception," had never put colored persons on the jury lists, it was to be presumed that his failure to do so was because of their race, color or previous condition of servitude, and that it was the duty of the grand jury to indict him for that offense. In the face of this ruling, no defense could be made by the accused, although he may have exercised at all times his best judgment in the selection of qualified persons, unless he could prove, what in most cases would be impossible, that in a county of many thousand inhabitants there was not a colored person qualified to serve as a juror. With this ruling there could be no necessity of alleging in the indictment anything beyond the general failure to put colored persons on the jury list, a fact which could not be disputed; and it would sufficiently inform the accused that he must be prepared, in order to rebut the presumption of guilt, to prove that there were no persons of the colored race in the county qualified to act as jurors. It is difficult to speak of this ruling in the language of moderation.

My second position is, that the 4th section of the Act of 1875, so far as it applies to the selection of jurors in the State Courts, is unconstitutional and void. Previous to the late Amendments, it would not have been contended, by any one familiar with the Constitution, that Congress was vested with any power to exercise supervision over the conduct of state officers in the discharge of their duties under the laws of the state, and prescribe a punishment for disregarding its directions. It would have been conceded that the selection of jurors was a subject exclusively for regulation by the States; that it was for them to determine who should act as jurors in their courts, from what class they should be taken, and what qualifications they should possess; and that their officers in carrying out the laws in this respect were responsible only to them. The States could have abolished jury trials altogether, and required all controversies to be submitted to the courts without their intervention. The 6th and 7th Amendments, in which jury trials are mentioned, apply only to the Federal Courts, as has been repeatedly adjudged. . . .

The 13th and 14th Amendments are relied upon, as already stated, to support the legislation in question. . . .

I cannot think I am mistaken in saying that a change so radical in the relation between the federal and state authorities, as would justify legislation interfering with the independent action of the different departments of the state governments, in all matters over which the States retain jurisdiction, was never contemplated by the recent Amendments. The People, in adopting them, did not suppose they were altering the fundamental theory of their dual system of governments. The discussions attending their consideration in Congress, and before the People, when presented to the Legislatures of the States for adoption, can be successfully appealed to in support of this assertion. The Union was preserved at a fearful cost of life and property. The institution of slavery in a portion of the country was the cause of constant irritation and crimination between the People of the States where it existed and those of the free States, which finally led to a rupture between them and to the civil war. As the war progressed, its sacrifices and burdens filled the People of the loyal States with a determination that not only should the Union be preserved, but that the institution which, in their judgment, had threatened its dissolution should be abolished. The Emancipation Proclamation of President Lincoln expressed this determination, though placed on the ground of military necessity. The 13th Amendment carried it into the organic law. That Amendment prohibits slavery and involuntary servitude, except for crime, within the United States, or any place subject to their jurisdiction. Its language is not restricted to the slavery of any particular class. It applies to all men; and embraces in its comprehensive language not merely that form of slavery which consists in the denial of personal rights to the slave, and subjects him to the condition of a chattel, but also serfage, vassalage, peonage, villeinage and every other form of compulsory service for the benefit, pleasure or caprice of others.

It was intended to render everyone within the domain of the Republic a freeman, with the right to follow the ordinary pursuits of life without other restraints than such as are applied to all others, and to enjoy equally with them the earnings of his labor. But it confers no political rights; it leaves the States free, as before its adoption, to determine who shall hold their offices and participate in the administration of their laws. A similar prohibition of slavery and involuntary servitude was in the Constitution of several States previous to its adoption by the United States; and it was never held to confer any political rights. . . .

. . . In the consideration of questions growing out of these Amendments much confusion has arisen from a failure to distinguish between the civil and the political rights of citizens. Civil rights are absolute and personal. Political rights, on the other hand, are conditioned and dependent upon the discretion of the elective or appointing power, whether that be the People acting through the ballot, or one of the departments of their government. The civil rights of the individual are never to be withheld, and may be always judicially enforced. The political rights which he may enjoy, such as holding office and discharging a public trust, are qualified because their possession depends on his fitness, to be adjudged by those whom society has clothed with the elective authority. The 13th and 14th Amendments were designed to secure the civil rights of all persons, of every race, color and condition; but they left to the States to determine to whom the possession of political powers should be intrusted. This is manifest from the fact that when it was desired to confer political power upon the newly made citizens of the States, as was done by inhibiting the denial to them of the suffrage on account of race, color or previous condition of servitude, a new amendment was required.

The doctrine of the District Judge, for which the counsel contend, would lead to some singular results. If, when a colored person is accused of a criminal offense, the presence of persons of his race on the jury by which he is to be tried is essential to secure to him the equal protection of the laws, it would seem that the presence of such persons on the Bench would be equally essential, if the court should consist of more than one judge, as in many cases it may; and if it should consist of a single judge, that such protection would be impossible. A similar objection might be raised to the composition of any appellate court to which the case, after verdict, might be carried.

The position that, in cases where the rights of colored persons are concerned, justice will not be done to them unless they have a mixed jury, is founded upon the notion that in such cases white persons will not be fair and honest jurors. If this position be correct, there ought not to be any white persons on the jury where the interests of colored persons only are involved. That jury would not be an honest or fair one, of which any of its members should be governed in his judgment by other considerations than the law and the evidence, and that decision would hardly be considered just, which should be reached by a sort of compromise, in which the prejudices of one race were set off against the prejudices of the other. To be consistent, those who hold this notion should contend that, in cases affecting members of the colored race only, the juries should be composed entirely of colored persons, and that the presiding judge should be of the same race. To this result the doctrine asserted by the District Court logically leads. . . .

. . . Those who regard the independence of the States in all their reserved powers—and this includes the independence of their Legislative, Judicial and Executive Departments—as essential to the successful maintenance of our form of government, cannot fail to view, with the gravest apprehension for the future, the indictment, in a court of the United States, of a judicial officer of a State for the manner in which he has discharged his duties under her laws, and of which she makes no complaint. The proceeding is a gross offense to the State; it is an attack upon her sovereignty, in matters over which she has never surrendered her jurisdiction. The doctrine which sustains it, carried to its logical results, would degrade and sink her to the level of a mere local municipal corporation; for if Congress can render an officer of a State criminally liable for the manner in which he discharges his duties under her laws, it can prescribe the nature and extent of the penalty to which he shall be subjected on conviction; it may imprison him for life, or punish him by removal from office. And if it can make the exclusion of persons from jury service on account of race or color a criminal offense, it can make their exclusion from office on that account also criminal; and, adopting the doctrine of the District Judge in this case, the failure to appoint them to office will be presumptive evidence of their exclusion on that ground. To such a result are we logically led. The legislation of Congress is founded, and is sustained by this court, as it seems to me, upon a theory as to what constitutes the equal protection of the laws, which is purely speculative, not warranted by any experience of the country, and not in accordance with the understanding of the people as to the meaning of those terms since the organization of the government.

I am authorized to say that Mr. Justice Clifford concurs with me in this opinion.

The Sinking Fund Cases

99 U.S. 700 (1879)

The Fourteenth Amendment is of course not the only constitutional provision susceptible to activist or anti-activist interpretation. The same basic problems that produced the Granger legislation and *Munn* v. *Illinois* also moved Congress to act. As of 1870, public

land and monetary grants accounted for about sixty percent of the
construction cost of our "private" railroads. A large part of the
balance of the cost was met by railroad bonds. The well-known
corruption in railroad finances led Congress to require that twenty-
five percent of the earnings of two congressionally chartered railroads be set aside as a sinking fund for the retirement of their
bonded indebtedness to the United States. There had been no such
requirement in the original charters of incorporation.

MR. CHIEF JUSTICE WAITE delivered the opinion of the Court.

The single question presented by the case of the Union Pacific Railroad Company is as to the constitutionality of that
part of the act of May 7, 1878, which establishes in the treasury of the United States a sinking-fund. The validity of the
rest of the act is not necessarily involved.

It is our duty, when required in the regular course of judicial
proceedings, to declare an act of Congress void if not within
the legislative power of the United States; but this declaration
should never be made except in a clear case. Every possible
presumption is in favor of the validity of a statute, and this
continues until the contrary is shown beyond a rational doubt.
One branch of the government cannot encroach on the domain
of another without danger. The safety of our institutions depends in no small degree on a strict observance of this salutary
rule.

The United States cannot any more than a State interfere
with private rights, except for legitimate governmental purposes. They are not included within the constitutional prohibition which prevents States from passing laws impairing the
obligation of contracts, but equally with the States they are
prohibited from depriving persons or corporations of property
without due process of law. They cannot legislate back to
themselves, without making compensation, the lands they have
given this corporation to aid in the construction of its railroad.
Neither can they by legislation compel the corporation to dis-

charge its obligations in respect to the subsidy bonds otherwise than according to the terms of the contract already made in that connection. The United States are as much bound by their contracts as are individuals. If they repudiate their obligations, it is as much repudiation, with all the wrong and reproach that term implies, as it would be if the repudiator had been a State or a municipality or a citizen. No change can be made in the title created by the grant of the lands, or in the contract for the subsidy bonds, without the consent of the corporation. All this is indisputable.

The contract of the company in respect to the subsidy bonds is to pay both principal and interest when the principal matures, unless the debt is sooner discharged by the application of one-half the compensation for transportation and other services rendered for the government, and the five per cent of net earnings as specified in the charter. This was decided in *Union Pacific Railroad Co.* v. *United States*, 91 U.S. 72. The precise point to be determined now is, whether a statute which requires the company in the management of its affairs to set aside a portion of its current income as a sinking-fund to meet this and other mortgage debts when they mature, deprives the company of its property without due process of law, or in any other way improperly interferes with vested rights.

This corporation is a creature of the United States. It is a private corporation created for public purposes, and its property is to a large extent devoted to public uses. It is, therefore, subject to legislative control so far as its business affects the public interests. *Chicago, Burlington, & Quincy Railroad Co.* v. *Iowa*, 94 U.S. 155.

It is unnecessary to decide what power Congress would have had over the charter if the right of amendment had not been reserved; for, as we think, that reservation has been made. In the act of 1862, sect. 18, it was accompanied by an explanatory statement showing that this had been done "the better to accomplish the object of this act, namely, to promote the public interest and welfare by the construction of said railroad and telegraph line, and keeping the same in working order, and to secure to the government at all times (but especially in time of war) the use and benefits of the same for postal, military, and other purposes," and by an injunction that it should be used with "due regard for the rights of said companies." In the act of 1864, however, there is nothing except the simple words (sect. 22) "that Congress may at any time alter, amend, and repeal this act." Taking both acts together, and giving the explanatory statement in that of 1862 all the effect it can be entitled to, we are of the opinion that Congress not only retains, but has given special notice of its intention to retain, full and complete power to make such alterations and amendments of the charter as come within the just scope of legislative power. That this power has a limit, no one can doubt. All agree that it cannot be used to take away property already acquired under the operation of the charter, or to deprive the corporation of the fruits actually reduced to possession of contracts lawfully made; but, as was said by this Court, through Mr. Justice Clifford, in *Miller* v. *The State* (15 Wall. 498), "it may safely be affirmed that the reserved power may be exercised, and to almost any extent, to carry into effect the original purposes of the grant, or to secure the due administration of its affairs, so as to protect the rights of stockholders and of creditors, and for the proper disposition of its assets;" and again, in *Holyoke Company* v. *Lyman* (id. 519), "to protect the rights of the public and of the corporators, or to promote the due administration of the affairs of the corporation." Mr. Justice Field, also speaking for the court, was even more explicit when, in *Tomlinson* v. *Jessup* (id. 459), he said, "the reservation affects the entire relation between the State and the corporation, and places under legislative control all rights, privileges, and immunities derived by its charter directly from the State;" and again, as late as *Railroad Company* v. *Maine* (96 U.S. 510), "by the reservation . . . the State retained the power to alter it [the charter] in all particulars constituting the grant to the new company, formed under it, of corporate rights, privileges, and immunities." Mr. Justice Swayne, in *Shields* v. *Ohio* (95 U.S. 324), says, by way of limitation, "The alterations must be reasonable; they must be made in good faith, and be consistent with the object and scope of the act of incorporation. Sheer oppression and wrong cannot be inflicted under the guise of amendment or alteration." The rules as here laid down are fully sustained by authority. Further citations are unnecessary.

Giving full effect to the principles which have thus been authoritatively stated, we think it safe to say, that whatever rules Congress might have prescribed in the original charter for the government of the corporation in the administration of its affairs, it retained the power to establish by amendment. In so doing it cannot undo what has already been done, and it cannot unmake contracts that have already been made, but it may provide for what shall be done in the future, and may direct what preparation shall be made for the due performance of contracts already entered into. It might originally have prohibited the borrowing of money on mortgage, or it might have said that no bonded debt should be created without ample provision by sinking-fund to meet it at maturity. Not having done so at first, it cannot now by direct legislation vacate mortgages already made under the powers originally granted, nor release debts already contracted. A prohibition now against contracting debts will not avoid debts already incurred. An amendment making it unlawful to issue bonds payable at a distant day, without at the same time establishing a fund for their ultimate redemption, will not invalidate a bond already out. All such legislation will be confined in its operation to the future. . . .

The United States occupy towards this corporation a twofold relation,—that of sovereign and that of creditor. *United States* v. *Union Pacific Railroad Co.*, 98 U.S. 569. Their rights as sovereign are not crippled because they are creditors, and their privileges as creditors are not enlarged by the charter because of their sovereignty. They cannot, as creditors, demand payment of what is due them before the time limited by the contract. Neither can they, as sovereign or creditors, require the company to pay the other debts it owes before they mature. But out of regard to the rights of the subsequent lien-holders and stockholders, it is not only their right, but their duty, as sovereign to see to it that the current stockholders do not, in the administration of the affairs of the corporation, appropriate to their own use that which in equity belongs to others. A legislative regulation which does no more than require them to submit to their just contribution towards the payment of a bonded debt cannot in any sense be said to deprive them of their property without due process of law. . . .

The question still remains, whether the particular provision of this statute now under consideration comes within this rule. It establishes a sinking-fund for the payment of debts when they mature, but does not pay the debts. The original contracts of loan are not changed. They remain as they were before, and are only to be met at maturity. All that has been done is to make it the duty of the company to lay by a portion of its current net income to meet its debts when they do fall due. In this way the current stockholders are prevented to some extent from depleting the treasury for their own benefit, at the expense of those who are to come after them. This is no more for the benefit of the creditors than it is for the corporation itself. It tends to give permanency to the value of the stock and bonds, and is in the direct interest of a faithful administration of affairs. It simply compels the managers for the time being to do what they ought to do voluntarily. The fund to be created is not so much for the security of the creditors as the ultimate protection of the public and the corporators.

To our minds it is a matter of no consequence that the Secretary of the Treasury is made the sinking-fund agent and the treasury of the United States the depository, or that the investment is to be made in the public funds of the United States. This does not make the deposit a payment of the debt due the United States. The duty of the manager of every sinking-fund is to seek some safe investment for the moneys as they accumulate in his hands, so that when required they may be promptly available. Certainly no objection can be made to the security of this investment. In fact, we do not understand that complaint is made in this particular. The objection is to the creation of the fund and not to the investment, if that investment is not in law a payment. . . .

Not to pursue this branch of the inquiry any further, it is sufficient now to say that we think the legislation complained of may be sustained on the ground that it is a reasonable regulation of the administration of the affairs of the corporation, and promotive of the interests of the public and the corporators. It takes nothing from the corporation or the stockholders which actually belongs to them. It oppresses no one, and inflicts no wrong. It simply gives further assurance of the continued solvency and prosperity of a corporation in which the public are so largely interested, and adds another guaranty to the permanent and lasting value of its vast amount of securities.

The legislation is also warranted under the authority by way of amendment to change or modify the rights, privileges, and immunities granted by the charter. The right of the stockholders to a division of the earnings of the corporation is a privilege derived from the charter. When the charter and its amendments first became laws, and the work on the road was undertaken, it was by no means sure that the enterprise would prove a financial success. No statutory restraint was then put upon the power of declaring dividends. It was not certain that the stock would ever find a place on the list of marketable securities, or that there would be any bonds subsequent in lien to that of the United States which could need legislative or other protection. Hence, all this was left unprovided for in the charter and its amendments as originally granted, and the reservation of the power of amendment inserted so as to enable the government to accommodate its legislation to the requirements of the public and the corporation as they should be developed in the future. Now it is known that the stock of the company has found its way to the markets of the world; that large issues of bonds have been made beyond what was originally contemplated, and that the company has gone on for years dividing its earnings without any regard to its increasing debt, or to the protection of those whose rights may be endangered if this practice is permitted to continue. For this reason Congress has interfered, and, under its reserved power, limited the privilege of declaring dividends on current earnings, so as to confine the stockholders to what is left after suitable provision has been made for the protection of creditors and stockholders against the disastrous consequences of a constantly increasing debt. As this increase cannot be kept down by payment unless voluntarily made by the corporation, the next best thing has been done, that is to say, a fund safely invested, which increases as the debt increases, has been established and set apart to meet the debt when the time comes that payment can be required.

No objection has ever been made by the State to this action by Congress. On the contrary, the State, by implication at least, has given its assent to what was done, for in 1864 it passed "An Act to aid in carrying out the provisions of the Pacific railroad and telegraph act of Congress," and thereby confirmed and vested in the company "all the rights, privileges, franchises, power, and authority conferred upon, granted to, or vested in said company by said act of Congress," and repealed "all laws or parts of laws inconsistent or in conflict with . . . the rights and privileges herein (therein) granted." Hittell's Laws, sect. 4798; Acts of 1863-64, 471. Inasmuch as by the Constitution of California then in force (art. 4, sect. 31) corporations, except for municipal purposes, could not be created by special act, but must be formed under general laws, the legal effect of this act is probably little more than a legislative recognition by the State of what had been done by the United States with one of the State corporations. . . .

Judgment affirmed.
Decree affirmed.

MR. JUSTICE FIELD, MR. JUSTICE STRONG, and MR. JUSTICE BRADLEY, dissented. . . .

MR. JUSTICE FIELD. I also dissent from the judgment of the court in these cases.

The decision will, in my opinion, tend to create insecurity in the title to corporate property in the country. It, in effect, determines that the general government, in its dealings with the Pacific Railroad Companies, is under no legal obligation to fulfil its contracts, and that whether it shall do so is a question of policy and not of duty. It also seems to me to recognize the right of the government to appropriate by legislative decree the earnings of those companies, without judicial inquiry and determination as to its claim to such earnings, thus sanctioning the exercise of judicial functions in its own cases. And in respect to the Central Pacific Company it asserts a supremacy of the Federal over the State government in the control of the corporation which, in my judgment, is subversive of the rights of the State. I therefore am constrained to add some suggestions to those presented by my associates, Justices Strong and Bradley. In what I have to say I shall confine myself chiefly to the case of the Central Pacific Company. That company is a State corporation, and is the successor of a corporation of the same name, created before the railroad acts of Congress were passed, and of four other corporations organized under the laws of the State. No sovereign attributes possessed by the general government were exercised in calling into existence the original company, or any of the companies with which it is now consolidated. They all derived their powers and capacities from the State, and held them at its will.

The relation of the general government to the Pacific companies is twofold: that of sovereign in its own territory and that of contractor. As sovereign, its power extends to the enforcement of such acts and regulations by the companies as will insure, in the management of their roads, and conduct of their officers in its territory, the safety, convenience, and comfort of the public. It can exercise such control in its territory over all common carriers of passengers and property. As a contractor it is bound by its engagements equally with a private individual; it cannot be relieved from them by any assertion of its sovereign authority. . . .

It is not material, in the view I take of the subject, whether the deposit of this large sum in the treasury of the creditor be termed a payment, or something else. It is the exaction from the company of money for which the original contract did not stipulate, which constitutes the objectionable feature of the act of 1878. The act thus makes a great change in the liabilities of the company. Its purpose, however, disguised, is to coerce the payment of money years in advance of the time prescribed by the contract. That such legislation is beyond the power of Congress I cannot entertain a doubt. The clauses of the original acts reserving a right to Congress to alter or amend them do not, in my judgment, justify the legislation. The power reserved under these clauses is declared to be for a specific purpose. The language in the act of 1862 is as follows: "And the better to accomplish the object of this act, to promote the public interest and welfare by the construction of said railroad and telegraph line, and keeping the same in working order, and to secure to the government at all times (but particularly in time of war) the use and benefits of the same for postal, military, and other purposes, Congress may at any time—having due regard for the rights of said companies named herein—add to, alter, amend, or repeal this act." Sect. 18. The language of the amendatory act of 1864 is more general: "That Congress may at any time alter, amend, or repeal this act." The two acts are to be read together; they deal with the same subject; and are to be treated as if passed at the same time. *Prescott* v. *Railroad Company*, 16 Wall. 603. The limitations, therefore, imposed upon the exercise of the power of alteration and amendment in the act of 1862 must be held to apply to the power reserved in the act of 1864. They are not repealed, either expressly or impliedly, by any thing in the latter act. If this be so, the legislation of 1878 can find no support in the clauses. The conditions upon which the reserved power could be exercised under them did not then exist. The road and telegraph had years before been constructed, and always kept in working order; and the government has at all times been secured in their use and benefits for postal, military, and other purposes.

But if the reserved power of alteration and amendment be considered as freed from the limitations designated, it cannot be exerted to affect the contract so far as it has been executed, or the rights vested under it. When the road was completed in the manner prescribed and accepted, the company became entitled as of right to the land and subsidy bonds stipulated. The title to the land was perfect on the issue of the patents; the title to the bonds vested on their delivery. Any alteration of the acts under the reservation clauses, or their repeal, could not revoke the title to the land or recall the bonds or change the right of the company to either. So far as these are concerned the contract was, long before the act of 1878, an executed and closed transaction, and they were as much beyond the reach of the government as any other property vested in private proprietorship. The right to hold the subsidy bonds for the period at which they are to run without paying or advancing money on them before their maturity, except as originally provided, or furnishing other security than that originally stipulated, was, on their delivery, as perfect as the right to hold the title to the land patented unincumbered by future liens of the government. Any alteration or amendment could only operate for the future and affect subsequent acts of the company: it could have no operation upon that which had already been done and vested. . . .

The object of a reservation of this kind in acts of incorporation is to insure to the government control over corporate franchises, rights, and privileges which, in its sovereign or legislative capacity, it may call into existence, not to interfere with contracts which the corporation created by it may make. Such is the purport of our language in *Tomlinson* v. *Jessup,* where we state the object of the reservation to be "to prevent a grant of *corporate* rights and privileges in a form which will preclude legislative interference with their exercise, if the public interest should at any time require such interference," and that "the reservation affects the entire relation between the State and corporation, and places under legislative control all rights, privileges, and immunities *derived by its charter directly from the State."* 15 Wall. 454. The same thing we repeated, with greater distinctness, in *Railroad Company* v. *Maine,* where we said that by the reservation the State retained the power to alter the act incorporating the company, in all particulars *constituting the grant to it of corporate rights, privileges, and immunities;* and that "the existence of the corporation, and its franchises and immunities, derived directly from the State, were thus kept under its control." But we added, that "rights and interests acquired by the company, *not constituting a part of the contract of incorporation,* stand upon a different footing." 96 U.S. 499.

Now, there was no grant by the United States to the Central Pacific Company of corporate rights, privileges, and immunities. No attribute of sovereignty was exercised by them in its creation. It took its life, and all its attributes and capacities, from the State. Whatever powers, rights, and privileges it acquired from the United States it took under its contract with them, and not otherwise. The relation between the parties being that of contractors, the rights and obligations of both, as already stated, are to be measured by the terms and conditions of the contract. And when the government of the United States entered into that contract, it laid aside its sovereignty and put itself on terms of equality with its contractor. It was then but a civil corporation, as incapable as the Central Pacific of releasing itself from its obligations, or of finally determining their extent and character. It could not, as justly observed by one of the counsel who argued this case, "*release itself and hold the other party* to the contract. It could not change its *obligations* and hold its *rights* unchanged. It cannot bind itself as a *civil corporation,* and loose itself by its sovereign legislative power." This principle is aptly expressed by the great conservative statesman, Alexander Hamilton, in his report to Congress on the public credit, in 1795: "When a government," he observes, "enters into a contract with an individual, it deposes, as to the matter of the contract, its constitutional authority, and exchanges the character of legislator for that of a moral agent, with the same rights and obligations as an individual. Its promises may be justly considered out of its *power to legislate,* unless in aid of them. It is, in theory, impossible to reconcile the two ideas of a *promise which obliges* with a power *to make a law which can vary the effect of it.*" Hamilton's Works, vol. iii. pp. 518, 519.

When, therefore, the government of the United States entered into the contract with the Central Pacific, it could no more than a private corporation or a private individual finally construe and determine the extent of the company's rights and liabilities. If it had cause of complaint against the company, it could not undertake itself, by legislative decree, to redress the grievance, but was compelled to seek redress as all other civil corporations are compelled, through the judicial tribunals. If the company was wasting its property, of which no allegation is made, or impairing the security of the government, the remedy by suit was ample. To declare that one of two contracting parties is entitled, under the contract between them, to the payment of a greater sum than is admitted to be payable, or to other or greater security than that given, is not a legislative function. It is judicial action; it is the exercise of judicial power,—and all such power, with respect to any transaction arising under the laws of the United States, is vested by the Constitution in the courts of the country.

THE TRIUMPH OF LAISSEZ-FAIRE

ACTIVISM (1888–1936)

Lochner v. *New York*

198 U.S. 45 (1905)

A New York law limited employment in bakeries to a maximum of sixty hours per week and ten hours per day. The Court's opinion reflects the full flowering of Mr. Justice Field's earlier dissenting efforts. Chief Justice Waite's approach is here reflected in Holmes's dissent.

MR. JUSTICE PECKHAM . . . delivered the opinion of the court. . . .

The statute necessarily interferes with the right of contract between the employer and employés, concerning the number of hours in which the latter may labor in the bakery of the employer. The general right to make a contract in relation to his business is part of the liberty of the individual protected by the Fourteenth Amendment of the federal Constitution. *Allgeyer* v. *Louisiana*, 165 U.S. 578. Under that provision no state can deprive any person of life, liberty, or property without due process of law. The right to purchase or to sell labor is part of the liberty protected by this amendment, unless there are circumstances which exclude the right. There are, however, certain powers, existing in the sovereignty of each state in the Union, somewhat vaguely termed police powers, the exact description and limitation of which have not been attempted by the courts. Those powers, broadly stated, and without, at present, any attempt at a more specific limitation, relate to the safety, health, morals and general welfare of the public. Both property and liberty are held on such reasonable conditions as may be imposed by the governing power of the state in the exercise of those powers, and with such conditions the Fourteenth Amendment was not designed to interfere. . . .

The state, therefore, has power to prevent the individual from making certain kinds of contracts, and in regard to them the federal Constitution offers no protection. If the contract be one which the state, in the legitimate exercise of its police power, has the right to prohibit, it is not prevented from prohibiting it by the Fourteenth Amendment. Contracts in violation of a statute, either of the federal or state government, or a contract to let one's property for immoral purposes, or to do any other unlawful act, could obtain no protection from the federal Constitution, as coming under the liberty of person or of free contract. Therefore, when the state, by its legislature, in the assumed exercise of its police powers, has passed an act which seriously limits the right to labor or the right of contract in regard to their means of livelihood between persons who are *sui juris* (both employer and employé), it becomes of great importance to determine which shall prevail—the right of the individual to labor for such time as he may choose, or the right of the state to prevent the individual from laboring, or from entering into any contract to labor, beyond a certain time prescribed by the state.

This court has recognized the existence and upheld the exercise of the police powers of the states in many cases which might fairly be considered as border ones, and it has, in the course of its determination of questions regarding the asserted invalidity of such statutes, on the ground of their violation of the rights secured by the federal Constitution, been guided by rules of a very liberal nature, the application of which has resulted, in numerous instances, in upholding the validity of state statutes thus assailed. Among the later cases where the state law has been upheld by this court is that of *Holden* v. *Hardy*, 169 U.S. 366. A provision in the act of the legislature of Utah was there under consideration, the act limiting the employment of workmen in all underground mines or work- ings, to eight hours per day, "except in cases of emergency, where life or property is in imminent danger." It also limited the hours of labor in smelting and other institutions for the reduction or refining of ores or metals to eight hours per day, except in like cases of emergency. The act was held to be a valid exercise of police powers of the state. A review of many of the cases on the subject, decided by this and other courts, as given in the opinion. It was held that the kind of employ- ment, mining, smelting, etc., and the character of the employés in such kinds of labor, were such as to make it reasonable and proper for the state to interfere to prevent the employés from being constrained by the rules laid down by the proprietors in regard to labor. . . .

It must, of course, be conceded that there is a limit to the valid exercise of the police power by the state. There is no dispute concerning this general proposition. Otherwise the Fourteenth Amendment would have no efficacy and the legis- latures of the states would have unbounded power, and it would be enough to say that any piece of legislation was en- acted to conserve the morals, the health, or the safety of the people; such legislation would be valid, no matter how abso- lutely without foundation the claim might be. The claim of the police power would be a mere pretext,—become another and delusive name for the supreme sovereignty of the state to be exercised free from constitutional restraint. This is not contended for. In every case that comes before this court, therefore, where legislation of this character is concerned, and where the protection of the federal Constitution is sought, the question necessarily arises: Is this a fair, reasonable, and appropriate exercise of the police power of the state, or is it an unreasonable, unnecessary, and arbitrary interference with the right of the individual to his personal liberty, or to enter into those contracts in relation to labor which may seem to him appropriate or necessary for the support of himself and his family? Of course the liberty of contract relating to labor includes both parties to it. The one has as much right to purchase as the other to sell labor.

This is not a question of substituting the judgment of the court for that of the legislature. If the act be within the power of the state it is valid, although the judgment of the court might be totally opposed to the enactment of such a law. But the question would still remain: Is it within the police power of the state? and that question must be answered by the court.

The question whether this act is valid as a labor law, pure and simple, may be dismissed in a few words. There is no reasonable ground for interfering with the liberty of person or the right of free contract, by determining the hours of labor, in the occupation of a baker. There is no contention that bakers as a class are not equal in intelligence and capacity to men in other trades or manual occupations, or that they are not able to assert their rights and care for themselves without the protecting arm of the state, interfering with their independence of judgment and of action. They are in no sense wards of the state. Viewed in the light of a purely labor law, with no reference whatever to the question of health, we think that a law like the one before us involves neither the safety, the morals, nor the welfare, of the public, and that the interest of the public is not in the slightest degree affected by such an act. The law must be upheld, if at all, as a law pertaining to the health of the individual engaged in the occupation of a baker. It does not affect any other portion of the public than those who are engaged in that occupation. Clean and wholesome bread does not depend upon whether the baker works but ten hours per day or only sixty hours a week. The limitation of the hours of labor does not come within the police power on that ground.

It is a question of which of two powers or rights shall prevail,—the power of the state to legislate or the right of the individual to liberty of person and freedom of contract. The mere assertion that the subject relates, though but in a remote degree, to the public health, does not necessarily render the enactment valid. The act must have a more direct relation, as a means to an end, and the end itself must be appropriate and legitimate, before an act can be held to be valid which interferes with the general right of an individual to be free in his person and in his power to contract in relation to his own labor. . . .

We think that there can be no fair doubt that the trade of a baker, in and of itself, is not an unhealthy one to that degree which would authorize the legislature to interfere with the right to labor, and with the right of free contract on the part of the individual, either as employer or employé. In looking through statistics regarding all trades and occupations, it may be true that the trade of a baker does not appear to be as healthy as some other trades, and is also vastly more healthy than still others. To the common understanding the trade of a baker has never been regarded as an unhealthy one. Very likely physicians would not recommend the exercise of that or of any other trade as a remedy for ill health. Some occupations are more healthy than others, but we think there are none which might not come under the power of the legislature to supervise and control the hours of working therein, if the mere fact that the occupation is not absolutely and perfectly healthy is to confer that right upon the legislative department of the government. It might be safely affirmed that almost all occupations more or less affect the health. There must be more than the mere fact of the possible existence of some small amount of unhealthiness to warrant legislative interference with liberty. It is unfortunately true that labor, even in any department, may possibly carry with it the seeds of unhealthiness. But are we all, on that account, at the mercy of legislative majorities? . . .

We do not believe in the soundness of the views which uphold this law. On the contrary, we think that such a law as this, although passed in the assumed exercise of the police power, and as relating to the public health, or the health of the employés named, is not within that power, and is invalid. The act is not, within any fair meaning of the term, a health law, but is an illegal interference with the rights of individuals, both employers and employés, to make contracts regarding labor upon such terms as they may think best, or which they may agree upon with the other parties to such contracts.

Statutes of the nature of that under review, limiting the hours in which grown and intelligent men may labor to earn their living, are mere meddlesome interferences with the rights of the individual, and they are not saved from condemnation by the claim that they are passed in the exercise of the police power. . . .

It was further urged . . . that restricting the hours of labor in the case of bakers was valid because it tended to cleanliness on the part of the workers, as a man was more apt to be cleanly when not overworked, and if cleanly then his "output" was also more likely to be so. . . . We do not admit the reasoning to be sufficient to justify the claimed right of such interference. The state in that case would assume the position of a supervisor, or *pater familias,* over every act of the individual, and its right of governmental interference with his hours of labor, his hours of exercise, the character thereof, and the extent to which it shall be carried would be recognized and upheld. In our judgment it is not possible in fact to discover the connection between the number of hours a baker may work in the bakery and the healthy quality of the bread made by the workman. The connection, if any exists, is too shadowy and thin to build any argument for the interference of the legislature. If the man works ten hours a day it is all right, but if ten and a half or eleven his health is in danger and his bread may be unhealthful, and, therefore, he shall not be permitted to do it. This, we think, is unreasonable and entirely arbitrary. . . .

This interference on the part of the legislatures of the several states with the ordinary trades and occupations of the people seems to be on the increase. . . .

It is impossible for us to shut our eyes to the fact that many of the laws of this character, while passed under what is claimed to be the police power for the purpose of protecting the public health or welfare, are, in reality, passed from other motives. We are justified in saying so when, from the character of the law and the subject upon which it legislates, it is apparent that the public health or welfare bears but the most remote relation to the law. The purpose of a statute must be determined from the natural and legal effect of the language employed; and whether it is or is not repugnant to the Constitution of the United States must be determined from the natural effect of such statutes when put into operation, and not from their proclaimed purpose.

Reversed.

Mr. Justice Harlan, with whom Mr. Justice White and Mr. Justice Day concurred, [dissented].

Mr. Justice Holmes, dissenting.

I regret sincerely that I am unable to agree with the judgment in this case, and that I think it my duty to express my dissent.

This case is decided upon an economic theory which a large part of the country does not entertain. If it were a question whether I agreed with that theory, I should desire to study it further and long before making up my mind. But I do not conceive that to be my duty, because I strongly believe that my agreement or disagreement has nothing to do with the right of a majority to embody their opinions in law. It is settled by various decisions of this court that state Constitutions and state laws may regulate life in many ways which we as legislators might think as injudicious, or if you like as tyrannical as this, and which, equally with this, interfere with the liberty to contract. Sunday laws and usury laws are ancient examples. A more modern one is the prohibition of lotteries. The liberty of the citizen to do as he likes so long as he does not interfere with the liberty of others to do the same, which has been a shibboleth for some well-known writers, is interfered with by school laws, by the postoffice, by every state or municipal institution which takes his money for purposes thought desirable, whether he likes it or not. The fourteenth amendment does not enact Mr. Herbert Spencer's Social Statics. The other day we sustained the Massachusetts vaccination law. *Jacobson* v. *Massachusetts,* 197 U.S. 11. . . . United States and state statutes and decisions cutting down the liberty to contract by way of combination are familiar to this court. *Northern Securities Co.* v. *United States,* 193 U.S. 197. . . . Two years ago we upheld the prohibition of sales of stock on margins, or for future delivery, in the Constitution of California. *Otis* v. *Parker,* 187 U.S. 606. . . . The decision sustaining an eight-hour law for miners is still recent. *Holden* v. *Hardy,* 169 U.S. 366. . . . Some of these laws embody convictions or prejudices which judges are likely to share. Some may not. But a Constitution is not intended to embody a particular economic theory, whether of paternalism and the organic relation of the citizen to the state or of *laissez faire.* It is made for people of fundamentally differing views, and the accident of our finding certain opinions natural and familiar, or novel, and even shocking, ought not to conclude our judgment upon the question whether statutes embodying them conflict with the Constitution of the United States.

General propositions do not decide concrete cases. The decision will depend on a judgment or intuition more subtle than any articulate major premise. But I think that the proposition just stated, if it is accepted, will carry us far toward the end. Every opinion tends to become a law. I think that the word "liberty," in the Fourteenth Amendment, is perverted when it is held to prevent the natural outcome of a dominant opinion, unless it can be said that a rational and fair man necessarily would admit that the statute proposed would infringe fundamental principles as they have been understood by the traditions of our people and our law. It does not need research to show that no such sweeping condemnation can be passed upon the statute before us. A reasonable man might think it a proper measure on the score of health. Men whom I certainly could not pronounce unreasonable would uphold it as a first instalment of a general regulation of the hours of work. Whether in the latter aspect it would be open to the charge of inequality I think it unnecessary to discuss.

Whitney v. California

274 U.S. 357 (1927)

Miss Anita Whitney, heiress to a famous fortune, was convicted of violating a state criminal-syndicalism law by helping to organize, and being a member of, a group advocating sabotage and other unlawful acts of violence as a means of accomplishing industrial or political change. The Court held first that the jury's verdict was conclusive on the issue of whether the defendant had helped organize and had joined the group knowing its syndicalist program (since this was a question of *fact*). The Court then turned to the *legal* issue: Was the state law constitutional? On this question, note the Court's respect for the presumption of constitutionality, and its inability to find the act "unreasonable or arbitrary." Compare the Court's attitude on these points with the majority position in *Lochner*.

Note the Holmes-Brandeis reference to the scope of the Fourteenth Amendment; their special respect for free utterance; and—this respect notwithstanding—their refusal to violate the Rule of Law, which compelled them to uphold the conviction. As they saw it, the Supreme Court's only function in cases of this type was to correct errors of law—i.e., *errors made by the lower court*. Here they could find no such error, though they make it clear that in their view *plaintiff* should have raised the clear-and-present-danger test at the trial level. Had this been done, and had the trial judge erred in applying it, Holmes and Brandeis would no doubt have dissented, as in *Gitlow* v. *New York*.[79]

MR. JUSTICE SANFORD delivered the opinion of the court:

By a criminal information filed in the superior court of Alameda county, California, the plaintiff in error was charged, in five counts, with violations of the Criminal Syndicalism Act of that state. Statutes 1919, chap. 188, p. 281. She was tried, convicted on the first count, and sentenced to imprisonment. The judgment was affirmed by the district court of appeal. 57 Cal. App. 449. Her petition to have the case heard by the supreme court was denied. Id. 453. And the case was brought here on a writ of error which was allowed by the presiding justice of the court of appeal, the highest court of the state in which a decision could be had. Judicial Code, §237.

On the first hearing in this court, the writ of error was dismissed for want of jurisdiction. 269 U.S. 530. Thereafter, a petition for rehearing was granted (269 U.S. 538), and the case

---

[79] 268 U.S. 652 (1925). The Supreme Court, of course, does not sit to correct the strategic "errors," or miscalculations, of litigants. Counsel for Miss Whitney did not raise the clear-and-present-danger issue, presumably because in that day it would not have been helpful (considering the Court's prior use of it). Miss Whitney wanted to win more than a Holmes-Brandeis dissent!

was again heard and reargued both as to the jurisdiction and the merits.

The pertinent provisions of the Criminal Syndicalism Act are:

"Section 1. The term 'criminal syndicalism' as used in this act is hereby defined as any doctrine or precept advocating, teaching or aiding and abetting the commission of crime, sabotage (which word is hereby defined as meaning wilful and malicious physical damage or injury to physical property), or unlawful acts of force and violence or unlawful methods of terrorism as a means of accomplishing a change in industrial ownership or control, or effecting any political change.

"Sec. 2. Any person who: . . . (4) Organizes or assists in organizing, or is or knowingly becomes a member of, any organization, society, group or assemblage of persons organized or assembled to advocate, teach or aid and abet criminal syndicalism. . . .

"Is guilty of a felony and punishable by imprisonment."

The first count of the information, on which the conviction was had, charged that on or about November 28, 1919, in Alameda county, the defendant, in violation of the Criminal Syndicalism Act, "did then and there unlawfully, wilfully, wrongfully, deliberately and feloniously organize and assist in organizing, and was, is, and knowingly became a member of an organization, society, group and assemblage of persons organized and assembled to advocate, teach, aid and abet criminal syndicalism." . . .

The following facts, among many others, were established on the trial by undisputed evidence: The defendant, a resident of Oakland, in Alameda county, California, had been a member of the Local Oakland branch of the Socialist Party. This Local sent delegates to the national convention of the Socialist Party held in Chicago in 1919, which resulted in a split between the "radical" group and the old-wing Socialists. The "radicals,"— to whom the Oakland delegates adhered,—being ejected, went to another hall, and formed the Communist Labor Party of America. Its Constitution provided for the membership of persons subscribing to the principles of the party and pledging themselves to be guided by its platform, and for the formation of state organizations conforming to its platform as the supreme declaration of the party. In its "Platform and Program" the party declared that it was in full harmony with "the revolutionary working class parties of all countries" and adhered to the principles of Communism laid down in the Manifesto of the Third International at Moscow, and that its purpose was "to create a unified revolutionary working class movement in America," organizing the workers as a class, in a revolutionary class struggle to conquer the capitalist state, for the overthrow of capitalist rule, the conquest of political power and the establishment of a working class government, the dictatorship of the proletariat, in place of the state machinery of the capitalists, which should make and enforce the laws, reorganize society on the basis of Communism and bring about the Communist Commonwealth—advocated, as the most important means of capturing state power, the action of the masses, proceeding from the shops and factories, the use of the political machinery of the capitalist state being only secondary; the organization of the workers into "revolutionary industrial unions;" propaganda pointing out their revolutionary nature and possibilities; and great industrial battles showing the value of the strike as a political weapon—commended the propaganda and example of the Industrial Workers of the World and their struggles and sacrifices in the class war—pledged support and co-operation to "the revolutionary industrial proletariat of America" in their struggles against the capitalist class—cited the Seattle and Winnipeg strikes and the numerous strikes all over the country, "proceeding without the authority of the old reactionary trade union officials," as manifestations of the new tendency—and recommended that strikes of national importance be supported and given a political character, and that propagandists and organizers be mobilized "who cannot only teach, but actually help to put in practice, the principles of revolutionary industrial unionism and Communism."

Shortly thereafter the Local Oakland withdrew from the Socialist Party, and sent accredited delegates, including the defendant, to a convention held in Oakland in November, 1919, for the purpose of organizing a California branch of the Communist Labor Party. The defendant, after taking out a temporary membership in the Communist Labor Party, attended this convention as a delegate and took an active part in its proceedings. She was elected a member of the credentials committee, and, as its chairman, made a report to the convention upon which the delegates were seated. She was also appointed a member of the resolutions committee, and, as such, signed the following resolution in reference to political action, among others proposed by the committee: "The C.L.P. of California fully recognizes the value of political action as a means of spreading communist propaganda; it insists that in proportion to the development of the economic strength of the working class, it, the working class, must also develop its political power. The C.L.P. of California proclaims and insists that the capture of political power, locally or nationally by the revolutionary working class can be of tremendous assistance to the workers in their struggle of emancipation. Therefore, we again urge the workers who are possessed of the right of franchise to cast their votes for the party which represents their immediate and final interest—the C.L.P.—at all elections, being fully convinced of the utter futility of obtaining any real measure of justice or freedom under officials elected by parties owned and controlled by the capitalist class." The minutes show that this resolution, with the others proposed by the committee, was read by its chairman to the convention before the committee on the constitution had submitted its report. According to the recollection of the defendant, however, she herself read this resolution. Thereafter, before the report of the committee on the constitution had been acted upon, the defendant was elected an alternate member of the state executive committee. The constitution, as finally read, was then adopted. This provided that the organization should be named the Communist Labor Party of California; that it should be "affiliated with" the Communist Labor Party of America, and subscribe to its program, platform and constitution, and "through this affiliation" be "joined with the Communist International of Moscow;" and that the qualifications for membership should be those prescribed in the national constitution. The proposed resolutions were later taken up and all adopted, except that on political action, which caused a lengthy debate, resulting in its defeat and the acceptance of the national program in its place. After this action, the defendant, without, so far as appears, making any protest, remained in the convention until it adjourned. She later attended as an alternate member one or two meetings of the state executive committee in San Jose and San Francisco, and stated, on the trial, that she was then a member of the Communist Labor Party. She also testified that it was not her intention that the Communist Labor Party of California should be an instrument of terrorism or violence, and that it was not her purpose or that of the convention to violate any known law.

In the light of this preliminary statement, we now take up, in so far as they require specific consideration, the various grounds upon which it is here contended that the Syndicalism Act and its application in this case is repugnant to the due process and equal protection clauses of the 14th Amendment.

1. While it is not denied that the evidence warranted the jury in finding that the defendant became a member of and assisted in organizing the Communist Labor Party of California, and that this was organized to advocate, teach, aid or abet criminal syndicalism as defined by the act, it is urged that the act, as here construed and applied, deprived the de-

fendant of her liberty without due process of law in that it
has made her action in attending the Oakland convention
unlawful by reason of "a subsequent event brought about
against her will, by the agency of others," with no showing
of a specific intent on her part to join in the forbidden purpose
of the association, and merely because, by reason of a lack
of "prophetic" understanding, she failed to foresee the quality
that others would give to the convention. The argument is, in
effect, that the character of the state organization could not
be forecast when she attended the convention; that she had
no purpose of helping to create an instrument of terrorism and
violence; that she "took part in formulating and presenting to
the convention a resolution which, if adopted, would have
committed the new organization to a legitimate policy of political reform by the use of the ballot;" that it was not until after
the majority of the convention turned out to be "contrary
minded, and other less temperate policies prevailed" that the
convention could have taken on the character of criminal syndicalism; and that, as this was done over her protest, her mere
presence in the convention, however violent the opinions expressed therein, could not thereby become a crime. This contention, while advanced in the form of a constitutional
objection to the act, is in effect nothing more than an effort
to review the weight of the evidence for the purpose of showing that the defendant did not join and assist in organizing the
Communist Labor Party of California with a knowledge of its
unlawful character and purpose. This question, which is foreclosed by the verdict of the jury,—sustained by the court of
appeal over the specific objection that it was not supported by
the evidence,—is one of fact merely which is not open to review in this court, involving as it does no constitutional question whatever. . . .

2. It is clear that the Syndicalism Act is not repugnant to
the due process clause by reason of vagueness and uncertainty
of definition. It has no substantial resemblance to the statutes

held void for uncertainty under the 14th and 5th Amendments in International Harvester Co. v. Kentucky, 234 U.S. 216, 221; and United States v. L. Cohen Grocery Co., 255 U.S. 81, 89, because not fixing an ascertainable standard of guilt. The language of §2, subd. 4, of the act under which the plaintiff in error was convicted is clear; the definition of "criminal syndicalism" specific. . . .

3. Neither is the Syndicalism Act repugnant to the equal protection clause, on the ground that as its penalties are confined to those who advocate a resort to violent and unlawful methods as a means of changing industrial and political conditions, it arbitrarily discriminates between such persons and those who may advocate a resort to these methods as a means of maintaining such conditions. . . .

4. Nor is the Syndicalism Act as applied in this case repugnant to the due process clause as a restraint of the rights of free speech, assembly, and association.

That the freedom of speech which is secured by the Constitution does not confer an absolute right to speak, without responsibility, whatever one may choose, or an unrestricted and unbridled license giving immunity for every possible use of language and preventing the punishment of those who abuse this freedom; and that a state in the exercise of its police power may punish those who abuse this freedom by utterances inimical to the public welfare, tending to incite to crime, disturb the public peace, or endanger the foundations of organized government and threaten its overthrow by unlawful means, is not open to question. Gitlow v. New York, 268 U.S. 652, 666–668, and cases cited.

By enacting the provisions of the Syndicalism Act the state has declared, through its legislative body, that to knowingly be or become a member of or assist in organizing an association to advocate, teach or aid and abet the commission of crimes or unlawful acts of force, violence or terrorism as a means of accomplishing industrial or political changes, involves such danger to the public peace and the security of the state, that these acts should be penalized in the exercise of its police power. That determination must be given great weight. Every presumption is to be indulged in favor of the validity of the statute (Mugler v. Kansas, 123 U.S. 623, 661), and it may not be declared unconstitutional unless it is an arbitrary or unreasonable attempt to exercise the authority vested in the state in the public interest (Great Northern R. Co. v. Clara City, 246 U.S. 434, 439).

The essence of the offense denounced by the act is the combining with others in an association for the accomplishment of the desired ends through the advocacy and use of criminal and unlawful methods. It partakes of the nature of a criminal conspiracy. See People v. Steelik, 187 Cal. 376. That such united and joint action involves even greater danger to the public peace and security than the isolated utterances and acts of individuals, is clear. We cannot hold that, as here applied, the act is an unreasonable or arbitrary exercise of the police power of the state, unwarrantably infringing any right of free speech, assembly or association, or that those persons are protected from punishment by the due process clause who abuse such rights by joining and furthering an organization thus menacing the peace and welfare of the state.

We find no repugnancy in the Syndicalism Act as applied in this case to either the due process or equal protection clause of the 14th Amendment, on any of the grounds upon which its validity has been here challenged.

The order dismissing the writ of error will be vacated and set aside, and the judgment of the Court of Appeal affirmed.

Mr. Justice Brandeis, concurring:

Miss Whitney was convicted of the felony of assisting in organizing, in the year 1919, the Communist Labor Party of California, of being a member of it, and of assembling with it. These acts are held to constitute a crime, because the party was formed to teach criminal syndicalism. The statute which made these acts a crime restricted the right of free speech and of assembly theretofore existing. The claim is that the statute, as applied, denied to Miss Whitney the liberty guaranteed by the 14th Amendment.

The felony which the statute created is a crime very unlike the old felony of conspiracy or the old misdemeanor of unlawful assembly. The mere act of assisting in forming a society for teaching syndicalism, of becoming a member of it, or of assembling with others for that purpose is given the dynamic quality of crime. There is guilt although the society may not contemplate immediate promulgation of the doctrine. Thus the accused is to be punished, not for attempt, incitement or conspiracy, but for a step in preparation, which, if it threatens the public order at all, does so only remotely. The novelty in the prohibition introduced is that the statute aims, not at the practice of criminal syndicalism, nor even directly at the preaching of it, but at association with those who propose to preach it.

Despite arguments to the contrary which had seemed to me persuasive, it is settled that the due process clause of the 14th Amendment applies to matters of substantive law as well as to matters of procedure. Thus all fundamental rights comprised within the term "liberty" are protected by the Federal Constitution from invasion by the states. The right of free speech, the right to teach, and the right of assembly are, of course, fundamental rights. [Citations omitted.] These may not be denied or abridged. But, although the rights of free speech and assembly are fundamental, they are not in their nature absolute. Their exercise is subject to restriction, if the particular restriction proposed is required in order to protect the state from destruction or from serious injury, political, economic or moral. That the necessity which is essential to a valid restriction does not exist unless speech would produce, or is intended to produce, a clear and imminent danger of some substantive evil which the state constitutionally may seek to prevent has been settled. See Schenck v. United States, 249 U.S. 47, 52.

It is said to be the function of the legislature to determine whether at a particular time and under the particular circumstances the formation of, or assembly with, a society organized to advocate criminal syndicalism constitutes a clear and present danger of substantive evil; and that by enacting the law here in question the legislature of California determined that question in the affirmative. Compare Gitlow v. New York, 268 U.S. 652, 668–671. The legislature must obviously decide, in the first instance, whether a danger exists which calls for a particular protective measure. But where a statute is valid only in case certain conditions exist, the enactment of the statute cannot alone establish the facts which are essential to its validity. Prohibitory legislation has repeatedly been held invalid, because unnecessary, where the denial of liberty involved was that of engaging in a particular business. The power of the courts to strike down an offending law is no less when the interests involved are not property rights, but the fundamental personal rights of free speech and assembly.

This court has not yet fixed the standard by which to determine when a danger shall be deemed clear; how remote the danger may be and yet be deemed present; and what degree of evil shall be deemed sufficiently substantial to justify resort to abridgment of free speech and assembly as the means of protection. To reach sound conclusions on these matters, we must bear in mind why a state is, ordinarily, denied the power to prohibit dissemination of social, economic and political doctrine which a vast majority of its citizens believes to be false and fraught with evil consequence.

Those who won our independence believed that the final end of the state was to make men free to develop their faculties; and that in its government the deliberative forces should prevail over the arbitrary. They valued liberty both as an end and as a means. They believed liberty to be the secret of happiness and courage to be the secret of liberty. They believed that freedom to think as you will and to speak as you think are means indispensable to the discovery and spread of political truth; that without free speech and assembly discussion would be futile; that with them, discussion affords ordinarily adequate protection against the dissemination of noxious doctrine; that the greatest menace to freedom is an inert people; that public discussion is a political duty; and that this should be a fundamental principle of the American government. They recognized the risks to which all human institutions are subject. But they knew that order cannot be secured merely through fear of punishment for its infraction; that it is hazardous to discourage thought, hope and imagination; that fear breeds repression; that repression breeds hate; that hate menaces stable government; that the path of safety lies in the opportunity to discuss freely supposed grievances and proposed remedies; and that the fitting remedy for evil counsels is good ones. Believing in the power of reason as applied through public discussion, they eschewed silence coerced by law—the argument of force in its worst form. Recognizing the occasional tyrannies of governing majorities, they amended the Constitution so that free speech and assembly should be guaranteed.

Fear of serious injury cannot alone justify suppression of free speech and assembly. Men feared witches and burned women. It is the function of speech to free men from the bondage of irrational fears. To justify suppression of free speech there must be reasonable ground to fear that serious evil will result if free speech is practiced. There must be reasonable ground to believe that the danger apprehended is imminent. There must be reasonable ground to believe that the evil to be prevented is a serious one. Every denunciation of existing law tends in some measure to increase the probability that there will be violation of it. Condonation of a breach enhances the probability. Expressions of approval add to the probability. Propagation of the criminal state of mind by teaching syndicalism increases it. Advocacy of lawbreaking heightens it still further. But even advocacy of violation, however reprehensible morally, is not a justification for denying free speech where the advocacy falls short of incitement and there is nothing to indicate that the advocacy would be immediately acted on. The wide difference between advocacy and incitement, between preparation and attempt, between assembling and conspiracy, must be borne in mind. In order to support a finding of clear and present danger it must be shown either that immediate serious violence was to be expected or was advocated, or that the past conduct furnished reason to believe that such advocacy was then contemplated.

Those who won our independence by revolution were not cowards. They did not fear political change. They did not exalt order at the cost of liberty. To courageous, self-reliant men, with confidence in the power of free and fearless reasoning applied through the processes of popular government, no danger flowing from speech can be deemed clear and present, unless the incidence of the evil apprehended is so imminent that it may befall before there is opportunity for full discussion. If there be time to expose through discussion the falsehood and fallacies, to avert the evil by the processes of education, the remedy to be applied is more speech, not enforced silence. Only an emergency can justify repression. Such must be the rule if authority is to be reconciled with freedom. Such, in my opinion, is the command of the Constitution. It is, therefore, always open to Americans to challenge a law abridging free speech and assembly by showing that there was no emergency justifying it.

Moreover, even imminent danger cannot justify resort to prohibition of these functions essential to effective democracy, unless the evil apprehended is relatively serious. Prohibition of free speech and assembly is a measure so stringent that it would be inappropriate as the means for averting a relatively trivial harm to society. A police measure may be unconstitutional merely because the remedy, although effective as means of protection, is unduly harsh or oppressive. Thus, a state might, in the exercise of its police power, make any trespass upon the land of another a crime, regardless of the results or of the intent or purpose of the trespasser. It might, also, punish an attempt, a conspiracy, or an incitement to commit the trespass. But it is hardly conceivable that this court would hold constitutional a statute which punished as a felony the mere voluntary assembly with a society formed to teach that pedestrians had the moral right to cross unenclosed, unposted, waste lands and to advocate their doing so, even if there was imminent danger that advocacy would lead to a trespass. The fact that speech is likely to result in some violence or in destruction of property is not enough to justify its suppression. There must be the probability of serious injury to the state. Among freemen, the deterrents ordinarily to be applied to prevent crime are education and punishment for violations of the law, not abridgment of the rights of free speech and assembly.

The California Syndicalism Act recites, in §4:

"Inasmuch as this act concerns and is necessary to the immediate preservation of the public peace and safety, for the reason that at the present time large numbers of persons are going from place to place in this state advocating, teaching and practicing criminal syndicalism, this act shall take effect upon approval by the governor."

This legislative declaration satisfies the requirement of the Constitution of the state concerning emergency legislation. Re McDermott, 180 Cal. 783. But it does not preclude inquiry into the question whether, at the time and under the circumstances, the conditions existed which are essential to validity under the Federal Constitution. As a statute, even if not void on its face, may be challenged because invalid as applied (Dahnke-Walker Mill. Co. v. Bondurant, 257 U.S. 282), the result of such an inquiry may depend upon the specific facts of the particular case. Whenever the fundamental rights of free speech and assembly are alleged to have been invaded, it must remain open to a defendant to present the issue whether there actually did exist at the time a clear danger; whether the danger, if any, was imminent; and whether the evil apprehended was one so substantial as to justify the stringent restriction interposed by the legislature. The legislative declaration, like the fact that the statute was passed and was sustained by the highest court of the state, creates merely a rebuttable presumption that these conditions have been satisfied.

Whether, in 1919, when Miss Whitney did the things complained of, there was in California such clear and present danger of serious evil, might have been made the important issue in the case. She might have required that the issue be determined either by the court or the jury. She claimed below that the statute as applied to her violated the Federal Constitution; but she did not claim that it was void because there was no clear and present danger of serious evil, nor did she request that the existence of these conditions of a valid measure thus restricting the rights of free speech and assembly be passed upon by the court or a jury. On the other hand, there was evidence on which the court or jury might have found that such danger existed. I am unable to assent to the suggestion in the opinion of the court that assembling with a political party, formed to advocate the desirability of a proletarian revolution by mass action at some date necessarily far in the future, is not a right within the protection of the 14th Amendment. In the present case, however, there was other testimony which tended to establish the existence of a conspiracy, on the part of members of the International Workers of the World, to commit present serious crimes; and likewise to show that such a conspiracy would be furthered by the activity of the society of which Miss Whitney was a member. Under these circumstances the judgment of the state court cannot be disturbed.

Our power of review in this case is limited not only to the question whether a right guaranteed by the Federal Constitution was denied (Murdock v. Memphis, 20 Wall. 590; Montana ex rel. Haire v. Rice, 204 U.S. 291, 301); but to the particular claims duly made below, and denied (Seaboard Air Line R. Co. v. Duvall, 225 U.S. 477, 485–488). We lack here the power occasionally exercised on review of judgments of lower federal courts to correct in criminal cases vital errors, although the objection was not taken in the trial court. Wiborg v. United States, 163 U.S. 632, 658–660; Clyatt v. United States, 197 U.S. 207, 221, 222. This is a writ of error to a state court. Because we may not inquire into the errors now alleged, I concur in affirming the judgment of the state court.

MR. JUSTICE HOLMES joins in this opinion.

Adair v. *United States*

208 U.S. 161 (1908)

Finding that a major source of difficulty in the railroad industry was the anti-union activity of management, Congress in 1898 prohibited the railroads from discriminating against union members and from requiring workers to sign "yellow dog" contracts (agreements not to remain or become union members). This case arose when the validity of the act was challenged. Here, it will be seen, the Court apparently found laissez-faire embedded in the Due Process Clause of the Fifth Amendment and also in the Commerce Clause (Art. 1, Sec. 8).

Mr. Justice HARLAN delivered the opinion of the court. . . .

The first inquiry is whether the part of the tenth section of the act of 1898 upon which the first count of the indictment was based is repugnant to the Fifth Amendment of the Constitution declaring that no person shall be deprived of liberty or property without due process of law. In our opinion that section, in the particular mentioned, is an invasion of the personal liberty, as well as of the right of property, guaranteed by that Amendment. Such liberty and right embraces the right to make contracts for the purchase of the labor of others and equally the right to make contracts for the sale of one's own labor; each right, however, being subject to the fundamental condition that no contract, whatever its subject matter, can be sustained which the law, upon reasonable grounds, forbids as inconsistent with the public interests or as hurtful to the public order or as detrimental to the common good. . . . It was the right of the defendant to prescribe the terms upon which the services of Coppage would be accepted, and it was the right of Coppage to become or not, as he chose, an employee of the railroad company upon the terms offered to him. Mr. Cooley, in his treatise on Torts, p. 278, well says: "It is a part of every man's civil rights that he be left at liberty to refuse business relations with any person whomsoever, whether the refusal rests upon reason, or is the result of whim, caprice, prejudice or malice. With his reasons neither the public nor third persons have any legal concern. It is also his right to have business relations with any one with whom he can make contracts, and if he is wrongfully deprived of this right by others, he is entitled to redress." . . .

While, as already suggested, the rights of liberty and property guaranteed by the Constitution against deprivation without due process of law, is subject to such reasonable restraints as the common good or the general welfare may require, it is not within the functions of government—at least in the absence of contract between the parties—to compel any person in the course of his business and against his will to accept or retain the personal services of another, or to compel any person, against his will, to perform personal services for another. The right of a person to sell his labor upon such terms as he deems proper is, in its essence, the same as the right of the purchaser of labor to prescribe the conditions upon which he will accept such labor from the person offering to sell it. So the right of the employee to quit the service of the employer, for whatever reason, is the same as the right of the employer, for whatever reason, to dispense with the services of such employee. It was the legal right of the defendant Adair—however unwise such a course might have been—to discharge Coppage because of his being a member of a labor organization, as it was the legal right of Coppage, if he saw fit to do so—however unwise such a course on his part might have been—to quit the service in which he was engaged, because the defendant employed some persons who were not members of a labor organization. In all such particulars the employer and the employee have equality of right, and any legislation that disturbs that equality is an arbitrary interference with the liberty of contract which no government can legally justify in a free land. These views find support in adjudged cases, . . . Of course, if the parties by contract fix the period of service, and prescribe the conditions upon which the contract may be terminated, such contract would control the rights of the parties as between themselves, and for any violation of those provisions the party wronged would have his appropriate civil action. And it may be—but upon that point we express no opinion—that in the case of a labor contract between an employer engaged in interstate commerce and his employee, Congress could make it a crime for either party without sufficient or just excuse or notice to disregard the terms of such contract or to refuse to perform it. In the absence, however, of a valid contract between the parties controlling their conduct towards each other and fixing a period of service, it cannot be, we repeat, that an employer is under any legal obligation, against his will, to retain an employee in his personal service any more than an employee can be compelled, against his will, to remain in the personal service of another. So far as this record discloses the facts the defendant, who seemed to have authority in the premises, did not agree to keep Coppage in service for any particular time, nor did Coppage agree to remain in such service a moment longer than he chose. The latter was at liberty to quit the service without assigning any reason for his leaving. And the defendant was at liberty, in his discretion, to discharge Coppage from service without giving any reason for so doing. . . .

But it is suggested that the authority to make it a crime for an agent or officer of an interstate carrier, having authority in the premises from his principal, to discharge an employee from service to such carrier, simply because of his membership in a labor organization, can be referred to the power of Congress to regulate interstate commerce, without regard to any question of personal liberty or right of property arising under the Fifth Amendment. This suggestion can have no bearing in the present discussion unless the statute, in the particular just stated, is within the meaning of the Constitution a regulation of commerce among the States. If it be not, then clearly the Government cannot invoke the commerce clause of the Constitution as sustaining the indictment against Adair.

Let us inquire what is commerce, the power to regulate which is given to Congress?

. . . The power to regulate interstate commerce is the power to prescribe rules by which such commerce must be governed. Of course, as has been often said, Congress has a large discretion in the selection or choice of the means to be employed in the regulation of interstate commerce, and such discretion is not to be interfered with except where that which is done is in plain violation of the Constitution. Northern Securities Co. v. United States, 193 U.S. 197, and authorities there cited. In this connection we may refer to Johnson v. Railroad, 196 U.S. 1, relied on in argument, which case arose under the act of Congress of March 2, 1893, 27 Stat. 531, c. 196. That act required carriers engaged in interstate commerce to equip their cars used in such commerce with automatic couplers and continuous brakes, and their locomotives with driving wheel brakes. But the act upon its face showed that its object was to promote the safety of employees and travelers upon railroads; and this court sustained its validity upon the ground that it manifestly had reference to interstate commerce and was calculated to subserve the interests of such commerce by affording protection to employees and travelers. It was held that there was a substantial connection between the object sought to be attained by the act and the means provided to accomplish that object. So, in regard to Employers' Liability Cases, 207 U.S. 463, decided at the present term. In that case the court sustained the authority of Congress, under its power to regulate interstate commerce, to prescribe the rule of liability, as between interstate carriers and its employees in such interstate commerce, in cases of personal injuries received by employees while actually engaged in such commerce. The decision on this point was placed on the ground that a rule of that character would have direct reference to the conduct of interstate commerce, and would, therefore, be within the competency of Congress to establish for commerce among the States, but not as to commerce completely internal to a State. Manifestly, any rule prescribed for the conduct of interstate commerce, in order to be within the competency of Congress under its power to regulate commerce among the States, must have some real or substantial relation to or connection with the commerce regulated. But what possible legal or logical connection is there between an employee's membership in a labor organization and the carrying on of interstate commerce? Such relation to a labor organization cannot have, in itself and in the eye of the law, any bearing upon the commerce with which the employee is connected by his labor and services. Labor associations, we assume, are organized for the general purpose of improving or bettering the conditions and conserving the interests of its members as wage-earners—an object entirely legitimate and to be commended rather than condemned. But surely those associations as labor organizations have nothing to do with interstate commerce as such. One who engages in the service of an interstate carrier will, it must be assumed, faithfully perform his duty, whether he be a member or not a member of a labor organization. His fitness for the position in which he labors and his diligence in the discharge of his duties cannot in law or sound reason depend in any degree upon his being or not being a member of a labor organization. It cannot be assumed that his fitness is assured, or his diligence increased, by such membership, or that he is less fit or less diligent because of his not being a member of such an organization. It is the employee as a man and not as a member of a labor organization who labors in the service of an interstate carrier. Will it be said that the provision in question had its origin in the apprehension, on the part of Congress, that if it did not show more consideration for members of labor organizations than for wage-earners who were not members of such organizations, or if it did not insert in the statute some such provision as the one here in question, members of labor organizations would, by illegal or violent measures, interrupt or impair the freedom of commerce among the States? We will not indulge in any such conjectures, nor make them, in whole or in part, the basis of our decision. We could not do so consistently with the respect due to a coördinate department of the Government. We could not do so without imputing to Congress the purpose to accord to one class of wage-earners privileges withheld from another class of wage-earners engaged, it may be, in the same kind of labor and serving the same employer. Nor will we assume, in our consideration of this case, that members of labor organizations will, in any considerable numbers, resort to illegal methods for accomplishing any particular object they have in view.

Looking alone at the words of the statute for the purpose of ascertaining its scope and effect, and of determining its validity, we hold that there is no such connection between interstate commerce and membership in a labor organization as to authorize Congress to make it a crime against the United States for an agent of an interstate carrier to discharge an employee because of such membership on his part. If such a power exists in Congress it is difficult to perceive why it might not, by absolute regulation, require interstate carriers, under penalties, to employ in the conduct of its interstate business only members of labor organizations, or only those who are not members of such organizations—a power which could not be recognized as existing under the Constitution of the United States. No such rule of criminal liability as that to which we have referred can be regarded as, in any just sense, a regulation of interstate commerce. We need scarcely repeat what this court has more than once said, that the power to regulate interstate commerce, great and paramount as that power is, cannot be exerted in violation of any fundamental right secured by other provisions of the Constitution. Gibbons v. Ogden, 9 Wheat. 1, 196; Lottery Case, 188 U.S. 321, 353.

It results, on the whole case, that the provision of the statute under which the defendant was convicted must be held to be repugnant to the Fifth Amendment and as not embraced by nor within the power of Congress to regulate interstate commerce, but under the guise of regulating interstate commerce and as applied to this case it arbitrarily sanctions an illegal invasion of the personal liberty as well as the right of property of the defendant Adair. . . .

The judgment must be reversed, with directions to set aside the verdict and judgment of conviction, sustain the demurrer to the indictment, and dismiss the case.

It is so ordered.

MR. JUSTICE MOODY did not participate in the decision of this case.

MR. JUSTICE MCKENNA, dissenting . . .

MR. JUSTICE HOLMES, dissenting.
I also think that the statute is constitutional, and but for the decision of my brethren I should have felt pretty clear about it.

As we all know, there are special labor unions of men engaged in the service of carriers. These unions exercise a direct influence upon the employment of labor in that business, upon the terms of such employment and upon the business itself. Their very existence is directed specifically to the business, and their connection with it is at least as intimate and important as that of safety couplers, and, I should think, as the liability of master to servant, matters which, it is admitted, Congress might regulate, so far as they concern commerce among the States. I suppose that it hardly would be denied that some of the relations of railroads with unions of railroad employees are closely enough connected with commerce to justify legislation by Congress. If so, legislation to prevent the exclusion of such unions from employment is sufficiently near.

The ground on which this particular law is held bad is not so much that it deals with matters remote from commerce among the States, as that it interferes with the paramount individual rights, secured by the Fifth Amendment. The section is, in substance, a very limited interference with freedom of contract, no more. It does not require the carriers to employ any one. It does not forbid them to refuse to employ any one, for any reason they deem good, even where the notion of a choice of persons is a fiction and wholesale employment is necessary upon general principles that it might be proper to control. The section simply prohibits the more powerful party to exact certain undertakings, or to threaten dismissal or unjustly discriminate on certain grounds against those already employed. I hardly can suppose that the grounds on which a contract lawfully may be made to end are less open to regulation than other terms. So I turn to the general question whether the employment can be regulated at all. I confess that I think that the right to make contracts at will that has been derived from the word liberty in the amendments has been stretched to its extreme by the decisions; but they agree that sometimes the right may be restrained. Where there is, or generally is

believed to be, an important ground of public policy for restraint the Constitution does not forbid it, whether this court
agrees or disagrees with the policy pursued. It cannot be
doubted that to prevent strikes, and, so far as possible, to foster
its scheme of arbitration, might be deemed by Congress an
important point of policy, and I think it impossible to say that
Congress might not reasonably think that the provision in
question would help a good deal to carry its policy along. But
suppose the only effect really were to tend to bring about the
complete unionizing of such railroad laborers as Congress can
deal with, I think that object alone would justify the act. I
quite agree that the question what and how much good labor
unions do, is one on which intelligent people may differ,—I
think that laboring men sometimes attribute to them advantages, as many attribute to combinations of capital disad-
vantages, that really are due to economic conditions of a far
wider and deeper kind—but I could not pronounce it unwarranted if Congress should decide that to foster a strong union
was for the best interest, not only of the men, but of the railroads and the country at large.

Di Santo v. Pennsylvania

273 U.S. 34 (1927)

For the reasons indicated in the opinion of Mr. Justice Brandeis,
the state sought by a licensing system to prevent fraud in the sale
of steamship tickets for passage to and from foreign countries. Di
Santo was prosecuted for violation of this measure.

Obviously, for activists the Commerce Clause was a two-edged
sword. It could be read narrowly, as in *Adair,* to defeat national
legislation; and it could be read broadly, as in *Di Santo,* to defeat
state legislation. The net result would be constitutionalization of
laissez-faire.

This case is included here to emphasize what might be called the conceptual, or magic-phrase, approach of the activist majority— and the more pragmatic approach of the anti-activist dissenters. Note how the majority opinion deals in abstractions, avoiding any reference to the concrete problems that instigated the legislation in question.

MR. JUSTICE BUTLER delivered the opinion of the Court: . . .

The soliciting of passengers and the sale of steamship tickets and orders for passage between the United States and Europe constitute a well-recognized part of foreign commerce. . . . A state statute which by its necessary operation directly interferes with or burdens foreign commerce is a prohibited regulation and invalid, regardless of the purpose with which it was passed. . . . Such legislation cannot be sustained as an exertion of the police power of the state to prevent possible fraud. . . . The Congress has complete and paramount authority to regulate foreign commerce and, by appropriate measures, to protect the public against the frauds of those who sell these tickets and orders. The sales here in question are related to foreign commerce as directly as are sales made in ticket offices maintained by the carriers and operated by their servants and employees. The license fee and other things imposed by the act on plaintiff in error, who initiates for his principals a transaction in foreign commerce, constitute a direct burden on that commerce. This case is controlled by *Texas Transport Co. v. New Orleans,* 264 U.S. 150, and *McCall v. California,* 136 U.S. 104.

Judgment reversed.

MR. JUSTICE BRANDEIS, with whom Mr. Justice Holmes concurs, dissenting:

The statute is an exertion of the police power of the state. Its evident purpose is to prevent a particular species of fraud and imposition found to have been practiced in Pennsylvania upon persons of small means, unfamiliar with our language and institutions. Much of the immigration into the United States is effected by arrangements made here for remittance of the means of travel. The individual immigrant is often an advance guard. After gaining a foothold here, he has his wife and children, aged parents, brothers, sisters or other relatives follow. To this end he remits steamship tickets or orders for transportation. The purchase of the tickets involves trust in the dealer. This is so not only because of the nature of the transaction, but also because a purchaser when unable to pay the whole price at one time makes successive deposits on account, the ticket or order not being delivered until full payment is made. The facilities for remitting both cash and steamship tickets are commonly furnished by private bankers of the same nationality as the immigrant. It was natural that the supervision of persons engaged in the business of supplying steamship tickets should be committed by the statute to the commissioner of banking.

Although the purchase made is of an ocean steamship ticket, the transaction regulated is wholly intrastate—as much so as if the purchase were of local real estate or of local theater tickets. There is no purpose on the part of the state to regulate foreign commerce. The statute is not an obstruction to foreign commerce. It does not discriminate against foreign commerce. It places no direct burden upon such commerce. It does not affect the commerce except indirectly. Congress could, of course, deal with the subject, because it is connected with foreign commerce. But it has not done so. Nor has it legislated on any allied subject. Thus, there can be no contention that Congress has occupied the field. And obviously, also, this is not a case in which the silence of Congress can be interpreted as a prohibition of state action—as a declaration that in the sale of ocean steamship tickets fraud may be practiced without let or hindrance. If Pennsylvania must submit to seeing its citizens defrauded, it is not because Congress has so willed, but because the Constitution so commands. I cannot believe that it does. . . .

Mr. Justice Stone, dissenting: . . .

In this case the traditional test of the limit of state action by inquiring whether the interference with commerce is direct or indirect seems to me too mechanical, too uncertain in its application, and too remote from actualities, to be of value. In thus making use of the expressions, "direct" and "indirect interference" with commerce, we are doing little more than using labels to describe a result rather than any trustworthy formula by which it is reached. . . .

I am not persuaded that the regulation here is more than local in character or that it interposes any barrier to commerce. Until Congress undertakes the protection of local communities from the dishonesty of the sellers of steamship tickets, it would seem that there is no adequate ground for holding that the regulation here involved is a prohibited interference with commerce.

Mr. Justice Holmes and Mr. Justice Brandeis concur in this opinion.

LIBERTARIAN ACTIVISM (1937–?) —

THE MEANING OF

THE FOURTEENTH AMENDMENT

The Great Depression confirmed what many had long believed: laissez-faire could no longer be the supreme and "natural" law of the land. Legislatures had known this for decades. The Supreme Court discovered it in the spring of 1937. Since then, no state or national legislation has suffered judicial veto to promote laissez-faire.

The Fieldian revolution has gone full cycle. Chief Justice Waite's view that economic policy is a matter for legislatures and the voters again prevails. Since Mr. Justice McReynolds' departure from the bench in 1941, there has not been even a laissez-faire dissent. But the old Fieldian activists were followed by a new group of libertarian activists. As Thomas Reed Powell observed, "Four of the Roosevelt appointees were as determined in *their* direction, as four of their predecessors were determined by attraction to the opposite pole."

Of the "great dissenters" in the days of laissez-faire activism, only Harlan Stone remained on the bench to see the new libertarian activism after 1936. At the close of a long career, spanning the two quite different eras of judicial Justice, he wrote to a trusted friend:

> My more conservative brethren in the old days [read their preferences into legislation and] into the Constitution as well. . . . The pendulum has now swung to the other extreme and history is repeating itself. The Court is now in as much danger of becoming a legislative and Constitution-making body, enacting into law its own predilections, as it was then.[80]

A great constitutional issue of our day, then, comes to this: Is judicial self-restraint a sound general principle, or is it relevant only with respect to economic issues? Shall the division of authority between the judges and the people vary with the importance of the issue at stake—

---

[80] Quoted in Alpheus T. Mason, *Security Through Freedom* (Ithaca, N.Y.: Cornell University Press, 1955), pp. 145–146.

"important" matters being settled by judges, the rest being left to the people?[81]

We turn now to the "new" Court's response to these problems in the context of the Fourteenth Amendment. We trace, in short, Mr. Justice Black's struggle with his colleagues as to the meaning of the 1868 amendment. (Compare with this the "old" Court's struggle with Mr. Justice Field.)

Palko v. *Connecticut*

302 U.S. 319 (1937)

In a state trial court Palko was found guilty of second-degree murder and sentenced to life imprisonment. Believing that the trial court had committed errors to Palko's advantage, the state appealed, as authorized by state legislation. A new trial resulted, notwithstanding Palko's plea of double jeopardy. The second trial brought a conviction of first-degree murder and a death sentence. Palko appealed, on the theory that the prohibition in the Fifth Amend-

---

[81] The Fields and the Blacks, of course, would decide what is, and what is not, important. In the orthodox view, the judicial role does not turn upon the supposed importance of the matter in issue, but upon whether (when the Constitution leaves room for doubt) the Court is prepared to hold that the people have *plainly* departed from their own basic and traditional values (the reasonable-man standard).

Neither approach escapes judicial judgment (or discretion). The crucial question perhaps is this: Which has a greater tendency to promote decision in terms of community, rather than merely personal, values? The premise of this question is Mr. Justice Holmes's view that "The first requirement of a sound body of law is that it should correspond with the actual feelings and demands of the community, whether right or wrong." (Oliver Wendell Holmes, *The Common Law* [Boston: Little, Brown and Company, 1881], p. 41.)

ment against double jeopardy is included in the Fourteenth Amendment as a limitation upon the states.

This case is crucial, because it is the culmination of a long period of development in the judicial effort to find a key to the vague generalities of the Fourteenth Amendment. The Court's opinion reflects the Common Law tradition at its best. In the years since 1868, some elements of the Bill of Rights had been "absorbed" into the Civil War Amendment, just as others had been rejected. With the cautious creativity of a great common lawyer, Mr. Justice Cardozo found a rational pattern in the time-tested, piece-by-piece efforts of many different judges over a long period of years. This pattern—the *Palko* rule—was adopted as a rule or principle of decision. To put it briefly, the general provisions of the Fourteenth Amendment protect only those principles "of justice so rooted in the traditions and conscience of our people as to be ranked as fundamental." Other, less basic, matters are within the province of local self-government. This approach permitted the Court to uphold a legislative estimate of contemporary needs. It was clear enough to yield a high degree of predictability for future cases, yet sufficiently flexible to accommodate the unknowable future. Above all, its potential for accommodation and growth was geared to the community's sense of values (as in the reasonable-man approach)—not to the private preferences of a few independent judges. All this is possible, no doubt, because the *Palko* rule reflects not one man's genius but the combined efforts of many men with varying experiences in different eras. *It should be noted that Mr. Justice Black was a member of the majority in this case.*

Appeal from the Supreme Court of Errors of Connecticut.

MR. JUSTICE CARDOZO delivered the opinion of the Court:

A statute of Connecticut permitting appeals in criminal cases to be taken by the state is challenged by appellant as an infringement of the Fourteenth Amendment. . . .

1. The execution of the sentence will not deprive appellant

of his life without the process of law assured to him by the Fourteenth Amendment of the Federal Constitution.

The argument for appellant is that whatever is forbidden by the Fifth Amendment is forbidden by the Fourteenth also. The Fifth Amendment, which is not directed to the states, but solely to the federal government, creates immunity from double jeopardy. No person shall be "subject for the same offense to be twice put in jeopardy of life or limb." The Fourteenth Amendment ordains, "nor shall any State deprive any person of life, liberty, or property, without due process of law." To retry a defendant, though under one indictment and only one, subjects him, it is said, to double jeopardy in violation of the Fifth Amendment, if the prosecution is one on behalf of the United States. From this the consequence is said to follow that there is a denial of life or liberty without due process of law, if the prosecution is one on behalf of the People of a State. Thirty-five years ago a like argument was made to this court in *Dreyer v. Illinois,* 187 U.S. 71, 85, and was passed without consideration of its merits as unnecessary to a decision. The question is now here.

We do not find it profitable to mark the precise limits of the prohibition of double jeopardy in federal prosecutions. The subject was much considered in *Kepner v. United States,* 195 U.S. 100, decided in 1904 by a closely divided court. The view was there expressed for a majority of the court that the prohibition was not confined to jeopardy in a new and independent case. It forbade jeopardy in the same case if the new trial was at the instance of the government and not upon defendant's motion. Cf. *Trono v. United States,* 199 U.S. 521. All this may be assumed for the purpose of the case at hand, though the dissenting opinions (195 U.S. 100, 134, 137) show how much was to be said in favor of a different ruling. Right-minded men, as we learn from those opinions, could reasonably, even if mistakenly, believe that a second trial was lawful in prosecutions subject to the Fifth Amendment, if it was all in the same case. Even more plainly, right-minded men could reasonably believe that in espousing that conclusion they were not favoring a practice repugnant to the conscience of mankind. Is double jeopardy in such circumstances, if double jeopardy it must be called, a denial of due process forbidden to the States? The tyranny of labels, *Snyder v. Massachusetts,* 291 U.S. 97, 114, must not lead us to leap to a conclusion that a word which in one set of facts may stand for oppression or enormity is of like effect in every other.

We have said that in appellant's view the Fourteenth Amendment is to be taken as embodying the prohibitions of the Fifth. His thesis is even broader. Whatever would be a violation of the original bill of rights (Amendments I to VIII) if done by the federal government is now equally unlawful by force of the Fourteenth Amendment if done by a state. There is no such general rule.

The Fifth Amendment provides, among other things, that no person shall be held to answer for a capital or otherwise infamous crime unless on presentment or indictment of a grand jury. This court has held that, in prosecutions by a state, presentment or indictment by a grand jury may give way to informations at the instance of a public officer. *Hurtado v. California,* 110 U.S. 516; *Gaines v. Washington,* 277 U.S. 81, 86. The Fifth Amendment provides also that no person shall be compelled in any criminal case to be a witness against himself. This court has said that, in prosecutions by a state, the exemption will fail if the state elects to end it. *Twining v. New Jersey,* 211 U.S. 78, 106, 111, 112. Cf. *Snyder v. Massachusetts, supra,* p. 105; *Brown v. Mississippi,* 297 U.S. 278, 285. The Sixth Amendment calls for a jury trial in criminal cases and the Seventh for a jury trial in civil cases at common law where the value in controversy shall exceed twenty dollars. This court has ruled that consistently with those amendments trial by jury may be modified by a state or abolished altogether. *Walker v. Sauvinet,* 92 U.S. 90; *Maxwell v. Dow,* 176 U.S. 581; *New York Central R. Co. v. White,* 243 U.S. 188, 208; *Wagner Electric Co. v. Lyndon,* 262 U.S. 226, 232. As to the Fourth Amendment, one should refer to *Weeks v. United States,* 232 U.S. 383, 398, and as to other provisions of the Sixth, to *West v. Louisiana,* 194 U.S. 258.

On the other hand, the due process clause of the Fourteenth Amendment may make it unlawful for a state to abridge by its statutes the freedom of speech which the First Amendment safeguards against encroachment by the Congress, *De Jonge v. Oregon,* 299 U.S. 353, 364; *Herndon v. Lowry,* 301 U.S. 242, 259; or the like freedom of the press, *Grosjean v. American Press Co.,* 297 U.S. 233; *Near v. Minnesota,* 283 U.S. 697, 707; or the free exercise of religion, *Hamilton v. Regents of University,* 293 U.S. 245, 262; cf. *Grosjean v. American Press Co., supra; Pierce v. Society of Sisters,* 268 U.S. 510; or the right of peaceable assembly, without which speech would be unduly trammeled, *De Jonge v. Oregon, supra; Herndon v. Lowry, supra;* or the right of one accused of crime to the benefit of counsel. *Powell v. Alabama,* 287 U.S. 45. In these and other situations immunities that are valid as against the federal government by force of the specific pledges of particular amendments have been found to be implicit in the concept of ordered liberty, and thus, through the Fourteenth Amendment, become valid as against the states.

The line of division may seem to be wavering and broken if there is a hasty catalogue of the cases on the one side and the other. Reflection and analysis will induce a different view. There emerges the perception of a rationalizing principle which gives to discrete instances a proper order and coherence. The right to trial by jury and the immunity from prosecution except as the result of an indictment may have value and importance. Even so, they are not of the very essence of a scheme of ordered liberty. To abolish them is not to violate a "principle of justice so rooted in the traditions and conscience of our people as to be ranked as fundamental." *Snyder v. Massachusetts, supra,* p. 105; *Brown v. Mississippi, supra,* p. 285; *Hebert v. Louisiana,* 272 U.S. 312, 316. Few would be so narrow or provincial as to maintain that a fair and enlightened system of justice would be impossible without them. What is true of jury trials and indictments is true also, as the cases show, of the immunity from compulsory self-incrimination. *Twining v. New Jersey, supra.* This too might be lost, and justice still be done. Indeed, today as in the past there are students of our penal system who look upon the immunity as a mischief rather than a benefit, and who would limit its scope, or destroy it altogether. No doubt there would remain the need to give protection against torture, physical or mental. *Brown v. Mississippi, supra.* Justice, however, would not perish if the accused were subject to a duty to respond to orderly inquiry. The exclusion of these immunities and privileges from the privileges and immunities protected against the action of the states has not been arbitrary or casual. It has been dictated by a study and appreciation of the meaning, the essential implications, of liberty itself.

We reach a different plane of social and moral values when we pass to the privileges and immunities that have been taken over from the earlier articles of the federal bill of rights and brought within the Fourteenth Amendment by a process of absorption. These in their origin were effective against the federal government alone. If the Fourteenth Amendment has absorbed them, the process of absorption has had its source in the belief that neither liberty nor justice would exist if they were sacrificed. *Twining v. New Jersey, supra,* p. 99. This is true, for illustration, of freedom of thought and speech. Of that freedom one may say that it is the matrix, the indispensable condition, of nearly every other form of freedom. With rare

aberrations a pervasive recognition of that truth can be traced
in our history, political and legal. So it has come about that
the domain of liberty, withdrawn by the Fourteenth Amendment from encroachment by the states, has been enlarged by
latter-day judgments to include liberty of the mind as well as
liberty of action. . . . Fundamental too in the concept of due
process, and so in that of liberty, is the thought that condemnation shall be rendered only after trial. *Scott v. McNeal*, 154
U.S. 34; *Blackmer v. United States*, 284 U.S. 421. The hearing,
moreover, must be a real one, not a sham or a pretense. *Moore
v. Dempsey*, 261 U.S. 86; *Mooney v. Holohan*, 294 U.S. 103.
For that reason, ignorant defendants in a capital case were
held to have been condemned unlawfully when in truth,
though not in form, they were refused the aid of counsel. *Powell v. Alabama, supra,* pp. 67, 68. The decision did not turn
upon the fact that the benefit of counsel would have been
guaranteed to the defendants by the provisions of the sixth
Amendment if they had been prosecuted in a federal court.
The decision turned upon the fact that in the particular situation laid before us in the evidence the benefit of counsel was
essential to the substance of a hearing.

Our survey of the cases serves, we think, to justify the statement that the dividing line between them, if not unfaltering
throughout its course, has been true for the most part to a
unifying principle. On which side of the line the case made
out by the appellant has appropriate location must be the next
inquiry and the final one. Is that kind of double jeopardy to
which the statute has subjected him a hardship so acute and
shocking that our polity will not endure it? Does it violate
those "fundamental principles of liberty and justice which lie
at the base of all our civil and political institutions"? *Hebert
v. Louisiana, supra.* The answer surely must be "no." What the
answer would have to be if the state were permitted after a
trial free from error to try the accused over again or to bring

another case against him, we have no occasion to consider. We deal with the statute before us and no other. The state is not attempting to wear the accused out by a multitude of cases with accumulated trials. It asks no more than this, that the case against him shall go on until there shall be a trial free from the corrosion of substantial legal error. *State v. Felch,* 92 Vt. 477; *State v. Lee, supra.* This is not cruelty at all, nor even vexation in any immoderate degree. If the trial had been infected with error adverse to the accused, there might have been review at his instance, and, as often as necessary to purge the vicious taint. A reciprocal privilege, subject at all times to the discretion of the presiding judge (*State v. Carabetta,* 106 Conn. 114; 137 Atl. 394), has now been granted to the state. There is here no seismic innovation. The edifice of justice stands, its symmetry, to many, greater than before.

2. The conviction of appellant is not in derogation of any privileges or immunities that belong to him as a citizen of the United States.

There is argument in his behalf that the privileges and immunities clause of the Fourteenth Amendment as well as the due process clause has been flouted by the judgment.

Maxwell v. Dow, supra, p. 584, gives all the answer that is necessary.

The judgment is affirmed.

Mr. Justice Butler dissents.

[Note: *Connecticut General Life Insurance Company* v. *Johnson,* 303 U.S. 77 (1938), found a certain state tax invalid under the Due Process Clause. Only Mr. Justice Black dissented. He did so on the ground that the word "person" in the Fourteenth Amendment does not include corporations. The Court, he said, "should now overrule previous decisions which interpreted the Fourteenth Amendment to include corporations." His position apparently was based on Charles Beard's "conspiracy theory" of the amendment.

As to the validity of this view, see Howard J. Graham, "The Conspiracy Theory," *Yale Law Journal,* 47 (1938), 371.]

Polk Co. v. *Glover*

305 U.S. 5 (1938)

To protect a local industry from fraudulent competition, Florida required that every container of citrus fruit or juice produced in Florida must have stamped into it or embossed upon it the word "Florida." Non-Florida producers were prohibited from so using that word. Here a Florida producer sought "due process" relief, on the ground that the law imposed an undue economic burden upon him. The trial court dismissed the complaint. On appeal, the Supreme Court held that the case should have been heard. That is, the plaintiff should have had an opportunity to prove, if he could, that the law was beyond support by reasonable minds. (The Court's *per curiam* opinion does not spell this out, but earlier cases, and the dissenter's reference to them, make it clear that this Holmesian test was what the majority had in mind.) Only Mr. Justice Black was not satisfied with this repudiation of the old laissez-faire "preferred position" for material interests. In his neo-activist view, apparently, substantive economic interests would have absolutely no protection under the Fourteenth Amendment. Note his emphasis upon the presumption of validity (the Court's position, of course, is not to the contrary on this point), and his repudiation of it in civil-liberty cases.

MR. JUSTICE BLACK, dissenting:

The important consequences of this remand raise far more than mere questions of procedure. State laws are continually subjected to constitutional attacks by those who do not wish to obey them. Accordingly, it becomes increasingly important to protect State governments from needless expensive burdens and suspensions of their laws incident to Federal Court injunctions issued on allegations that show no right to relief. The operation of this Florida law has been suspended. Complaints seeking to invalidate and suspend the operation of State laws by invoking the "vague contours" of due process can irreparably injure State governments if we accept as a "salutary principle" the rule that all such complaints—though failing to state a cause of action—raise "grave constitutional questions" which require that "the essential facts shall be determined." Under this declared "salutary principle" specially applying to bills attacking the constitutionality of legislative acts, such bills must be defended against even though they fail to state a cause of action. This is contrary to the traditional general rule that fatally defective bills are dismissed on motion (formerly demurrer) in order to prevent needless litigation, delay and expense. The application of this special principle to bills attacking State legislation seriously undermines the historical presumption of the validity of State acts. A refusal to determine whether or not the allegations of the bill are sufficient to strike down an act until evidence has been heard adds a special burden to the defense of State legislation, as though legislation were to be presumed invalid. I do not believe this principle leads to salutary results and I am of the opinion that we should now determine whether the allegations of the bill, if proven, would entitle petitioners to relief.

Even according to the presently prevailing interpretation of the Due Process Clause of the Fourteenth Amendment, I do not believe that the averments of petitioners' bill can sustain invalidation of this duly enacted Florida statute. The statute contains a legislative finding that "certain persons, firms and corporations in the State of Florida" had engaged "in the practice" of deceiving customers into the belief that non-Florida canned citrus products had been produced in Florida. The legislature further found that this practice operated to "the injury and detriment of the producers and canners of citrus fruit and citrus juices in the State of Florida . . ." and concluded that an effective method to prevent this fraudulent practice was to require the publication of the truth upon labels and containers. Averments of petitioners' bill, in their strongest light, go no further than to dent this legislative finding. They say to require publication of the truth in this manner on the cans and labels is burdensome and violates the Due Process Clause of the Fourteenth Amendment. They further charge here that this finding of the legislature is a "feigned" assumption and that "the facts alleged [in petitioners' bill] not only show the nonexistence of any basis for such assumption but demonstrates that the law will cause serious injury to the packer and marked curtailment of the sale of citrus products grown and canned in Florida." Petitioners' argument for reversal largely involves "this disputed question as to the existence of facts concerning the basis for the law, and . . . the preamble statement of the alleged evil which gave rise to its enactment. . . ."

Because, it is said, the embossing and labelling requirements raise grave constitutional issues, the State of Florida will be required to defend against two issues raised by petitioners' bill. The State must answer the charges: first, that—contrary to the legislative finding—there was no fraudulent practice under which the dealers in canned citrus products were led to believe that they were buying Florida products when in fact the canned goods were produced outside that State; second, that truthful labelling and embossing as required by the statute would financially injure citrus growers, producers, canners and the people of Florida rather than benefit them as found by the legislature.

In attacking the legislative finding that the act would bestow benefits on the State of Florida, petitioners allege that the law would require petitioners to spend extra money for labels; might cause them to lose some business; would afford the op-

portunity for spoiling and swelling of some cans on the theory
that embossing without spoiling is difficult and could weaken
the tin of containers thereby permitting acid to corrode the
steel underneath the tin; that petitioners will suffer loss because they have on their hands cans that have not been embossed; and that Florida already has laws adequate to protect
itself from fraudulent sales.

With reference to a State law regulating containers (for
lard) this Court has already said:

"This may involve a change of packing by the company and
the cost of that change, but this is a sacrifice the law can
require to protect from the deception of the old method."

The real issue raised by petitioners' bill is not the cost incident to changing from the old method of labelling and embossing, but whether the Florida legislature—convinced that
fraud existed—had the constitutional right to determine the
policy which it believed would protect the people of Florida
from that fraud. The cause is now sent back to a Federal
District Court to review the facts underlying the policy enacted
into law by the legislature.

Under our constitutional plan of government, the exclusive
power of determining the wisdom of this policy rested with
the legislature of Florida subject to the veto power of Florida's
governor. This Court has taken judicial notice of the fact that
citrus fruits support one of the great industries of the State of
Florida and held that it "was competent for the legislature (of
Florida) to find that it was essential for the success of that
industry that its reputation be preserved in other States where-
in such fruits find their most extensive market." The legislators
of Florida are peculiarly qualified to determine the policies
relating to one of their State's greatest industries. Legislatures,
under our system, determine the necessity for regulatory laws,
considering both the evil and the benefits that may result.
Unless prohibited by constitutional limitations, their decisions
as to policy are final. In weighing conflicting arguments on the

wisdom of legislation they are not confined within the narrow boundaries of a particular controversy between litigants. Their inquiries are not subject to the strict rules of evidence which have been found essential in proceedings before courts. Legislators may personally survey the field and obtain data and a broad perspective which the necessary limitations of court litigation make impossible.

The legislative history of the Florida statute under review indicates that it was given the careful and cautious consideration which regulation of one of the State's major industries deserved. Companion measures were offered in the Florida House and Senate on the same day—April 28, 1937. In the House the measure was referred to the Committee on Citrus Fruits. The existence of such a standing committee is itself indicative of a legislative procedure designed to give careful consideration to the legislation concerning this important industry. May 4, 1937, the House Committee voted to report the bill, favorably, sixteen ayes, no nays, six members absent. June 1, the bill was made the special order of business and on June 2, the companion Senate bill previously passed by that body by a vote of twenty-four to one was substituted for the House measure and passed by a vote of seventy to nothing.

In the face of this history, petitioners insist that this statute duly passed by the legislature and signed by the Governor of Florida violates the Due Process Clause as an unreasonable, capricious, unjust, harsh and arbitrary measure. Therefore, if petitioners are to obtain relief on this theory it must be found that this statute was "fixed or arrived at through an exercise of will, or by caprice, without consideration or adjustment with reference to principles, circumstances or significance"; or that it was "despotic, autocratic (or) high-handed"; or that it is "irrational, senseless" or passed by those "not endowed with reasoning ability; non-conformable to reason"; or that it is capricious or freakish which "denotes an impulsive seemingly causeless change of mind, like that of a child or a lunatic."

The cause is remanded for the court below to determine whether the legislative requirement that cans and labels be truthfully marked is arbitrary, unreasonable, capricious, unjust or harsh. This makes it necessary for the court to weigh and pass upon the relative judgment, poise and reasoning ability of the one legislator who voted against the law, as contrasted with the ninety-four legislators and the governor who favored it. I do not believe that obedience to this carefully considered legislative enactment would violate any of petitioners' property rights without due process of law or that—even under prevailing doctrine—the averments of the complaint indicate that no known or supposed facts could sustain it. The allegations of the complaint in this cause raise no more than questions of policy for legislative determination, which the Florida legislature has already considered and which can be presented to other legislatures in the future.

The majority opinion apparently does not decide that Florida has no power to require that the origin of citrus products canned in Florida shall be truthfully shown. Petitioners' bill insists that Florida exercised its power so unwisely as to violate rights of property without due process, because, as alleged, canning frauds did not exist, and could be prevented by a wiser statute, less expensive and burdensome to petitioners. Thus they challenge the wisdom of the Florida legislation. On remand of petitioners' bill which fails to show that the Florida law is invalid, may the Court, on evidence outside the bill, hold that the law violates due process because the court is convinced that the legislature might have chosen a wiser, less expensive and less burdensome regulation? If a court in this case and under this bill has this power, the final determination of the wisdom and choice of legislative policy has passed from legislatures—elected by and responsible to the people— to the courts. I believe in the language of the *Powell* case that since all that has been "said of this legislation is that it is unwise, or unnecessarily oppressive to those" canning citrus products, that "petitioners' appeal must be to the legislature . . . not to the judiciary." I would affirm.

[Note: For more recent cases demonstrating Mr. Justice Black's *anti-activism* where business (as distinct from libertarian) claims are involved, see, for example, *Ferguson* v. *Skrupa*, 372 U.S. 726 (1963); *Morey* v. *Doud*, 354 U.S. 457 (1957); *United States* v. *Causby*, 328 U.S. 256 (1946). But note the new economic activism in the interpretation of statutes in cases involving claims against business (see pp. 439–467, below).

In *Hague* v. *CIO*, 307 U.S. 496 (1939), the Court upheld a free-speech claim, apparently under the *Palko*–Due-Process rule. In a separate opinion, Justices Roberts and Black put the same result in terms of the "privileges and immunities of citizens of the United States" (rather than the Due Process Clause of the same amendment). See footnote 41, above, and related text.]

Bridges v. California

and

Times-Mirror v. Superior Court

314 U.S. 252 (1941)

Bridges, an *alien*, and Times-Mirror, a *corporation*, claimed protection, under the Fourteenth Amendment, for freedom of utterance. In *Connecticut General*, Mr. Justice Black had insisted that corporations were not entitled to Fourteenth Amendment protection; and in *Hague* he had rejected Due Process and relied upon the "Privileges and Immunities" of *citizens* clause as the shield for free utterance.

Mr. Justice Black delivered the opinion of the Court:

These two cases, while growing out of different circumstances and concerning different parties, both relate to the scope of our national constitutional policy safeguarding free speech and a free press. All of the petitioners were adjudged guilty and fined for contempt of court by the Superior Court of Los Angeles County. Their conviction rested upon comments pertaining to pending litigation which were published in newspapers. In the Superior Court and later in the California Supreme Court, petitioners challenged the state's action as an abridgment, prohibited by the Federal Constitution, of freedom of speech and of the press, but the Superior Court overruled this contention, and the Supreme Court affirmed. The importance of the constitutional question prompted us to grant certiorari. 309 U.S. 649; 310 U.S. 623.

In brief, the state courts asserted and exercised a power to punish petitioners for publishing their views concerning cases not in all respects finally determined, upon the following chain of reasoning: California is invested with the power and duty to provide an adequate administration of justice; by virtue of this power and duty, it can take appropriate measures for providing fair judicial trials free from coercion or intimidation; included among such appropriate measures is the common law procedure of punishing certain interferences and obstructions through contempt proceedings; this particular measure, devolving upon the courts of California by reason of their creation as courts, includes the power to punish for publications made outside the court room if they tend to interfere with the fair and orderly administration of justice in a pending case; the trial court having found that the publications had such a tendency, and there being substantial evidence to support the finding, the punishments here imposed were an appropriate exercise of the state's power; in so far as these punishments constitute a restriction on liberty of expression, the public interest in that liberty was properly subordinated to the public interest in judicial impartiality and decorum.

If the inference of conflict raised by the last clause be correct, the issue before us is of the very gravest moment. For free speech and fair trials are two of the most cherished policies of our civilization, and it would be a trying task to choose between them. But even if such a conflict is not actually raised by the question before us, we are still confronted with the delicate problems entailed in passing upon the deliberations of the highest court of a state. This is not, however, solely an issue between state and nation, as it would be if we were called upon to mediate in one of those troublous situations where each claims to be the repository of a particular sovereign power. To be sure, the exercise of power here in question was by a state judge. But in deciding whether or not the sweeping constitutional mandate against any law "abridging the freedom of speech or of the press" forbids it, we are necessarily measuring a power of all American courts, both state and federal, including this one.

I

It is to be noted at once that we have no direction by the legislature of California that publications outside the court room which comment upon a pending case in a specified manner should be punishable. As we said in Cantwell v. Connecticut, 310 U.S. 296, 307, 308, such a "declaration of the State's policy would weigh heavily in any challenge of the law as infringing constitutional limitations." But as we also said there, the problem is different where "the judgment is based on a common law concept of the most general and undefined nature." Id. 308. . . . For here the legislature of California has not appraised a particular kind of situation and found a specific danger sufficiently imminent to justify a restriction on a particular kind of utterance. The judgments below, therefore, do not come to us encased in the armor wrought by prior legislative deliberation. Under such circumstances, this Court has said that "it must necessarily be found, as an original question" that the specified publications involved created "such likelihood of bringing about the substantive evil as to deprive [them] of the constitutional protection." Gitlow v. New York, 268 U.S. 652, 671.

How much "likelihood" is another question, "a question of proximity and degree" that cannot be completely captured in a formula. In Schenck v. United States, however, this Court said that there must be a determination of whether or not "the words used are used in such circumstances and are of such a nature as to create a clear and present danger that they will bring about the substantive evils." We recognize that this statement, however helpful, does not comprehend the whole problem. As Mr. Justice Brandeis said in his concurring opinion in Whitney v. California, 274 U.S. 357, 374: "This Court has not yet fixed the standard by which to determine when a danger shall be deemed clear; how remote the danger may be and yet be deemed present."

Nevertheless, the "clear and present danger" language of the Schenck Case has afforded practical guidance in a great variety of cases in which the scope of constitutional protections of freedom of expression was in issue. It has been utilized by either a majority or minority of this Court in passing upon the constitutionality of convictions under espionage acts, Schneck v. United States, supra; Abrams v. United States, 250 U.S. 616; under a criminal syndicalism act, Whitney v. California, 274 U.S. 357, supra; under an "anti-insurrection" act, Herndon v. Lowry, 301 U.S. 242, supra; and for breach of the peace at common law, Cantwell v. Connecticut, 310 U.S. 296, supra. And very recently we have also suggested that "clear and present danger" is an appropriate guide in determining the constitutionality of restrictions upon expression where the substantive evil sought to be prevented by the restriction is "de-

struction of life or property, or invasion of the right of privacy."
Thornhill v. Alabama, 310 U.S. 88, 105.

Moreover, the likelihood, however great, that a substantive
evil will result cannot alone justify a restriction upon freedom
of speech or the press. The evil itself must be "substantial,"
Brandeis, J., concurring in Whitney v. California, supra (274
U.S. 374); it must be "serious," id. 376. And even the expression of "legislative preferences or beliefs" cannot transform
minor matters of public inconvenience or annoyance into substantive evils of sufficient weight to warrant the curtailment of
liberty of expression. Schneider v. Irvington, 308 U.S. 147, 161.

What finally emerges from the "clear and present danger"
cases is a working principle that the substantive evil must be
extremely serious and the degree of imminence extremely high
before utterances can be punished. Those cases do not purport to mark the furthermost constitutional boundaries of protected expression, nor do we here. They do no more than
recognize a minimum compulsion of the Bill of Rights. For
the First Amendment does not speak equivocally. It prohibits
any law "abridging the freedom of speech or of the press."
It must be taken as a command of the broadest scope that
explicit language, read in the context of a liberty-loving society, will allow.

II

Before analyzing the punished utterances and the circumstances surrounding their publication, we must consider an
argument which, if valid, would destroy the relevance of the
foregoing discussion to this case. In brief, this argument is that
the publications here in question belong to a special category
marked off by history, a category to which the criteria of
constitutional immunity from punishment used where other
types of utterances are concerned are not applicable. For, the
argument runs, the power of judges to punish by contempt
out-of-court publications tending to obstruct the orderly and

fair administration of justice in a pending case was deeply rooted in English common law at the time the Constitution was adopted. That this historical contention is dubious has been persuasively argued elsewhere. Fox, Contempt of Court, passim, e.g., 207. See also Stansbury, Trial of James H. Peck, 430. In any event it need not detain us, for to assume that English common law in this field became ours is to deny the generally accepted historical belief that "one of the objects of the Revolution was to get rid of the English common law on liberty of speech and of the press." Schofield, Freedom of the Press in the United States, 9 Publications Amer. Sociol. Soc., 67, 76.

More specifically, it is to forget the environment in which the First Amendment was ratified. In presenting the proposals which were later embodied in the Bill of Rights, James Madison, the leader in the preparation of the First Amendment, said: "Although I know whenever the great rights, the trial by jury, freedom of the press, or liberty of conscience, come in question in that body [Parliament], the invasion of them is resisted by able advocates, yet their Magna Charta does not contain any one provision for the security of those rights, respecting which the people of America are most alarmed. The freedom of the press and rights of conscience, those choicest privileges of the people, are unguarded in the British Constitution." 1 Annals of Congress 1789–1790, 434. And Madison elsewhere wrote that "the state of the press . . . under the common law, cannot . . . be the standard of its freedom in the United States." VI Writings of James Madison 1790–1802, 387.

There are no contrary implications in any part of the history of the period in which the First Amendment was framed and adopted. No purpose in ratifying the Bill of Rights was clearer than that of securing for the people of the United States much greater freedom of religion, expression, assembly, and petition than the people of Great Britain had ever enjoyed. It cannot be denied, for example, that the religious test oath or the restrictions upon assembly then prevalent in England would have been regarded as measures which the Constitution prohibited the American Congress from passing. And since the same unequivocal language is used with respect to freedom of the press, it signifies a similar enlargement of that concept as well. . . .

The implications of subsequent American history confirm such a construction of the First Amendment. To be sure, it occurred no more to the people who lived in the decades following Ratification than it would to us now that the power of courts to protect themselves from disturbances and disorder in the court room by use of contempt proceedings could seriously be challenged as conflicting with constitutionally secured guarantees of liberty. In both state and federal courts, this power has been universally recognized. See Anderson v. Dunn, 6 Wheat. 204, 227. But attempts to expand it in the post-Ratification years evoked popular reactions that bespeak a feeling of jealous solicitude for freedom of the press. In Pennsylvania and New York, for example, heated controversies arose over alleged abuses in the exercise of the contempt power, which in both places culminated in legislation practically forbidding summary punishment for publications. See Nelles and King, Contempt by Publication, 28 Columbia L. Rev. 401, 409–422.

In the federal courts, there was the celebrated case of Judge Peck, recently referred to by this Court in Nye v. United States, 313 U.S. 33, 45. The impeachment proceedings against him, it should be noted, and the strong feelings they engendered, were set in motion by his summary punishment of a lawyer for publishing comment on a case which was on appeal at the time of publication and which raised the identical issue of several other cases then pending before him. Here again legislation was the outcome, Congress proclaiming in a statute expressly captioned "An Act *declaratory* of the law concerning contempts of court," that the power of federal courts to inflict summary punishment for contempt "shall not be construed to extend to any cases except the misbehaviour of . . . persons in the presence of the said courts, or so near thereto as to obstruct the administration of justice. . . ." When recently called upon to interpret this statute, we overruled the earlier decision of this Court in Toledo Newspaper Co. v. United States, 247 U.S. 402, in the belief that it improperly enlarged the stated area of summary punishment. Nye v. United States, supra. Here, as in the Nye Case, we need not determine whether the statute was intended to demarcate the full power permissible under the Constitution to punish by contempt proceedings. But we do find in the enactment viewed in its historical context, a respect for the prohibitions of the First Amendment, not as mere guides to the formulation of policy, but as commands the breach of which cannot be tolerated.

We are aware that although some states have by statute or decision expressly repudiated the power of judges to punish publications as contempts on a finding of mere tendency to interfere with the orderly administration of justice in a pending case, other states have sanctioned the exercise of such a power. (See Nelles and King, loc. cit. supra, 536–562, for a collection and discussion of state cases.) But state power in this field was not tested in this Court for more than a century. Not until 1925, with the decision in Gitlow v. New York, 268 U.S. 652, supra, did this Court recognize in the Fourteenth Amendment the application to the states of the same standards of freedom of expression as, under the First Amendment, are applicable to the federal government. And this is the first time since 1925 that we have been called upon to determine the constitutionality of a state's exercise of the contempt power in this kind of situation. Now that such a case is before us, we cannot allow the mere existence of other untested state decisions to destroy the historic constitutional meaning of freedom of speech and of the press.

History affords no support for the contention that the criteria applicable under the Constitution to other types of utterances are not applicable, in contempt proceedings, to out-of-court publications pertaining to a pending case.

III

We may appropriately begin our discussion of the judgments below by considering how much, as a practical matter, they would affect liberty of expression. It must be recognized that public interest is much more likely to be kindled by a controversial event of the day than by a generalization, however penetrating, of the historian or scientist. Since they punish utterances made during the pendency of a case, the judgments below therefore produce their restrictive results at the precise time when public interest in the matters discussed would naturally be at its height. Moreover, the ban is likely to fall not only at a crucial time but upon the most important topics of discussion. Here, for example, labor controversies were the topics of some of the publications. Experience shows that the more acute labor controversies are, the more likely it is that in some aspect they will get into court. It is therefore the controversies that command most interest that the decisions below would remove from the arena of public discussion.

No suggestion can be found in the Constitution that the freedom there guaranteed for speech and the press bears an inverse ratio to the timeliness and importance of the ideas seeking expression. Yet, it would follow as a practical result of the decisions below that anyone who might wish to give public expression to his views on a pending case involving no matter what problem of public interest, just at the time his audience would be most receptive, would be as effectively discouraged as if a deliberate statutory scheme of censorship had been adopted. Indeed, perhaps more so, because under a legislative specification of the particular kinds of expressions prohibited and the circumstances under which the prohibitions are to operate, the speaker or publisher might at least have an authoritative guide to the permissible scope of comment, instead of being compelled to act at the peril that judges might find in the utterance a "reasonable tendency" to obstruct justice in a pending case.

This unfocussed threat is, to be sure, limited in time, terminating as it does upon final disposition of the case. But this does not change its censorial quality. An endless series of moratoria on public discussion, even if each were very short, could hardly be dismissed as an insignificant abridgement of freedom of expression. And to assume that each would be short is to overlook the fact that the "pendency" of a case is frequently a matter of months or even years rather than days or weeks.

For these reasons we are convinced that the judgments below result in a curtailment of expression that cannot be dismissed as insignificant. If they can be justified at all, it must be in terms of some serious substantive evil which they are designed to avert. The substantive evil here sought to be averted has been variously described below. It appears to be double: disrespect for the judiciary; and disorderly and unfair administration of justice. The assumption that respect for the judiciary can be won by shielding judges from published criticism wrongly appraises the character of American public opinion. For it is a prized American privilege to speak one's mind, although not always with perfect good taste, on all public institutions. And an enforced silence, however limited, solely in the name of preserving the dignity of the bench, would probably engender resentment, suspicion, and contempt much more than it would enhance respect.

The other evil feared, disorderly and unfair administration of justice, is more plausibly associated with restricting publications which touch upon pending litigation. The very word "trial" connotes decisions on the evidence and arguments properly advanced in open court. Legal trials are not like elections, to be won through the use of the meeting-hall, the radio, and the newspaper. But we cannot start with the assumption that publications of the kind here involved actually do threaten to change the nature of legal trials, and that to preserve judicial impartiality, it is necessary for judges to have a contempt power by which they can close all channels of public expression to all matters which touch upon pending cases. We must therefore turn to the particular utterances here in question and the circumstances of their publication to determine to what extent the substantive evil of unfair administration of justice was a likely consequence, and whether the degree of likelihood was sufficient to justify summary punishment.

The Los Angeles Times Editorials. The Times-Mirror Company, publisher of the Los Angeles Times, and L. D. Hotchkiss, its managing editor, were cited for contempt for the publication of three editorials. Both found by the trial court to be responsible for one of the editorials, the company and Hotchkiss were each fined $100. The company alone was held responsible for the other two, and was fined $100 more on account of one, and $300 more on account of the other.

The $300 fine presumably marks the most serious offense. The editorial thus distinguished was entitled "Probation for Gorillas?". After vigorously denouncing two members of a labor union who had previously been found guilty of assaulting nonunion truck drivers, it closes with the observation: "Judge A. A. Scott will make a serious mistake if he grants probation to Matthew Shannon and Kennan Holmes. This community needs the example of their assignment to the jute mill." Judge Scott had previously set a day (about a month after the publication) for passing upon the application of Shannon and Holmes for probation and for pronouncing sentence.

The basis for punishing the publication as contempt was by

the trial court said to be its "inherent tendency" and by the Supreme Court its "reasonable tendency" to interfere with the orderly administration of justice in an action then before a court for consideration. In accordance with what we have said on the "clear and present danger" cases, neither "inherent tendency" nor "reasonable tendency" is enough to justify a restriction of free expression. But even if they were appropriate measures, we should find exaggeration in the use of those phrases to describe the facts here.

From the indications in the record of the position taken by the Los Angeles Times on labor controversies in the past, there could have been little doubt of its attitude toward the probation of Shannon and Holmes. In view of the paper's long-continued militancy in this field, it is inconceivable that any judge in Los Angeles would expect anything but adverse criticism from it in the event probation were granted. Yet such criticism after final disposition of the proceedings would clearly have been privileged. Hence, this editorial, given the most intimidating construction it will bear, did no more than threaten future adverse criticism which was reasonably to be expected anyway in the event of a lenient disposition of the pending case. To regard it, therefore, as in itself of substantial influence upon the course of justice would be to impute to judges a lack of firmness, wisdom, or honor, which we cannot accept as a major premise. . . .

The other two editorials publication of which was fined below are set out in the lower margin. With respect to these two editorials, there is no divergence of conclusions among the members of this Court. We are all of the opinion that, upon any fair construction, their possible influence on the course of justice can be dismissed as negligible, and that the Constitution compels us to set aside the convictions as unpermissible exercises of the state's power. In view of the foregoing discussion of "Probation for Gorillas?", analysis of these editorials and their setting is deemed unnecessary.

The Bridges Telegram.   While a motion for a new trial was pending in a case involving a dispute between an A.F. of L. union and a C.I.O. union of which Bridges was an officer, he either caused to be published or acquiesced in the publication of a telegram which he had sent to the Secretary of Labor. The telegram referred to the judge's decision as "outrageous"; said that attempted enforcement of it would tie up the port of Los Angeles and involve the entire Pacific Coast; and concluded with the announcement that the C.I.O. union, representing some twelve thousand members, did "not intend to allow state courts to override the majority vote of members in choosing its officers and representatives and to override the National Labor Relations Board."

Apparently Bridges' conviction is not rested at all upon his use of the word "outrageous." The remainder of the telegram fairly construed appears to be a statement that if the court's decree should be enforced there would be a strike. It is not claimed that such a strike would have been in violation of the terms of the decree, nor that in any other way it would have run afoul of the law of California. On no construction, therefore, can the telegram be taken as a threat either by Bridges or the union to follow an illegal course of action.

Moreover, this statement of Bridges was made to the Secretary of Labor, who is charged with official duties in connection with the prevention of strikes. Whatever the cause might be, if a strike was threatened or possible the Secretary was entitled to receive all available information. Indeed, the Supreme Court of California recognized that, publication in the newspapers aside, in sending the message to the Secretary, Bridges was exercising the right of petition to a duly accredited representative of the United States government, a right protected by the First Amendment. . . .

In looking at the reason advanced in support of the judgment of contempt, we find that here, too, the possibility of causing unfair disposition of a pending case is the major justification asserted. And here again the gist of the offense, according to the court below, is intimidation.

Let us assume that the telegram could be construed as an announcement of Bridges' intention to call a strike, something which, it is admitted, neither the general law of California nor the court's decree prohibited. With an eye on the realities of the situation, we cannot assume that Judge Schmidt was unaware of the possibility of a strike as a consequence of his decision. If he was not intimidated by the facts themselves, we do not believe that the most explicit statement of them could have sidetracked the course of justice. Again, we find exaggeration in the conclusion that the utterance even "tended" to interfere with justice. If there was electricity in the atmosphere, it was generated by the facts; the charge added by the Bridges telegram can be dismissed as negligible. The words of Mr. Justice Holmes, spoken in reference to very different facts, seem entirely applicable here: "I confess that I cannot find in all this or in the evidence in the case anything that would have affected a mind of reasonable fortitude, and still less can I find there anything that obstructed the administration of justice in any sense that I possibly can give to those words." Toledo Newspaper Co. v. United States, 247 U.S. 425.

Reversed.

MR. JUSTICE FRANKFURTER, with whom concurred the CHIEF JUSTICE, MR. JUSTICE ROBERTS and MR. JUSTICE BYRNES, dissenting:

Our whole history repels the view that it is an exercise of one of the civil liberties secured by the Bill of Rights for a leader of a large following or for a powerful metropolitan newspaper to attempt to overawe a judge in a matter immediately pending before him. The view of the majority deprives California of means for securing to its citizens justice according to law—means which, since the Union was founded, have been the possession, hitherto unchallenged, of all the states. This sudden break with the uninterrupted course of constitutional history has no constitutional warrant. To find justification for such deprivation of the historic powers of the states is to misconceive the idea of freedom of thought and speech as guaranteed by the Constitution.

We are not even vouchsafed reference to the specific provision of the Constitution which renders states powerless to insist upon trial by courts rather than trial by newspapers. So far as the Congress of the United States is concerned, we are referred to the First Amendment. That is specific. But we are here dealing with limitations upon California—with restraints upon the states. To say that the protection of freedom of speech of the First Amendment is absorbed by the Fourteenth does not say enough. Which one of the various limitations upon state power introduced by the Fourteenth Amendment absorbs the First? Some provisions of the Fourteenth Amendment apply only to citizens and one of the petitioners here is an alien; some of its provisions apply only to natural persons, and another petitioner here is a corporation. See *Hague* v. *C.I.O.*, 307 U.S. 496, 514, and cases cited. Only the Due Process Clause assures constitutional protection of civil liberties to aliens and corporations. Corporations cannot claim for themselves the "liberty" which the Due Process Clause guarantees. That clause protects only their property. *Pierce* v. *Society of Sisters*, 268 U.S. 510, 535. The majority opinion is strangely silent in failing to avow the specific constitutional provision upon which its decision rests.

These are not academic debating points or technical niceties. Those who have gone before us have admonished us "that in a free representative government nothing is more fundamental than the right of the people through their appointed servants to govern themselves in accordance with their own will, except so far as they have restrained themselves by constitutional limits specifically established, and that in our peculiar dual form of government nothing is more fundamental than the full power of the State to order its own affairs and govern its own people, except so far as the Federal Constitution expressly or by fair implication has withdrawn that power. The power of the people of the States to make and alter their laws at pleasure is the greatest security for liberty and justice . . . We are not invested with the jurisdiction to pass upon the expediency, wisdom or justice of the laws of the States as declared by their courts, but only to determine their conformity with the Federal Constitution and the paramount laws enacted pursuant to it. Under the guise of interpreting the Constitution we must take care that we do not import into the discussion our own personal views of what would be wise, just and fitting rules of government to be adopted by a free people and confound them with constitutional limitations." *Twining* v. *New Jersey*, 211 U.S. 78, 106–07.

A trial is not a "free trade in ideas," nor is the best test of truth in a courtroom "the power of the thought to get itself accepted in the competition of the market." Compare Mr. Justice Holmes in Abrams v. United States, 250 U.S. 616, 630. A court is a forum with strictly defined limits for discussion. It is circumscribed in the range of its inquiry and in its methods by the Constitution, by laws, and by age-old traditions. Its judges are restrained in their freedom of expression by historic compulsions resting on no other officials of government. They are so circumscribed precisely because judges have in their keeping the enforcement of rights and the protection of liberties which, according to the wisdom of the ages, can only be enforced and protected by observing such methods and traditions. . . .

It is trifling with great issues to suggest that the question before us is whether eighteenth-century restraints upon the freedom of the press should now be revived. The question is rather whether nineteenth- and twentieth-century American institutions should be abrogated by judicial fiat. . . .

We are charged here with the duty, always delicate, of sitting in judgment on state power. We must be fastidiously careful not to make our private views the measure of constitutional authority. To be sure, we are here concerned with an appeal to the great liberties which the Constitution assures to all our people, even against state denial. When a substantial claim of an abridgment of these liberties is advanced, the presumption of validity that belongs to an exercise of state power must not be allowed to impair such a liberty or to check our close examination of the merits of the controversy. But the utmost protection to be accorded to freedom of speech and of the press cannot displace our duty to give due regard also to the state's power to deal with what may essentially be local situations. . . .

By the constitution of California as authoritatively construed by its Supreme Court and therefore as binding upon this Court as though ratified by all the voters of California, the citizens of that state have chosen to place in its courts the power, as we have defined it, to insure impartial justice. If the citizens of California have other desires, if they want to permit the free play of modern publicity in connection with pending litigation, it is within their easy power to say so and to have their way. They have ready means of amending their constitution and they have frequently made use of them. We are, after all, sitting over three thousand miles away from a great state without intimate knowledge of its habits and its needs in a matter which does not cut across the affirmative powers of the national government. Some play of policy must be left to the states in the task of accommodating individual rights and the overriding public well-being which makes those rights possible. How are we to know whether an easy-going or stiffer view of what affects the actual administration of justice is appropriate to local circumstances? How are we to say that California has no right to model its judiciary upon the qualities and standards attained by the English administration of justice, and to use means deemed appropriate to that end by English courts? It is surely an arbitrary judgment to say that the Due Process Clause denies California that right. For respect for "the liberty of the subject" though not explicitly written into a constitution, is so deeply embedded in the very texture of English feeling and conscience that it survives, as the pages of Hansard abundantly prove, the exigencies of the life and death struggle of the British people. See, e.g., Carr, Concerning English Administrative Law, chap. 3 ("Crisis Legislation").

The rule of law applied in these cases by the California court forbade publications having "a reasonable tendency to interfere with the orderly administration of justice in pending actions." To deny that this age-old formulation of the prohibition against interference with dispassionate adjudication is properly confined to the substantive evil is not only to turn one's back on history but also to indulge in an idle play on words unworthy of constitutional adjudication. It was urged before us that the words "reasonable tendency" had a fatal pervasiveness, and that their replacement by "clear and present danger" was required to state a constitutionally permissible rule of law. . . . Our duty is not ended with the recitation of phrases that are the short-hand of a complicated historic process. The phrase "clear and present danger" is merely a justification for curbing utterance where that is warranted by the substantive evil to be prevented. The phrase itself is an expression of tendency and not of accomplishment, and the literary difference between it and "reasonable tendency" is not of constitutional dimension. . . .

It is suggested that threats, by discussion, to untrammeled decisions by courts are the most natural expressions when public feeling runs highest. But it does not follow that states are left powerless to prevent their courts from being subverted by outside pressure when the need for impartiality and fair proceeding is greatest. To say that the framers of the Consti-

tution sanctified veiled violence through coercive speech
directed against those charged with adjudications is not merely
to make violence an ingredient of justice; it mocks the very
ideal of justice by respecting its forms while stultifying its
uncontaminated exercise.

We turn to the specific cases before us:

The earliest editorial involved in No. 3, "Sit-strikers Convicted," commented upon a case the day after a jury had
returned a verdict and the day before the trial judge was to
pronounce sentence and hear motions for a new trial and applications for probation. On its face the editorial merely expressed exulting approval of the verdict, a completed action
of the court, and there is nothing in the record to give it additional significance. The same is true of the second editorial,
"Fall of an Ex-Queen," which luridly draws a moral from a
verdict of guilty in a sordid trial and which was published
eight days prior to the day set for imposing sentence. In both
instances imposition of sentences was immediately pending at
the time of publication, but in neither case was there any
declaration, direct or sly, in regard to this. As the special
guardian of the Bill of Rights this Court is under the heaviest
responsibility to safeguard the liberties guaranteed from any
encroachment, however astutely disguised. The Due Process
Clause of the Fourteenth Amendment protects the right to
comment on a judicial proceeding, so long as this is not done
in a manner interfering with the impartial disposition of a
litigation. There is no indication that more was done in these
editorials; they were not close threats to the judicial function
which a state should be able to restrain. We agree that the
judgment of the state court in this regard should not stand.

"Probation for Gorillas?", the third editorial, is a different
matter. . . .

This editorial was published three days after the trial judge
had fixed the time for sentencing and for passing on an application for probation, and a month prior to the date set. It

consisted of a sustained attack on the defendants, with an explicit demand of the judge that they be denied probation and be sent "to the jute mill." This meant, in California idiom, that in the exercise of his discretion the judge should treat the offense as a felony, with all its dire consequences, and not as a misdemeanor. Under the California Penal Code the trial judge had wide discretion in sentencing the defendants: he could sentence them to the county jail for one year or less, or to the state penitentiary for two years. The editorial demanded that he take the latter alternative and send the defendants to the "jute mill" of the state penitentiary. A powerful newspaper admonished a judge, who within a year would have to secure popular approval if he desired continuance in office, that failure to comply with its demands would be "a serious mistake." Clearly, the state court was justified in treating this as a threat to impartial adjudication. . . .

In No. 1, Harry R. Bridges challenges a judgment by the Superior Court of California fining him $125 for contempt. He was president of the International Longshoremen's and Warehousemen's Union, an affiliate of the Committee for Industrial Organization, and also West Coast director for the C.I.O. The I.L.W.U. was largely composed of men who had withdrawn from the International Longshoremen's Association, an affiliate of the American Federation of Labor. In the fall of 1937 the rival longshoremen's unions were struggling for control of a local in San Pedro Harbor. The officers of this local, carrying most of its members with them, sought to transfer the allegiance of the local to I.L.W.U. Thereupon, longshoremen remaining in I.L.A. brought suit in the Superior Court of Los Angeles county against the local and its officers. On January 21, 1938, Judge Schmidt, sitting in the Superior Court, enjoined the officers from working on behalf of I.L.W.U. and appointed a receiver to conduct the affairs of the local as an affiliate of the A.F. of L., by taking charge of the outstanding bargaining agreements of the local and of its hiring hall, which

is the physical mainstay of such a union. Judge Schmidt
promptly stayed enforcement of his decree, and on January
24th the defendants in the injunction suit moved for a new
trial and for vacation of the judgment. In view of its local
setting, the case aroused great public interest. The waterfront
situation on the Pacific Coast was also watched by the United
States Department of Labor, and Bridges had been in communication with the Secretary of Labor concerning the difficulties.
On the same day that the motion for new trial was filed,
Bridges sent the Secretary the following wire concerning
Judge Schmidt's decree: . . .

This Telegram duly found its way into the metropolitan
newspapers of California. Bridges' responsibility for its publication is clear. His publication of the telegram in the Los
Angeles and San Francisco papers is the basis of Bridges'
conviction for contempt.

The publication of the telegram was regarded by the state
supreme court as "a threat that if an attempt was made to
enforce the decision, the ports of the entire Pacific Coast would
be tied up" and "a direct challenge to the court that 11,000
longshoremen on the Pacific Coast would not abide by its
decision." This occurred immediately after counsel had moved
to set aside the judgment which was criticized, so unquestionably there was a threat to litigation obviously alive. It
would be inadmissible dogmatism for us to say that in the
context of the immediate case—the issues at stake, the environment in which the judge, the petitioner and the community
were moving, the publication here made, at the time and in the
manner it was made—this could not have dominated the
mind of the judge before whom the matter was pending.
Here too the state court's judgment should not be overturned.

The fact that the communication to the Secretary of Labor
may have been privileged does not constitutionally protect
whatever extraneous use may have been made of the communication. It is said that the possibility of a strike, in case

of an adverse ruling, must in any event have suggested itself to the private thoughts of a sophisticated judge. Therefore the publication of the Bridges' telegram, we are told, merely gave that possibility public expression. To afford constitutional shelter for a definite attempt at coercing a court into a favorable decision because of the contingencies of frustration to which all judicial action is subject, is to hold, in effect, that the Constitution subordinates the judicial settlement of conflicts to the unfettered indulgence of violent speech. The mere fact that after an unfavorable decision men may, upon full consideration of their responsibilities as well as their rights, engage in a strike or a lockout, is a poor reason for denying a state the power to protect its courts from being bludgeoned by serious threats while a decision is hanging in the judicial balance. A vague, undetermined possibility that a decision of a court may lead to a serious manifestation of protest is one thing. The impact of a definite threat of action to prevent a decision is a wholly different matter. . . .

The question concerning the narrow power we recognize always is—was there a real and substantial threat to the impartial decision by a court of a case actively pending before it? The threat must be close and direct; it must be directed towards a particular litigation. The litigation must be immediately pending. When a case is pending is not a technical, lawyer's problem, but is to be determined by the substantial realities of the specific situation. Danger of unbridled exercise of judicial power because of immunity from speech which is coercing is a figment of groundless fears. In addition to the internal censor of conscience, professional standards, the judgment of fellow judges and the bar, the popular judgment exercised in elections, the power of appellate courts, including this Court, there is the corrective power of the press and of public comment free to assert itself fully immediately upon completion of judicial conduct. Because courts, like other agencies, may at times exercise power arbitrarily and have done so, resort to this Court is open to determine whether, under the guise of protecting impartiality in specific litigation, encroachments have been made upon the liberties of speech and press. But instances of past arbitrariness afford no justification for reversing the course of history and denying the states power to continue to use time-honored safeguards to assure unbullied adjudications. All experience justifies the states in acting upon the conviction that a wrong decision in a particular case may best be forestalled or corrected by more rational means than coercive intrusion from outside the judicial process. . . .

[Note: In *Wheeling Steel Corp.* v. *Glander,* 337 U.S. 562 (1949), where only material interests were at stake, Mr. Justice Black again insisted that corporations are not "persons" for purposes of the Fourteenth Amendment.]

West Virginia State Board of Education

v. Barnette

319 U.S. 624 (1943)

In *Minersville School District* v. *Gobitis,* 310 U.S. 586 (1940), Mr. Justice Black and seven of his colleagues upheld a compulsory flag salute in public schools. Only Mr. Justice Stone dissented. Thereafter, Justices Murphy, Rutledge, and Jackson were appointed to the Supreme Court. In this case the flag-salute issue rose again. Mr. Justice Frankfurter's dissenting opinion is the classic modern statement of the anti-activist position in a civil-liberty case.

MR. JUSTICE JACKSON delivered the opinion of the Court:
    Following the decision by this Court on June 3, 1940, in Minersville School Dist. v. Gobitis, 310 U.S. 586, the West Virginia legislature amended its statutes to require all schools

therein to conduct courses of instruction in history, civics, and in the Constitutions of the United States and of the State "for the purpose of teaching, fostering and perpetuating the ideals, principles and spirit of Americanism, and increasing the knowledge of the organization and machinery of the government." Appellant Board of Education was directed, with advice of the State Superintendent of Schools, to "prescribe the courses of study covering these subjects" for public schools. The Act made it the duty of private, parochial and denominational schools to prescribe courses of study "similar to those required for the public schools."

The Board of Education on January 9, 1942, adopted a resolution containing recitals taken largely from the Court's Gobitis opinion and ordering that the salute to the flag become "a regular part of the program of activities in the public schools," that all teachers and pupils "shall be required to participate in the salute honoring the Nation represented by the Flag; provided, however, that refusal to salute the Flag be regarded as an Act of insubordination, and shall be dealt with accordingly."

The resolution originally required the "commonly accepted salute to the Flag" which it defined. Objections to the salute as "being too much like Hitler's" were raised by the Parent and Teachers Association, the Boy and Girl Scouts, the Red Cross, and the Federation of Women's Clubs. Some modification appears to have been made in deference to these objections, but no concession was made to Jehovah's Witnesses. What is now required is the "stiff-arm" salute, the saluter to keep the right hand raised with palm turned up while the following is repeated: "I pledge allegiance to the Flag of the United States of America and to the Republic for which it stands; one Nation, indivisible, with liberty and justice for all."

Failure to conform is "insubordination" dealt with by expulsion. Readmission is denied by statute until compliance. Meanwhile the expelled child is "unlawfully absent" and may be proceeded against as a delinquent. His parents or guardians are liable to prosecution, and if convicted are subject to fine not exceeding $50 and jail term not exceeding thirty days.

Appellees, citizens of the United States and of West Virginia, brought suit in the United States District Court for themselves and others similarly situated asking its injunction to restrain enforcement of these laws and regulations against Jehovah's Witnesses. The Witnesses are an unincorporated body teaching that the obligation imposed by law of God is superior to that of laws enacted by temporal government. Their religious beliefs include a literal version of Exodus, Chapter 20, verses 4 and 5, which says: "Thou shalt not make unto thee any graven image, or any likeness of anything that is in heaven above, or that is in the earth beneath, or that is in the water under the earth; thou shalt not bow down thyself to them, nor serve them." They consider that the flag is an "image" within this command. For this reason they refuse to salute it.

Children of this faith have been expelled from school and are threatened with exclusion for no other cause. Officials threaten to send them to reformatories maintained for criminally inclined juveniles. Parents of such children have been prosecuted and are threatened with prosecutions for causing delinquency.

The Board of Education moved to dismiss the complaint setting forth these facts and alleging that the law and regulations are an unconstitutional denial of religious freedom, and of freedom of speech, and are invalid under the "due process" and "'equal protection" clauses of the Fourteenth Amendment to the Federal Constitution. The cause was submitted on the pleadings to a District Court of three judges. It restrained enforcement as to the plaintiffs and those of that class. The Board of Education brought the case here by direct appeal.

This case calls upon us to reconsider a precedent decision, as the Court throughout its history often has been required to do. Before turning to the Gobitis Case, however, it is desirable to notice certain characteristics by which this controversy is distinguished.

The freedom asserted by these appellees does not bring them into collision with rights asserted by any other individual. It is such conflicts which most frequently require intervention of the State to determine where the rights of one end and those of another begin. But the refusal of these persons to participate in the ceremony does not interfere with or deny rights of others to do so. Nor is there any question in this case that their behavior is peaceable and orderly. The sole conflict is between authority and rights of the individual. The State asserts power to condition access to public education on making a prescribed sign and profession and at the same time to coerce attendance by punishing both parent and child. The latter stand on a right of self-determination in matters that touch individual opinion and personal attitude.

As the present Chief Justice said in dissent in the Gobitis Case, the State may "require teaching by instruction and study of all in our history and in the structure and organization of our government, including the guaranties of civil liberty, which tend to inspire patriotism and love of country." 310 U.S. at 604. Here, however, we are dealing with a compulsion of students to declare a belief. They are not merely made acquainted with the flag salute so that they may be informed as to what it is or even what it means. The issue here is whether this slow and easily neglected route to aroused loyalties constitutionally may be short-cut by substituting a compulsory salute and slogan. This issue is not prejudiced by the Court's previous holding that where a State, without compelling attendance, extends college facilities to pupils who voluntarily enroll, it may prescribe military training as part of the course without offense to the Constitution. It was held that those who take

advantage of its opportunities may not on ground of conscience refuse compliance with such conditions. Hamilton v.
University of California, 293 U.S. 245. In the present case
attendance is not optional. That case is also to be distinguished
from the present one because, independently of college privileges or requirements, the State has power to raise militia and
impose the duties of service therein upon its citizens.

There is no doubt that, in connection with the pledges, the
flag salute is a form of utterance. Symbolism is a primitive but
effective way of communicating ideas. The use of an emblem
or flag to symbolize some system, idea, institution, or personality, is a short cut from mind to mind. Causes and nations,
political parties, lodges and ecclesiastical groups seek to knit
the loyalty of their followings to a flag or banner, a color or
design. The State announces rank, function, and authority
through crowns and maces, uniforms and black robes; the
church speaks through the Cross, the Crucifix, the altar and
shrine and clerical raiment. Symbols of State often convey
political ideas just as religious symbols come to convey theo-
logical ones. Associated with many of these symbols are appropriate gestures of acceptance or respect: a salute, a bowed
or bared head, a bended knee. A person gets from a symbol
the meaning he puts into it, and what is one man's comfort and
inspiration is another's jest and scorn. . . .

Whether the First Amendment to the Constitution will permit officials to order observance of ritual of this nature does
not depend upon whether as a voluntary exercise we would
think it to be good, bad, or merely innocuous. Any credo of
nationalism is likely to include what some disapprove or to
omit what others think essential and to give off different overtones as it takes on different accents or interpretations. If
official power exists to coerce acceptance of any patriotic
creed, what it shall contain cannot be decided by courts, but
must be largely discretionary with the ordaining authority,
whose power to prescribe would no doubt include power to

amend. Hence validity of the asserted power to force an American citizen publicly to profess any statement of belief or to engage in any ceremony of assent to one, presents questions of power that must be considered independently of any idea we may have as to the utility of the ceremony in question.

Nor does the issue as we see it turn on one's possession of particular religious views or the sincerity with which they are held. While religion supplies appellees' motive for enduring the discomforts of making the issue in this case, many citizens who do not share these religious views hold such a compulsory rite to infringe constitutional liberty of the individual. It is not necessary to inquire whether nonconformist beliefs will exempt from the duty to salute unless we first find power to make the salute a legal duty.

The Gobitis decision, however, *assumed*, as did the argument in that case and in this, that power exists in the State to impose the flag salute discipline upon school children in general. The Court only examined and rejected a claim based on religious beliefs of immunity from an unquestioned general rule. The question which underlies the flag salute controversy is whether such a ceremony so touching matters of opinion and political attitude may be imposed upon the individual by official authority under powers committed to any political organization under our Constitution. We examine rather than assume existence of this power and, against this broader definition of issues in this case, re-examine specific grounds assigned for the Gobitis decision.

1.   It was said that the flag-salute controversy confronted the Court with "the problem which Lincoln cast in memorable dilemma: 'Must a government of necessity be too *strong* for the liberties of its people, or too *weak* to maintain its own existence?'" and that the answer must be in favor of strength. Minersville School Dist. v. Gobitis, supra, 310 U.S. at 596.

We think these issues may be examined free of pressure or restraint growing out of such considerations.

It may be doubted whether Mr. Lincoln would have thought that the strength of government to maintain itself would be impressively vindicated by our confirming power of the state to expel a handful of children from school. Such oversimplification, so handy in political debate, often lacks the precision necessary to postulates of judicial reasoning. If validly applied to this problem, the utterance cited would resolve every issue of power in favor of those in authority and would require us to override every liberty thought to weaken or delay execution of their policies.

Government of limited power need not be anemic government. Assurance that rights are secure tends to diminish fear and jealousy of strong government, and by making us feel safe to live under it makes for its better support. Without promise of a limiting Bill of Rights it is doubtful if our Constitution could have mustered enough strength to enable its ratification. To enforce those rights today is not to choose weak government over strong government. It is only to adhere as a means of strength to individual freedom of mind in preference to officially disciplined uniformity for which history indicates a disappointing and disastrous end.

The subject now before us exemplifies this principle. Free public education, if faithful to the ideal of secular instruction and political neutrality, will not be partisan or enemy of any class, creed, party, or faction. If it is to impose any ideological discipline, however, each party or denomination must seek to control, or failing that, to weaken the influence of the educational system. Observance of the limitations of the Constitution will not weaken Government in the field appropriate for its exercise.

2. It was also considered in the Gobitis Case that functions of educational officers in states, counties and school districts were such that to interfere with their authority "would in effect make us the school board for the country." Id. at 598.

The Fourteenth Amendment, as now applied to the States,

protects the citizen against the State itself and all of its creatures—Boards of Education not excepted. These have, of course, important, delicate, and highly discretionary functions, but none that they may not perform within the limits of the Bill of Rights. That they are educating the young for citizenship is reason for scrupulous protection of Constitutional freedoms of the individual, if we are not to strangle the free mind at its source and teach youth to discount important principles of our government as mere platitudes.

Such Boards are numerous and their territorial jurisdiction often small. But small and local authority may feel less sense of responsibility to the Constitution, and agencies of publicity may be less vigilant in calling it to account. . . . There are village tyrants as well as village Hampdens, but none who acts under color of law is beyond the Constitution.

3.   The Gobitis opinion reasoned that this is a field "where courts possess no marked and certainly no controlling competence," that it is committed to the legislatures as well as the courts to guard cherished liberties and that it is constitutionally appropriate to "fight out the wise use of legislative authority in the forum of public opinion and before legislative assemblies rather than to transfer such a contest to the judicial arena," since all the "effective means of inducing political changes are left free." Id. 310 U.S. at 597, 598, 600.

The very purpose of a Bill of Rights was to withdraw certain subjects from the vicissitudes of political controversy, to place them beyond the reach of majorities and officials and to establish them as legal principles to be applied by the courts. One's right to life, liberty, and property, to free speech, a free press, freedom of worship and assembly, and other fundamental rights may not be submitted to vote; they depend on the outcome of no elections.

In weighing arguments of the parties it is important to distinguish between the due process clause of the Fourteenth Amendment as an instrument for transmitting the principles of the First Amendment and those cases in which it is applied for its own sake. The test of legislation which collides with the Fourteenth Amendment, because it also collides with the principles of the First, is much more definite than the test when only the Fourteenth is involved. Much of the vagueness of the due process clause disappears when the specific prohibitions of the First become its standard. The right of a State to regulate, for example, a public utility may well include, so far as the due process test is concerned, power to impose all of the restrictions which a legislature may have a "rational basis" for adopting. But freedoms of speech and of press, of assembly, and of worship may not be infringed on such slender grounds. They are susceptible of restriction only to prevent grave and immediate danger to interests which the state may lawfully protect. It is important to note that while it is the Fourteenth Amendment which bears directly upon the State it is the more specific limiting principles of the First Amendment that finally govern this case.

Nor does our duty to apply the Bill of Rights to assertions of official authority depend upon our possession of marked competence in the field where the invasion of rights occurs. True, the task of translating the majestic generalities of the Bill of Rights, conceived as part of the pattern of liberal government in the eighteenth century, into concrete restraints on officials dealing with the problems of the twentieth century, is one to disturb self-confidence. These principles grew in soil which also produced a philosophy that the individual was the center of society, that his liberty was attainable through mere absence of governmental restraints, and that government should be entrusted with few controls and only the mildest supervision over men's affairs. We must transplant these rights to a soil in which the laissez-faire concept or principle of noninterference has withered at least as to economic affairs, and social advancements are increasingly sought through closer integration of society and through expanded and strengthened governmental controls. These changed conditions often deprive precedents of reliability and cast us more than we would choose upon our own judgment. But we act in these matters not by authority of our competence but by force of our commissions. We cannot, because of modest estimates of our competence in such specialties as public education, withhold the judgment that history authenticates as the function of this Court when liberty is infringed.

4. Lastly, and this is the very heart of the Gobitis opinion, it reasons that "national unity is the basis of national security," that the authorities have "the right to select appropriate means for its attainment," and hence reaches the conclusion that such compulsory measures toward "national unity" are constitutional. Id. at 595. Upon the verity of this assumption depends our answer in this case.

National unity as an end which officials may foster by persuasion and example is not in question. The problem is whether under our Constitution compulsion as here employed is a permissible means for its achievement.

Struggles to coerce uniformity of sentiment in support of some end thought essential to their time and country have been waged by many good as well as by evil men. Nationalism is a relatively recent phenomenon but at other times and places the ends have been racial or territorial security, support of a dynasty or regime, and particular plans for saving souls. As first and moderate methods to attain unity have failed, those bent on its accomplishment must resort to an ever increasing severity. As governmental pressure toward unity becomes greater, so strife becomes more bitter as to whose unity it shall be. Probably no deeper division of our people could proceed from any provocation than from finding it necessary to choose what doctrine and whose program public educational officials shall compel youth to unite in embracing. Ultimate futility of such attempts to compel coherence is the lesson of every such effort from the Roman drive to stamp out

Christianity as a disturber of its pagan unity, the Inquisition, as a means to religious and dynastic unity, the Siberian exiles as a means to Russian unity, down to the fast failing efforts of our present totalitarian enemies. Those who begin coercive elimination of dissent soon find themselves exterminating dissenters. Compulsory unification of opinion achieves only the unanimity of the graveyard.

It seems trite but necessary to say that the First Amendment to our Constitution was designed to avoid these ends by avoiding these beginnings. There is no mysticism in the American concept of the State or of the nature or origin of its authority. We set up government by consent of the governed, and the Bill of Rights denies those in power any legal opportunity to coerce that consent. Authority here is to be controlled by public opinion, not public opinion by authority.

The case is made difficult not because the principles of its decision are obscure but because the flag involved is our own. Nevertheless, we apply the limitations of the Constitution with no fear that freedom to be intellectually and spiritually diverse or even contrary will disintegrate the social organization. To believe that patriotism will not flourish if patriotic ceremonies are voluntary and spontaneous instead of a compulsory routine is to make an unflattering estimate of the appeal of our institutions to free minds. We can have intellectual individualism and the rich cultural diversities that we owe to exceptional minds only at the price of occasional eccentricity and abnormal attitudes. When they are so harmless to others or to the State as those we deal with here, the price is not too great. But freedom to differ is not limited to things that do not matter much. That would be a mere shadow of freedom. The test of its substance is the right to differ as to things that touch the heart of the existing order.

If there is any fixed star in our constitutional constellation, it is that no official, high or petty, can prescribe what shall be orthodox in politics, nationalism, religion, or other matters of opinion or force citizens to confess by word or act their faith therein. If there are any circumstances which permit an exception, they do not now occur to us.

We think the action of the local authorities in compelling the flag salute and pledge transcends constitutional limitations on their power and invades the sphere of intellect and spirit which it is the purpose of the First Amendment to our Constitution to reserve from all official control.

The decision of this Court in Minersville School Dist. v. Gobitis and the holdings of those few per curiam decisions which preceded and foreshadowed it are overruled, and the judgment enjoining enforcement of the West Virginia Regulation is affirmed.

[Mr. Justice Black wrote a concurring opinion in which his brother Douglas joined. Mr. Justice Murphy also wrote a concurring opinion.]

MR. JUSTICE ROBERTS and MR. JUSTICE REED adhere to the views expressed by the Court in Minersville School Dist. v. Gobitis, 310 U.S. 586, and are of the opinion that the judgment below should be reversed.

MR. JUSTICE FRANKFURTER, dissenting:

One who belongs to the most vilified and persecuted minority in history is not likely to be insensible to the freedoms guaranteed by our Constitution. Were my purely personal attitude relevant I should wholeheartedly associate myself with the general libertarian views in the Court's opinion, representing as they do the thought and action of a lifetime. But as judges we are neither Jew nor Gentile, neither Catholic nor agnostic. We owe equal attachment to the Constitution and are equally bound by our judicial obligations whether we derive our citizenship from the earliest or the latest immigrants to these shores. As a member of this Court I am not justified in writing my private notions of policy into the Constitution, no matter how deeply I may cherish them or how mischievous I may deem their disregard. The duty of a judge who must decide which of two claims before the Court shall prevail, that of a State to enact and enforce laws within its general competence or that of an individual to refuse obedience because of the demands of his conscience, is not that of the ordinary person. It can never be emphasized too much that one's own opinion about the wisdom or evil of a law should be excluded altogether when one is doing one's duty on the bench. The only opinion of our own even looking in that direction that is material is our opinion whether legislators could in reason have enacted such a law. In the light of all the circumstances, including the history of this question in this Court, it would require more daring than I possess to deny that reasonable legislators could have taken the action which is before us for review. Most unwillingly, therefore, I must differ from my brethren with regard to legislation like this. I cannot bring my mind to believe that the "liberty" secured by the Due Process Clause gives this Court authority to deny to the State of West Virginia the attainment of that which we all recognize as a legitimate legislative end, namely, the promotion of good citizenship, by employment of the means here chosen. . . .

The admonition that judicial self-restraint alone limits arbitrary exercise of our authority is relevant every time we are asked to nullify legislation. The Constitution does not give us greater veto power when dealing with one phase of "liberty" than with another, or when dealing with grade school regulations than with college regulations that offend conscience, as was the case in Hamilton v. University of California, 293 U.S. 245. In neither situation is our function comparable to that of a legislature or are we free to act as though we were a super-legislature. Judicial self-restraint is equally necessary whenever an exercise of political or legislative power is challenged. There is no warrant in the constitutional basis of this Court's authority for attributing different rôles to it depending upon the nature of the challenge to the legislation. Our power does not vary according to the particular provision of the Bill of Rights which is invoked. The right not to have property taken without just compensation has, so far as the scope of judicial power is concerned, the same constitutional dignity as the right to be protected against unreasonable searches and seizures, and the latter has no less claim than freedom of the press or freedom of speech, or religious freedom. In no instance is this Court the primary protector of the particular liberty that is invoked. This Court has recognized, what hardly could be denied, that all the provisions of the first ten Amendments are "specific" prohibitions, United States v. Carolene Products Co., 304 U.S. 144, 152, note 4. But each specific Amendment, in so far as embraced within the Fourteenth Amendment, must be equally respected, and the function of this Court does not differ in passing on the constitutionality of legislation challenged under different Amendments. . . .

The reason why from the beginning even the narrow judicial authority to nullify legislation has been viewed with a jealous eye is that it serves to prevent the full play of the democratic process. The fact that it may be an undemocratic aspect of our scheme of government does not call for its rejection or its disuse. But it is the best of reasons, as this Court has frequently recognized, for the greatest caution in its use. . . .

Under our constitutional system the legislature is charged solely with civil concerns of society. If the avowed or intrinsic legislative purpose is either to promote or to discourage some religious community or creed, it is clearly within the constitutional restrictions imposed on legislatures and cannot stand. But it by no means follows that legislative power is wanting whenever a general non-discriminatory civil regulation in fact touches conscientious scruples or religious beliefs of an individual or a group. Regard for such scruples or beliefs undoubtedly presents one of the most reasonable claims for the exertion of legislative accommodation. It is, of course, beyond our power to rewrite the State's requirement, by providing exemptions for those who do not wish to participate in the flag salute or by making some other accommodations to meet their scruples. That wisdom might suggest the making of such accommodations and that school administration would not find it too difficult to make them and yet maintain the ceremony for those not refusing to conform, is outside our province to suggest. Tact, respect, and generosity toward variant views will always commend themselves to those charged with the duties of legislation so as to achieve a maximum of good will and to require a minimum of unwilling submission to a general law. But the real question is, who is to make such accommodations, the courts or the legislature? . . .

Conscientious scruples, all would admit, cannot stand against every legislative compulsion to do positive acts in conflict with such scruples. We have been told that such compulsions override religious scruples only as to major concerns of the state. But the determination of what is major and what is minor itself raises questions of policy. For the way in which men equally guided by reason appraise importance goes to the very heart of policy. Judges should be very diffident in setting their judgment against that of a state in determining what is and what is not a major concern, what means are appropriate to proper ends, and what is the total social cost in striking the balance of imponderables. . . .

The constitutional protection of religious freedom terminated disabilities, it did not create new privileges. It gave religious equality, not civil immunity. Its essence is freedom from conformity to religious dogma, not freedom from conformity to law because of religious dogma. Religious loyalties may be exercised without hindrance from the state, the state may not exercise that which except by leave of religious loyalties is within the domain of temporal power. Otherwise each individual could set up his own censor against obedience to laws conscientiously deemed for the public good by those whose business it is to make laws.

The prohibition against any religious establishment by the

government placed denominations on an equal footing—it assured freedom from support by the government to any mode of worship and the freedom of individuals to support any mode of worship. Any person may therefore believe or disbelieve what he pleases. He may practice what he will in his own house of worship or publicly within the limits of public order. But the lawmaking authority is not circumscribed by the variety of religious beliefs, otherwise the constitutional guaranty would be not a protection of the free exercise of religion but a denial of the exercise of legislation.

The essence of the religious freedom guaranteed by our Constitution is therefore this: no religion shall either receive the state's support or incur its hostility. Religion is outside the sphere of political government. This does not mean that all matters on which religious organizations or beliefs may pronounce are outside the sphere of government. Were this so, instead of the separation of church and state, there would be the subordination of the state on any matter deemed within the sovereignty of the religious conscience. Much that is the concern of temporal authority affects the spiritual interests of men. But it is not enough to strike down a nondiscriminatory law that it may hurt or offend some dissident view. It would be too easy to cite numerous prohibitions and injunctions to which laws run counter if the variant interpretations of the Bible were made the tests of obedience to law. The validity of secular laws cannot be measured by their conformity to religious doctrines. It is only in a theocratic state that ecclesiastical doctrines measure legal right or wrong.

When dealing with religious scruples we are dealing with an almost numberless variety of doctrines and beliefs entertained with equal sincerity by the particular groups for which they satisfy man's needs in his relation to the mysteries of the universe. There are in the United States more than 250 distinctive established religious denominations. In the state of Pennsylvania there are 120 of these, and in West Virginia as many as

65. But if religious scruples afford immunity from civic obedience to laws, they may be invoked by the religious beliefs of any individual even though he holds no membership in any sect or organized denomination. Certainly this Court cannot be called upon to determine what claims of conscience should be recognized and what should be rejected as satisfying the "religion" which the Constitution protects. That would indeed resurrect the very discriminatory treatment of religion which the Constitution sought forever to forbid.

Consider the controversial issue of compulsory Bible-reading in public schools. The educational policies of the states are in great conflict over this, and the state courts are divided in their decisions on the issue whether the requirement of Bible-reading offends constitutional provisions dealing with religious freedom. The requirement of Bible-reading has been justified by various state courts as an appropriate means of inculcating ethical precepts and familiarizing pupils with the most lasting expression of great English literature. Is this Court to overthrow such variant state educational policies by denying states the right to entertain such convictions in regard to their school systems, because of a belief that the King James version is in fact a sectarian text to which parents of the Catholic and Jewish faiths and of some Protestant persuasions may rightly object to having their children exposed? On the other hand the religious consciences of some parents may rebel at the absence of any Bible-reading in the schools. See Washington ex rel. Clithero v. Showalter, 284 U.S. 573. Or is this Court to enter the old controversy between science and religion by unduly defining the limits within which a state may experiment with its school curricula? The religious consciences of some parents may be offended by subjecting their children to the Biblical account of creation, while another state may offend parents by prohibiting a teaching of biology that contradicts such Biblical account. Compare Scopes v. State, 154 Tenn. 105. What of conscientious objections to what is devoutly felt by parents to

be the poisoning of impressionable minds of children by chau-
vinistic teaching of history? This is very far from a fanciful
suggestion for in the belief of many thoughtful people nationalism is the seed-bed of war.

There are other issues in the offing which admonish us of the
difficulties and complexities that confront states in the duty of
administering their local school systems. All citizens are taxed
for the support of public schools although this Court has denied the right of a state to compel all children to go to such
schools and has recognized the right of parents to send
children to privately maintained schools. Parents who are
dissatisfied with the public schools thus carry a double educational burden. Children who go to public school enjoy in many
states derivative advantages such as free textbooks, free lunch,
and free transportation in going to and from school. What of
the claims for equality of treatment of those parents who, because of religious scruples, cannot send their children to public schools? What of the claim that if the right to send children
to privately maintained schools is partly an exercise of religious
conviction, to render effective this right it should be accompanied by equality of treatment by the state in supplying free
textbooks, free lunch, and free transportation to children who
go to private schools? What of the claim that such grants are
offensive to the cardinal constitutional doctrine of separation
of church and state?

These questions assume increasing importance in view of
the steady growth of parochial schools both in number and in
population. I am not borrowing trouble by adumbrating these
issues nor am I parading horrible examples of the consequences of today's decision. I am aware that we must decide
the case before us and not some other case. But that does not
mean that a case is dissociated from the past and unrelated to
the future. We must decide this case with due regard for what
went before and no less regard for what may come after. Is it
really a fair construction of such a fundamental concept as the

right freely to exercise one's religion that a state cannot choose
to require all children who attend public school to make the
same gesture of allegiance to the symbol of our national life
because it may offend the conscience of some children, but
that it may compel all children to attend public school to listen
to the King James version although it may offend the consciences of their parents? And what of the larger issue of
claiming immunity from obedience to a general civil regulation
that has a reasonable relation to a public purpose within the
general competence of the state? See Pierce v. Society of
Sisters, 268 U.S. 510, 535. . . .

One's conception of the Constitution cannot be severed from
one's conception of a judge's function in applying it. The Court
has no reason for existence if it merely reflects the pressures of
the day. Our system is built on the faith that men set apart for
this special function, freed from the influences of immediacy
and from the deflections of worldly ambition, will become able
to take a view of longer range than the period of responsibility
entrusted to Congress and legislatures. We are dealing with
matters as to which legislators and voters have conflicting
views. Are we as judges to impose our strong convictions on
where wisdom lies? That which three years ago had seemed to
five successive Courts to lie within permissible areas of legislation is now outlawed by the deciding shift of opinion of two
Justices. What reason is there to believe that they or their
successors may not have another view a few years hence? Is
that which was deemed to be of so fundamental a nature as to
be written into the Constitution to endure for all times to be
the sport of shifting winds of doctrine? Of course, judicial
opinions, even as to questions of constitutionality, are not im-
mutable. As has been true in the past, the Court will from time
to time reverse its position. But I believe that never before
these Jehovah's Witnesses cases (except for minor deviations
subsequently retraced) has this Court overruled decisions so as
to restrict the powers of democratic government. Always here-

tofore, it has withdrawn narrow views of legislative authority so as to authorize what formerly it had denied.

In view of this history it must be plain that what thirteen Justices found to be within the constitutional authority of a state, legislators cannot be deemed unreasonable in enacting. Therefore, in denying to the states what heretofore has received such impressive judicial sanction, some other tests of unconstitutionality must surely be guiding the Court than the absence of a rational justification for the legislation. But I know of no other test which this Court is authorized to apply in nullifying legislation.

In the past this Court has from time to time set its views of policy against that embodied in legislation by finding laws in conflict with what was called the "spirit of the Constitution." Such undefined destructive power was not conferred on this Court by the Constitution. Before a duly enacted law can be judicially nullified, it must be forbidden by some explicit restriction upon political authority in the Constitution. Equally inadmissible is the claim to strike down legislation because to us as individuals it seems opposed to the "plan and purpose" of the Constitution. That is too tempting a basis for finding in one's personal views the purposes of the Founders.

The uncontrollable power wielded by this Court brings it very close to the most sensitive areas of public affairs. As appeal from legislation to adjudication becomes more frequent, and its consequences more far-reaching, judicial self-restraint becomes more and not less important, lest we unwarrantably enter social and political domains wholly outside our concern. I think I appreciate fully the objections to the law before us. But to deny that it presents a question upon which men might reasonably differ appears to me to be intolerance. And since men may so reasonably differ, I deem it beyond my constitutional power to assert my view of the wisdom of this law against the view of the State of West Virginia.

Jefferson's opposition to judicial review has not been accepted by history, but it still serves as an admonition against confusion between judicial and political functions. As a rule of judicial self-restraint, it is still as valid as Lincoln's admonition. For those who pass laws not only are under duty to pass laws. They are also under duty to observe the Constitution. And even though legislation relates to civil liberties, our duty of deference to those who have the responsibility for making the laws is no less relevant or less exacting. And this is so especially when we consider the accidental contingencies by which one man may determine constitutionality and thereby confine the political power of the Congress of the United States and the legislatures of forty-eight states. The attitude of judicial humility which these considerations enjoin is not an abdication of the judicial function. It is a due observance of its limits. Moreover, it is to be borne in mind that in a question like this we are not passing on the proper distribution of political power as between the states and the central government. We are not discharging the basic function of this Court as the mediator of powers within the federal system. To strike down a law like this is to deny a power to all government. . . .

Of course patriotism cannot be enforced by the flag salute. But neither can the liberal spirit be enforced by judicial invalidation of illiberal legislation. Our constant preoccupation with the constitutionality of legislation rather than with its wisdom tends to preoccupation of the American mind with a false value. The tendency of focussing attention on constitutionality is to make constitutionality synonymous with wisdom, to regard a law as all right if it is constitutional. Such an attitude is a great enemy of liberalism. Particularly in legislation affecting freedom of thought and freedom of speech much which should offend a free-spirited society is constitutional. Reliance for the most precious interests of civilization, therefore, must be found outside of their vindication in courts of law. Only a persistent positive translation of the faith of a free society into the convictions and habits and actions of a community is the ultimate reliance against unabated temptations to fetter the human spirit.

[Note: If in the *Barnette* case Mr. Justice Jackson took an activist stand, he seems to have become more restrained after his experience in the Nürnberg trials.

In *Zorach* v. *Clauson*, 343 U.S. 306 (1952), the Court upheld "released time" sectarian religious instruction for public-school children. Justices Black, Frankfurter, and Jackson dissented. Is Mr. Justice Frankfurter's position here compatible with his position in the *Flag Salute* cases?]

Prince v. *Massachusetts*

312 U.S. 158 (1944)

This case must have been particularly trying for the libertarian activists, because it involved a clash between two liberal claims: freedom from child labor, and (absolute?) freedom of religion.

Mr. Justice Rutledge delivered the opinion of the Court:

The case brings for review another episode in the conflict between Jehovah's Witnesses and state authority. This time Sarah Prince appeals from convictions for violating Massachusetts' child labor laws, by acts said to be a rightful exercise of her religious convictions.

When the offenses were committed she was the aunt and custodian of Betty M. Simmons, a girl nine years of age. Originally there were three separate complaints. They were, shortly, for (1) refusal to disclose Betty's identity and age to a public officer whose duty was to enforce the statutes; (2) furnishing her with magazines, knowing she was to sell them unlawfully, that is, on the street; and (3) as Betty's custodian, permitting her to work contrary to law. The complaints were made, respectively, pursuant to §§ 79, 80 and 81 of Chapter 149, Gen. Laws of Mass. (Ter. Ed.). The Supreme Judicial Court reversed the conviction under the first complaint on state grounds; but sustained the judgments founded on the other two. 313 Mass. 223, 46 N.E. 2d 755. They present the only questions for our decision. These are whether §§ 80 and 81, as applied, contravene the Fourteenth Amendment by denying or abridging appellant's freedom of religion and by denying to her the equal protection of the laws.

Sections 80 and 81 form parts of Massachusetts' comprehensive child labor law. They provide methods for enforcing the prohibitions of § 69, which is as follows:

"No boy under twelve and no girl under eighteen shall sell, expose or offer for sale any newspapers, magazines, periodicals or any other articles of merchandise of any description, or exercise the trade of bootblack or scavenger, or any other trade, in any street or public place."

Sections 80 and 81, so far as pertinent, read:

"Whoever furnishes or sells to any minor any article of any description with the knowledge that the minor intends to sell such article in violation of any provision of sections sixty-nine to seventy-three, inclusive, or after having received written notice to this effect from any officer charged with the enforcement thereof, or knowingly procures or encourages any minor to violate any provisions of said sections, shall be punished by a fine of not less than ten nor more than two hundred dollars or by imprisonment for not more than two months, or both." § 80.

"Any parent, guardian or custodian having a minor under his control who compels or permits such minor to work in violation of any provision of sections sixty to seventy-four, inclusive, . . . shall for a first offense be punished by a fine of not less than two nor more than ten dollars or by imprisonment for not more than five days, or both; . . ." § 81.

The story told by the evidence has become familiar. It

hardly needs repeating, except to give setting to the variations introduced through the part played by a child of tender years. Mrs. Prince, living in Brockton, is the mother of two young sons. She also has legal custody of Betty Simmons, who lives with them. The children too are Jehovah's Witnesses and both Mrs. Prince and Betty testified they were ordained ministers. The former was accustomed to go each week on the streets of Brockton to distribute "Watchtower" and "Consolation," according to the usual plan. She had permitted the children to engage in this activity previously, and had been warned against doing so by the school attendance officer, Mr. Perkins. But, until December 18, 1941, she generally did not take them with her at night.

That evening, as Mrs. Prince was preparing to leave her home, the children asked to go. She at first refused. Childlike, they resorted to tears; and, motherlike, she yielded. Arriving downtown, Mrs. Prince permitted the children "to engage in the preaching work with her upon the sidewalks." That is, with specific reference to Betty, she and Mrs. Prince took positions about twenty feet apart near a street intersection. Betty held up in her hand, for passers-by to see, copies of "Watch Tower" and "Consolation." From her shoulder hung the usual canvas magazine bag, on which was printed: "Watchtower and Consolation 5¢ per copy." No one accepted a copy from Betty that evening and she received no money. Nor did her aunt. But on other occasions, Betty had received funds and given out copies.

Mrs. Prince and Betty remained until 8:45 p.m. A few minutes before this, Mr. Perkins approached Mrs. Prince. A discussion ensued. He inquired and she refused to give Betty's name. However, she stated the child attended the Shaw School. Mr. Perkins referred to his previous warnings and said he would allow five minutes for them to get off the street. Mrs. Prince admitted she supplied Betty with the magazines and said, "[N]either you nor anybody else can stop me . . . This child is exercising her God-given right and her constitutional right to preach the gospel, and no creature has a right to interfere with God's commands." However, Mrs. Prince and Betty departed. She remarked as she went, "I'm not going through this any more. We've been through it time and time again. I'm going home and put the little girl to bed." It may be added that testimony, by Betty, her aunt and others, was offered at the trials, and was excluded, to show that Betty believed it was her religious duty to perform this work and failure would bring condemnation "to everlasting destruction at Armageddon."

As the case reaches us, the questions are no longer open whether what the child did was a "sale" or an "offer to sell" within § 69 or was "work" within § 81. The state court's decision has foreclosed them adversely to appellant as a matter of state law. The only question remaining therefore is whether, as construed and applied, the statute is valid. Upon this the court said: "We think that freedom of the press and of religion is subject to incidental regulation to the slight degree involved in the prohibition of the selling of religious literature in streets and public places by boys under twelve and girls under eighteen, and in the further statutory provisions herein considered, which have been adopted as means of enforcing that prohibition." 313 Mass. 223, 229, 46 N.E. 2d 755, 758.

Appellant does not stand on freedom of the press. Regarding it as secular, she concedes it may be restricted as Massachusetts has done. Hence, she rests squarely on freedom of religion under the First Amendment, applied by the Fourteenth to the states. She buttresses this foundation, however, with a claim of parental right as secured by the due process clause of the latter Amendment. Cf. *Meyer* v. *Nebraska*, 262 U.S. 390. These guaranties, she thinks, guard alike herself and the child in what they have done. Thus, two claimed liberties are at stake. One is the parent's, to bring up the child in the way he should go, which for appellant means to teach him the tenets and the practices of their faith. The other freedom is the child's, to observe these; and among them is "to preach the gospel . . . by public distribution" of "Watchtower" and "Consolation," in conformity with the scripture: "A little child shall lead them."

If by this position appellant seeks for freedom of conscience a broader protection than for freedom of the mind, it may be doubted that any of the great liberties insured by the First Article can be given higher place than the others. All have preferred position in our basic scheme. *Schneider* v. *State*, 308 U.S. 147; *Cantwell* v. *Connecticut*, 310 U.S. 296. All are interwoven there together. Differences there are, in them and in the modes appropriate for their exercise. But they have unity in the charter's prime place because they have unity in their human sources and functionings. Heart and mind are not identical. Intuitive faith and reasoned judgment are not the same. Spirit is not always thought. But in the everyday business of living, secular or otherwise, these variant aspects of personality find inseparable expression in a thousand ways. They cannot be altogether parted in law more than in life.

To make accommodation between these freedoms and an exercise of state authority always is delicate. It hardly could be more so than in such a clash as this case presents. On one side is the obviously earnest claim for freedom of conscience and religious practice. With it is allied the parent's claim to authority in her own household and in the rearing of her children. The parent's conflict with the state over control of the child and his training is serious enough when only secular matters are concerned. It becomes the more so when an element of religious conviction enters. Against these sacred private interests, basic in a democracy, stand the interests of society to protect the welfare of children, and the state's assertion of authority to that end, made here in a manner conceded valid if only secular things were involved. The last is no mere corporate concern of official authority. It is the interest of youth itself, and of the whole community, that children be both safeguarded from abuses and given opportunities for growth into free and independent well-developed men and citizens. Between contrary pulls of such weight, the safest and most objective recourse is to the lines already marked out, not precisely but for guides, in narrowing the no man's land where this battle has gone on.

The rights of children to exercise their religion, and of parents to give them religious training and to encourage them in the practice of religious belief, as against preponderant sentiment and assertion of state power voicing it, have had recognition here, most recently in *West Virginia State Board of Education* v. *Barnette,* 319 U.S. 624. Previously in *Pierce* v. *Society of Sisters,* 268 U.S. 510, this Court had sustained the parent's authority to provide religious with secular schooling, and the child's right to receive it, as against the state's requirement of attendance at public schools. And in *Meyer* v. *Nebraska,* 262 U.S. 390, children's rights to receive teaching in languages other than the nation's common tongue were guarded against the state's encroachment. It is cardinal with us that the custody, care and nurture of the child reside first in the parents, whose primary function and freedom include preparation for obligations the state can neither supply nor hinder. *Pierce* v. *Society of Sisters, supra.* And it is in recognition of this that these decisions have respected the private realm of family life which the state cannot enter.

But the family itself is not beyond regulation in the public interest, as against a claim of religious liberty. *Reynolds* v. *United States,* 98 U.S. 145; *Davis* v. *Beason,* 133 U.S. 333. And neither rights of religion nor rights of parenthood are beyond limitation. Acting to guard the general interest in youth's well being, the state as *parens patriae* may restrict the parent's control by requiring school attendance, regulating or prohibiting the child's labor and in many other ways. Its authority is not nullified merely because the parent grounds his claim to control the child's course of conduct on religion or conscience. Thus, he cannot claim freedom from compulsory vaccination for the child more than for himself on religious grounds. The right to practice religion freely does not include liberty to expose the community or the child to communicable disease or the latter to ill health or death. *People* v. *Pierson,* 176 N.Y. 201, 68 N.E. 243. The catalogue need not be lengthened. It is sufficient to show what indeed appellant hardly disputes, that the state has a wide range of power for limiting parental freedom and authority in things affecting the child's welfare; and that this includes, to some extent, matters of conscience and religious conviction.

But it is said the state cannot do so here. This, first, because when state action impinges upon a claimed religious freedom, it must fall unless shown to be necessary for or conducive to the child's protection against some clear and present danger, cf. *Schenck* v. *United States,* 249 U.S. 47; and, it is added, there was no such showing here. The child's presence on the street, with her guardian, distributing or offering to distribute the magazines, it is urged, was in no way harmful to her, nor in any event more so than the presence of many other children at the same time and place, engaged in shopping and other activities not prohibited. Accordingly, in view of the preferred position the freedoms of the First Article occupy, the statute in its present application must fall. It cannot be sustained by any presumption of validity. Cf. *Schneider* v. *State,* 308 U.S. 147. And, finally, it is said, the statute is, as to children, an absolute prohibition, not merely a reasonable regulation, of the denounced activity.

Concededly a statute or ordinance identical in terms with § 69, except that it is applicable to adults or all persons generally, would be invalid. *Young* v. *California,* 308 U.S. 147; *Nichols* v. *Massachusetts,* 308 U.S. 147; *Jamison* v. *Texas,* 318 U.S. 413; *Murdock* v. *Pennsylvania,* 319 U.S. 105; *Martin* v. *City of Struthers,* 319 U.S. 141. But the mere fact a state could not wholly prohibit this form of adult activity, whether characterized locally as a "sale" or otherwise, does not mean it cannot do so for children. Such a conclusion granted would mean that a state could impose no greater limitation upon child labor than upon adult labor. Or, if an adult were free to enter dance halls, saloons, and disreputable places generally, in order to discharge his conceived religious duty to admonish or dissuade persons from frequenting such places, so would be a child with similar convictions and objectives, if not alone then in the parent's company, against the state's command.

The state's authority over children's activities is broader than over like actions of adults. This is peculiarly true of public activities and in matters of employment. A democratic society rests, for its continuance, upon the healthy, well-rounded growth of young people into full maturity as citizens, with all that implies. It may secure this against impeding restraints and dangers within a broad range of selection. Among evils most appropriate for such action are the crippling effects of child employment, more especially in public places, and the possible harms arising from other activities subject to all the diverse influences of the street. It is too late now to doubt that legislation appropriately designed to reach such evils is within the state's police power, whether against the parent's claim to control of the child or one that religious scruples dictate contrary action.

It is true children have rights, in common with older people, in the primary use of highways. But even in such use streets afford dangers for them not affecting adults. And in other uses, whether in work or in other things, this difference may be magnified. This is so not only when children are unaccompanied but certainly to some extent when they are with their parents. What may be wholly permissible for adults therefore may not be so for children, either with or without their parents' presence.

Street preaching, whether oral or by handing out literature, is not the primary use of the highway, even for adults. While for them it cannot be wholly prohibited, it can be regulated within reasonable limits in accommodation to the primary and other incidental uses. But, for obvious reasons, notwithstanding appellant's contrary view, the validity of such a prohibition applied to children not accompanied by an older person hardly would seem open to question. The case reduces itself therefore to the question whether the presence of the child's guardian puts a limit to the state's power. That fact may lessen the likelihood that some evils the legislation seeks to avert will occur. But it cannot forestall all of them. The zealous though lawful exercise of the right to engage in propagandizing the community, whether in religious, political or other matters, may and at times does create situations difficult enough for adults to cope with and wholly inappropriate for children, especially of tender years, to face. Other harmful possibilities could be stated, of emotional excitement and psychological or physical injury. Parents may be free to become martyrs themselves. But it does not follow they are free, in identical circumstances, to make martyrs of their children before they have reached the age of full and legal discretion when they can make that choice for themselves. Massachusetts has determined that an absolute prohibition, though one limited to streets and public places and to the incidental uses proscribed, is necessary to accomplish its legitimate objectives. Its power to attain them is broad enough to reach these peripheral instances in which the parent's supervision may reduce but cannot eliminate entirely the ill effects of the prohibited conduct. We think that with reference to the public proclaiming of religion, upon the streets and in other similar public places, the power of the state to control the conduct of children reaches beyond the scope of its authority over adults, as is true in the case of other freedoms, and the rightful boundary of its power has not been crossed in this case.

In so ruling we dispose also of appellant's argument founded upon denial of equal protection. It falls with that based on denial of religious freedom, since in this instance the one is but another phrasing of the other. Shortly, the contention is that the street, for Jehovah's Witnesses and their children, is their church, since their conviction makes it so; and to deny them access to it for religious purposes as was done here has the same effect as excluding altar boys, youthful choristers, and other children from the edifices in which they practice their religious beliefs and worship. The argument hardly needs more than statement, after what has been said, to refute it. However Jehovah's Witnesses may conceive them, the public highways have not become their religious property merely by their assertion. And there is no denial of equal protection in excluding their children from doing there what no other children may do.

Our ruling does not extend beyond the facts the case presents. We neither lay the foundation "for any [that is, every] state intervention in the indoctrination and participation of children in religion" which may be done "in the name of their health and welfare" nor give warrant for "every limitation on their religious training and activities." The religious training and indoctrination of children may be accomplished in many ways, some of which, as we have noted, have received constitutional protection through decisions of this Court. These and all others except the public proclaiming of religion on the streets, if this may be taken as either training or indoctrination of the proclaimer, remain unaffected by the decision.

The judgment is

Affirmed.

Mr. Justice Murphy, dissenting:

This attempt by the state of Massachusetts to prohibit a child from exercising her constitutional right to practice her religion on the public streets cannot, in my opinion, be sustained. . . .

As the opinion of the Court demonstrates, the power of the state lawfully to control the religious and other activities of children is greater than its power over similar activities of adults. But that fact is no more decisive of the issue posed by this case than is the obvious fact that the family itself is subject to reasonable regulation in the public interest. We are concerned solely with the reasonableness of this particular prohibition of religious activity by children.

In dealing with the validity of statutes which directly or indirectly infringe religious freedom and the right of parents to encourage their children in the practice of a religious belief, we are not aided by any strong presumption of the constitutionality of such legislation. *United States* v. *Carolene Products Co.*, 304 U.S. 144, 152, note 4. On the contrary, the human freedoms enumerated in the First Amendment and carried over into the Fourteenth Amendment are to be presumed to be invulnerable and any attempt to sweep away those freedoms is prima facie invalid. It follows that any restriction or prohibition must be justified by those who deny that the freedoms have been unlawfully invaded. The burden was therefore on the state of Massachusetts to prove the reasonableness and necessity of prohibiting children from engaging in religious activity of the type involved in this case.

The burden in this instance, however, is not met by vague references to the reasonableness underlying child labor legislation in general. The great interest of the state in shielding minors from the evil vicissitudes of early life does not warrant every limitation on their religious training and activities. The reasonableness that justifies the prohibition of the ordinary distribution of literature in the public streets by children is not necessarily the reasonableness that justifies such a drastic restriction when the distribution is part of their religious faith. *Murdock* v. *Pennsylvania, supra,* 111. If the right of a child to practice its religion in that manner is to be forbidden by constitutional means, there must be convincing proof that such a practice constitutes a grave and immediate danger to the state or to the health, morals or welfare of the child. *West Virginia State Board of Education* v. *Barnette,* 319 U.S.

624, 639. The vital freedom of religion, which is "of the very essence of a scheme of ordered liberty," *Palko* v. *Connecticut,* 302 U.S. 319, 325, cannot be erased by slender references to the state's power to restrict the more secular activities of children.

The state, in my opinion, has completely failed to sustain its burden of proving the existence of any grave or immediate danger to any interest which it may lawfully protect. There is no proof that Betty Simmons' mode of worship constituted a serious menace to the public. It was carried on in an orderly, lawful manner at a public street corner. And "one who is rightfully on a street which the state has left open to the public carries with him there as elsewhere the constitutional right to express his views in an orderly fashion. This right extends to the communication of ideas by handbills and literature as well as by the spoken word." *Jamison* v. *Texas,* 318 U.S. 13, 416. The sidewalk, no less than the cathedral or the evangelist's tent, is a proper place, under the Constitution, for the orderly worship of God. Such use of the streets is as necessary to the Jehovah's Witnesses, the Salvation Army and others who practice religion without benefit of conventional shelters as is the use of the streets for purposes of passage. . . .

Mr. Justice Jackson:

The novel feature of this decision is this: the Court holds that a state may apply child labor laws to restrict or prohibit an activity of which, as recently as last term, it held: "This form of religious activity occupies the same high estate under the First Amendment as do worship in the churches and preaching from the pulpits. It has the same claim to protection as the more orthodox and conventional exercises of religion." ". . . the mere fact that the religious literature is 'sold' by itinerant preachers rather than 'donated' does not transform evangelism into a commercial enterprise. If it did, then the passing of the collection plate in church would make the church service a commercial project. The constitutional rights of those spreading their religious beliefs through the spoken and printed word are not to be gauged by standards governing retailers or wholesalers of books." *Murdock* v. *Pennsylvania*, 319 U.S. 105, 109, 111.

It is difficult for me to believe that going upon the streets to accost the public is the same thing for application of public law as withdrawing to a private structure for religious worship. But if worship in the churches and the activity of Jehovah's Witnesses on the streets "occupy the same high estate" and have the "same claim to protection" it would seem that child labor laws may be applied to both if to either. If the *Murdock* doctrine stands along with today's decision, a foundation is laid for any state intervention in the indoctrination and participation of children in religion, provided it is done in the name of their health or welfare.

This case brings to the surface the real basis of disagreement among members of this Court in previous Jehovah's Witness cases. *Murdock* v. *Pennsylvania*, 319 U.S. 105; *Martin* v. *Struthers*, 319 U.S. 141; *Jones* v. *Opelika*, 316 U.S. 584, 319 U.S. 103; *Douglas* v. *Jeannette*, 319 U.S. 157. Our basic difference seems to be as to the method of establishing limitations which of necessity bound religious freedom.

My own view may be shortly put: I think the limits begin to operate whenever activities begin to affect or collide with liberties of others or of the public. Religious activities which concern only members of the faith are and ought to be free— as nearly absolutely free as anything can be. But beyond these, many religious denominations or sects engage in collateral and secular activities intended to obtain means from unbelievers to sustain the worshippers and their leaders. They raise money, not merely by passing the plate to those who voluntarily attend services or by contributions by their own people, but by solicitations and drives addressed to the public by holding public dinners and entertainments, by various kinds of sales and Bingo games and lotteries. All such money-raising activities on a public scale are, I think, Caesar's affairs and may be regulated by the state so long as it does not discriminate against one because he is doing them for a religious purpose, and the regulation is not arbitrary and capricious, in violation of other provisions of the Constitution.

The Court in the *Murdock* case rejected this principle of separating immune religious activities from secular ones in declaring the disabilities which the Constitution imposed on local authorities. Instead, the Court now draws a line based on age that cuts across both true exercise of religion and auxiliary secular activities. I think this is not a correct principle for defining the activities immune from regulation on grounds of religion, and *Murdock* overrules the grounds on which I think affirmance should rest. I have no alternative but to dissent from the grounds of affirmance of a judgment which I think was rightly decided, and upon right grounds, by the Supreme Judicial Court of Massachusetts. 313 Mass. 223.

MR. JUSTICE ROBERTS and MR. JUSTICE FRANFURTER join in this opinion.

[*Quaere:* Where in the Fourteenth Amendment or in the Bill of Rights is the provision that allows the state greater control over children than over adults? If there is such a provision, why was it not decisive, *or even mentioned,* in the Barnette *Flag Salute* case?]

Adamson v. *California*

332 U.S. 46 (1947)

This case marks the "culmination" of Mr. Justice Black's apparent effort to find a precise, noneconomic, and libertarian "interpretation" of the vague generalities of the Fourteenth Amendment. The problem was this: In a state criminal case, the prosecutor had commented to the jury on the defendant's failure to testify in his own defense. Such comment is forbidden in federal prosecutions as a violation of the defendant's privilege against self-incrimination under the Fifth Amendment. (The theory presumably is that a prosecutor's observations "convert" the defendant's silence into a "confession.") The Court upheld the conviction, finding no violation of fundamental justice as contemplated by the *Palko* principle. Mr. Justice Frankfurter's concurring opinion is a defense of the *Palko* approach in the face of Mr. Justice Black's activist dissent.

Mr. Justice Reed delivered the opinion of the Court.

The appellant, Adamson, a citizen of the United States, was convicted, without recommendation for mercy, by a jury in a Superior Court of the State of California of murder in the first degree. After considering the same objections to the conviction that are pressed here, the sentence of death was affirmed by the Supreme Court of the state. 27 Cal.2d 478, 165 P.2d 3. Review of that judgment by this Court was sought and allowed under Judicial Code § 237, 28 U.S.C. § 344. The provisions of California law which were challenged in the state proceedings as invalid under the Fourteenth Amendment to the Federal Constitution are those of the state constitution and penal code in the margin. They permit the failure of a defendant to explain or to deny evidence against him to be commented upon by court and by counsel and to be considered by court and jury. The defendant did not testify. As the trial court gave its instructions and the District Attorney argued the case in accordance with the constitutional and statutory provisions just referred to, we have for decision the question of their constitutionality in these circumstances under the limitations of § 1 of the Fourteenth Amendment.

The appellant was charged in the information with former convictions for burglary, larceny and robbery and pursuant to § 1025, California Penal Code, answered that he had suffered the previous convictions. This answer barred allusion to these charges of convictions on the trial. Under California's interpretation of § 1025 of the Penal Code and § 2051 of the Code of Civil Procedure, however, if the defendant, after answering affirmatively charges alleging prior convictions, takes the witness stand to deny or explain away other evidence that has been introduced "the commission of these crimes could have been revealed to the jury on cross-examination to impeach his testimony." People v. Adamson, 27 Cal.2d 478, 494, 165 P.2d 3, 11. . . . This forces an accused who is a repeated offender to choose between the risk of having his prior offenses disclosed to the jury or of having it draw harmful inferences from uncontradicted evidence that can only be denied or explained by the defendant.

In the first place, appellant urges that the provision of the Fifth Amendment that no person "shall be compelled in any criminal case to be a witness against himself" is a fundamental national privilege or immunity protected against state abridgment by the Fourteenth Amendment or a privilege or immunity secured, through the Fourteenth Amendment, against deprivation by state action because it is a personal right, enumerated in the federal Bill of Rights.

Secondly, appellant relies upon the due process of law clause of the Fourteenth Amendment to invalidate the provisions of the California law . . . and as applied (a) because comment on failure to testify is permitted, (b) because appellant was forced to forego testimony in person because of danger of disclosure of his past convictions through cross-examination and (c) because the presumption of innocence was infringed by the shifting of the burden of proof to appellant in permitting comment on his failure to testify.

We shall assume, but without any intention thereby of ruling upon the issue, that state permission by law to the court, counsel and jury to comment upon and consider the failure of defendant "to explain or to deny by his testimony any evidence or facts in the case against him" would infringe defendant's privilege against self-incrimination under the Fifth Amendment if this were a trial in a court of the United States under a similar law. Such an assumption does not determine appellant's rights under the Fourteenth Amendment. It is settled law that the clause of the Fifth Amendment protecting a person against being compelled to be a witness against himself, is not made effective by the Fourteenth Amendment as a protection against state action on the ground that freedom from testimonial compulsion is a right of national citizenship, or because it is a personal privilege or immunity secured by the Federal Constitution as one of the rights of man that are listed in the Bill of Rights.

The reasoning that leads to those conclusions starts with the unquestioned premise that the Bill of Rights, when adopted, was for the protection of the individual against the federal government and its provisions were inapplicable to similar actions done by the states. Barron v. Baltimore, 7 Pet. 243. . . . With the adoption of the Fourteenth Amendment, it was suggested that the dual citizenship recognized by its first sentence, secured for citizens federal protection for their elemental privileges and immunities of state citizenship. The Slaughter-House Cases decided, contrary to the suggestion, that these rights, as privileges and immunities of state citizenship, remained under the sole protection of the state governments. This Court, without the expression of a contrary view upon that phase of the issues before the Court, has approved this determination. . . . The power to free defendants in state trials from self-incrimination was specifically determined to be beyond the scope of the privileges and immunities clause of the Fourteenth Amendment in Twining v. New Jersey, 211 U.S. 78, 91–98. "The privilege against self-incrimination may be withdrawn and the accused put upon the stand as a witness for the state." The Twining case likewise disposed of the contention that freedom from testimonial compulsion, being specifically granted by the Bill of Rights, is a federal privilege or immunity that is protected by the Fourteenth Amendment against state invasion. This Court held that the inclusion in the Bill of Rights of this protection against the power of the national government did not make the privilege a federal privilege or immunity secured to citizens by the Constitution against state action. . . . After declaring that state and national citizenship co-exist in the same person, the Fourteenth Amendment forbids a state from abridging the privileges and immunities of citizens of the United States. As a matter of words, this leaves a state free to abridge, within the limits of the due process clause, the privileges and immunities flowing from state citizenship. This reading of the Federal Constitution has heretofore found favor with the majority of this Court as a natural and logical interpretation. It accords with the constitutional doctrine of federalism by leaving to the states the responsibility of dealing with the privileges and immunities of their citizens except those inherent in national citizenship. It is the construction placed upon the amendment by justices whose own experience had given them contemporaneous knowledge of the purposes that led to the adoption of the Fourteenth Amendment. This construction has become embedded in our federal system as a functioning element in preserving the balance between national and state power. We reaffirm the conclusion of the Twining and Palko cases that protection against self-incrimination is not a privilege or immunity of national citizenship.

Appellant secondly contends that if the privilege against self-incrimination is not a right protected by the privileges and immunities clause of the Fourteenth Amendment against state action, this privilege, to its full scope under the Fifth Amendment, inheres in the right to a fair trial. A right to a fair trial is a right admittedly protected by the due process clause of the Fourteenth Amendment. Therefore, appellant argues, the due process clause of the Fourteenth Amendment protects his privilege against self-incrimination. The due process clause of the Fourteenth Amendment, however, does not draw all the rights of the federal Bill of Rights under its protection. That contention was made and rejected in Palko v. Connecticut, 302 U.S. 319, 323. It was rejected with citation of the cases excluding several of the rights, protected by the Bill of Rights, against infringement by the National Government. Nothing has been called to our attention that either the framers of the Fourteenth Amendment or the states that adopted intended its due process clause to draw within its scope the earlier amendments to the Constitution. Palko held that such provisions of the Bill of Rights as were "implicit in the concept of ordered liberty," 302 U.S. at page 325, became secure from state interference by the clause. But it held nothing more.

Specifically, the due process clause does not protect, by virtue of its mere existence, the accused's freedom from giving testimony by compulsion in state trials that is secured to him against federal interference by the Fifth Amendment. . . . For a state to require testimony from an accused is not necessarily a breach of a state's obligation to give a fair trial. Therefore, we must examine the effect of the California law applied in this trial to see whether the comment on failure to testify violates the protection against state action that the due process clause does grant to an accused. The due process clause forbids compulsion to testify by fear of hurt, torture or exhaustion. It forbids any other type of coercion that falls within the scope of due process. California follows Anglo-American legal tradition in excusing defendants in criminal prosecutions from compulsory testimony. Cf. Wigmore (3d Ed.) § 2252. That is a matter of legal policy and not because of the requirements of due process under the Fourteenth Amendment. So our inquiry is directed, not at the broad question of the constitutionality of compulsory testimony from the accused under the due process clause, but to the constitutionality of the provision

of the California law that permits comment upon his failure
to testify. It is, of course, logically possible that while an
accused might be required, under appropriate penalties, to
submit himself as a witness without a violation of due process,
comment by judge or jury on inferences to be drawn from his
failure to testify, in jurisdictions where an accused's privilege
against self-incrimination is protected, might deny due process.
For example, a statute might declare that a permitted refusal
to testify would compel an acceptance of the truth of the
prosecution's evidence.

Generally, comment on the failure of an accused to testify
is forbidden in American jurisdictions. . . . California, however, is one of a few states that permit limited comment upon
a defendant's failure to testify. That permission is narrow.
The California law . . . authorizes comment by court and
counsel upon the "failure of the defendant to explain or to
deny by his testimony any evidence or facts in the case against
him." This does not involve any presumption, rebuttable or
irrebuttable, either of guilt or of the truth of any fact, that is
offered in evidence. Compare Tot v. United States, 319 U.S.
463, 470. It allows inferences to be drawn from proven facts.
Because of this clause, the court can direct the jury's attention
to whatever evidence there may be that a defendant could
deny and the prosecution can argue as to inferences that may
be drawn from the accused's failure to testify. . . . There is
here no lack of power in the trial court to adjudge and no
denial of a hearing. California has prescribed a method for
advising the jury in the search for truth. However sound may
be the legislative conclusion that an accused should not be
compelled in any criminal case to be a witness against himself,
we see no reason why comment should not be made upon his
silence. It seems quite natural that when a defendant has
opportunity to deny or explain facts and determines not to do
so, the prosecution should bring out the strength of the evidence by commenting upon defendant's failure to explain or

deny it. The prosecution evidence may be of facts that may be beyond the knowledge of the accused. If so, his failure to testify would have little if any weight. But the facts may be such as are necessarily in the knowledge of the accused. In that case a failure to explain would point to an inability to explain.

Appellant sets out the circumstances of this case, however, to show coercion and unfairness in permitting comment. The guilty person was not seen at the place and time of the crime. There was evidence, however, that entrance to the place or room where the crime was committed might have been obtained through a small door. It was freshly broken. Evidence showed that six fingerprints on the door were petitioner's. Certain diamond rings were missing from the deceased's possession. There was evidence that appellant, some time after the crime, asked an unidentified person whether the latter would be interested in purchasing a diamond ring. As has been stated, the information charged other crimes to appellant and he admitted them. His argument here is that he could not take the stand to deny the evidence against him because he would be subjected to a cross-examination as to former crimes to impeach his veracity and the evidence so produced might well bring about his conviction. Such cross-examination is allowable in California. . . . Therefore, appellant contends the California statute permitting comment denies him due process.

It is true that if comment were forbidden, an accused in this situation could remain silent and avoid evidence of former crimes and comment upon his failure to testify. We are of the view, however, that a state may control such a situation in accordance with its own ideas of the most efficient administration of criminal justice. The purpose of due process is not to protect an accused against a proper conviction but against an unfair conviction. When evidence is before a jury that threatens conviction, it does not seem unfair to require him to choose between leaving the adverse evidence unexplained and subjecting himself to impeachment through disclosure of former crimes. Indeed, this is a dilemma with which any defendant may be faced. If facts, adverse to the defendant, are proven by the prosecution, there may be no way to explain them favorably to the accused except by a witness who may be vulnerable to impeachment on cross-examination. The defendant must then decide whether or not to use such a witness. The fact that the witness may also be the defendant makes the choice more difficult but a denial of due process does not emerge from the circumstances.

There is no basis in the California law for appellant's objection on due process or other grounds that the statutory authorization to comment on the failure to explain or deny adverse testimony shifts the burden of proof or the duty to go forward with the evidence. Failure of the accused to testify is not an admission of the truth of the adverse evidence. Instructions told the jury that the burden of proof remained upon the state and the presumption of innocence with the accused. Comment on failure to deny proven facts does not in California tend to supply any missing element of proof of guilt. . . . It only directs attention to the strength of the evidence for the prosecution or to the weakness of that for the defense. The Supreme Court of California called attention to the fact that the prosecutor's argument approached the borderline in a statement that might have been construed as asserting "that the jury should infer guilt solely from defendant's silence." That court felt that it was improbable the jury was misled into such an understanding of their power. We shall not interfere with such a conclusion. People v. Adamson, supra, 27 Cal.2d 494, 495, 165 P.2d 3, 12. . . .

We find no other error that gives ground for our intervention in California's administration of criminal justice.

Affirmed.

MR. JUSTICE FRANKFURTER [concurring]. . . .

Between the incorporation of the Fourteenth Amendment into the Constitution and the beginning of the present membership of the Court—a period of 70 years—the scope of that Amendment was passed upon by 43 judges. Of all these judges, only one, who may respectfully be called an eccentric exception, ever indicated the belief that the Fourteenth Amendment was a shorthand summary of the first eight Amendments theretofore limiting only the Federal Government, and that due process incorporated those eight Amendments as restrictions upon the powers of the States. Among these judges were not only those who would have to be included among the greatest in the history of the Court, but—it is especially relevant to note—they included those whose services in the cause of human rights and the spirit of freedom are the most conspicuous in our history. It is not invidious to single out Miller, Davis, Bradley, Waite, Matthews, Gray, Fuller, Holmes, Brandeis, Stone and Cardozo (to speak only of the dead) as judges who were alert in safeguarding and promoting the interests of liberty and human dignity through law. But they were also judges mindful of the relation of our federal system to a progressively democratic society and therefore duly regardful of the scope of authority that was left to the States even after the Civil War. And so they did not find that the Fourteenth Amendment, concerned as it was with matters fundamental to the pursuit of justice, fastened upon the States procedural arrangements which, in the language of Mr. Justice Cardozo, only those who are "narrow or provincial" would deem essential to "a fair and enlightened system of justice." Palko v. Connecticut, 302 U.S. 319, 325. To suggest that it is inconsistent with a truly free society to begin prosecutions without an indictment, to try petty civil cases without the paraphernalia of a common law jury, to take into consideration that one who has full opportunity to make a defense remains silent is, in de Tocqueville's phrase, to confound the familiar with the necessary.

The short answer to the suggestion that the provision of the Fourteenth Amendment, which ordains "nor shall any State deprive any person of life, liberty, or property, without due process of law," was a way of saying that every State must thereafter initiate prosecutions through indictment by a grand jury, must have a trial by a jury of 12 in criminal cases, and must have trial by such a jury in common law suits where the amount in controversy exceeds $20, is that it is a strange way of saying it. It would be extraordinarily strange for a Constitution to convey such specific commands in such a roundabout and inexplicit way. After all, an amendment to the Constitution should be read in a " 'sense most obvious to the common understanding at the time of its adoption.' . . . For it was for public adoption that it was proposed." . . . Those reading the English language with the meaning which it ordinarily conveys, those conversant with the political and legal history of the concept of due process, those sensitive to the relations of the States to the central government as well as the relation of some of the provisions of the Bill of Rights to the process of justice, would hardly recognize the Fourteenth Amendment as a cover for the various explicit provisions of the first eight Amendments. Some of these are enduring reflections of experience with human nature, while some express the restricted views of Eighteenth-Century England regarding the best methods for the ascertainment of facts. The notion that the Fourteenth Amendment was a covert way of imposing upon the States all the rules which it seemed important to Eighteenth Century statesmen to write into the Federal Amendments, was rejected by judges who were themselves witnesses of the process by which the Fourteenth Amendment became part of the Constitution. Arguments that may now be adduced to prove that the first eight Amendments were concealed within the historic phrasing of the Fourteenth Amendment were not unknown at the time of its adoption. A surer estimate of their bearing was possible for judges at the time than distorting distance is likely to vouchsafe. Any evidence of design or purpose not contemporaneously known could hardly have influenced those who ratified the Amendment. Remarks of a particular proponent of the Amendment, no matter how influential, are not to be deemed part of the Amendment. What was submitted for ratification was his proposal, not his speech. Thus, at the time of the ratification of the Fourteenth Amendment the constitutions of nearly half of the ratifying States did not have the rigorous requirements of the Fifth Amendment for instituting criminal proceedings through a grand jury. It could hardly have occurred to these States that by ratifying the Amendment they uprooted their established methods for prosecuting crime and fastened upon themselves a new prosecutorial system.

Indeed, the suggestion that the Fourteenth Amendment incorporates the first eight Amendments as such is not unambiguously urged. Even the boldest innovator would shrink from suggesting to more than half the States that they may no longer initiate prosecutions without indictment by grand jury, or that thereafter all the States of the Union must furnish a jury of 12 for every case involving a claim above $20. There is suggested merely a selective incorporation of the first eight Amendments into the Fourteenth Amendment. Some are in and some are out, but we are left in the dark as to which are in and which are out. Nor are we given the calculus for determining which go in and which stay out. If the basis of selection is merely that those provisions of the first eight Amendments are incorporated which commend themselves to individual justices as indispensable to the dignity and happiness of a free man, we are thrown back to a merely subjective test. The protection against unreasonable search and seizure might have primacy for one judge, while trial by a jury of 12 for every claim above $20 might appear to another as an ultimate need in a free society. In the history of thought "natural law" has a much longer and much better founded meaning and justification than such subjective selection of the first eight Amendments for incorporation into the Fourteenth. If all that is meant is that due process contains within itself certain minimal standards which are "of the very essence of a scheme of ordered liberty," Palko v. Connecticut, 302 U.S. 319, 325, putting upon this Court the duty of applying these standards from time to time, then we have merely arrived at the insight which our predecessors long ago expressed. We are called upon to apply to the difficult issues of our own day the wisdom afforded by the great opinions in this field. . . . This guidance bids us to be duly mindful of the heritage of the past, with its great lessons of how liberties are won and how they are lost. As judges charged with the delicate task of subjecting the government of a continent to the Rule of Law we must be particularly mindful that it is "a *constitution* we are expounding," so that it should not be imprisoned in what are merely legal forms even though they have the sanction of the Eighteenth Century. . . .

And so, when, as in a case like the present, a conviction in a State court is here for review under a claim that a right protected by the Due Process Clause of the Fourteenth Amendment has been denied, the issue is not whether an infraction of one of the specific provisions of the first eight Amendments is disclosed by the record. The relevant question is whether the criminal proceedings which resulted in conviction deprived the accused of the due process of law to which the United States Constitution entitled him. Judicial review of that guaranty of the Fourteenth Amendment inescapably imposes upon this Court an exercise of judgment upon the whole course of the proceedings in order to ascertain whether they offend those canons of decency and fairness which express the notions of justice of English-speaking peoples even toward those charged with the most heinous offenses. These standards of justice are not authoritatively formulated anywhere as though they were prescriptions in a pharmacopoeia. But neither does the application of the Due Process Clause imply that judges are wholly at large. The judicial judgment in applying the Due Process Clause must move within the limits of accepted notions of justice and is not to be based upon the idiosyncrasies of a merely personal judgment. The fact that judges among themselves may differ whether in a particular case a trial offends accepted notions of justice is not disproof that general rather than idiosyncratic standards are applied. An important safeguard against such merely individual judgment is an alert deference to the judgment of the State court under review.

MR. JUSTICE BLACK, dissenting. . . .

This decision reasserts a constitutional theory spelled out in Twining v. New Jersey, 211 U.S. 78, that this Court is endowed by the Constitution with boundless power under "natural law" periodically to expand and contract constitutional standards to conform to the Court's conception of what at a particular time constitutes "civilized decency" and "fundamental principles of liberty and justice." Invoking this Twining rule, the Court concludes that although comment upon testimony in a federal court would violate the Fifth Amendment, identical comment in a state court does not violate today's fashion in civilized decency and fundamentals and is therefore not prohibited by the Federal Constitution as amended.

The Twining case was the first, as it is the only decision of this Court, which has squarely held that states were free, notwithstanding the Fifth and Fourteenth Amendments, to extort evidence from one accused of crime. I agree that if Twining be reaffirmed, the result reached might appropriately follow. But I would not reaffirm the Twining decision. I think that decision and the "natural law" theory of the Constitution upon which it relies, degrade the constitutional safeguards of the Bill of Rights and simultaneously appropriate for this Court a broad power which we are not authorized by the Constitution to exercise. Furthermore, the Twining decision rested on

previous cases and broad hypotheses which have been under-
cut by intervening decisions of this Court. See Corwin, The
Supreme Court's Construction of the Self-Incrimination
Clause, 29 Mich.L.Rev. 1, 191, 202. My reasons for believing
that the Twining decision should not be revitalized can best
be understood by reference to the constitutional, judicial, and
general history that preceded and followed the case. That
reference must be abbreviated far more than is justified but
for the necessary limitations of opinion-writing. . . .

My study of the historical events that culminated in the
Fourteenth Amendment, and the expressions of those who
sponsored and favored, as well as those who opposed its submission and passage, persuades me that one of the chief objects that the provisions of the Amendment's first section,
separately, and as a whole, were intended to accomplish was
to make the Bill of Rights applicable to the states. With full
knowledge of the import of the Barron decision, the framers
and backers of the Fourteenth Amendment proclaimed its
purpose to be to overturn the constitutional rule that case had
announced. This historical purpose has never received full
consideration or exposition in any opinion of this Court interpreting the Amendment. . . .

For this reason, I am attaching to this dissent, an appendix
which contains a resumé, by no means complete, of the
Amendment's history. In my judgment that history conclu-
sively demonstrates that the language of the first section of the
Fourteenth Amendment, taken as a whole, was thought by
those responsible for its submission to the people, and by those
who opposed its submission, sufficiently explicit to guarantee
that thereafter no state could deprive its citizens of the privileges and protections of the Bill of Rights. Whether this Court
ever will, or whether it now should, in the light of past decisions, give full effect to what the Amendment was intended to
accomplish is not necessarily essential to a decision here. However that may be, our prior decisions, including Twining, do

not prevent our carrying out that purpose, at least to the extent of making applicable to the states, not a mere part, as the Court has, but the full protection of the Fifth Amendment's provision against compelling evidence from an accused to convict him of crime. And I further contend that the "natural law" formula which the Court uses to reach its conclusion in this case should be abandoned as an incongruous excrescence on our Constitution. I believe that formula to be itself a violation of our Constitution, in that it subtly conveys to courts, at the expense of legislatures, ultimate power over public policies in fields where no specific provision of the Constitution limits legislative power. . . .

I cannot consider the Bill of Rights to be an outworn 18th Century "strait jacket" as the Twining opinion did. Its provisions may be thought outdated abstractions by some. And it is true that they were designed to meet ancient evils. But they are the same kind of human evils that have emerged from century to century wherever excessive power is sought by the few at the expense of the many. In my judgment the people of no nation can lose their liberty so long as a Bill of Rights like ours survives and its basic purposes are conscientiously interpreted, enforced and respected so as to afford continuous protection against old, as well as new, devices and practices which might thwart those purposes. I fear to see the consequences of the Court's practice of substituting its own concepts of decency and fundamental justice for the language of the Bill of Rights as its point of departure in interpreting and enforcing that Bill of Rights. If the choice must be between the selective process of the Palko decision applying some of the Bill of Rights to the States, or the Twining rule applying none of them, I would choose the Palko selective process. But rather than accept either of these choices, I would follow what I believe was the original purpose of the Fourteenth Amendment—to extend to all the people of the nation the complete protection of the Bill of Rights. To hold that this Court can determine what, if any, provisions of the Bill of Rights will be enforced, and if so to what degree, is to frustrate the great design of a written Constitution.

Conceding the possibility that this Court is now wise enough to improve on the Bill of Rights by substituting natural law concepts for the Bill of Rights, I think the possibility is entirely too speculative to agree to take that course. I would therefore hold in this case that the full protection of the Fifth Amendment's proscription against compelled testimony must be afforded by California. This I would do because of reliance upon the original purpose of the Fourteenth Amendment.

It is an illusory apprehension that literal application of some or all of the provisions of the Bill of Rights to the States would unwisely increase the sum total of the powers of this Court to invalidate state legislation. The Federal Government has not been harmfully burdened by the requirement that enforcement of federal laws affecting civil liberty conform literally to the Bill of Rights. Who would advocate its repeal? It must be conceded, of course, that the natural-law-due-process formula, which the Court today reaffirms, has been interpreted to limit substantially this Court's power to prevent state violations of the individual civil liberties guaranteed by the Bill of Rights. But this formula also has been used in the past and can be used in the future, to license this Court, in considering regulatory legislation, to roam at large in the broad expanses of policy and morals and to trespass, all too freely, on the legislative domain of the States as well as the Federal Government.

Since Marbury v. Madison, 1 Cranch 137, was decided, the practice has been firmly established for better or worse, that courts can strike down legislative enactments which violate the Constitution. This process, of course, involves interpretation, and since words can have many meanings, interpretation obviously may result in contraction or extension of the original purpose of a constitutional provision thereby affecting policy. But to pass upon the constitutionality of statutes by looking to the particular standards enumerated in the Bill of Rights and other parts of the Constitution is one thing; to invalidate statutes because of application of "natural law" deemed to be above and undefined by the Constitution is another. "In the one instance, courts proceeding within clearly marked constitutional boundaries seek to execute policies written into the Constitution; in the other they roam at will in the limitless area of their own beliefs as to reasonableness and actually select policies, a responsibility which the Constitution entrusts to the legislative representatives of the people." Federal Power Commission v. Natural Gas Pipeline Co., 315 U.S. 575, 599, 601, n. 4.

MR. JUSTICE DOUGLAS joins in this opinion.

MR. JUSTICE MURPHY, with whom MR. JUSTICE RUTLEDGE concurs, dissenting.

While in substantial agreement with the views of MR. JUSTICE BLACK, I have one reservation and one addition to make.

I agree that the specific guarantees of the Bill of Rights should be carried over intact into the first section of the Fourteenth Amendment. But I am not prepared to say that the latter is entirely and necessarily limited by the Bill of Rights. Occasions may arise where a proceeding falls so far short of conforming to fundamental standards of procedure as to warrant constitutional condemnation in terms of a lack of due process despite the absence of a specific provision in the Bill of Rights.

That point, however, need not be pursued here inasmuch as the Fifth Amendment is explicit in its provision that no person shall be compelled in any criminal case to be a witness against himself. That provision, as MR. JUSTICE BLACK demonstrates, is a constituent part of the Fourteenth Amendment. . . .

[Note: In *Winters* v. *New York*, 333 U.S. 507 (1948), about a year after his *Adamson* dissent, Mr. Justice Black voted to strike down a state criminal law for excessive vagueness. Where among the "specific" provisions of the Bill of Rights, as allegedly incorporated in the Fourteenth Amendment, is statutory vagueness mentioned? Similar difficulties are presented, for example, in *Griffin* v. *Illinois*, 351 U.S. 12 (1956), and *Poe* v. *Ullman*, 367 U.S. 496 (1961).

How can unequal legislative districts raise an Equal Protection problem, if that and related clauses in the Fourteenth Amendment incorporate, and mean, no more and no less than the Bill of Rights? (See *Reynolds* v. *Sims*, below.)

Mr. Justice Black apparently abandoned *Palko* because in his view its "imprecision" leaves (and burdens) judges with too much discretion. Does his *Adamson* effort resolve this difficulty? Is it possible to make law sufficiently precise to cover explicitly all future cases? Were not Plato and Aristotle amazingly "modern" in their discussions of rule and discretion?

Mr. Justice Douglas was the only one who joined in Black's *Adamson* dissent. In *Poe* v. *Ullman*, 367 U.S. 497 (1961), he explicitly abandoned that position in favor of the Murphy-Rutledge view in *Adamson*. No doubt he recognized that his earlier view was not compatible with his stand in *Poe* and his anticipated position in *Reynolds* v. *Sims*.

Are Mr. Justice Stone's dissenting comments on the old activist use of labels in the *Di Santo* case relevant with respect to modern activism as seen in the post-1936 Due Process cases?]

Frank v. *Maryland*

358 U.S. 360 (1959)

Acting without a search warrant, a health inspector found evidence of rodent infection in Frank's yard, and requested permission to inspect his house. Frank refused. He was prosecuted and found guilty of violating a state law requiring the opening of one's house to daytime inspection on demand of an inspector having cause to suspect a serious health hazard. The Supreme Court affirmed the conviction. This case is particularly interesting in its revelation of how differently activist and anti-activist judges may read history.

MR. JUSTICE FRANKFURTER delivered the opinion of the Court. . . .

The history of the constitutional protection against official invasion of the citizen's home makes explicit the human concerns which it was meant to respect. In years prior to the Revolution leading voices in England and the Colonies protested against the ransacking by Crown officers of the homes of citizens in search of evidence of crime or of illegally imported goods. The vivid memory by the newly independent Americans of these abuses produced the Fourth Amendment as a safeguard against such arbitrary official action by officers of the new Union, as like provisions had already found their way into State Constitutions.

In 1765, in England, what is properly called the great case of *Entick v. Carrington,* 19 Howell's State Trials, col. 1029, announced the principle of English law which became part of the Bill of Rights and whose basic protection has become imbedded in the concept of due process of law. It was there decided that English law did not allow officers of the Crown to break into a citizen's home, under cover of a general executive warrant, to search for evidence of the utterance of libel. Among the reasons given for that decision were these:

> "It is very certain, that the law obligeth no man to accuse himself; because the necessary means of compelling self-accusation, falling upon the innocent as well as the guilty, would be both cruel and unjust; and it should seem, that search for evidence is disallowed upon the same principle. There too the innocent would be confounded with the guilty." *Id.* at col. 1073.

These were not novel pronouncements to the colonists. A few years earlier, in Boston, revenue officers had been authorized

to use Writs of Assistance, empowering them to search suspected places, including private houses, for smuggled goods.
In 1761 the validity of the use of the Writs was contested in the
historic proceedings in Boston. James Otis attacked the Writ of
Assistance because its use placed "the liberty of every man in
the hands of every petty officer." His powerful argument so
impressed itself first on his audience and later on the people of
all the Colonies that President Adams was in retrospect moved
to say that "American Independence was then and there born."
Many years later this Court, in *Boyd* v. *United States,* 116 U. S.
616, carefully reviewed this history and pointed out, as did
Lord Camden in *Entick* v. *Carrington,* that

> ". . . the 'unreasonable searches and seizures' condemned in
> the Fourth Amendment are almost always made for the purpose
> of compelling a man to give evidence against himself, which in
> criminal cases is condemned in the Fifth Amendment; and com-
> pelling a man 'in a criminal case to be a witness against himself,'
> which is condemned in the Fifth Amendment, throws light on
> the question as to what is an 'unreasonable search and seizure'
> within the meaning of the Fourth Amendment." 116 U. S., at
> 633.

Against this background two protections emerge from the
broad constitutional proscription of official invasion. The first
of these is the right to be secure from intrusion into personal
privacy, the right to shut the door on officials of the state unless their entry is under proper authority of law. The second,
and intimately related protection, is self-protection: the right to
resist unauthorized entry which has as its design the securing
of information to fortify the coercive power of the state against
the individual, information which may be used to effect a
further deprivation of life or liberty or property. Thus, evidence of criminal action may not, save in very limited and
closely confined situations, be seized without a judicially issued
search warrant. It is this aspect of the constitutional protection
to which the quoted passages from *Entick* v. *Carrington* and

Boyd v. *United States* refer. Certainly it is not necessary to accept any particular theory of the interrelationship of the Fourth and Fifth Amendments to realize what history makes plain, that it was on the issue of the right to be secure from searches for evidence to be used in criminal prosecutions or for forfeitures that the great battle for fundamental liberty was fought. While these concerns for individual rights were the historic impulses behind the Fourth Amendment and its analogues in state constitutions, the application of the Fourth Amendment and the extent to which the essential right of privacy is protected by the Due Process Clause of the Fourteenth Amendment are of course not restricted within these historic bounds.

But giving the fullest scope to this constitutional right to privacy, its protection cannot be here invoked. The attempted inspection of appellant's home is merely to determine whether conditions exist which the Baltimore Health Code proscribes. If they do appellant is notified to remedy the infringing conditions. No evidence for criminal prosecution is sought to be seized. Appellant is simply directed to do what he could have been ordered to do without any inspection, and what he cannot properly resist, namely, act in a manner consistent with the maintenance of minimum community standards of health and well-being, including his own. Appellant's resistance can only be based, not on admissible self-protection, but on a rarely voiced denial of any official justification for seeking to enter his home. The constitutional "liberty" that is asserted is the absolute right to refuse consent for an inspection designed and pursued solely for the protection of the community's health, even when the inspection is conducted with due regard for every convenience of time and place.

The power of inspection granted by the Baltimore City Code is strictly limited, more exacting than the analogous provisions of many other municipal codes. Valid grounds for suspicion of the existence of a nuisance must exist. Certainly the presence of a pile of filth in the back yard combined with the run-down condition of the house gave adequate grounds for such suspicion. The inspection must be made in the day time. Here was no midnight knock on the door, but an orderly visit in the middle of the afternoon with no suggestion that the hour was inconvenient. Moreover, the inspector has no power to force entry and did not attempt it. A fine is imposed for resistance, but officials are not authorized to break past the unwilling occupant.

Thus, not only does the inspection touch at most upon the periphery of the important interests safeguarded by the Fourteenth Amendment's protection against official intrusion, but it is hedged about with safeguards designed to make the least possible demand on the individual occupant, and to cause only the slightest restriction on his claims of privacy. Such a demand must be assessed in the light of the needs which have produced it.

Inspection without a warrant, as an adjunct to a regulatory scheme for the general welfare of the community and not as a means of enforcing the criminal law, has antecedents deep in our history. For more than 200 years Maryland has empowered its officers to enter upon ships, carriages, shops, and homes in the service of the common welfare. . . .

Affirmed.

Mr. Justice Douglas, with whom the Chief Justice [Warren], Mr. Justice Black and Mr. Justice Brennan concur, dissenting. . . .

The Court misreads history when it relates the Fourth Amendment primarily to searches for evidence to be used in criminal prosecutions. That certainly is not the teaching of *Entick* v. *Carrington,* 19 Howell's St. Tr. col. 1029. At that time—1765—it was the search for the nonconformist that led British officials to ransack private homes. The commands of our First Amendment (as well as the prohibitions of the Fourth and the Fifth) reflect the teachings of *Entick* v. *Carrington, supra.* These three amendments are indeed closely related, safeguarding not only privacy and protection against self-incrimination but "conscience and human dignity and freedom of expression as well." See *Ullman* v. *United States,* 350 U.S. 422, 445 *et seq.* (dissent); *Feldman* v. *United States,* 322 U.S. 487, 499 (dissent). It is only in that setting that *Entick* v. *Carrington, supra,* can be understood, as evidenced by Lord Camden's long review of the oppressive practices directed at the press by the Star Chamber, the Long Parliament, and the Licensing Acts. 19 Howell's St. Tr. cols. 1069–1072. It was in the setting of freedom of expression that Lord Camden denounced the general warrants. Taylor, The American Constitution (1911), p. 234, gives the correct interpretation of that historical episode:

> "In the effort to destroy the freedom of the press, by a strained exercise of the prerogative a general warrant was issued in 1763 for the discovery and apprehension of the authors and printers (not named) of the obnoxious No. 45 of the *North Briton,* which commented in severe and offensive terms on the King's Speech at the prorogation of Parliament and upon the unpopular Peace of Paris recently (February 10, 1763) concluded. Forty-nine persons, including Wilkes, were arrested under the general warrant; and when it was ascertained that Wilkes was the author, an information for libel was filed against him on which a verdict was obtained. In suits afterward brought against the Under-Secretary of State who had issued the general warrant, Wilkes, and Dryden Leach, one of the printers arrested on suspicion, obtained verdicts for damages. When the matter came before the King's Bench in 1765, Lord Mansfield and the other three judges pronounced the general warrant illegal, declaring that 'no degree of antiquity could give sanction to a usage bad in itself.'" And see 2 Paterson, Liberty of the Subject (1877), pp. 129–132.

This history, also recounted in *Boyd* v. *United States,* 116 U.S. 616, 625–626, was, in the words of Mr. Justice Bradley, "fresh in the memories of those who achieved our independence and established our form of government." The Fourth Amendment thus has a much wider frame of reference than mere criminal prosecutions. . . .

The well-known protest of the elder Pitt against invasion of the home by the police, had nothing to do with criminal proceedings.

> "The poorest man may in his cottage bid defiance to all the force of the Crown. It may be frail—its roof may shake—the wind may blow through it—the storm may enter, the rain may enter—but the King of England cannot enter—all his force dares not cross the threshold of the ruined tenement!"

While this statement did not specifically refer to the general warrant, it was said in reference to the danger of excise officers entering private homes to levy the "Cyder Tax." 15 Hansard, Parliamentary History of England (1753–1765) p. 1307.

Some of the statutes which James Otis denounced did not involve criminal proceedings. They in the main regulated customs and allowed forfeitures of goods shipped into the Colonies in violation of English shipping regulations. The twenty-dollar forfeiture involved here is no different in substance from the ones that Otis and the colonists found so objectionable. For their objection went not to the amount or size of the forfeiture but to the lawless manner in which it was collected. "Every man prompted by revenge, ill humour, or wantonness to inspect the inside of his neighbour's house, may get a writ of assistance." Tudor, Life of James Otis (1823), p. 68. It was not the search that was vicious. It was the *absence of a warrant issued on a showing of probable cause* that Otis denounced—the precise situation we have here:

> "Now one of the most essential branches of English liberty is the freedom of one's house. A man's house is his castle; and whilst he is quiet, he is as well guarded as a prince in his castle. This writ, if it should be declared legal, would totally annihilate

this privilege. Custom-house officers may enter our houses when they please; we are commanded to permit their entry. Their menial servants may enter, may break locks, bars, and every thing in their way. . . ."

[*Quaere*: Which of the two *Frank* views is the more sound as a matter of history; which, as a matter of public policy? Is the language of the Constitution, plus the gloss of history, sufficiently clear to justify a judicial veto of legislative policy in the context of this case?]

Gideon v. *Wainwright*

372 U.S. (1962)

From time to time, as in *Bridges* and *Baker*, Mr. Justice Black's libertarian activism has prevailed. Yet prior to 1962 it was for the most part a minority position, supported largely by Mr. Justice Douglas—at first with Justices Murphy and Rutledge, and then, after their departure, with Chief Justice Warren and Mr. Justice Brennan. (The alignment of the judges in *Frank* v. *Maryland* was typical during the late 1950's). After Mr. Justice Frankfurter retired, and was replaced by Mr. Justice Goldberg in 1962, it soon became clear that for the first time libertarian activism had obtained majority status. Thereafter, Mr. Justice Harlan became the chief spokesman for the anti-activist position. *Gideon* and the four cases that follow reveal the magnitude of the new activist "revolution."

MR. JUSTICE BLACK delivered the opinion of the Court.
    Petitioner was charged in a Florida state court with having broken and entered a poolroom with intent to commit a misdemeanor. This offense is a felony under Florida law. Appearing in court without funds and without a lawyer, petitioner

asked the court to appoint counsel for him, whereupon the following colloquy took place:

> "The COURT: Mr. Gideon, I am sorry, but I cannot appoint Counsel to represent you in this case. Under the laws of the State of Florida, the only time the Court can appoint Counsel to represent a Defendant is when that person is charged with a capital offense. I am sorry, but I will have to deny your request to appoint Counsel to defend you in this case.
>
> "The DEFENDANT: The United States Supreme Court says I am entitled to be represented by Counsel."

Put to trial before a jury, Gideon conducted his defense about as well as could be expected from a layman. He made an opening statement to the jury, cross-examined the State's witnesses, presented witnesses in his own defense, declined to testify himself, and made a short argument "emphasizing his innocence to the charge contained in the Information filed in this case." The jury returned a verdict of guilty, and petitioner was sentenced to serve five years in the state prison. Later, petitioner filed in the Florida Supreme Court this habeas corpus petition attacking his conviction and sentence on the ground that the trial court's refusal to appoint counsel for him denied him rights "guaranteed by the Constitution and the Bill of Rights by the United States Government." Treating the petition for habeas corpus as properly before it, the State Supreme Court, "upon consideration thereof" but without an opinion, denied all relief. Since 1942, when Betts v. Brady, 316 U.S. 455, was decided by a divided Court, the problem of a defendant's federal constitutional right to counsel in a state court has been a continuing source of controversy and litigation in both state and federal courts. To give this problem another review here, we granted certiorari. 370 U.S. 908. Since Gideon was proceeding *in forma pauperis,* we appointed counsel to represent him and requested both sides to discuss in their briefs and oral arguments the following: "Should this

Court's holding in Betts v. Brady, 316 U.S. 455, be reconsidered?"

I.

The facts upon which Betts claimed that he had been unconstitutionally denied the right to have counsel appointed to assist him are strikingly like the facts upon which Gideon here bases his federal constitutional claim. . . . Like Gideon, Betts sought release by habeas corpus, alleging that he had been denied the right to assistance of counsel in violation of the Fourteenth Amendment. Betts was denied any relief, and on review this Court affirmed. It was held that a refusal to appoint counsel for an indigent defendant charged with a felony did not necessarily violate the Due Process Clause of the Fourteenth Amendment, which for reasons given the Court deemed to be the only applicable federal constitutional provision. The Court said:

> "Asserted denial [of due process] is to be tested by an appraisal of the totality of facts in a given case. That which may, in one setting, constitute a denial of fundamental fairness, shocking to the universal sense of justice, may, in other circumstances, and in the light of other considerations, fall short of such denial." 316 U.S., at 462.

. . . Since the facts and circumstances of the two cases are so nearly indistinguishable, we think the Betts v. Brady holding if left standing would require us to reject Gideon's claim that the Constitution guarantees him the assistance of counsel. Upon full reconsideration we conclude that Betts v. Brady should be overruled.

II.

. . . We accept Betts v. Brady's assumption, based as it was on our prior cases, that a provision of the Bill of Rights which is "fundamental and essential to a fair trial" is made obligatory upon the States by the Fourteenth Amendment. We think the Court in Betts was wrong, however, in concluding that the Sixth Amendment's guarantee of counsel is not one of these fundamental rights. Ten years before Betts v. Brady, this Court, after full consideration of all the historical data examined in Betts, had unequivocally declared that "the right to the aid of counsel is of this fundamental character." Powell v. Alabama, 287 U.S. 45, 68 (1932). While the Court at the close of its Powell opinion did by its language, as this Court frequently does, limit its holding to the particular facts and circumstances of that case, its conclusions about the fundamental nature of the right to counsel are unmistakable. Several years later, in 1936, the Court reemphasized what it had said about the fundamental nature of the right to counsel. . . .

In light of these and many other prior decisions of this Court, it is not surprising that the Betts Court, when faced with the contention that "one charged with crime, who is unable to obtain counsel, must be furnished counsel by the state," conceded that "[e]xpressions in the opinions of this court lend color to the argument . . ." 316 U.S., at 462–463. The fact is that in deciding as it did—that "appointment of counsel is not a fundamental right, essential to a fair trial"—the Court in Betts v. Brady made an abrupt break with its own well-considered precedents. In returning to these old precedents, sounder we believe than the new, we but restore constitutional principles established to achieve a fair system of justice. Not only these precedents but also reason and reflection require us to recognize that in our adversary system of criminal justice, any person haled into court, who is too poor to hire a lawyer, cannot be assured a fair trial unless counsel is provided for him. This seems to us to be an obvious truth. Governments, both state and federal, quite properly spend vast sums of money to establish machinery to try defendants accused of crime. Lawyers to prosecute are everywhere deemed essential to protect the public's interest in an orderly society. Similarly, there are few defendants charged with crime, few indeed, who fail to hire the best lawyers they can get to prepare and present their defenses. That government hires lawyers to prosecute and defendants who have the money hire lawyers to defend are the strongest indications of the widespread belief that lawyers in criminal courts are necessities, not luxuries. The right of one charged with crime to counsel may not be deemed fundamental and essential to fair trials in some countries, but it is in ours. From the very beginning, our state and national constitutions and laws have laid great emphasis on procedural and substantive safeguards designed to assure fair trials before impartial tribunals in which every defendant stands equal before the law. This noble ideal cannot be realized if the poor man charged with crime has to face his accusers without a lawyer to assist him. . . . The Court in Betts v. Brady departed from the sound wisdom upon which the Court's holding in Powell v. Alabama rested. Florida, supported by two other States, has asked that Betts v. Brady be left intact. Twenty-two States, as friends of the Court, argue that Betts was "an anachronism when handed down" and that it should now be overruled. We agree. . . .

Reversed.

[Justices Douglas and Clark wrote concurring opinions.]

Mr. Justice Harlan, concurring.

I agree that Betts v. Brady should be overruled, but consider it entitled to a more respectful burial than has been accorded, at least on the part of those of us who were not on the Court when that case was decided.

I cannot subscribe to the view that Betts v. Brady represented "an abrupt break with its own well-considered precedents." . . . In 1932, in Powell v. Alabama, 287 U.S. 45, a capital case, this Court declared that under the particular facts there presented . . . the state court had a duty to assign counsel for the trial as a necessary requisite of due process of law. It is evident that these limiting facts were not added to the opinion as an afterthought; they were repeatedly emphasized . . . and were clearly regarded as important to the result.

Thus when this Court, a decade later, decided Betts v. Brady, it did no more than to admit of the possible existence of special circumstances in noncapital as well as capital trials, while at the same time to insist that such circumstances be shown in order to establish a denial of due process. The right to appointed counsel had been recognized as being considerably broader in federal prosecutions, see Johnson v. Zerbst, 304 U.S. 458, but to have imposed these requirements on the States would indeed have been "an abrupt break" with the almost immediate past. The declaration that the right to appointed counsel in state prosecutions, as established in Powell v. Alabama, was not limited to capital cases was in truth not a departure from, but an extension of, existing precedent.

The principles declared in Powell and in Betts, however, had a troubled journey throughout the years that have followed first the one case and then the other. Even by the time of the Betts decision, dictum in at least one of the Court's opinions had indicated that there was an absolute right to the services of counsel in the trial of state capital cases. . . .

In noncapital cases, the "special circumstances" rule has continued to exist in form while its substance has been substantially and steadily eroded. In the first decade after Betts, there were cases in which the Court found special circumstances to be lacking, but usually by a sharply divided vote. However, no such decision has been cited to us, and I have found none, after Quicksall v. Michigan, 339 U.S. 660, decided in 1950. At the same time, there have been not a few cases in which special circumstances were found in little or nothing more than the "complexity" of the legal questions presented, although those questions were often of only routine difficulty. The Court has come to recognize, in other words, that the mere existence of a serious criminal charge constituted in itself special circumstances requiring the services of counsel at trial. In truth the Betts v. Brady rule is no longer a reality.

This evolution, however, appears not to have been fully recognized by many state courts, in this instance charged with the front-line responsibility for the enforcement of constitutional rights. To continue a rule which is honored by this Court only with lip service is not a healthy thing and in the long run will do disservice to the federal system.

The special circumstances rule has been formally abandoned in capital cases, and the time has now come when it should be similarly abandoned in non-capital cases, at least as to offenses which, as the one involved here, carry the possibility of a substantial prison sentence. (Whether the rule should extend to *all* criminal cases need not now be decided.) This indeed does no more than to make explicit something that has long since been foreshadowed in our decisions.

In agreeing with the Court that the right to counsel in a case such as this should now be expressly recognized as a fundamental right embraced in the Fourteenth Amendment, I wish to make a further observation. When we hold a right or immunity, valid against the Federal Government, to be "implicit in the concept of ordered liberty" and thus valid against the States, I do not read our past decisions to suggest that by so holding, we automatically carry over an entire body of federal law and apply it in full sweep to the States. Any such concept would disregard the frequently wide disparity between the legitimate interests of the States and of the Federal Government, the divergent problems that they face, and the significantly different consequences of their actions. Cf. Roth v. United States, 354 U.S. 476, 496–508 (separate opinion of this writer). In what is done today I do not understand the Court to depart from the principles laid down in Palko v. Connecticut, 302 U.S. 319, or to embrace the concept that the Fourteenth Amendment "incorporates" the Sixth Amendment as such.

On these principles I join in the judgment of the Court.

[Note: At the time of the American Revolution it was long-settled English law that one accused of felony had no right to *employ* counsel in his defense. The purpose of the Sixth Amendment, apparently, was to kill this tradition, not to require government to supply counsel for indigents. "It is clear that the federal courts never thought they were required by the Sixth Amendment to appoint counsel for indigent defendants at any time before *Johnson v. Zerbst* in 1938." (William M. Beaney, *The Right to Counsel in American Courts* [Ann Arbor, Mich.: University of Michigan Press, 1955], p. 77.)

In *Betts* v. *Brady,* 316 U.S. 455 (1942), the Supreme Court refused to impose the *Zerbst* tour de force upon the states. In its view, of course, the Fourteenth Amendment required fairness in state trials; but it was not convinced that absence of counsel meant inevitably that a trial was unfair. Thus, under the *Betts* fairness rule, a state convict was entitled to federal relief only upon a reasonable showing that in fact he suffered from want of legal assistance. Absent a proper waiver, the *Zerbst* and *Gideon* rules, on the other hand, open the jail doors for all indigent convicts tried without counsel, regardless of the fairness or unfairness of their trials (to say nothing of guilt or innocence).

Of course, all indigents accused of crime should have adequate legal assistance; but court-appointed (i.e., unpaid, often young and inexperienced) lawyers do not seem to be an adequate solution. That is why the Department of Justice has repeatedly urged Congress to appropriate funds to meet this pressing need. In the Criminal Justice Act of 1964, Congress complied, but only with respect to federal cases. *Gideon*, like *Green* v. *United States*, 355 U.S. 184 (1957), is a classic example of the activist technique of overruling precedent while purporting not to do so. See J. H. Israel, "*Gideon* v. *Wainwright:* The 'Art of Overruling,'" 1963 *Supreme Court Review*, 211.]

Malloy v. *Hogan*

84 S. Ct. 1489 (1964)

MR. JUSTICE BRENNAN delivered the opinion of the Court.

In this case we are asked to reconsider prior decisions holding that the privilege against self-incrimination is not safeguarded against state action by the Fourteenth Amendment.

Twining v. New Jersey, 211 U.S. 78; Adamson v. California, 332 U.S. 46.

The petitioner was arrested during a gambling raid in 1959 by Hartford, Connecticut, police. He pleaded guilty to the crime of pool-selling, a misdemeanor, and was sentenced to one year in jail and fined $500. The sentence was ordered to be suspended after 90 days, at which time he was to be placed on probation for two years. About 16 months after his guilty plea, petitioner was ordered to testify before a referee appointed by the Superior Court of Hartford County to conduct an inquiry into alleged gambling and other criminal activities in the county. The petitioner was asked a number of questions related to events surrounding his arrest and conviction. He refused to answer any question "on the grounds it may tend to incriminate me." The Superior Court adjudged him in contempt, and committed him to prison until he was willing to answer the questions. Petitioner's application for a writ of habeas corpus was denied by the Superior Court, and the Connecticut Supreme Court of Errors affirmed. 150 Conn. 220; 187 A.2d 744. The latter court held that the Fifth Amendment's privilege against self-incrimination was not available to a witness in a state proceeding, that the Fourteenth Amendment extended no privilege to him, and that the petitioner had not properly invoked the privilege available under the Connecticut Constitution. We granted certiorari. 373 U.S. 948. We reverse. We hold that the Fourteenth Amendment guaranteed the petitioner the protection of the Fifth Amendment's privilege against self-incrimination, and that under the applicable federal standard, the Connecticut Supreme Court of Errors erred in holding that the privilege was not properly invoked.

The extent to which the Fourteenth Amendment prevents state invasion of rights enumerated in the first eight Amendments has been considered in numerous cases in this Court since the Amendment's adoption in 1868. Although many Justices have deemed the Amendment to incorporate all eight of the Amendments, the view which has thus far prevailed dates from the decision in 1897 in Chicago, B. & Q. R. Co. v. Chicago, 166 U.S. 226, which held that the Due Process Clause requires the States to pay just compensation for private property taken for public use. It was on the authority of that decision that the Court said in 1908 in Twining v. New Jersey, supra, that "it is possible that some of the personal rights safeguarded by the first eight Amendments against national action may also be safeguarded against state action, because a denial of them would be a denial of due process of law." 211 U.S., at 99.

The Court has not hesitated to re-examine past decisions according the Fourteenth Amendment a less central role in the preservation of basic liberties than that which was contemplated by its Framers when they added the Amendment to our constitutional scheme. Thus, although the Court as late as 1922 said that "neither the Fourteenth Amendment nor any other provision of the Constitution of the United States imposes upon the States any restrictions about 'freedom of speech' . . .," Prudential Ins. Co. of America v. Cheek, 259 U.S. 530, 543, three years later Gitlow v. New York 268 U.S. 652, initiated a series of decisions which today holds immune from state invasion every First Amendment protection for the cherished rights of mind and spirit—the freedoms of speech, press, religion, assembly, association, and petition for redress of grievances.

Similarly, Palko v. Connecticut, 302 U.S. 319, decided in 1938, suggested that the rights secured by the Fourth Amendment, were not protected against state action, citing at 302 U.S. 324, the statement of the Court in 1914 in Weeks v. United States, 232 U.S. 383, 398, that "the 4th Amendment is not directed to individual misconduct of [state] officials." In 1961, however, the Court held that in the light of later decisions, it was taken as settled that ". . . the Fourth Amendment's right of privacy has been declared enforceable against the States through the Due Process Clause of the Fourteenth. . . ." Mapp v. Ohio, 367 U.S. 643, 655. Again, although the Court held in 1942 that in a state prosecution for a noncapital offense, "appointment of counsel is not a fundamental right," Betts v. Brady, 316 U.S. 455, 471; cf. Powell v. Alabama, 287 U.S. 45, only last Term this decision was re-examined and it was held that provision of counsel in all criminal cases was "a fundamental right, essential to a fair trial," and thus was made obligatory on the States by the Fourteenth Amendment. Gideon v. Wainwright, 372 U.S. 335, 344–345.

We hold today that the Fifth Amendment's exception from compulsory self-incrimination is also protected by the Fourteenth Amendment against abridgment by the States. Decisions of the Court since Twining and Adamson have departed from the contrary view expressed in those cases. We discuss first the decisions which forbid the use of coerced confessions in state criminal prosecutions.

Brown v. Mississippi, 297 U.S. 278, was the first case in which the Court held that the Due Process Clause prohibited the States from using the accused's coerced confessions against him. The Court in Brown felt impelled, in light of Twining, to say that its conclusion did not involve the privilege against self-incrimination. "Compulsion by torture to extort a confession is a different matter." 297 U.S. 285. But this distinction was soon abandoned, and today the admissibility of a confession in a state criminal prosecution is tested by the same standard applied in federal prosecutions since 1897, when, in Bram v. United States, 168 U.S. 532, the Court held that "In criminal trials, in the courts of the United States, wherever a question arises whether a confession is incompetent because not voluntary, the issue is controlled by that portion of the Fifth Amendment to the constitution of the United States commanding that no person 'shall be compelled in any criminal case to be a witness against himself.'" Id., 168 U.S. at 542. Under this test, the constitutional inquiry is not whether the conduct of state officers in obtaining the confession was shocking, but whether the confession is "free and voluntary; that is, [it] must not be extracted by any sort of threats or violence, nor obtained by any direct or implied promises, however slight, nor by the

exertion of any improper influence. . . ." Id., 168 U.S. at 542–
543. . . . In other words the person must not have been compelled to incriminate himself. We have held inadmissible even
a confession secured by so mild a whip as the refusal, under
certain circumstances, to allow a suspect to call his wife until
he confessed. Haynes v. Washington, 373 U.S. 503.

The marked shift to the federal standard in state cases began
with Lisenba v. California, 314 U.S. 219, where the Court
spoke of accused's "free choice to admit, to deny, or to refuse
to answer." Id., 314 U.S. at 241. . . . The shift reflects recognition that the American system of criminal prosecution is accusatorial, not inquisitorial, and that the Fifth Amendment
privilege is its essential mainstay. Rogers v. Richmond, 365 U.S.
534, 541. Governments, state and federal, are thus constitutionally compelled to establish guilt by evidence independently
and freely secured, and may not by coercion prove a charge
against an accused out of his own mouth. Since the Fourteenth
Amendment prohibits the States from inducing a person to
confess through "sympathy falsely aroused," Spano v. New
York, supra, 360 U.S. at p. 323, or other like inducement far
short of "compulsion by torture," Haynes v. Washington, supra, it follows *a fortiori* that it also forbids the States to resort
to imprisonment, as here, to compel him to answer questions
that might incriminate him. The Fourteenth Amendment secures against state invasion the same privilege that the Fifth
Amendment guarantees against federal infringement—the
right of a person to remain silent unless he chooses to speak in
the unfettered exercise of his own will, and to suffer no
penalty, as held in Twining, for such silence.

This conclusion is fortified by our recent decision in Mapp v.
Ohio, 367 U.S. 643, overruling Wolf v. Colorado, supra, which
had held "that in a prosecution in a State court for a State
crime the Fourteenth Amendment does not forbid the admission of evidence obtained by an unreasonable search and
seizure," 338 U.S., at 33. Mapp held that the Fifth Amendment
privilege against self-incrimination implemented the Fourth

Amendment in such cases, and that the two guarantees of personal security conjoined in the Fourteenth Amendment to make the exclusionary rule obligatory upon the States. We relied upon the great case of Boyd v. United States, 116 U.S. 616, decided in 1886, which, considering the Fourth and Fifth Amendments as running "almost into each other," id., 116 U.S., at 630, held that "Breaking into a house and opening boxes and drawers are circumstances of aggravation; but any forcible and compulsory extortion of a man's own testimony, or of his private papers to be used as evidence to convict him of crime, or to forfeit his goods, is within the condemnation of [those Amendments]. . . ." 116 U.S., at 630. We said in Mapp:

> "We find that, as to the Federal Government, the Fourth and Fifth Amendments and, as to the States, the freedom from unconscionable invasions of privacy and the freedom from convictions based upon coerced confessions do enjoy an 'intimate relation' in their perpetuation of 'principles of humanity and civil liberty [secured] . . . only after years of struggle.' Bram v United States, 1897, 168 U.S. 532, 543–544. . . . The philosophy of each Amendment and of each freedom is complementary to, although not dependent upon, that of the other in its sphere of influence—the very least that together they assure in either sphere is that no man is to be convicted on unconstitutional evidence." 367 U.S. 656–657.

In thus returning to the Boyd view that the privilege is one of the "principles of a free government," 116 U.S., at 632, Mapp necessarily repudiated the Twining concept of the privilege as a mere rule of evidence "best defended not as an unchangeable principle of universal justice, but as a law proved by experience to be expedient." 211 U.S., at 113.

The respondent State of Connecticut concedes in its brief that under our decisions, particularly those involving coerced confessions, "the accusatorial system has become a fundamental part of the fabric of our society and, hence, is enforceable against the States." The State urges, however, that the availability of the federal privilege to a witness in a state inquiry is to be determined according to a less stringent standard than is applicable in a federal proceeding. We disagree. We have held that the guarantees of the First Amendment, Gitlow v. New York, supra; Cantwell v. Connecticut, supra; Louisiana ex rel. Gremillion v. N.A.A.C.P., supra, the prohibition of unreasonable searches and seizures of the Fourth Amendment, Ker v. California, infra, and the right to counsel guaranteed by the Sixth Amendment, Gideon v. Wainwright, supra, are all to be enforced against the States under the Fourteenth Amendment according to the same standards that protect those personal rights against federal encroachment. In the coerced confession cases, involving the policies of the privilege itself, there has been no suggestion that a confession might be considered coerced if used in a federal but not a state tribunal. The Court thus has rejected the notion that the Fourteenth Amendment applies to the states only a "watered-down, subjective version of the individual guarantees of the Bill of Rights," Ohio ex rel. Eaton v. Price, 364 U.S. 263, 275 (dissenting opinion). If Cohen v. Hurley, 366 U.S. 117, and Adamson v. California, supra, suggest such an application of the privilege against self-incrimination, that suggestion cannot survive recognition of the degree to which the Twining view of the privilege has been eroded. What is accorded is a privilege of refusing to incriminate one's self, and the feared prosecution may be by either federal or state authorities. Murphy v. Waterfront Comm'n, ante. It would be incongruous to have different standards determine the validity of a claim of privilege based on the same feared prosecution, depending on whether the claim was asserted in a state or federal court. Therefore, the same standards must determine whether an accused's silence in either a federal or state proceeding is justified.

We turn to the petitioner's claim that the State of Connecticut denied him the protection of his federal privilege. It must be considered irrelevant that the petitioner was a witness in a statutory inquiry and not a defendant in a criminal prosecution, for it has long been settled that the privilege protects witnesses in similar federal inquiries. Counselman v. Hitchcock, 142 U.S. 547; McCarthy v. Arndstein, 266 U.S. 34; Hoffman v. United States, 341 U.S. 479. We recently elaborated the content of the federal standard in Hoffman:

> "The privilege afforded not only extends to answers that would in themselves support a conviction . . . but likewise embraces those which would furnish a link in the chain of evidence needed to prosecute . . . if the witness, upon interposing his claim, were required to prove the hazard . . . he would be compelled to surrender the very protection which the privilege is designed to guarantee. To sustain the privilege, it need only be evident from the implications of the question, in the setting in which it is asked, that a responsive answer to the question or an explanation of why it cannot be answered might be dangerous because injurious disclosure could result." 341 U.S., at 486–487.

We also said that, in applying that test, the judge must be

> " 'perfectly clear, from a careful consideration of all the circumstances in the case, that the witness is mistaken, and that the answer[s] cannot possibly have such tendency' to incriminate." 341 U.S., at 488.

The State of Connecticut argues that the Connecticut courts properly applied the federal standards to the facts of this case. We disagree.

The investigation in the course of which petitioner was questioned began when the Superior Court in Hartford County appointed the Honorable Ernest A. Inglis, formerly Chief Justice of Connecticut, to conduct an inquiry into whether there was reasonable cause to believe that crimes, including gambling, were being committed in Hartford County. Petitioner appeared on January 16 and 25, 1961, and in both instances he was asked substantially the same questions about the circumstances surrounding his arrest and conviction for pool-selling in late 1959. The questions which petitioner refused to answer may be summarized as follows: (1) for whom did he work on September 11, 1959; (2) who selected and paid his counsel in connection with his arrest on that date and subsequent conviction; (3) who selected and paid his bondsman; (4) who paid his fine; (5) what was the name of the tenant in the apartment in which he was arrested; and (6) did he know John Bergoti. The Connecticut Supreme Court of Errors ruled that the answers to these questions could not tend to incriminate him because the defenses of double jeopardy and the running of the one-year statute of limitations on misdemeanors would defeat any prosecution growing out of his answers to the first five questions. As for the sixth question, the court held that petitioner's failure to explain how a revelation of his relationship with Bergoti would incriminate him vitiated his claim to the protection of the privilege afforded by state law.

The conclusions of the Court of Errors, tested by the federal standard, fails to take sufficient account of the setting in which the questions were asked. The interrogation was part of a wide-ranging inquiry into crime, including gambling, in Hartford. It was admitted on behalf of the State at oral argument— and indeed it is obvious from the questions themselves—that the State desired to elicit from the petitioner the identity of the person who ran the pool-selling operation in connection with which he had been arrested in 1959. It was apparent that petitioner might apprehend that if this person were still engaged in unlawful activity, disclosure of his name might furnish a link in a chain of evidence sufficient to connect the petitioner with a more recent crime for which he might still be prosecuted.

Analysis of the sixth question, concerning whether petitioner knew John Bergoti, yields a similar conclusion. In the context of the inquiry, it should have been apparent to the referee that Bergoti was suspected by the State to be involved in some way in the subject matter of the investigation. An affirmative answer to the question might well have either connected petitioner with a more recent crime, or at least have operated as a waiver of his privilege with reference to his relationship with a possible criminal. See Rogers v. United States, 340 U.S. 367. We conclude, therefore, that as to each of the questions, it was "evident from the implications of the question, in the setting in which it [was] asked, that a responsive answer to the question or an explanation of why it [could not] be answered might be dangerous because injurious disclosure could result," Hoffman v. United States, supra, 341 U.S. 486–487; see Singleton v. United States, 343 U.S. 944.

Reversed.

While MR. JUSTICE DOUGLAS joins the opinion of the Court, he also adheres to his concurrence in Gideon v. Wainwright, 372 U.S. 335, 345.

MR. JUSTICE HARLAN, whom MR. JUSTICE CLARK joins, dissenting.

Connecticut has adjudged this petitioner in contempt for refusing to answer questions in a state inquiry. The courts of the State, whose laws embody a privilege against self-incrimination, refused to recognize the petitioner's claim of privilege, finding that the questions asked him were not incriminatory. This Court now holds the contempt adjudication unconstitutional because, it is decided: (1) the Fourteenth Amendment makes the Fifth Amendment privilege against self-incrimination applicable to the States; (2) the federal standard justifying a claim of this privilege likewise applies to the States; and (3) judged by that standard the petitioner's claim of privilege should have been upheld.

Believing that the reasoning behind the Court's decision carries extremely mischievous, if not dangerous consequences for our federal system in the realm of criminal law enforcement, I must dissent. The importance of the issue presented and the serious incursion which the Court makes on time-honored, basic constitutional principles justifies a full exposition of my reasons.

I.

I can only read the Court's opinion as accepting in fact what it rejects in theory: the application to the States, via the Fourteenth Amendment, of the forms of federal criminal procedure embodied within the first eight Amendments to the Constitution. While it is true that the Court deals today with only one aspect of state criminal procedure, and rejects the wholesale "incorporation" of such federal constitutional requirements, the logical gap between the Court's premises and its novel constitutional conclusion can, I submit, be bridged only by the additional premise that the Due Process Clause of the Fourteenth Amendment is a shorthand directive to this Court to pick and choose among the provisions of the first eight Amendments and apply those chosen, freighted with their entire accompanying body of federal doctrine, to law enforcement in the States.

I accept and agree with the proposition that continuing re-examination of the constitutional conception of Fourteenth Amendment "due process" of law is required, and that development of the community's sense of justice may in time lead to expansion of the protection which due process affords. In particular in this case, I agree that principles of justice to which due process gives expression, as reflected in decisions of this Court, prohibit a State, as the Fifth Amendment prohibits the Federal Government, from imprisoning a person *solely* because he refuses to give evidence which may incriminate him under the laws of the State. I do not understand, however, how this process of re-examination, which must refer always to the guiding standard of due process of law, including, of course, reference to the particular guarantees of the Bill of Rights, can be short-circuited by the simple device of incorporating into due process, without critical examination, the whole body of law which surrounds a specific prohibition directed against the Federal Government. The consequence of such an approach to due process as it pertains to the States is inevitably disregard of all relevant differences which may exist between state and federal criminal law and its enforcement. The ultimate result is compelled uniformity, which is inconsistent with the purpose of our federal system and which is achieved either by encroachment on the States' sovereign powers or by dilution in federal law enforcement of the specific protections found in the Bill of Rights.

II.

As recently as 1961, this Court reaffirmed that "the Fifth Amendment's privilege against self-incrimination," ante, p. 1491, was not applicable against the States. Cohen v. Hurley, 366 U.S. 117. The question had been most fully explored in Twining v. New Jersey, 211 U.S. 78. Since 1908, when Twining was decided, this Court has adhered to the view there expressed that "the exemption from compulsory self-incrimination in the courts of the states is not secured by any part of the Federal Constitution," 211 U.S., at 114; Snyder v. Commonwealth of Massachusetts, 291 U.S. 97, 105; Brown v. Mississippi, 297 U.S. 278, 285; Palko v. Connecticut, 302 U.S. 319, 324; Adamson v. California, supra; Knapp v. Schweitzer, 357 U.S. 371, 374; Cohen v. Hurley, supra. Although none of these cases involved a commitment to prison for refusing to incriminate oneself under state law, and they are relevantly distinguishable from this case on that narrow ground, it is perfectly clear from them that until today it has been regarded as settled law that the Fifth Amendment privilege did not, by any process of reasoning, apply *as such* to the States.

The Court suggests that this consistent line of authority has been undermined by the concurrent development of constitutional doctrine in the areas of coerced confessions and search and seizure. That is *post facto* reasoning at best. Certainly there has been no intimation until now that Twining has been tacitly overruled.

It was in Brown v. Mississippi, supra, that this Court first prohibited the use of a coerced confession in a state criminal trial. The petitioners in Brown had been tortured until they confessed. The Court was hardly making an artificial distinction when it said:

"... [T]he question of the right of the state to withdraw the privilege against self-incrimination is not here involved. The compulsion to which the quoted statements [from Twining and Snyder, supra,] refer is that of the *processes of justice* by which the accused may be called as a witness and required to testify. *Compulsion by torture* to extort a confession is a different matter." 297 U.S., at 285. (Emphasis supplied.)[1]

The majority is simply wrong when it asserts that this perfectly understandable distinction "was soon abandoned," ante, p. . . . In none of the cases cited, ante, pp. . . . , in which was developed the full sweep of the constitutional prohibition against the use of coerced confessions at state trials, was there anything to suggest that the Fifth Amendment was being made applicable to state proceedings. In Lisenba v. California, 314 U.S. 219, 62 S.Ct. 280, the privilege against self-incrimination is not mentioned. The relevant question before the Court was whether "the evidence [of coercion] requires that we set aside the finding of two courts and a jury and adjudge the admission of the confessions so fundamentally unfair, so contrary to the common concept of ordered liberty as to amount to a taking of life without due process of law." Id., 314 U.S. at 238. The question was the same in Ashcraft v. Tennessee, 322 U.S. 143; the

---

[1] Nothing in the opinion in Brown supports the Court's intimation here, ante, p. . . . , that if Twining had not been on the books, reversal of the convictions would have been based on the Fifth Amendment. The Court made it plain in Brown that it regarded the trial use of a confession extracted by torture as on a par with domination of a trial by a mob, see, e.g., Moore v. Dempsey, 261 U.S. 86, where the trial "is a mere pretense," 297 U.S. 286.

Court there adverted to the "third degree," e.g., id., 322 U.S. at 150, note 5, and "secret inquisitorial practices," id., 322 U.S. at 152. Malinski v. New York, 324 U.S. 401, is the same; the privilege against self-incrimination is not mentioned.[2] So too in Spano v. New York, 360 U.S. 315; Lynumn v. Illinois, 372 U.S. 528; and Haynes v. Washington, 373 U.S. 503. Finally, in Rogers v. Richmond, 365 U.S. 534, although the Court did recognize that "ours is an accusatorial and not an inquisitorial system," id., 365 U.S. at 541, it is clear that the Court was concerned only with the problem of coerced confessions, see id.; the opinion includes nothing to support the Court's assertion here, ante, p. . . . , that "the Fifth Amendment privilege is . . . [the] essential mainstay" of our system.

In Adamson, supra, the Court made it explicit that it did not regard the increasingly strict standard for determining the admissibility at trial of an out-of-court confession as undermining the holding of Twining. After stating that "the due process clause does not protect, by virtue of its mere existence the accused's freedom from giving testimony by compulsion in state trials that is secured to him against federal interference by the Fifth Amendment," the Court said: "The due process clause forbids compulsion to testify by fear of hurt, torture or exhaustion. It forbids any other type of coercion that falls within the scope of due process." 332 U.S., at 54 (footnotes omitted). Plainly, the Court regarded these two lines of cases

---

[2] "And so, when a conviction in a state court is properly here for review, under a claim that a right protected by the Fourteenth Amendment has been denied, the question is not whether the record can be found to disclose an infraction of one of the specific provisions of the first eight amendments. To come concretely to the present case, the question is not whether the record permits a finding, by a tenuous process of psychological assumptions and reasoning, that Malinski by means of a confession was forced to self-incrimination in defiance of the Fifth Amendment. The exact question is whether the criminal proceedings which resulted in his conviction deprived him of the due process of law by which he was constitutionally entitled to have his guilt determined." Malinski, supra, 324 U.S. at 416 (opinion of Frankfurter, J.).

as distinct. See also Palko v. Connecticut, supra, 302 U.S., at 326, to the same effect. Cohen, supra, which adhered to Twining, was decided after all but a few of the confession cases which the Court mentions.

The coerced confession cases are relevant to the problem of this case not because they overruled Twining *sub silentio,* but rather because they applied the same standard of fundamental fairness which is applicable here. The recognition in them that federal supervision of state criminal procedures must be directly based on the requirements of due process is entirely inconsistent with the theory here espoused by the majority. The parallel treatment of federal and state cases involving coerced confessions resulted from the fact that the same demand of due process was applicable in both; it was not the consequence of the automatic engrafting of federal law construing constitutional provisions inapplicable to the States onto the Fourteenth Amendment.

The decision in Mapp v. Ohio, 367 U.S. 643, that evidence unconstitutionally seized, see Wolf v. Colorado, 338 U.S. 25, 28, may not be used in a state criminal trial furnishes no "fortification," see ante, p. . . . , for today's decision. The very passage from the Mapp opinion which the Court quotes, ante, p. . . . , makes explicit the distinct bases of the exclusionary rule as applied in federal and state courts:

> "We find that, as to the Federal Government, the Fourth and Fifth Amendments and, as to the States, the freedom from unconscionable invasions of privacy and the freedom from convictions based upon coerced confessions do enjoy an 'intimate relation' in their perpetuation of 'principles of humanity and civil liberty [secured] . . . only after years of struggle.' Bram v. United States, 1897, 168 U.S. 532, 543–544." 367 U.S., at 656–657 (footnote omitted). See also id., 367 U.S. at 655.

Although the Court discussed Boyd v. United States, 116 U.S. 616, a federal case involving both the Fourth and Fifth Amendments, nothing in Mapp supports the statement, ante,

p. . . . , that the Fifth Amendment was part of the basis for extending the exclusionary rule to the States. The elaboration of Mapp in Ker v. California, 374 U.S. 23, did in my view make the Fourth Amendment applicable to the States through the Fourteenth; but there is nothing in it to suggest that the Fifth Amendment went along as baggage.

III.

The previous discussion shows that this Court's decisions do not dictate the "incorporation" of the Fifth Amendment's privilege against self-incrimination into the Fourteenth Amendment. Approaching the question more broadly, it is equally plain that the line of cases exemplified by Palko v. Connecticut, supra, in which this Court has reconsidered the requirements which the Due Process Clause imposes on the States in the light of current standards, furnishes no general theoretical framework for what the Court does today.

The view of the Due Process Clause of the Fourteenth Amendment which this Court has consistently accepted and which has "thus far prevailed," ante, p. . . . , is that its requirements are as "old as a principle of civilized government," Munn v. Illinois, 94 U.S. 113, 123, the specific applications of which must be ascertained "by the gradual process of judicial inclusion and exclusion . . . ," Davidson v. New Orleans, 96 U.S. 97, 104. Due process requires "observance of those general rules established in our system of jurisprudence for the security of private rights." Hagar v. Reclamation District No. 108, 111 U.S. 701, 708. See Hurtado v. California, 110 U.S. 516, 537.

> "This court has never attempted to define with precision the words 'due process of law'. . . . It is sufficient to say that there are certain immutable principles of justice, which inhere in the very idea of free government, which no member of the Union may disregard. . . ." Holden v. Hardy, 169 U.S. 366, 389.

It followed from this recognition that due process encompassed the fundamental safeguards of the individual against the abusive exercise of governmental power that some of the restraints on the Federal Government which were specifically enumerated in the Bill of Rights applied also against the States. But, while inclusion of a particular provision in the Bill of Rights might provide historical evidence that the right involved was traditionally regarded as fundamental, inclusion of the right in due process was otherwise entirely independent of the first eight Amendments:

> ". . . [I]t is possible that some of the personal rights safeguarded by the first eight Amendments against national action may also be safeguarded against state action, because a denial of them would be a denial of due process of law. . . . *If this is so, it is not because those rights are enumerated in the first eight Amendments, but because they are of such a nature that they are included in the conception of due process of law.*" Twining, supra, 211 U.S. at 99. (Emphasis supplied.)

Relying heavily on Twining, Mr. Justice Cardozo provided what may be regarded as a classic expression of this approach in Palko v. Connecticut, supra. After considering a number of individual rights (including the right not to incriminate oneself) which were "not of the very essence of a scheme of ordered liberty," id., 302 U.S. at 325, he said:

> "We reach a different plane of social and moral values when we pass to the privileges and immunities that have been taken over from the earlier articles of the Federal Bill of Rights and brought within the Fourteenth Amendment by a process of absorption. These in their origin were effective against the federal government alone. If the Fourteenth Amendment has absorbed them, the process of absorption has had its source in the belief that neither liberty nor justice would exist if they were sacrificed." Id., 302 U.S. at 326.

Further on, Mr. Justice Cardozo made the independence of the Due Process Clause from the provisions of the first eight Amendments explicit:

> "Fundamental . . . in the concept of due process, and so in that of liberty, is the thought that condemnation shall be rendered

only after trial. Scott v. McNeal, 154 U.S. 34; Blackmer v. United States, 284 U.S. 421. The hearing, moreover, must be a real one, not a sham or a pretense. Moore v. Dempsey, 261 U.S. 86; Mooney v. Holohan, 294 U.S. 103. For that reason, ignorant defendants in a capital case were held to have been condemned unlawfully when in truth, though not in form, they were refused the aid of counsel. Powell v. Alabama, supra, 287 U.S. 45, at pages 67, 68. The decision did not turn upon the fact that the benefit of counsel would have been guaranteed to the defendants by the provisions of the Sixth Amendment if they had been prosecuted in a federal court. The decision turned upon the fact that in the particular situation laid before us in the evidence the benefit of counsel was essential to the substance of a hearing." Id., 302 U.S. at 327.

It is apparent that Mr. Justice Cardozo's metaphor of "absorption" was *not* intended to suggest the transplantation of case law surrounding the specifics of the first eight Amendments to the very different soil of the Fourteenth Amendment's Due Process Clause. For, as he made perfectly plain, what the Fourteenth Amendment requires of the States does not basically depend on what the first eight Amendments require of the Federal Government.

Seen in proper perspective, therefore, the fact that First Amendment protections have generally been given equal scope in the federal and state domains or that in some areas of criminal procedure the Due Process Clause demands as much of the States as the Bill of Rights demands of the Federal Government, is only tangentially relevant to the question now before us. It is toying with constitutional principles to assert that the Court has "rejected the notion that the Fourteenth Amendment applies to the states only a 'watered-down, subjective version of the Bill of Rights,'" ante, p. . . . . What the Court has with the single exception of the Ker case, supra, p. . . . ; see infra, p. . . . , consistently rejected is the notion that the Bill of Rights, as such, applies to the States in any aspect at all.

If one attends to those areas to which the Court points, ante, p. . . . , in which the prohibitions against the state and federal governments have moved in parallel tracks, the cases in fact reveal again that the Court's usual approach has been to ground the prohibitions against state action squarely on due process, without intermediate reliance on any of the first eight Amendments. Although more recently the Court has referred to the First Amendment to describe the protection of free expression against state infringement, earlier cases leave no doubt that such references are "shorthand" for doctrines developed by another route. In Gitlow v. New York, 268 U.S. 652, 666, for example, the Court said:

> "For present purposes we may and do assume that freedom of speech and of the press—which are protected by the First Amendment from abridgment by Congress—are among the fundamental personal rights and 'liberties' protected by the due process clause of the Fourteenth Amendment from impairment by the States."

The Court went on to consider the extent of those freedoms in the context of state interests. MR. JUSTICE HOLMES, in dissent, said:

> "The general principle of free speech, it seems to me, must be taken to be included in the Fourteenth Amendment, in view of the scope that has been given to the word 'liberty' as there used, although perhaps it may be accepted with a somewhat larger latitude of interpretation than is allowed to Congress by the sweeping language that governs or ought to govern the laws of the United States." Id., 268 U.S. at 672.

CHIEF JUSTICE HUGHES, in De Jonge v. Oregon, 299 U.S. 353, 364, gave a similar analysis:

> "Freedom of speech and of the press are fundamental rights which are safeguarded by the due process clause of the Fourteenth Amendment of the Federal Constitution. . . . The right of peaceable assembly is a right cognate to those of free speech

and free press and is equally fundamental. As this Court said in United States v. Cruikshank, 92 U.S. 542, 552: 'The very idea of a government, republican in form, implies a right on the part of its citizens to meet peaceably for consultation in respect to public affairs and to petition for a redress of grievances.' The First Amendment of the Federal Constitution expressly guarantees that right against abridgment by Congress. But explicit mention there does not argue exclusion elsewhere. For the right is one that cannot be denied without violating those fundamental principles of liberty and justice which lie at the base of all civil and political institutions—principles which the Fourteenth Amendment embodies in the general terms of its due process clause. . . ."

The coerced confession and search and seizure cases have already been considered. The former, decided always directly on grounds of fundamental fairness furnish no support for the Court's present views. Ker v. California, *supra*, did indeed incorporate the Fourth Amendment's protection against invasions of privacy into the Due Process Clause. But that case should be regarded as the exception which proves the rule. The right to counsel in state criminal proceedings, which this Court assured in Gideon v. Wainwright, 372 U.S. 335, does not depend on the Sixth Amendment. In Betts v. Brady, 316 U.S. 455, 462, this Court had said:

"Due process of law is secured against invasion by the federal Government by the Fifth Amendment and is safeguarded against state action in identical words by the Fourteenth. The phrase formulates a concept less rigid and more fluid than those envisaged in other specific and particular provisions of the Bill of Rights. Its application is less a matter of rule. Asserted denial is to be tested by an appraisal of the totality of facts in a given case. That which may, in one setting, constitute a denial of fundamental fairness, shocking to the universal sense of justice, may, in other circumstances, and in the light of other considerations, fall short of such denial." (Footnote omitted.)

Although Gideon overruled Betts, the constitutional approach in both cases was the same. Gideon was based on the Court's conclusion, contrary to that reached in Betts, that the appointment of counsel for an indigent criminal defendant *was* essential to the conduct of a fair trial, and was therefore, part of due process. 372 U.S., at 342-345.

The Court's approach in the present case is in fact nothing more or less than "incorporation" in snatches. If, however, the Due Process Clause *is* something more than a reference to the Bill of Rights and protects only those rights which derive from fundamental principles, as the majority purports to believe, it is just as contrary to precedent and just as illogical to incorporate the provisions of the Bill of Rights one at a time as it is to incorporate them all at once.

IV.

The Court's undiscriminating approach to the Due Process Clause carries serious implications for the sound working of our federal system in the field of criminal law.

The Court concludes, almost without discussion, that "the same standards must determine whether an accused's silence in either a federal or state proceeding is justified," ante, p. . . . . About all that the Court offers in explanation of this conclusion is the observation that it would be "incongruous" if different standards governed the assertion of a privilege to remain silent in state and federal tribunals. Such "incongruity," however, is at the heart of our federal system. The powers and responsibilities of the state and federal governments are not congruent; under our Constitution, they are not intended to be. Why should it be thought, as an *a priori* matter, that limitations on the investigative power of the States are in all respects identical with limitations on the investigative power of the Federal Government? This certainly does not follow from the fact that we deal here with constitutional requirements; for the provisions of the Constitution which are construed are different.

As the Court pointed out in Abbate v. United States, 359 U.S. 187, 195, "the States under our federal system have the principal responsibility for defining and prosecuting crimes." The Court endangers this allocation of responsibility for the prevention of crime when it applies to the States doctrines developed in the context of federal law enforcement, without any attention to the special problems which the States as a group or particular States may face. If the power of the States to deal with local crime is unduly restricted, the likely consequence is a shift of responsibility in this area to the Federal Government, with its vastly greater resources. Such a shift, if it occurs, may in the end serve to weaken the very liberties which the Fourteenth Amendment safeguards by bringing us closer to the monolithic society which our federalism rejects. Equally dangerous to our liberties is the alternative of watering down protections against the Federal Government embodied in the Bill of Rights so as not unduly to restrict the powers of the States. The dissenting opinion in Aguilar v. Texas, supra, evidences that this danger is not imaginary. See my concurring opinion in Aguilar, 377 U.S. at——.

Rather than insisting, almost by rote, that the Connecticut court, in considering the petitioner's claim of privilege, was required to apply the "federal standard," the Court should have fulfilled its responsibility under the Due Process Clause by inquiring whether the proceedings below met the demands of fundamental fairness which due process embodies. Such an approach may not satisfy those who see in the Fourteenth Amendment a set of easily applied "absolutes" which can afford a haven from unsettling doubt. It is, however, truer to the spirit which requires this Court constantly to re-examine fundamental principles and at the same time enjoins it from reading its own preferences into the Constitution.

The Connecticut Supreme Court of Errors gave full and careful consideration to the petitioner's claim that he would incriminate himself if he answered the questions put to him. It noted that its decisions "from a time antedating the adoption of . . . [the Connecticut] constitution in 1818" had upheld a privilege to refuse to answer incriminating questions. 150 Conn. 220, 223, 187 A.2d 744, 746. Stating that federal cases treating the Fifth Amendment privilege had "persuasive force" in interpreting its own constitutional provision, and citing Hoffman v. United States, 341 U.S. 479, in particular, the Supreme Court of Errors described the requirements for assertion of the privilege by quoting from one of its own cases, id., 150 Conn. at 225, 187 A.2d at 747:

> "[A] witness . . . has the right to refuse to answer any question which would tend to incriminate him. But a mere claim on his part that the evidence will tend to incriminate him is not sufficient. . . . [He having] made his claim, it is then . . . [necessary for the judge] to determine in the exercise of a legal discretion whether, from the circumstances of the case and the nature of the evidence which the witness is called upon to give, there is reasonable ground to apprehend danger of criminal liability from his being compelled to answer. That danger 'must be real and appreciable, with reference to the ordinary operation of law in the ordinary course of things—not a danger of an imaginary and unsubstantial character, having reference to some extraordinary and barely possible contingency, so improbable that no reasonable man would suffer it to influence his conduct. We think that a merely remote and naked possibility, out of the ordinary course of law and such as no reasonable man would be affected by, should not be suffered to obstruct the administration of justice. The object of the law is to afford to a party, called upon to give evidence in a proceeding *inter alios,* protection against being brought by means of his own evidence within the penalties of the law. But it would be to convert a salutary protection into a means of abuse if it were to be held that a mere imaginary possibility of danger, however, remote and improbable, was sufficient to justify the withholding of evidence essential to the ends of justice.' Cockburn, C. J., in Regina v. Boyes, 1 B. & S. 311, 330. . . ." McCarthy v. Clancy, 110 Conn. 482, 488–489, 148 A. 551, 555.

The court carefully applied the above standard to each question which the petitioner was asked. It dealt first with the question whether he knew John Bergoti. The court said:

> "Bergoti is nowhere described or in any way identified, either as to his occupation, actual or reputed, or as to any criminal record he may have had. . . . Malloy made no attempt even to suggest to the court how an answer to the question whether he knew Bergoti could possibly incriminate him. . . . On this state of the record the question was proper, and Malloy's claim of privilege, made without explanation, was correctly overruled. Malloy 'chose to keep the door tightly closed and to deny the court the smallest glimpse of the danger he apprehended. He cannot then complain that we see none.' In re Pillo, 11 N.J. 8, 22, 93 A.2d 176, 183. . . ." 150 Conn., at 226–227, 187 A.2d, at 748.

The remaining questions are summarized in the majority's opinion, *ante*, p. . . . All of them deal with the circumstances surrounding the petitioner's conviction on a gambling charge in 1959. The court declined to decide "whether, on their face and apart from any consideration of Malloy's immunity from prosecution, the questions should or should not have been answered in the light of his failure to give any hint of explanation as to how answers to them could incriminate him." 150 Conn., at 227, 187 A.2d, at 748. The court considered the State's claim that the petitioner's prior conviction was sufficient to clothe him with immunity from prosecution for other crimes to which the questions might pertain, but declined to rest its decision on that basis. Id., 150 Conn., at 227–229, 187 A.2d, at 748–749. The court concluded, however, that the running of the statute of limitations on misdemeanors committed in 1959 and the absence of any indication that Malloy had engaged in any crime other than a misdemeanor removed all appearance of danger of incrimination from the questions propounded concerning the petitioner's activities in 1959. The court summarized this conclusion as follows:

> "In all this, Malloy confounds vague and improbable possibilities of prosecution with reasonably appreciable ones. Under claims

like his, it would always be possible to work out some finespun and improbable theory from which an outside chance of prosecution could be envisioned. Such claims are not enough to support a claim of privilege, at least where, as here, a witness suggests no rational explanation of his fears of incrimination, and the questions themselves, under all the circumstances, suggest none." Id., 150 Conn. at 230–231, 187 A.2d at 750.

Peremptorily rejecting all of the careful analysis of the Connecticut court, this Court creates its own "finespun and improbable theory" about how these questions might have incriminated the petitioner. With respect to his acquaintance with Bergoti, this Court says only:

"In the context of the inquiry, it should have been apparent to the referee that Bergoti was suspected by the State to be involved in some way in the subject matter of the investigation. An affirmative answer to the question might well have either connected petitioner with a more recent crime, or at least have operated as a waiver of his privilege with reference to his relationship with a possible criminal." Ante, pp. . . .

The other five questions, treated at length in the Connecticut court's opinion, get equally short shrift from this Court; it takes the majority, unfamiliar with Connecticut law and far removed from the proceedings below, only a dozen lines to consider the questions and conclude that they were incriminating:

"The interrogation was a part of a wide-ranging inquiry into crime, including gambling, in Hartford. It was admitted on behalf of the State at oral argument—and indeed it is obvious from the questions themselves—that the State desired to elicit from the petitioner the identity of the person who ran the pool-selling operation in connection with which he had been arrested in 1959. It was apparent that petitioner might apprehend that if this person were still engaged in unlawful activity, disclosure of his name might furnish a link in a chain of evidence sufficient to connect the petitioner with a more recent crime for which he might still be prosecuted." (Footnote omitted.) Ante, p. . . .

I do not understand how anyone could read the opinion of the Connecticut court and conclude that the state law which was the basis of its decision or the decision itself was lacking in fundamental fairness. The truth of the matter is that under any standard—state or federal—the commitment for contempt was proper. Indeed, as indicated above, there is every reason to believe that the Connecticut court did apply the Hoffman standard quoted approvingly in the majority's opinion. I entirely agree with my Brother WHITE, post, pp. . . . , that if the matter is viewed only from the standpoint of the federal standard, such standard was fully satisfied. The Court's reference to a federal standard is, to put it bluntly, simply an excuse for the Court to substitute its own superficial assessment of the facts and state law for the careful and better informed conclusions of the state court. No one who scans the two opinions with an objective eye will, I think, reach any other conclusion.

I would affirm.

MR. JUSTICE WHITE, with whom MR. JUSTICE STEWART joins, dissenting. . . .

Baker v. *Carr*

369 U.S. 186 (1962)

This case presents the classic modern example of the difference between the activist and anti-activist outlooks. The Court repeatedly had refused to decide whether, and how, legislative seats should be reapportioned. Where, in the face of numerous conflicting theories of political representation, are to be found constitutional criteria for judgment? If a choice were made, what mode of judicial relief would be available? Should a Court venture so deeply into a "political thicket" traditionally reserved for the political processes? In *Baker* v. *Carr*, only the latter question was answered. But the

answer seemed to mean that the two others would have to be faced
—eventually.

Mr. Justice Brennan delivered the opinion of the Court.

This civil action was brought under 42 U.S.C. §§ 1983 and
1988 to redress the alleged deprivation of federal constitutional
rights. The complaint, alleging that by means of a 1901 statute
of Tennessee apportioning the members of the General Assembly among the State's 95 counties, "these plaintiffs and
others similarly situated, are denied the equal protection of
the laws accorded them by the Fourteenth Amendment to the
Constitution of the United States by virtue of the debasement
of their votes," was dismissed by a three-judge court convened
under 28 U.S.C. § 2281 in the Middle District of Tennessee.
The court held that it lacked jurisdiction of the subject matter
and also that no claim was stated upon which relief could be
granted. 179 F. Supp. 824. . . . We hold that the dismissal was
error, and remand the cause to the District Court for trial and
further proceedings consistent with this opinion.

The General Assembly of Tennessee consists of the Senate
with 33 members and the House of Representatives with 99
members. . . . Tennessee's standard for allocating legislative
representation among her counties is the total number of
qualified voters resident in the respective counties, subject only
to minor qualifications. Decennial reapportionment in compliance with the constitutional scheme was effected by the
General Assembly each decade from 1871 to 1901. . . . In 1901
the General Assembly . . . passed the Apportionment Act here
in controversy. In the more than 60 years since that action, all
proposals in both Houses of the General Assembly for reapportionment have failed to pass.

Between 1901 and 1961, Tennessee has experienced substantial growth and redistribution of her population. In 1901 the
population was 2,020,616, of whom 487,380 were eligible to
vote. The 1960 Federal Census reports the State's population

at 3,567,089, of whom 2,092,891 are eligible to vote. The relative standings of the counties in terms of qualified voters have changed significantly. It is primarily the continued application of the 1901 Apportionment Act to this shifted and enlarged voting population which gives rise to the present controversy.

. . . It is alleged that "because of the population changes since 1900, and the failure of the legislature to reapportion itself since 1901," the 1901 statute became "unconstitutional and obsolete." Appellants also argue that, because of the composition of the legislature effected by the 1901 apportionment act, redress in the form of a state constitutional amendment to change the entire mechanism for reapportioning, or any other change short of that, is difficult or impossible. The complaint concludes that "these plaintiffs and others similarly situated, are denied the equal protection of the laws accorded them by the Fourteenth Amendment to the Constitution of the United States by virtue of the debasement of their votes." They seek a declaration that the 1901 statute is unconstitutional and an injunction restraining the appellees from acting to conduct any further elections under it. They also pray that unless and until the General Assembly enacts a valid reapportionment, the District Court should either decree a reapportionment by mathematical application of the Tennessee constitutional formulae to the most recent Federal Census figures, or direct the appellees to conduct legislative elections, primary and general, at large. . . .

The District Court's Opinion and Order of Dismissal.

Because we deal with this case on appeal from an order of dismissal granted on appellees' motions, precise identification of the issues presently confronting us demands clear exposition of the grounds upon which the District Court rested in dismissing the case. . . .

The District Court's dismissal order . . . rested . . . upon lack of subject-matter jurisdiction and lack of a justiciable cause of action without attempting to distinguish between these grounds. . . . The court proceeded to explain its action as turning on the case's presenting a "question of the distribution of political strength for legislative purposes." For,

> "from a review of [numerous Supreme Court] . . . decisions there can be no doubt that the federal rule, as enunciated and applied by the Supreme Court, is that the federal courts, whether from a lack of jurisdiction or from the inappropriateness of the subject matter for judicial consideration, will not intervene in cases of this type to compel legislative reapportionment." . . .

The court went on to express doubts as to the feasibility of the various possible remedies sought by the plaintiffs. . . . Then it made clear that its dismissal reflected a view not of doubt that violation of constitutional rights was alleged, but of a court's impotence to correct that violation:

> "With the plaintiffs' argument that the legislature of Tennessee is guilty of a clear violation of the state constitution and of the rights of the plaintiffs the Court entirely agrees. It also agrees that the evil is a serious one which should be corrected without further delay. But even so the remedy in this situation clearly does not lie with the courts. It has long been recognized and is accepted doctrine that there are indeed some rights guaranteed by the Constitution for the violation of which the courts cannot give redress." . . .

In light of the District Court's treatment of the case, we hold today only (a) that the court possessed jurisdiction of the subject matter; (b) that a justiciable cause of action is stated upon which appellants would be entitled to appropriate relief; and (c) because appellees raise the issue before this Court, that the appellants have standing to challenge the Tennessee apportionment statutes. Beyond noting that we have no cause at this stage to doubt the District Court will be able to fashion relief if violations of constitutional rights are found, it is improper now to consider what remedy would be most appropriate if appellants prevail at the trial.

JURISDICTION OF THE SUBJECT MATTER.

The District Court was uncertain whether our cases withholding federal judicial relief rested upon a lack of federal jurisdiction or upon the inappropriateness of the subject matter for judicial consideration—what we have designated "nonjusticiability." The distinction between the two grounds is significant. In the instance of nonjusticiability, consideration of the cause is not wholly and immediately foreclosed; rather, the Court's inquiry necessarily proceeds to the point of deciding whether the duty asserted can be judicially identified and its breach judicially determined, and whether protection for the right asserted can be judicially molded. In the instance of lack of jurisdiction the cause either does not "arise under" the Federal Constitution, laws or treaties (or fall within one of the other enumerated categories of Art. III, § 2), or is not a "case or controversy" within the meaning of that section; or the cause is not one described by any jurisdictional statute. . . .

An unbroken line of our precedents sustains the federal courts' jurisdiction of the subject matter of federal constitutional claims of this nature. The first cases involved the redistricting of States for the purpose of electing Representatives to the Federal Congress. . . . When the Minnesota Supreme Court affirmed the dismissal of a suit to enjoin the Secretary of State of Minnesota from acting under Minnesota redistricting legislation, we reviewed the constitutional merits of the legislation and reversed the State Supreme Court. *Smiley* v. *Holm,* 285 U.S. 355. . . . When a three-judge District Court . . . permanently enjoined officers of the State of Mississippi from conducting an election of Representatives under a Mississippi redistricting act, we reviewed the federal questions on the merits and reversed the District Court. *Wood* v. *Broom*, 287 U.S. 1. . . .

The appellees refer to *Colegrove* v. *Green*, 328 U.S. 549, as authority that the District Court lacked jurisdiction of the subject matter. Appellees misconceive the holding of that case. The holding was precisely contrary to their reading of it. Seven members of the Court participated in the decision. Unlike many other cases in this field which have assumed without discussion that there was jurisdiction, all three opinions filed in *Colegrove* discussed the question. Two of the opinions expressing the views of four of the Justices, a majority, flatly held that there was jurisdiction of the subject matter. MR. JUSTICE BLACK joined by MR. JUSTICE DOUGLAS and MR. JUSTICE MURPHY stated: "It is my judgment that the District Court had jurisdiction. . . ." MR. JUSTICE RUTLEDGE, writing separately, expressed agreement with this conclusion. . . . Indeed, it is even questionable that the opinion of MR. JUSTICE FRANKFURTER, joined by JUSTICES REED and BURTON, doubted jurisdiction of the subject matter. . . .

Several subsequent cases similar to *Colegrove* have been decided by the Court in summary *per curiam* statements. None was dismissed for want of jurisdiction of the subject matter. . . .

Two cases decided with opinions after *Colegrove* likewise plainly imply that the subject matter of this suit is within District Court jurisdiction. In *MacDougall* v. *Green*, 335 U.S. 281, the District Court dismissed for want of jurisdiction . . . a suit to enjoin enforcement of the requirement that nominees for state-wide elections be supported by a petition signed by a minimum number of persons from at least 50 of the State's 102 counties. This Court's disagreement with that action is clear since the Court affirmed the judgment after a review of the merits and concluded that the particular claim there was without merit. In *South* v. *Peters*, 339 U.S. 276, we affirmed the dismissal of an attack on the Georgia "county unit" system but founded our action on a ground that plainly would not have been reached if the lower court lacked jurisdiction of the subject matter. . . . The express words of our holding were that "federal courts consistently refuse to exercise their equity powers in cases posing political issues arising from a state's geographical distribution of electoral strength among its political subdivisions." 339 U.S., at 277.

We hold that the District Court has jurisdiction of the subject matter of the federal constitutional claim asserted in the complaint. . . .

STANDING.

A federal court cannot "pronounce any statute, either of a state or of the United States, void, because irreconcilable with the constitution, except as it is called upon to adjudge the legal rights of litigants in actual controversies." Liverpool, N. Y. & P. Steamship Co. v. Commissioners of Emigration, 113 U.S. 33, 39. Have the appellants alleged such a personal stake in the outcome of the controversy so as to assure that concrete adverseness which sharpens the presentation of issues upon which the court so largely depends for illumination of difficult constitutional questions? This is the gist of the question of standing. It is, of course, a question of federal law.

The complaint was filed by residents of Davidson, Hamilton, Knox, Montgomery, and Shelby Counties. Each is a person allegedly qualified to vote for members of the General Assembly representing his county. These appellants sued "on their own behalf and on behalf of all qualified voters of their respective counties, and further, on behalf of all voters of the State of Tennessee who are similarly situated. . . ." The appellees are the Tennessee Secretary of State, Attorney General, Coordinator of Elections, and members of the State Board of Elections; the members of the State Board are sued in their own right and also as representatives of the County Election Commissioners whom they appoint.

We hold that the appellants do have standing to maintain this suit. Our decisions plainly support this conclusion. Many of the cases have assumed rather than articulated the premise in deciding the merits of similar claims. And Colegrove v. Green, supra, squarely held that voters who allege facts showing disadvantage to themselves as individuals have standing to sue. . . .

The injury which appellants assert is that [the 1901] classification disfavors the voters in the counties in which they reside, placing them in a position of constitutionally unjustifiable inequality *vis-à-vis* voters in irrationally favored counties. A citizen's right to a vote free of arbitrary impairment by state action has been judicially recognized as a right secured by the Constitution, when such impairment resulted from dilution by a false tally; . . . or by a refusal to count votes from arbitrarily selected precincts; . . . or by a stuffing of the ballot box. . . .

They are asserting "a plain, direct and adequate interest in maintaining the effectiveness of their votes," Coleman v. Miller, 307 U.S. at 438, 59 S.Ct. at p. 975 not merely a claim of "the right possessed by every citizen 'to require that the government be administered according to law . . .' ." Fairchild v. Hughes, 258 U.S. 126, 129. . . .

JUSTICIABILITY.

In holding that the subject matter of this suit was not justiciable, the District Court relied on *Colegrove* v. *Green, supra,* and subsequent *per curiam* cases. . . . We understand the District Court to have read the cited cases as compelling the conclusion that since the appellants sought to have a legislative apportionment held unconstitutional, their suit presented a "political question" and was therefore nonjusticiable. We hold that this challenge to an apportionment presents no nonjusticiable "political question." The cited cases do not hold the contrary.

Of course the mere fact that the suit seeks protection of a

political right does not mean it presents a political question. Such an objection "is little more than a play upon words." . . . Rather, it is argued that apportionment cases, whatever the actual wording of the complaint, can involve no federal constitutional right except one resting on the guaranty of a republican form of government, and that complaints based on that clause have been held to present political questions which are nonjusticiable.

We hold that the claim pleaded here neither rests upon nor implicates the Guaranty Clause and that its justiciability is therefore not foreclosed by our decisions of cases involving that clause. The District Court misinterpreted *Colegrove* v. *Green* and other decisions of this Court on which it relied. Appellants' claim that they are being denied equal protection is justiciable, and if "discrimination is sufficiently shown, the right to relief under the equal protection clause is not diminished by the fact that the discrimination relates to political rights." *Snowden* v. *Hughes*, 321 U.S. 1, 11. To show why we reject the argument based on the Guaranty Clause . . . we deem it necessary first to consider the contours of the "political question" doctrine.

Our discussion . . . requires review of a number of political question cases, in order to expose the attributes of the doctrine. . . . That review reveals that in the Guaranty Clause cases and in the other "political question" cases, it is the relationship between the judiciary and the coordinate branches of the Federal Government, and not the federal judiciary's relationship to the States, which gives rise to the "political question." . . .

The nonjusticiability of a political question is primarily a function of the separation of powers. . . . Prominent on the surface of any case held to involve a political question is found a textually demonstrable constitutional commitment of the issue to a coordinate political department; or a lack of judicially discoverable and manageable standards for resolving it; or the impossibility of deciding without an initial policy determination of a kind clearly for nonjudicial discretion; or the impossibility of a court's undertaking independent resolution without expressing lack of the respect due coordinate branches of government; or an unusual need for unquestioning adherence to a political decision already made; or the potentiality of embarrassment from multifarious pronouncements by various departments on one question.

Unless one of these formulations is inextricable from the case at bar, there should be no dismissal for nonjusticiability on the ground of a political question's presence. The doctrine of which we treat is one of "political questions," not one of "political cases." The courts cannot reject as "no law suit" a bona fide controversy as to whether some action denominated "political" exceeds constitutional authority. . . .

But it is argued that this case shares the characteristics of decisions that constitute a category not yet considered, cases concerning the Constitution's guaranty, in Art. IV, § 4, of a republican form of government. . . .

[The Court discusses *Luther* v. *Borden,* 7 How. 1 (1849), and other cases holding the republican guaranty provision judicially unenforceable.]

We conclude that the nonjusticiability of claims resting on the Guaranty Clause which arises from their embodiment of questions that were thought "political," can have no bearing upon the justiciability of the equal protection claim presented in this case. . . . We emphasize that it is the involvement in Guaranty Clause claims of the elements thought to define "political questions," and no other feature, which could render them nonjusticiable. Specifically, we have said that such claims are not held nonjusticiable because they touch matters of state governmental organization. . . . Only last Term, in *Gomillion* v. *Lightfoot,* 364 U.S. 339, we applied the Fifteenth Amendment to strike down a redrafting of municipal boundaries which effected a discriminatory impairment of voting rights, in the face of what a majority of the Court of Appeals thought to be a sweeping commitment to state legislatures of the power to draw and redraw such boundaries. . . .

We conclude that the complaint's allegations of a denial of

equal protection present a justiciable constitutional cause of action upon which appellants are entitled to a trial and a decision. The right asserted is within the reach of judicial protection under the Fourteenth Amendment.

The judgment of the District Court is reversed and the cause is remanded for further proceedings consistent with this opinion.

Reversed and remanded.

Mr. Justice Whittaker did not participate in the decision of this case.

Mr. Justice Douglas, concurring.

While I join the opinion of the Court and, like the Court, do not reach the merits, a word of explanation is necessary. I put to one side the problems of "political" questions involving the distribution of power between this Court, the Congress, and the Chief Executive. We have here a phase of the recurring problem of the relation of the federal courts to state agencies. More particularly, the question is the extent to which a State may weight one person's vote more heavily than it does another's. . . .

The traditional test under the Equal Protection Clause has been whether a State has made "an invidious discrimination," as it does when it selects "a particular race or nationality for oppressive treatment." See *Skinner* v. *Oklahoma,* 316 U.S. 535, 541. Universal equality is not the test; there is room for weighting. As we stated in *Williamson* v. *Lee Optical Co.,* 348 U.S. 483, 489, "The prohibition of the Equal Protection Clause goes no further than the invidious discrimination."

I agree with my Brother Clark that if the allegations in the complaint can be sustained a case for relief is established. We are told that a single vote in Moore County, Tennessee, is worth 19 votes in Hamilton County, that one vote in Stewart or in Chester County is worth nearly eight times a single vote in Shelby or Knox County. The opportunity to prove that an "invidious discrimination" exists should therefore be given the appellants. . . .

With the exceptions of *Colegrove* v. *Green*, 328 U.S. 549; *MacDougall* v. *Green*, 335 U.S. 281; *South* v. *Peters*, 339 U.S. 276, and the decisions they spawned, the Court has never thought that protection of voting rights was beyond judicial cognizance. Today's treatment of those cases removes the only impediment to judicial cognizance of the claims stated in the present complaint.

The justiciability of the present claims being established, any relief accorded can be fashioned in the light of well-known principles of equity.

MR. JUSTICE CLARK, concurring. . . .

I believe it can be shown that this case is distinguishable from earlier cases dealing with the distribution of political power by a State, that a patent violation of the Equal Protection Clause of the United States Constitution has been shown, and that an appropriate remedy may be formulated.

I.

I take the law of the case from *MacDougall* v. *Green*, 335 U.S. 281 (1948), which involved an attack under the Equal Protection Clause upon an Illinois election statute. The Court decided that case on its merits without hindrance from the "political question" doctrine. Although the statute under attack was upheld, it is clear that the Court based its decision upon the determination that the statute represented a rational state policy. It stated:

"It would be strange indeed, and doctrinaire, for this Court, applying such broad constitutional concepts as due process and equal protection of the laws, to deny a State the power to assure a *proper* diffusion of political initiative as between its thinly populated counties and those having concentrated masses, *in view of the fact that the latter have practical opportunities for exerting their political weight at the polls not available to the former.*" Id., at 284. (Emphasis supplied.)

The other cases upon which my Brethren dwell are all distinguishable or inapposite. The widely heralded case of *Colegrove* v. *Green* . . . was one not only in which the Court was bob-tailed but in which there was no majority opinion. Indeed, even the "political question" point in MR. JUSTICE FRANKFURTER's opinion was no more than an alternative ground. Moreover, the appellants did not present an equal protection argument. While it has served as a Mother Hubbard to most of the subsequent cases, I feel it was in that respect ill-cast and for all of these reasons put it to one side. Likewise, I do not consider the Guaranty Clause cases based on Art. I, § 4, of the Constitution, because it is not invoked here and it involves different criteria, as the Court's opinion indicates. . . . Finally, the Georgia county unit system cases, such as *South* v. *Peters* . . . reflect the viewpoint of *MacDougall*, i. e., to refrain from intervening where there is some rational policy behind the State's system.

II.

The controlling facts cannot be disputed. It appears from the record that 37% of the voters of Tennessee elect 20 of the 33 Senators while 40% of the voters elect 63 of the 99 members of the House. But this might not on its face be an "invidious discrimination," . . . for a "statutory discrimination will not be set aside if any state of facts reasonably may be conceived to justify it." *McGowan* v. *Maryland*, 366 U.S. 420, 426 (1961).

It is true that the apportionment policy incorporated in Tennessee's Constitution, i. e., state-wide numerical equality of representation with certain minor qualifications, is a rational one. . . . However, the root of the trouble is not in Tennessee's Constitution, for admittedly its policy has not been followed.

The discrimination lies in the action of Tennessee's Assembly in allocating legislative seats to counties or districts created by it. Try as one may, Tennessee's apportionment just cannot be made to fit the pattern cut by its Constitution. This was the finding of the District Court. The policy of the Constitution referred to by the dissenters, therefore, is of no relevance here. We must examine what the Assembly has done. The frequency and magnitude of the inequalities in the present districting admit of no policy whatever. . . . The apportionment picture in Tennessee is a topsy-turvical of gigantic proportion. . . . Tennessee's apportionment is a crazy quilt without rational basis. . . .

No one contends that mathematical equality among voters is required by the Equal Protection Clause. But certainly there must be some rational design to a State's districting. The discrimination here does not fit any pattern. . . . My Brother HARLAN contends that other proposed apportionment plans contain disparities. Instead of chasing those rabbits he should first pause long enough to meet appellants' proof of discrimination by showing that in fact the present plan follows a rational policy. Not being able to do this, he merely counters with such generalities as "classic legislative judgment," no "significant discrepancy," and "de minimis departures." I submit that even a casual glance at the present apportionment picture shows these conclusions to be entirely fanciful. If present representation has a policy at all, it is to maintain the *status quo* of invidious discrimination at any cost. . . .

III.

Although I find the Tennessee apportionment statute offends the Equal Protection Clause, I would not consider intervention by this Court into so delicate a field if there were any other relief available to the people of Tennessee. But the majority of the people of Tennessee have no "practical opportunities of exerting their political weight at the polls" to correct the existing "invidious discrimination." Tennessee has no initiative and referendum. I have searched diligently for other "practical opportunities" present under the law. I find none other than through the federal courts. The majority of the voters have been caught up in a legislative strait jacket. Tennessee has an "informed, civically militant electorate" and "an aroused popular conscience," but it does not sear "the conscience of the people's representatives." This is because the legislative policy has riveted the present seats in the Assembly to their respective constituencies, and by the votes of their incumbents a reapportionment of any kind is prevented. The people have been rebuffed at the hands of the Assembly; they have tried the constitutional convention route, but since the call must originate in the Assembly it, too, has been fruitless. They have tried Tennessee courts with the same result, and Governors have fought the tide only to flounder. It is said that there is recourse in Congress and perhaps that may be, but from a practical standpoint this is without substance. To date Congress has never undertaken such a task in any State. We therefore must conclude that the people of Tennessee are stymied and without judicial intervention will be saddled with the present discrimination in the affairs of their state government.

IV.

Finally, we must consider if there are any appropriate modes of effective judicial relief. The federal courts are, of course, not forums for political debate, nor should they resolve themselves into state constitutional conventions or legislative assemblies. Nor should their jurisdiction be exercised in the hope that such a declaration, as is made today, may have the direct effect of bringing on legislative action and relieving the courts of the problem of fashioning relief. To my mind this would be nothing less than blackjacking the Assembly into reapportioning the State. If judicial competence were lacking to fashion an effective decree, I would dismiss this appeal. However . . . I see no such difficulty in the position of this case. One plan might be to start with the existing assembly districts, consolidate some of them, and award the seats thus released to those counties suffering the most egregious discrimination. Other possibilities are present and might be more effective. But the plan here suggested would at least release the strangle hold now on the Assembly and permit it to redistrict itself. . . .

MR. JUSTICE STEWART, concurring.

The separate writings of my dissenting and concurring Brothers stray so far from the subject of today's decision as to convey, I think, a distressingly inaccurate impression of what the Court decides. For that reason, I think it appropriate, in joining the opinion of the Court, to emphasize in a few words what the opinion does and does not say. . . .

The complaint in this case asserts that Tennessee's system of apportionment is utterly arbitrary—without any possible justification in rationality. The District Court did not reach the merits of that claim, and this Court quite properly expresses no view on the subject. Contrary to the suggestion of my Brother HARLAN, the Court does not say or imply that "state legislatures must be so structured as to reflect with approximate equality the voice of every voter." . . . The Court does not say or imply that there is anything in the Federal Constitution "to prevent a State, acting not irrationally, from choosing any electoral legislative structure it thinks best suited to the interests, temper, and customs of its people." . . . And contrary to the suggestion of my Brother DOUGLAS, the Court most assuredly does not decide the question, "may a State weight the vote of one county or one district more heavily than it weights the vote in another?" . . .

My Brother CLARK has made a convincing prima facie showing that Tennessee's system of apportionment is in fact utterly arbitrary—without any possible justification in rationality. My Brother HARLAN has, with imagination and ingenuity, hypothesized possibly rational bases for Tennessee's system. But the merits of this case are not before us now. The defendants have not yet had an opportunity to be heard in defense of the State's system of apportionment; indeed, they have not yet even filed an answer to the complaint. As in other cases, the proper place for the trial is in the trial court, not here.

MR. JUSTICE FRANKFURTER, whom MR. JUSTICE HARLAN joins, dissenting.

The Court today reverses a uniform course of decision established by a dozen cases, including one by which the very claim now sustained was unanimously rejected only five years ago. The impressive body of rulings thus cast aside reflected the equally uniform course of our political history regarding the relationship between population and legislative representation—a wholly different matter from denial of the franchise to individuals because of race, color, religion or sex. Such a massive repudiation of the experience of our whole past in asserting destructively novel judicial power demands a detailed analysis of the role of this Court in our constitutional scheme. Disregard of inherent limits in the effective exercise of the Court's "judicial Power" not only presages the futility of judicial intervention in the essentially political conflict of forces by which the relation between population and representation has time out of mind been and now is determined. It may well impair the Court's position as the ultimate organ of "the supreme Law of the Land" in that vast range of legal problems, often strongly entangled in popular feeling, on which this Court must pronounce. The Court's authority—possessed neither of the purse nor the sword—ultimately rests on sustained public confidence in its moral sanction. Such feeling must be nourished by the Court's complete detachment, in fact and in appearance, from political entanglements and by abstention from injecting itself into the clash of political forces in political settlements.

A hypothetical claim resting on abstract assumptions is now for the first time made the basis for affording illusory relief for a particular evil even though it foreshadows deeper and more pervasive difficulties in consequence. The claim is hypothetical and the assumptions are abstract because the Court does not vouchsafe the lower courts—state and federal—guide-lines for formulating specific, definite, wholly unprecented remedies for the inevitable litigations that today's umbrageous disposition is bound to stimulate in connection with politically motivated reapportionments in so many States. In such a setting, to promulgate jurisdiction in the abstract is meaningless. It is as devoid of reality as "a brooding omnipresence in the sky" for it conveys no intimation what relief, if any, a District Court is capable of affording that would not invite legislatures to play ducks and drakes with the judiciary. For this Court to direct the District Court to enforce a claim to which the Court has over the years consistently found itself required to deny legal enforcement and at the same time to find it necessary to withhold any guidance to the lower court how to enforce this turnabout, new legal claim, manifests an odd—indeed an esoteric—conception of judicial propriety. One of the Court's supporting opinions, as elucidated by commentary, unwittingly affords a disheartening preview of the mathematical quagmire (apart from divers judicially inappropriate and elusive determinants), into which this Court today catapults the lower courts of the country without so much as adumbrating the basis for a legal calculus as a means of extrication. Even assuming the indispensable intellectual disinterestedness on the part of judges in such matters, they do not have accepted legal standards or criteria or even reliable analogies to draw upon for making judicial judgments. To charge courts with the task of accommodating the incommensurable factors of policy that underlie these mathematical puzzles is to attribute, however flatteringly, omnicompetence to judges. The Framers of the Constitution persistently rejected a proposal that embodied this assumption and Thomas Jefferson never entertained it.

Recently legislation, creating a district appropriately described as "an atrocity of ingenuity," is not unique. Considering the gross inequality among legislative electoral units within almost every State, the Court naturally shrinks from asserting that in districting at least substantial equality is a constitutional requirement, enforceable by courts. Room continues to be allowed for weighting. This of course implies that geography, economics, urban-rural conflict, and all the other non-legal factors which have throughout history entered into political districting are to some extent not to be ruled out in the undefined vista now opened up by review in the federal courts of state reapportionments. To some extent—aye, there's the rub. In effect, today's decision empowers the courts of the country to devise what should constitute the proper composition of the legislatures of the fifty States. If state courts should for one reason or another find themselves unable to discharge this task, the duty of doing so is put on the federal courts or on this Court, if State views do not satisfy this Court's notion of what is proper districting.

We were soothingly told at the bar of this Court that we need not worry about the kind of remedy a court could effectively fashion once the abstract constitutional right to have courts pass on a state-wide system of electoral districting is recognized as a matter of judicial rhetoric, because legislatures would heed the Court's admonition. This is not only an euphoric hope. It implies a sorry confession of judicial impotence in place of a frank acknowledgment that there is not under our Constitution a judicial remedy for every political mischief, for every undesirable exercise of legislative power. The Framers carefully and with deliberate forethought refused so to enthrone the judiciary. In this situation, as in others of like nature, appeal for relief does not belong here. Appeal must be to an informed, civically militant electorate. In a democratic society like ours, relief must come through an aroused popular conscience that sears the conscience of the people's representatives. In any event there is nothing judi-

cially more unseemly nor more self-defeating than for this
Court to make *in terrorem* pronouncements, to indulge in
merely empty rhetoric, sounding a word of promise to the
ear, sure to be disappointing to the hope. . . .

I.

In sustaining appellants' claim, based on the Fourteenth
Amendment, that the District Court may entertain this suit,
this Court's uniform course of decision over the years are
overruled or disregarded. Explicitly it begins with Colegrove
v. Green, supra, decided in 1946, but its roots run deep in
the Court's historic adjudicatory process.

. . . Both opinions joining in the result in Colegrove v. Green
agreed that considerations were controlling which dictated
denial of jurisdiction though not in the strict sense of want of
power. While the two opinions show a divergence of view
regarding some of these considerations, there are important
points of concurrence. Both opinions demonstrate a predominant concern, first, with avoiding federal judicial involvement
in matters traditionally left to legislative policymaking; second,
with respect to the difficulty—in view of the nature of the
problems of apportionment and its history in this country—of
drawing on or devising judicial standards for judgment, as
opposed to legislative determinations, of the part which mere
numerical equality among voters should play as a criterion for
the allocation of political power; and, third, with problems
of finding appropriate modes of relief—particularly, the problem of resolving the essentially political issue of the relative
merits of at-large elections and elections held in districts of
unequal population.

The broad applicability of these considerations—summarized in the loose shorthand phrase, "political question"—in
cases involving a State's apportionment of voting power among
its numerous localities has led the Court, since 1946, to recognize their controlling effect in a variety of situations. . . .

II.

The Colegrove doctrine, in the form in which repeated decisions have settled it, was not an innovation. It represents long judicial thought and experience. From its earliest opinions this Court has consistently recognized a class of controversies which do not lend themselves to judicial standards and judicial remedies. To classify the various instances as "political questions" is rather a form of stating this conclusion than revealing of analysis. Some of the cases so labelled have no relevance here. But from others emerge unifying considerations that are compelling. . . .

The influence of these converging considerations—the caution not to undertake decision where standards meet for judicial judgment are lacking, the reluctance to interfere with matters of state government in the absence of an unquestionable and effectively enforceable mandate, the unwillingness to make courts arbiters of the broad issues of political organization historically committed to other institutions and for whose adjustment the judicial process is ill-adapted—has been decisive of the settled line of cases, reaching back more than a century, which holds that Art. IV, § 4, of the Constitution, guaranteeing to the States "a Republican Form of Government," is not enforceable through the courts. . . .

III.

The present case involves all of the elements that have made the Guarantee Clause cases non-justiciable. It is, in effect, a Guarantee Clause claim masquerading under a different label. But it cannot make the case more fit for judicial action that appellants invoke the Fourteenth Amendment rather than Art. IV, § 4, where, in fact, the gist of their complaint is the same— unless it can be found that the Fourteenth Amendment speaks with greater particularity to their situation. . . .

What, then, is this question of legislative apportionment?

Appellants invoke the right to vote and to have their votes counted. But they are permitted to vote and their votes are counted. They go to the polls, they cast their ballots, they send their representatives to the state councils. Their complaint is simply that the representatives are not sufficiently numerous or powerful—in short, that Tennessee has adopted a basis of representation with which they are dissatisfied. Talk of "debasement" or "dilution" is circular talk. One cannot speak of "debasement" or "dilution" of the value of a vote until there is first defined a standard of reference as to what a vote should be worth. What is actually asked of the Court in this case is to choose among competing bases of representation—ultimately, really, among competing theories of political philosophy—in order to establish an appropriate frame of government for the State of Tennessee and thereby for all the States of the Union.

In such a matter, abstract analogies which ignore the facts of history deal in unrealities; they betray reason. This is not a case in which a State has, through a device however oblique and sophisticated, denied Negroes or Jews or redheaded persons a vote, or given them only a third or a sixth of a vote. That was Gomillion v. Lightfoot, 364 U.S. 339. What Tennessee illustrates is an old and still widespread method of representation—representation by local geographical division, only in part respective of population—in preference to others, others, forsooth, more appealing. Appellants contest this choice and seek to make this Court the arbiter of the disagreement. They would make the Equal Protection Clause the character of adjudication, asserting that the equality which it guarantees comports, if not the assurance of equal weight to every voter's vote, at least the basic conception that representation ought to be proportionate to population, a standard by reference to which the reasonableness of apportionment plans may be judged.

To find such a political conception legally enforceable in

the broad and unspecific guarantee of equal protection is to rewrite the Constitution. See Luther v. Borden, supra. Certainly, "equal protection" is no more secure a foundation for judicial judgment of the permissibility of varying forms of representative government than is "Republican Form." Indeed since "equal protection of the laws" can only mean an equality of persons standing in the same relation to whatever governmental action is challenged, the determination whether treatment is equal presupposes a determination concerning the nature of the relationship. This, with respect to apportionment, means an inquiry into the theoretic base of representation in an acceptably republican state. For a court could not determine the equal-protection issue without in fact first determining the Republican-Form issue, simply because what is reasonable for equal protection purposes will depend upon what frame of government, basically, is allowed. To divorce "equal protection" from "Republican Form" is to talk about half a question.

The notion that representation proportioned to the geographic spread of population is so universally accepted as a necessary element of equality between man and man that it must be taken to be the standard of a political equality preserved by the Fourteenth Amendment—that it is, in appellants' words "the basic principle of representative government" —is, to put it bluntly, not true. However desirable and however desired by some among the great political thinkers and framers of our government, it has never been generally practiced, today or in the past. It was not the English system, it was not the colonial system, it was not the system chosen for the national government by the Constitution, it was not the system exclusively or even predominantly practiced by the States at the time of adoption of the Fourteenth Amendment, it is not predominantly practiced by the States today. Unless judges, the judges of this Court, are to make their private views of political wisdom the measure of the Constitution— views which in all honesty cannot but give the appearance, if not reflect the reality, of involvement with the business of partisan politics so inescapably a part of apportionment controversies—the Fourteenth Amendment, "itself a historical product," . . . provides no guide for judicial oversight of the representation problem. . . .

The stark fact is that if among the numerous widely varying principles and practices that control state legislative apportionment today there is any generally prevailing feature, that feature is geographic inequality in relation to the population standard. . . .

Manifestly, the Equal Protection Clause supplies no clearer guide for judicial examination of apportionment methods than would the Guarantee Clause itself. Apportionment, by its character, is a subject of extraordinary complexity, involving— even after the fundamental theoretical issues concerning what is to be represented in a representative legislature have been fought out or compromised—considerations of geography, demography, electoral convenience, economic and social cohesions or divergencies among particular local groups, communications, the practical effects of political institutions like the lobby and the city machine, ancient traditions and ties of settled usage, respect for proven incumbents of long experience and senior status, mathematical mechanics, censuses compiling relevant data, and a host of others. . . .

IV.

Appellants, however, contend that the federal courts may provide the standard which the Fourteenth Amendment lacks by reference to the provisions of the constitution of Tennessee. . . .

This reasoning does not bear analysis. Like claims invoking state constitutional requirement have been rejected here and for good reason. It is settled that whatever federal consequences may derive from a discrimination worked by a state statute must be the same as if the same discrimination were written into the State's fundamental law. Nashville, C. & St. L. R. Co. v. Browning, 310 U.S. 362. . . .

. . . In all of the apportionment cases which have come before the Court, a consideration which has been weighty in determining their non-justiciability has been the difficulty or impossibility of devising effective judicial remedies in this class of case. . . .

Although the District Court had jurisdiction in the very restricted sense of power to determine whether it could adjudicate the claim, the case is of that class of political controversy which, by the nature of its subject, is unfit for federal judicial action. The judgment of the District Court, in dismissing the complaint for failure to state a claim on which relief can be granted, should therefore be affirmed.

Dissenting opinion of MR. JUSTICE HARLAN, whom MR. JUSTICE FRANKFURTER joins.

The dissenting opinion of MR. JUSTICE FRANKFURTER, in which I join, demonstrates the abrupt departure the majority makes from judicial history by putting the federal courts into this area of state concerns—an area which, in this instance, the Tennessee state courts themselves have refused to enter.

It does not detract from his opinion to say that the panorama of judicial history it unfolds, though evincing a steadfast underlying principle of keeping the federal courts out of these domains, has a tendency, because of variants in expression, to becloud analysis in a given case. With due respect to the majority, I think that has happened here.

Once one cuts through the thicket of discussion devoted to "jurisdiction," "standing," "justiciability," and "political question," there emerges a straightforward issue which, in my view, is determinative of this case. Does the complaint disclose a violation of a federal constitutional right, in other words, a claim over which a United States District Court would have jurisdiction under 28 U.S.C. § 1343(3) and 42 U.S.C. § 1983?

The majority opinion does not actually discuss this basic question, but, as one concurring Justice observes, seems to decide it *"sub silentio."* . . . However, in my opinion, appellants' allegations, accepting all of them as true, do not, parsed down or as a whole, show an infringement by Tennessee of any rights assured by the Fourteenth Amendment. Accordingly, I believe the complaint should have been dismissed for "failure to state a claim upon which relief can be granted." Fed.Rules Civ.Proc. rule 12(b)(6), 28 U.S.C.A.

It is at once essential to recognize this case for what it is. The issue here relates not to a method of state electoral apportionment by which seats in the *federal* House of Representatives are allocated, but solely to the right of a State to fix the basis of representation in its *own* legislature. Until it is first decided to what extent that right is limited by the Federal Constitution, and whether what Tennessee has done or failed to do in this instance runs afoul of any such limitation, we need not reach the issues of "justiciability" or "political question" or any of the other considerations which in such cases as Colegrove v. Green, 328 U.S. 549, led the Court to decline to adjudicate a challenge to a state apportionment affecting seats in the federal House of Representatives, in the absence of a controlling Act of Congress. . . .

I can find nothing in the Equal Protection Clause or elsewhere in the Federal Constitution which expressly or impliedly supports the view that state legislatures must be so structured as to reflect with approximate equality the voice of every voter. Not only is that proposition refuted by history, as shown by my brother FRANKFURTER, but it strikes deep into the heart of our federal system. Its acceptance would require us to turn our backs on the regard which this Court has always shown for the judgment of state legislatures and courts on matters of basically local concern.

In the last analysis, what lies at the core of this controversy is a difference of opinion as to the function of representative

government. It is surely beyond argument that those who have
the responsibility for devising a system of representation may
permissibly consider that factors other than bare numbers
should be taken into account. The existence of the United
States Senate is proof enough of that. To consider that we may
ignore the Tennessee Legislature's judgment in this instance
because that body was the product of an asymmetrical electoral apportionment would in effect be to assume the very
conclusion here disputed. Hence we must accept the present
form of the Tennessee Legislature as the embodiment of the
State's choice, or, more realistically, its compromise, between
competing political philosophies. The federal courts have not
been empowered by the Equal Protection Clause to judge
whether this resolution of the State's internal political conflict is desirable or undesirable, wise or unwise. . . .

In short, there is nothing in the Federal Constitution to
prevent a State, acting not irrationally, from choosing any
electoral legislative structure it thinks best suited to the interests, temper, and customs of its people. I would have thought
this proposition settled by MacDougall v. Green, 335 U.S.
281, at p. 283, in which the Court observed that to "assume
that political power is a function exclusively of numbers is to
disregard the practicalities of government," and reaffirmed by
South v. Peters, 339 U.S. 276. A State's choice to distribute
electoral strength among geographical units, rather than according to a census of population, is certainly no less a rational
decision of policy than would be its choice to levy a tax on
property rather than a tax on income. . . .

The claim that Tennessee's system of apportionment is so
unreasonable as to amount to a capricious classification of
voting strength stands up no better under dispassionate
analysis. . . .

A Federal District Court is asked to say that the passage of
time has rendered the 1901 apportionment obsolete to the

point where its continuance becomes vulnerable under the Fourteenth Amendment. But is not this matter one that involves a classic legislative judgment? Surely it lies within the province of a state legislature to conclude that an existing allocation of senators and representatives constitutes a desirable balance of geographical and demographical representation, or that in the interest of stability of government it would be best to defer for some further time the redistribution of seats in the state legislature.

Indeed, I would hardly think it unconstitutional if a state legislature's expressed reason for establishing or maintaining an electoral imbalance between its rural and urban population were to protect the State's agricultural interests from the sheer weight of numbers of those residing in its cities. . . .

From a reading of the majority and concurring opinions one will not find it difficult to catch the premises that underlie this decision. The fact that the appellants have been unable to obtain political redress of their asserted grievances appears to be regarded as a matter which should lead the Court to stretch to find some basis for judicial intervention. While the Equal Protection Clause is invoked, the opinion for the Court notably eschews explaining how, consonant with past decisions, the undisputed facts in this case can be considered to show a violation of that constitutional provision. The majority seems to have accepted the argument, pressed at the bar, that if this Court merely asserts authority in this field, Tennessee and other "malapportioning" States will quickly respond with appropriate political action, so that this Court need not be greatly concerned about the federal courts becoming further involved in these matters. At the same time the majority has wholly failed to reckon with what the future may hold in store if this optimistic prediction is not fulfilled. Thus, what the Court is doing reflects more an adventure in judicial experimentation than a solid piece of constitutional adjudication. . . .

Reynolds v. Sims
84 S. Ct. 1363 (1964)

In this case, and in the companion cases below, the Court had to face at least some of the issues left open in *Baker* v. *Carr.*

III.

MR. CHIEF JUSTICE WARREN delivered the opinion of the Court. . . .

A predominant consideration in determining whether a State's legislative apportionment scheme constitutes an invidious discrimination violative of rights asserted under the Equal Protection Clause is that the rights allegedly impaired are individual and personal in nature. As stated by the Court in *United States* v. *Bathgate,* 246 U.S. 220, 227, "the right to vote is personal. . . ." While the result of a court decision in a state legislative apportionment controversy may be to require the restructuring of the geographical distribution of seats in a state legislature, the judicial focus must be concentrated upon ascertaining whether there has been any discrimination against certain of the State's citizens which constitutes an impermissible impairment of their constitutionally protected right to vote. Like *Skinner* v. *Oklahoma,* 316 U.S. 535, such a case "touches a sensitive and important area of human rights," and "involves one of the basic civil rights of man," presenting questions of alleged "invidious discriminations . . . against groups or types of individuals in violation of the constitutional guaranty of just and equal laws." 316 U.S., at 536, 541. Undoubtedly, the right of suffrage is a fundamental matter in a free and democratic society. Especially since the right to exercise the franchise in a free and unimpaired manner is preservative of other basic civil and political rights, any alleged infringement of the right of citizens to vote must be carefully and meticulously scrutinized. Almost a century ago, in *Yick Wo* v. *Hopkins,* 118 U.S. 356, the Court referred to "the political franchise of voting" as "a fundamental political right, because preservative of all rights." 118 U.S., at 370.

Legislators represent people, not trees or acres. Legislators are elected by voters, not farms or cities or economic interests. As long as ours is a representative form of government, and our legislatures are those instruments of government elected directly by and directly representative of the people, the right to elect legislators in a free and unimpaired fashion is a bedrock of our political system. It could hardly be gainsaid that a constitutional claim had been asserted by an allegation that certain otherwise qualified voters had been entirely prohibited from voting for members of their state legislature. And, if a State should provide that the votes of citizens in one part of the State should be given two times, or five times, or 10 times the weight of votes of citizens in another part of the State, it could hardly be contended that the right to vote of those residing in the disfavored areas had not been effectively diluted. It would appear extraordinary to suggest that a state could be constitutionally permitted to enact a law providing that certain of the state's voters could vote two, five, or 10 times for their legislative representatives, while voters living elsewhere could vote only once. And it is inconceivable that a state law to the effect that, in counting votes for legislators, the votes of citizens in one part of the State would be multiplied by two, five, or 10, while the votes of persons in another area would be counted only at face value, could be constitutionally sustainable. Of course, the effect of state legislative districting schemes which give the same number of representatives to unequal numbers of constituents is identical. Overweighting and overvaluation of the votes of those living here has the certain effect of dilution and undervaluation of the votes of those living there. The resulting discrimination against those individual voters living in disfavored areas is easily demonstrable mathematically. Their right to vote is simply not the same right to vote as that of those living in a favored part of the State. Two, five, or 10 of them must vote before the effect of their voting is equivalent to that of their favored neighbor. Weighting the votes of citizens differently, by any method or means, merely because of where they happen to reside, hardly seems justifiable. One must be ever aware that the Constitution forbids "sophisticated as well as simple-minded modes of discrimination." *Lane* v. *Wilson*, 307 U.S. 268, 275, *Gomillion* v. *Lightfoot*, 364 U.S. 339, 342. As we stated in *Wesberry* v. *Sanders, supra:*

> "We do not believe that the Framers of the Constitution intended to permit the same vote-diluting discrimination to be accomplished through the device of districts containing widely varied numbers of inhabitants. To say that a vote is worth more in one district than in another would . . . run counter to our fundamental ideas of democratic government. . . ."

State legislatures are, historically, the fountainhead of representative government in this country. A number of them have their roots in colonial times, and substantially antedate the creation of our Nation and our Federal Government. In fact, the first formal stirrings of American political independence are to be found, in large part, in the views and actions of several of the colonial legislative bodies. With the birth of our National Government, and the adoption and ratification of the Federal Constitution, state legislatures retained a most important place in our Nation's governmental structure. But representative government is in essence self-government through the medium of elected representatives of the people, and each and every citizen has an inalienable right to full and effective participation in the political processes of his State's legislative bodies. Most citizens can achieve this participation only as qualified voters through the election of legislators to represent them. Full and effective participation by all citizens in state government requires, therefore, that each citizen has an equally effective voice in the election of members of his state legislature. Modern and viable state government needs, and the Constitution demands, no less.

Logically, in a society ostensibly grounded on representative government, it would seem reasonable that a majority of the people of a State could elect a majority of that State's legislators. To conclude differently, and to sanction minority control of state legislative bodies, would appear to deny majority rights in a way that far surpasses any possible denial of minority rights that might otherwise be thought to result. Since legislatures are responsible for enacting laws by which all citizens are to be governed, they should be bodies which are collectively responsive to the popular will. And the concept of equal protection has been traditionally viewed as requiring the uniform treatment of persons standing in the same relation to the governmental action questioned or challenged. With respect to the allocation of legislative representation, all voters, as citizens of a State, stand in the same relation regardless of where they live. Any suggested criteria for the differentiation of citizens are insufficient to justify any discrimination, as to the weight of their votes, unless relevant to the permissible purposes of legislative apportionment. Since the achieving of fair and effective representation for all citizens is concededly the basic aim of legislative apportionment, we conclude that the Equal Protection Clause guarantees the opportunity for equal participation by all voters in the election of state legislators. Diluting the weight of votes because of place of residence impairs basic constitutional rights under the Fourteenth Amendment just as much as invidious discriminations based upon factors such as race, *Brown* v. *Board of Education,* 347 U.S. 483, or economic status, *Griffin* v. *Illinois,* 351 U.S. 12, *Douglas* v. *California,* 372 U.S. 353. Our constitutional system amply provides for the protection of minorities by means other than giving them majority control of state legislatures. And the democratic ideals of equality and majority rule, which have served this Nation so well in the past, are hardly of any less significance for the present and the future.

We are told that the matter of apportioning representation in a state legislature is a complex and many-faceted one. We are advised that States can rationally consider factors other than population in apportioning legislative representation. We are admonished not to restrict the power of the States to impose differing views as to political philosophy on their citizens. We are cautioned about the dangers of entering into political thickets and mathematical quagmires. Our answer is this: a denial of constitutionally protected rights demands judicial protection; our oath and our office require no less of us. As stated in *Gomillion* v. *Lightfoot, supra:*

> "When a State exercises power wholly within the domain of state interest, it is insulated from federal judicial review. But such insulation is not carried over when state power is used as an instrument for circumventing a federally protected right."

To the extent that a citizen's right to vote is debased, he is that much less a citizen. The fact that an individual lives here or there is not a legitimate reason for overweighting or diluting the efficacy of his vote. The complexions of societies and civilizations change, often with amazing rapidity. A nation once primarily rural in character becomes predominantly urban. Representation schemes once fair and equitable become archaic and outdated. But the basic principle of representative government remains, and must remain, unchanged—the weight of a citizen's vote cannot be made to depend on where he lives. Population is, of necessity, the starting point for consideration and the controlling criterion for judgment in legislative apportionment controversies. A citizen, a qualified voter, is no more nor no less so because he lives in the city or on the farm. This is the clear and strong command of our Constitution's Equal Protection Clause. This is an essential part of the concept of a government of laws and not men. This is at the heart of Lincoln's vision of "government of the people, by the people, [and] for the people." The Equal Protection Clause demands no less than substantially equal state legislative representation for all citizens, of all places as well as of all races.

IV.

We hold that, as a basic constitutional standard, the Equal Protection Clause requires that the seats in both houses of a bicameral state legislature must be apportioned on a population basis. Simply stated, an individual's right to vote for state legislators is unconstitutionally impaired when its weight is in a substantial fashion diluted when compared with votes of citizens living in other parts of the State. Since, under neither the existing apportionment provisions nor under either of the proposed plans was either of the houses of the Alabama Legislature apportioned on a population basis, the District Court correctly held that all three of these schemes were constitutionally invalid. Furthermore, the existing apportionment, and also to a lesser extent the apportionment under the Crawford-Webb Act, presented little more than crazy quilts, completely lacking in rationality, and could be found invalid on that basis alone. Although the District Court presumably found the apportionment of the Alabama House of Representatives under the 67-Senator Amendment to be acceptable, we conclude that the deviations from a strict population basis are too egregious to permit us to find that that body, under this proposed plan, was apportioned sufficiently on a population basis so as to permit the arrangement to be constitutionally sustained. Although about 43% of the State's total population would be required to comprise districts which could elect a majority in that body, only 39 of the 106 House seats were actually to be distributed on a population basis, as each of Alabama's 67 counties was given at least one representative, and population-variance ratios of close to 5-to-1 would have existed. While mathematical nicety is not a constitutional requisite, one could hardly conclude that the Alabama House, under the proposed constitutional amendment, had been apportioned sufficiently on a population basis to be sustainable under the requirements of the Equal Protection Clause. And none of the other apportionments of seats in either of the bodies of the Alabama Legislature, under the three plans considered by the District Court, came nearly as close to approaching the required constitutional standard as did that of the House of Representatives under the 67-Senator Amendment.

Legislative apportionment in Alabama is signally illustrative and symptomatic of the seriousness of this problem in a number of the States. At the time this litigation was commenced, there had been no reapportionment of seats in the Alabama Legislature for over 60 years. Legislative inaction, coupled with the unavailability of any political or judicial remedy, had resulted, with the passage of years, in the perpetuated scheme becoming little more than an irrational anachronism. Consistent failure by the Alabama Legislature to comply with state constitutional requirements as to the frequency of reapportionment and the bases of legislative representation resulted in a minority strangle hold on the State Legislature. Inequality of representation in one house added to the inequality in the other. With the crazy-quilt existing apportionment virtually conceded to be invalid, the Alabama Legislature offered two proposed plans for consideration by the District Court, neither of which was to be effective until 1966 and neither of which provided for the apportionment of even one of the two houses on a population basis. We find that the court below did not err in holding that neither of these proposed reapportionment schemes, considered as a whole, "meets the necessary constitutional requirements." And we conclude that the District Court acted properly in considering these two proposed plans, although neither was to become effective until the 1966 election and the proposed constitutional amendment was scheduled to be submitted to the State's voters in November 1962.

Consideration by the court below of the two proposed plans was clearly necessary in determining whether the Alabama Legislature had acted effectively to correct the admittedly existing malapportionment, and in ascertaining what sort of judicial relief, if any, should be afforded.

V.

Since neither of the houses of the Alabama Legislature, under any of the three plans considered by the District Court, was apportioned on a population basis, we would be justified in proceeding no further. However, one of the proposed plans, that contained in the so-called 67-Senator Amendment, at least superficially resembles the scheme of legislative representation followed in the Federal Congress. Under this plan, each of Alabama's 67 counties is allotted one senator, and no counties are given more than one Senate seat. Arguably, this is analogous to the allocation of two Senate seats, in the Federal Congress, to each of the 50 States, regardless of population. Seats in the Alabama House, under the proposed constitutional amendment, are distributed by giving each of the 67 counties at least one, with the remaining 39 seats being allotted among the more populous counties on a population basis. This scheme, at least at first glance, appears to resemble that prescribed for the Federal House of Representatives, where the 435 seats are distributed among the States on a population basis, although each State, regardless of its population, is given at least one Congressman. Thus, although there are substantial differences in underlying rationale and result, the 67-Senator Amendment, as proposed by the Alabama Legislature, at least arguably presents for consideration a scheme analogous to that used for apportioning seats in Congress.

Much has been written since our decision in *Baker* v. *Carr* about the applicability of the so-called federal analogy to state legislative apportionment arrangements. After considering the matter, the court below concluded that no conceivable analogy could be drawn between the federal scheme and the apportionment of seats in the Alabama Legislature under the proposed constitutional amendment. We agree with the District Court, and find the federal analogy inapposite and irrelevant to state legislative districting schemes. Attempted reliance on the federal analogy appears often to be little more than an after-the-fact rationalization offered in defense of maladjusted state apportionment arrangements. The original constitutions of 36 of our States provided that representation in both houses of the state legislatures would be based completely, or predominantly, on population. And the Founding Fathers clearly had no intention of establishing a pattern or model for the apportionment of seats in state legislatures when the system of representation in the Federal Congress was adopted. Demonstrative of this is the fact that the Northwest Ordinance, adopted in the same year, 1787, as the Federal Constitution, provided for the apportionment of seats in territorial legislatures solely on the basis of population.

The system of representation in the two Houses of the Federal Congress is one ingrained in our Constitution, as part of the law of the land. It is one conceived out of compromise and concession indispensable to the establishment of our federal republic. Arising from unique historical circumstances, it is based on the consideration that in establishing our type of federalism a group of formerly independent States bound themselves together under one national government. Admittedly, the original 13 States surrendered some of their sovereignty in agreeing to join together "to form a more perfect Union." But at the heart of our constitutional system remains the concept of separate and distinct governmental entities which have delegated some, but not all, of their formerly held powers to the single national government. The fact that almost three-fourths of our present States were never in fact independently sovereign does not detract from our view that the so-called federal analogy is inapplicable as a sustaining precedent for state legislative apportionments. The developing history and growth of our republic cannot cloud the fact that, at the time of the inception of the system of representation in the Federal Congress, a compromise between the larger and smaller States on this matter averted a deadlock in the constitutional convention which had threatened to abort the birth of our Nation. In rejecting an asserted analogy to the federal electoral college in *Gray* v. *Sanders, supra,* we stated:

> "We think the analogies to the electoral college, to districting and redistricting, and to other phases of the problems of representation in state or federal legislatures or conventions are inapposite. The inclusion of the electoral college in the Constitution, as the result of specific historical concerns, validated the collegiate principle despite its inherent numerical inequality, but implied nothing about the use of an analogous system by a State in a statewide election. No such specific accommodation of the latter was ever undertaken, and therefore no validation of its numerical inequality ensued."

Political subdivisions of States—counties, cities, or whatever —never were and never have been considered as sovereign entities. Rather, they have been traditionally regarded as subordinate governmental instrumentalities created by the State to assist in the carrying out of state governmental functions. As stated by the Court in *Hunter* v. *City of Pittsburgh,* 207 U. S. 161, 178, these governmental units are "created as convenient agencies for exercising such of the governmental powers of the State as may be entrusted to them," and the "number, nature and duration of the powers conferred upon [them] . . . and the territory over which they shall be exercised rests in the absolute discretion of the State." The relationship of the States to the Federal Goverment could hardly be less analogous.

Thus, we conclude that the plan contained in the 67-Senator Amendment for apportioning seats in the Alabama Legislature cannot be sustained by recourse to the so-called federal analogy.

Nor can any other inequitable state legislative apportionment scheme be justified on such an asserted basis. This does not necessarily mean that such a plan is irrational or involves something other than a "republican form of government." We conclude simply that such a plan is impermissible for the States under the Equal Protection Clause, since perforce resulting, in virtually every case, in submergence of the equal-population principle in at least one house of a state legislature.

Since we find the so-called federal analogy inapposite to a consideration of the constitutional validity of state legislative apportionment schemes, we necessarily hold that the Equal Protection Clause requires both houses of a state legislature to be apportioned on a population basis. The right of a citizen to equal representation and to have his vote weighted equally with those of all other citizens in the election of members of one house of a bicameral state legislature would amount to little if States could effectively submerge the equal-population principle in the apportionment of seats in the other house. If such a scheme were permissible, an individual citizen's ability to exercise an effective voice in the only instrument of state government directly representative of the people might be almost as effectively thwarted as if neither house were apportioned on a population basis. Deadlock between the two bodies might result in compromise and concession on some issues. But in all too many cases the more probable result would be frustration of the majority will through minority veto in the house not apportioned on a population basis, stemming directly from the failure to accord adequate overall legislative representation to all of the State's citizens on a nondiscriminatory basis. In summary, we can perceive no constitutional difference, with respect to the geographical distribution of state legislative representation, between the two houses of a bicameral state legislature.

We do not believe that the concept of bicameralism is rendered anachronistic and meaningless when the predom-

inant basis of representation in the two state legislative bodies
is required to be the same—population. A prime reason for
bicameralism, modernly considered, is to insure mature and
deliberate consideration of, and to prevent precipitate action
on, proposed legislative measures. Simply because the controlling criterion for apportioning representation is required
to be the same in both houses does not mean that there will
be no differences in the composition and complexion of the
two bodies. Different constituencies can be represented in the
two houses. One body could be composed of single-member
districts while the other could have at least some multimember
districts. The length of terms of the legislators in the separate
bodies could differ. The numerical size of the two bodies
could be made to differ, even significantly, and the geographical size of districts from which legislators are elected could
also be made to differ. And apportionment in one house could
be arranged so as to balance off minor inequities in the representation of certain areas in the other house. In summary,
these and other factors could be, and are presently in many
States, utilized to engender differing complexions and collective attitudes in the two bodies of a state legislature, although
both are apportioned substantially on a population basis.

VI.

By holding that as a federal constitutional requisite both
houses of a state legislature must be apportioned on a population basis, we mean that the Equal Protection Clause requires that a State make an honest and good faith effort to
construct districts, in both houses of its legislature, as nearly
of equal population as is practicable. We realize that it is a
practical impossibility to arrange legislative districts so that
each one has an identical number of residents, or citizens, or
voters. Mathematical exactness or precision is hardly a work-
able constitutional requirement.

In *Wesberry* v. *Sanders, supra,* the Court stated that congressional representation must be based on population as nearly as is practicable. In implementing the basic constitutional principle of representative government as enunciated by the Court in *Wesberry*—equality of population among districts—some distinctions may well be made between congressional and state legislative representation. Since, almost invariably, there is a significantly larger number of seats in state legislative bodies to be distributed within a State than congressional seats, it may be feasible to use political subdivision lines to a greater extent in establishing state legislative districts than in congressional districting while still affording adequate representation to all parts of the State. To do so would be constitutionally valid, so long as the resulting apportionment was one based substantially on population and the equal-population principle was not diluted in any significant way. Somewhat more flexibility may therefore be constitutionally permissible with respect to state legislative apportionment than in congressional districting. Lower courts can and assuredly will work out more concrete and specific standards for evaluating state legislative apportionment schemes in the context of actual litigation. For the present, we deem it expedient not to attempt to spell out any precise constitutional tests. What is marginally permissible in one State may be unsatisfactory in another, depending on the particular circumstances of the case. Developing a body of doctrine on a case-by-case basis appears to us to provide the most satisfactory means of arriving at detailed constitutional requirements in the area of state legislative apportionment. Cf. *Slaughter-House Cases,* 16 Wall. 36, 78–79. Thus, we proceed to state here only a few rather general considerations which appear to us to be relevant.

A State may legitimately desire to maintain the integrity of various political subdivisions, insofar as possible, and provide for compact districts of contiguous territory in designing a legislative apportionment scheme. Valid considerations may underlie such aims. Indiscriminate districting, without any regard for political subdivision or natural or historical boundary lines, may be little more than an open invitation to partisan gerrymandering. Single-member districts may be the rule in one State, while another State might desire to achieve some flexibility by creating multimember or floterial districts. Whatever the means of accomplishment, the overriding objective must be substantial equality of population among the various districts, so that the vote of any citizen is approximately equal in weight to that of any other citizen in the State.

History indicates, however, that many States have deviated, to a greater or lesser degree, from the equal-population principle in the apportionment of seats in at least one house of their legislatures. So long as the divergences from a strict population standard are based on legitimate considerations incident to the effectuation of a rational state policy, some deviations from the equal-population principle are constitutionally permissible with respect to the apportionment of seats in either or both of the two houses of a bicameral state legislature. But neither history alone, nor economic or other sorts of group interests, are permissible factors in attempting to justify disparities from population-based representation. Citizens, not history or economic interests, cast votes. Considerations of area alone provide an insufficient justification for deviations from the equal-population principle. Again, people, not land or trees or pastures, vote. Modern developments and improvements in transportation and communications make rather hollow, in the mid-1960's, most claims that deviations from population-based representation can validly be based solely on geographical considerations. Arguments for allowing such deviations in order to insure effective representation for sparsely settled areas and to prevent legislative districts from becoming so large that the availability of access of citizens to their representatives is impaired are today, for the most part, unconvincing.

A consideration that appears to be of more substance in justifying some deviations from population-based representation in state legislatures is that of insuring some voice to political subdivisions, as political subdivisions. Several factors make more than insubstantial claims that a State can rationally consider according political subdivisions some independent representation in at least one body of the state legislature, as long as the basic standard of equality of population among districts is maintained. Local governmental entities are frequently charged with various responsibilities incident to the operation of state government. In many States much of the legislature's activity involves the enactment of so-called local legislation, directed only to the concerns of particular political subdivisions. And a State may legitimately desire to construct districts along political subdivision lines to deter the possibilities of gerrymandering. However, permitting deviations from population-based representation does not mean that each local governmental unit or political subdivision can be given separate representation, regardless of population. Carried too far, a scheme of giving at least one seat in one house to each political subdivision (for example, to each county) could easily result, in many States, in a total subversion of the equal-population principle in that legislative body. This would be especially true in a State where the number of counties is large and many of them are sparsely populated, and the number of seats in the legislative body being apportioned does not significantly exceed the number of counties. Such a result, we conclude, would be constitutionally impermissible. And careful judicial scrutiny must of course be given, in evaluating state apportionment schemes, to the character as well as the degree of deviations from a strict population basis. But if, even as a result of a clearly rational state policy of according some legislative representation to political subdivisions, population is submerged as the controlling consideration in the apportionment of seats in the particular legislative body, then the right of all of the State's citizens to cast an effective and adequately weighted vote would be unconstitutionally impaired.

VII.

One of the arguments frequently offered as a basis for upholding a State's legislative apportionment arrangement, despite substantial disparities from a population basis in either or both houses, is grounded on congressional approval, incident to admitting States into the Union, of state apportionment plans containing deviations from the equal-population principle. Proponents of this argument contend that congressional approval of such schemes, despite their disparities from population-based representation, indicate that such arrangements are plainly sufficient as establishing a "republican form of government." As we stated in *Baker* v. *Carr*, some questions raised under the Guaranty Clause are nonjusticiable, where "political" in nature and where there is a clear absence of judicially manageable standards. Nevertheless, it is not inconsistent with this view to hold that, despite congressional approval of state legislative apportionment plans at the time of admission into the Union, even though deviating from the equal-population principle here enunciated, the Equal Protection Clause can and does require more. And an apportionment scheme in which both houses are based on population can hardly be considered as failing to satisfy the Guaranty Clause requirement. Congress presumably does not assume, in admitting States into the Union, to pass on all constitutional questions relating to the character of state governmental organization. In any event, congressional approval, however well-considered, could hardly validate an unconstitutional state legislative apportionment. Congress simply lacks the constitutional power to insulate States from attack with respect to alleged deprivations of individual constitutional rights.

VIII.

That the Equal Protection Clause requires that both houses of a state legislature be apportioned on a population basis does not mean that States cannot adopt some reasonable plan for periodic revision of their apportionment schemes. Decennial reapportionment appears to be a rational approach to readjustment of legislative representation in order to take into account population shifts and growth. Reallocation of legislative seats every 10 years coincides with the prescribed practice in 41 of the States, often honored more in the breach than the observance, however. Illustratively, the Alabama Constitution requires decennial reapportionment, yet the last reapportionment of the Alabama Legislature, when this suit was brought, was in 1901. Limitations on the frequency of reapportionment are justified by the need for stability and continuity in the organization of the legislative system, although undoubtedly reapportioning no more frequently than every 10 years leads to some imbalance in the population of districts toward the end of the decennial period and also to the development of resistance to change on the part of some incumbent legislators. In substance, we do not regard the Equal Protection Clause as requiring daily, monthly, annual or biennial reapportionment, so long as a State has a reasonably conceived plan for periodic readjustment of legislative representation. While we do not intend to indicate that decennial reapportionment is a constitutional requisite, compliance with such an approach would clearly meet the minimal requirements for maintaining a reasonably current scheme of legislative representation. And we do not mean to intimate that more frequent reapportionment would not be constitutionally permissible or practicably desirable. But if reapportionment were accomplished with less frequency, it would assuredly be constitutionally suspect.

IX.

Although general provisions of the Alabama Constitution provide that the apportionment of seats in both houses of the Alabama Legislature should be on a population basis, other more detailed provisions clearly make compliance with both sets of requirements impossible. With respect to the operation of the Equal Protection Clause, it makes no difference whether a State's apportionment scheme is embodied in its constitution or in statutory provisions. In those States where the alleged malapportionment has resulted from noncompliance with state constitutional provisions which, if complied with, would result in an apportionment valid under the Equal Protection Clause, the judicial task of providing effective relief would appear to be rather simple. We agree with the view of the District Court that state constitutional provisions should be deemed violative of the Federal Constitution only when validly asserted constitutional rights could not otherwise be protected and effectuated. Clearly, courts should attempt to accommodate the relief ordered to the apportionment provisions of state constitutions insofar as is possible. But it is also quite clear that a state legislative apportionment scheme is no less violative of the Federal Constitution when it is based on state constitutional provisions which have been consistently complied with than when resulting from a noncompliance with state constitutional requirements. When there is an unavoidable conflict between the Federal and a State Constitution, the Supremacy Clause of course controls.

X.

We do not consider here the difficult question of the proper remedial devices which federal courts should utilize in state legislative apportionment cases. Remedial technique in this new and developing area of the law will probably often differ with the circumstances of the challenged apportionment and a variety of local conditions. It is enough to say now that, once a State's legislative apportionment scheme has been found to be unconstitutional, it would be the unusual case in which a court would be justified in not taking appropriate action to insure that no further elections are conducted under the invalid plan. However, under certain circumstances, such as where an impending election is imminent and a State's election machinery is already in progress, equitable considerations might justify a court in withholding the granting of immediately effective relief in a legislative apportionment case, even though the existing apportionment scheme was found invalid. In awarding or withholding immediate relief, a court is entitled to and should consider the proximity of a forthcoming election and the mechanics and complexities of state election laws, and should act and rely upon general equitable principles. With respect to the timing of relief, a court can reasonably endeavor to avoid a disruption of the election process which might result from requiring precipitate changes that could make unreasonable or embarrassing demands on a State in adjusting to the requirements of the court's decree. As stated by Mr. Justice Douglas, in concurring in *Baker* v. *Carr,* "any relief accorded can be fashioned in the light of well-known principles of equity."

We feel that the District Court in this case acted in a most proper and commendable manner. It initially acted wisely in declining to stay the impending primary election in Alabama, and properly refrained from acting further until the Alabama Legislature had been given an opportunity to remedy the admitted discrepancies in the State's legislative apportionment scheme, while initially stating some of its views to provide guidelines for legislative action. And it correctly recognized that legislative reapportionment is primarily a matter for legislative consideration and determination, and that judicial relief becomes appropriate only when a legislature fails to reapportion according to federal constitutional requisites in a timely fashion after having had an adequate opportunity to do so. Additionally, the court below acted with proper judicial restraint, after the Alabama Legislature had failed to act effectively in remedying the constitutional deficiencies in the State's legislative apportionment scheme, in ordering its own temporary reapportionment plan into effect, at a time sufficiently early to permit the holding of elections pursuant to that plan without great difficulty, and in prescribing a plan admittedly provisional in purpose so as not to usurp the primary responsibility for reapportionment which rests with the legislature.

We find, therefore, that the action taken by the District Court in this case, in ordering into effect a reapportionment of both houses of the Alabama Legislature for purposes of the 1962 primary and general elections, by using the best parts of the two proposed plans which it had found, as a whole, to be invalid, was an appropriate and well-considered exercise of judicial power. Admittedly, the lower court's ordered plan was intended only as a temporary and provisional measure and the District Court correctly indicated that the plan was invalid as a permanent apportionment. In retaining jurisdiction while deferring a hearing on the issuance of a final injunction in order to give the provisionally reapportioned legislature an opportunity to act effectively, the court below proceeded in a proper fashion. Since the District Court evinced its realization that its ordered reapportionment could not be sustained as the basis for conducting the 1966 election of Alabama legislators, and avowedly intends to take some further action should the reapportioned Alabama Legislature fail to enact a constitutionally valid, permanent apportionment scheme in the interim, we affirm the judgment below and remand the cases for further proceedings consistent with the views stated in this opinion.

It is so ordered.

MR. JUSTICE CLARK, concurring in the reversal.

The Court goes much beyond the necessities of this case in laying down a new "equal population" principle for state legislative apportionment. This principle seems to be an offshoot of *Gray* v. *Sanders*, 372 U.S. 368, 381 (1963), *i. e.*, "one person, one vote," modified by the "nearly as is practicable" admonition of *Wesberry* v. *Sanders*, 376 U.S. 1, 8 (1964). Whether "nearly as is practicable" means "one person, one vote" qualified by "approximately equal" or "some deviations" or by the impossibility of "mathematical nicety" is not clear from the majority's use of these vague and meaningless phrases. But whatever the standard, the Court applies it to each house of the State Legislature.

It seems to me that all that the Court need say in this case is that each plan considered by the trial court is "a crazy quilt," clearly revealing invidious discrimination in each house of the Legislature and therefore violative of the Equal Protection Clause. See my concurring opinion in *Baker* v. *Carr*, 369 U.S. 186, 253–258 (1962).

I, therefore, do not reach the question of the so-called "federal analogy." But in my view, if one house of the State Legislature meets the population standard, representation in the other house might include some departure from it so as to take into account, on a rational basis, other factors in order to afford some representation to the various elements of the State. See my dissenting opinion in *Lucas* v. *The Forty-fourth General Assembly of Colorado*, —— U.S. ——, decided this date.

MR. JUSTICE STEWART.

In this case all of the parties have agreed with the District

Court's finding that legislative inaction for some 60 years in
the face of growth and shifts in population has converted Alabama's legislative apportionment plan enacted in 1901 into
one completely lacking in rationality. Accordingly, for the
reasons stated in my dissenting opinion in *Lucas* v. *The Forty-
Fourth General Assembly of the State of Colorado, ante,*
p. ———, I would affirm the judgment of the District Court
holding that this apportionment violated the Equal Protection
Clause.

I also agree with the Court that it was proper for the District Court, in framing a remedy, to adhere as closely as practicable to the apportionments approved by the representatives
of the people of Alabama, and to afford the State of Alabama
full opportunity, consistent with the requirements of the Federal Constitution, to devise its own system of legislative apportionment.

Mr. Justice Harlan, dissenting.

In these cases the Court holds that seats in the legislatures
of six States are apportioned in ways that violate the Federal
Constitution. Under the Court's ruling it is bound to follow
that the legislatures in all but a few of the other 44 States
will meet the same fate. These decisions, with *Wesberry* v.
Sanders, 376 U.S. 1, involving congressional districting by
the States, and *Gray* v. *Sanders,* 372 U.S. 368, relating to
elections for statewide office, have the effect of placing basic
aspects of state political systems under the pervasive overlord-
ship of the federal judiciary. Once again, I must register my
protest.

PRELIMINARY STATEMENT.

Today's holding is that the Equal Protection Clause of the
Fourteenth Amendment requires every State to structure its
legislature so that all the members of each house represent
substantially the same number of people; other factors may

be given play only to the extent that they do not significantly encroach on this basic "population" principle. Whatever may be thought of this holding as a piece of political ideology— and even on that score the political history and practices of this country from its earliest beginnings leave wide room for debate (see the dissenting opinion of Frankfurter, J., in *Baker v. Carr*, 369 U.S. 186, 266, 301–323)—I think it demonstrable that the Fourteenth Amendment does not impose this political tenet on the States or authorize this Court to do so.

The Court's constitutional discussion, found in its opinion in the Alabama cases (Nos. 23, 27, 41, *ante*, p. ——) and more particularly at pages 26–33 thereof, is remarkable (as, indeed, is that found in the separate opinions of my Brothers STEWART and CLARK, *ante*, pp. ——, ——) for its failure to address itself at all to the Fourteenth Amendment as a whole or to the legislative history of the Amendment pertinent to the matter at hand. Stripped of aphorisms, the Court's argument boils down to the assertion that petitioners' right to vote has been invidiously "debased" or "diluted" by systems of apportionment which entitle them to vote for fewer legislators than other voters, an assertion which is tied to the Equal Protection Clause only by the constitutionally frail tautology that "equal" means "equal."

Had the Court paused to probe more deeply into the matter, it would have found that the Equal Protection Clause was never intended to inhibit the States in choosing any democratic method they pleased for the apportionment of their legislatures. This is shown by the language of the Fourteenth Amendment taken as a whole, by the understanding of those who proposed and ratified it, and by the political practices of the States at the time the Amendment was adopted. It is confirmed by numerous state and congressional actions since the adoption of the Fourteenth Amendment, and by the common understanding of the Amendment as evidenced by subsequent constitutional amendments and decisions of this Court before

Baker v. *Carr, supra,* made an abrupt break with the past in 1962.

The failure of the Court to consider any of these matters cannot be excused or explained by any concept of "developing" constitutionalism. It is meaningless to speak of constitutional "development" when both the language and history of the controlling provisions of the Constitution are wholly ignored. Since it can, I think, be shown beyond doubt that state legislative apportionments, as such, are wholly free of constitutional limitations, save such as may be imposed by the Republican Form of Government Clause (Const., Art. IV, § 4), the Court's action now bringing them within the purview of the Fourteenth Amendment amounts to nothing less than an exercise of the amending power by this Court.

So far as the Federal Constitution is concerned, the complaints in these cases should all have been dismissed below for failure to state a cause of action, because what has been alleged or proved shows no violation of any constitutional right.

Before proceeding to my argument it should be observed that nothing done in *Baker* v. *Carr, supra,* or in the two cases that followed in its wake, *Gray* v. *Sanders* and *Wesberry* v. *Sanders, supra,* from which the Court quotes at some length, forecloses the conclusion which I reach.

Baker decided only that claims such as those made here are within the competence of the federal courts to adjudicate. Although the Court stated as its conclusion that the allegations of a denial of equal protection presented "a justiciable constitutional cause of action," 369 U.S., at 237, it is evident from the Court's opinion that it was concerned all but exclusively with *justiciability* and gave no serious attention to the question whether the Equal Protection Clause touches state legislative apportionments. Neither the opinion of the Court nor any of the concurring opinions considered the relevant text of the Fourteenth Amendment or any of the historical materials bearing on that question. None of the materials was briefed or otherwise brought to the Court's attention.

In the *Gray* case the Court expressly laid aside the applicability to state legislative apportionments of the "one person, one vote" theory there found to require the striking down of the Georgia county unit system. See 372 U.S., at 376, and the concurring opinion of STEWART, J., joined by CLARK, J., *id.*, at 381–382.

In *Wesberry*, involving congressional districting, the decision rested on Art. I, § 2, of the Constitution. The Court expressly did not reach the arguments put forward concerning the Equal Protection Clause. See 376 U.S., at 8, note 10.

Thus it seems abundantly clear that the Court is entirely free to deal with the cases presently before it in light of materials now called to its attention for the first time. To these I now turn.

I.

A. *The Language of the Fourteenth Amendment.*

The Court relies exclusively on that portion of § 1 of the Fourteenth Amendment which provides that no State shall "deny to any person within its jurisdiction the equal protection of the laws," and disregards entirely the significance of § 2, which reads:

> "Representatives shall be apportioned among the several States according to their respective numbers, counting the whole number of persons in each State, excluding Indians not taxed. *But when the right to vote at any election for* the choice of electors for President and Vice President of the United States, Representatives in Congress, *the Executive and Judicial officers of a State, or the members of the Legislature thereof, is denied* to any of the male inhabitants of such State, being twenty-one years of age, and citizens of the United States, *or in any way abridged,* except for participation in rebellion, or other crime, the basis of representation therein shall be reduced in the proportion which

the number of such male citizens shall bear to the whole number of male citizens twenty-one years of age in such State." (Emphasis added.)

The Amendment is a single text. It was introduced and discussed as such in the Reconstruction Committee, which reported it to the Congress. It was discussed as a unit in Congress and proposed as a unit to the States, which ratified it as a unit. A proposal to split up the Amendment and submit each section to the States as a separate amendment was rejected by the Senate. Whatever one might take to be the application to these cases of the Equal Protection Clause if it stood alone, I am unable to understand the Court's utter disregard of the second section which expressly recognizes the States' power to deny "or in any way" abridge the right of their inhabitants to vote for "the members of the [State] Legislature," and its express provision of a remedy for such denial or abridgement. The comprehensive scope of the second section and its particular reference to the state legislatures precludes the suggestion that the first section was intended to have the result reached by the Court today. If indeed the words of the Fourteenth Amendment speak for themselves, as the majority's disregard of history seems to imply, they speak as clearly as may be against the construction which the majority puts on them. But we are not limited to the language of the Amendment itself.

B. *Proposal and Ratification of the Amendment.*

The history of the adoption of the Fourteenth Amendment provides conclusive evidence that neither those who proposed nor those who ratified the Amendment believed that the Equal Protection Clause limited the power of the States to apportion their legislatures as they saw fit. Moreover, the history demonstrates that the intention to leave this power undisturbed was deliberate and was widely believed to be essential to the adoption of the Amendment.

(i) *Proposal of the amendment in Congress.*—A resolution proposing what became the Fourteenth Amendment was reported to both houses of Congress by the Reconstruction Committee of Fifteen on April 30, 1866. The first two sections of the proposed amendment read:

"Sec. 1.   No State shall make or enforce any law which shall abridge the privileges or immunities of citizens of the United States; nor shall any State deprive any person of life, liberty, or property without due process of law; nor deny to any person within its jurisdiction the equal protection of the laws.

"Sec. 2.   Representatives shall be apportioned among the several States which may be included within this Union, according to their respective numbers, counting the whole number of persons in each State, excluding Indians not taxed. But whenever, in any State, the elective franchise shall be denied to any portion of its male citizens not less than twenty-one years of age, or in any way abridged except for participation in rebellion or other crime, the basis of representation in such State shall be reduced in the proportion which the number of such male citizens shall bear to the whole number of male citizens not less than twenty-one years of age."

In the House, Thaddeus Stevens introduced debate on the resolution on May 8. In his opening remarks, Stevens explained why he supported the resolution although it fell "far short" of his wishes:

"I believe it is all that can be obtained in the present state of public opinion. Not only Congress but the several States are to be consulted. Upon a careful survey of the whole ground, we did not believe that nineteen of the loyal States could be induced to ratify any proposition more stringent than this."

In explanation of this belief, he asked the House to remember "that three months since, and more, the committee reported and the House adopted a proposed amendment fixing the basis of representation in such way as would surely have secured the enfranchisement of every citizen at no distant period," but that proposal had been rejected by the Senate.

He then explained the impact of the first section of the proposed Amendment, particularly the Equal Protection Clause.

"This amendment . . . allows Congress to correct the unjust legislation of the States, so far that the law which operates upon one man shall operate *equally* upon all. Whatever law punishes a white man for a crime shall punish the black man precisely in the same way and to the same degree. Whatever law protects the white man shall afford 'equal' protection to the black man. Whatever means of redress is afforded to one shall be afforded to all. Whatever law allows the white man to testify in court shall allow the man of color to do the same. These are great advantages over their present codes. Now different degrees of punishment are inflicted, not on account of the magnitude of the crime, but according to the color of the skin. Now color disqualifies a man from testifying in courts, or being tried in the same way as white men. I need not enumerate these partial and oppressive laws. Unless the Constitution should restrain them those States will all, I fear, keep up this discrimination, and crush to death the hated freedmen."

He turned next to the second section, which he said he considered "the most important in the article." Its effect, he said, was to fix "the basis of representation in Congress." In unmistakable terms, he recognized the power of a State to withhold the right to vote:

"If any State shall exclude any of her adult male citizens from the elective franchise, or abridge that right, she shall forfeit her right to representation in the same proportion. The effect of this provision will be either to compel the States to grant universal suffrage or so to shear them of their power as to keep them forever in a hopeless minority in the national Government, both legislative and executive."

Closing his discussion of the second section, he noted his dislike for the fact that it allowed "the States to discriminate [with respect to the right to vote] among the same class, and receive proportionate credit in representation."

Toward the end of the debate three days later, Mr. Bingham, the author of the first section in the Reconstruction Committee and its leading proponent, concluded his discussion of it with the following:

> "Allow me, Mr. Speaker, in passing, to say that this amendment takes from no State any right that ever pertained to it. No State ever had the right, under the forms of law or otherwise, to deny to any freeman the equal protection of the laws or to abridge the privileges or immunities of any citizen of the Republic, although many of them have assumed and exercised the power, and that without remedy. *The amendment does not give, as the second section shows, the power to Congress of regulating suffrage in the several States.*" (Emphasis added.)

He immediately continued:

> "*The second section excludes the conclusion that by the first section suffrage is subjected to congressional law;* save, indeed, with this exception, that as the right in the people of each State to a republican government and to choose their Representatives in Congress is of the guarantees of the Constitution, by this amendment a remedy might be given directly for a case supposed by Madison, where treason might change a State government from a republican to a despotic government, and thereby deny suffrage to the people." (Emphasis added.)

He stated at another point in his remarks:

> "To be sure we all agree, and the great body of the people of this country agree, and the committee thus far in reporting measures of reconstruction agree, that *the exercise of the elective franchise, though it be one of the privileges of a citizen of the Republic, is exclusively under the control of the States.*" (Emphasis added.)

In the three days of debate which separate the opening and closing remarks, both made by members of the Reconstruction

Committee, every speaker on the resolution, with a single doubtful exception, assumed without question that, as Mr. Bingham said, *supra,* "the second section excludes the conclusion that by the first section suffrage is subjected to congressional law." The assumption was neither inadvertent nor silent. Much of the debate concerned the change in the basis of representation effected by the second section, and the speakers stated repeatedly, in express terms or by unmistakable implication, that the States retained the power to regulate suffrage within their borders. Attached as Appendix A hereto are some of those statements. The resolution was adopted by the House without change on May 10.

Debate in the Senate began on May 23, and followed the same pattern. Speaking for the Senate Chairman of the Reconstruction Committee, who was ill, Senator Howard, also a member of the Committee, explained the meaning of the Equal Protection Clause as follows:

"The last two clauses of the first section of the amendment disable a State from depriving not merely a citizen of the United States, but any person, whoever he may be, of life, liberty, or property without due process of law, or from denying to him the equal protection of the laws of the State. This abolishes all class legislation in the States and does away with the injustice of subjecting one caste of persons to a code not applicable to another. It prohibits the hanging of a black man for a crime for which the white man is not to be hanged. It protects the black man in his fundamental rights as a citizen with the same shield which it throws over the white man. Is it not time, Mr. President, that we extend to the black man, I had almost called it the poor privilege of the equal protection of the law? . . .

"But, sir, the first section of the proposed amendment does not give to either of these classes the right of voting. The right of suffrage is not, in law, one of the privileges or immunities thus secured by the Constitution. It is merely the creature of law. It has always been regarded in this country as the result of positive local law, not regarded as one of those fundamental rights lying at the basis of all society and without which a people cannot exist except as slaves, subject to a depotism [*sic*]." (Emphasis added.)

Discussing the second section, he expressed his regret that it did "not recognize the authority of the United States over the question of suffrage in the several States at all. . . ." He justified the limited purpose of the Amendment in this regard as follows:

"But, sir, it is not the question here what will we do; it is not the question what you, or I, or half a dozen other members of the Senate may prefer in respect to colored suffrage; it is not entirely the question what measure we can pass through the two Houses; but the question really is, what will the Legislatures of the various States to whom these amendments are to be submitted do in the premises; what is it likely will meet the general approbation of the people who are to elect the Legislatures, three fourths of whom must ratify our propositions before they have the force of constitutional provisions? . . .

"The committee were of opinion that the States are not yet prepared to sanction so fundamental a change as would be the concession of the right of suffrage to the colored race. We may as well state it plainly and fairly, so that there shall be no misunderstanding on the subject. It was our opinion that three fourths of the States of this Union could not be induced to vote to grant the right of suffrage, even in any degree or under any restriction, to the colored race. . . .

"*The second section leaves the right to regulate the elective franchise still with the States, and does not meddle with that right.*" (Emphasis added.)

There was not in the Senate, as there had been in the House, a closing speech in explanation of the Amendment. But because the Senate considered, and finally adopted, several changes in the first and second sections, even more attention was given to the problem of voting rights there than had been given in the House. In the Senate, it was fully understood by everyone that neither the first nor the second section interfered with the right of the States to regulate the elective franchise. Attached as Appendix B hereto are representative statements from the debates to that effect. After having changed the proposed amendment to the form in which it was adopted, the Senate passed the resolution on June 8, 1866. As changed, it passed in the House on June 13.

(ii) *Ratification by the "loyal" States.*—Reports of the debates in the state legislatures on the ratification of the Fourteenth Amendment are not generally available. There is, however, compelling indirect evidence. Of the 23 loyal States which ratified the Amendment before 1870, five had constitutional provisions for apportionment of at least one house of their respective legislatures which wholly disregarded the spread of population. Ten more had constitutional provisions which gave primary emphasis to population, but which applied also other principles, such as partial ratios and recognition of political subdivisions, which were intended to favor sparsely settled areas. Can it be seriously contended that the legislatures of these States, almost two-thirds of those concerned, would have ratified an amendment which might render their own States' constitutions unconstitutional.

Nor were these state constitutional provisions merely theoretical. In New Jersey, for example, Cape May County, with a population of 8,349, and Ocean County, with a population of 13,628, each elected one State Senator, as did Essex and Hudson Counties, with populations of 143,839 and 129,067, respectively. In the House, each county was entitled to one representative, which left 39 seats to be apportioned according to population. Since there were 12 counties besides the two already mentioned which had populations over 30,000, it is evident that there were serious disproportions in the House also. In New York, each of the 60 counties except Hamilton County was entitled to one of the 128 seats in the Assembly. This left 69 seats to be distributed among counties the populations of which ranged from 15,420 to 942,292. With seven more counties having populations over 100,000 and 13 others having populations over 50,000, the disproportion in the Assembly was necessarily large. In Vermont, after each county had been allocated one Senator, there were 16 seats remaining to be distributed among the larger counties. The smallest county had a population of 4,082; the largest had a population of 40,651 and there were 10 other counties with populations over 20,000.

(iii) *Ratification by the "reconstructed" States.*—Each of the 10 "reconstructed" States was required to ratify the Four-teenth Amendment before it was readmitted to the Union. The Constitution of each was scrutinized in Congress. Debates over readmission were extensive. In at least one instance, the problem of state legislative apportionment was expressly called to the attention of Congress. Objecting to the inclusion of Florida in the Act of June 25, 1868, Mr. Farnsworth stated on the floor of the House:

"I might refer to the apportionment of representatives. By this constitution representatives in the Legislature of Florida are ap-portioned in such a manner as to give to the sparsely-populated portions of the State the control of the Legislature. The sparsely-populated parts of the State are those where there are very few negroes, the parts inhabited by the white rebels, the men who, coming in from Georgia, Alabama, and other States, control the fortunes of their several counties. By this constitution every county in that State is entitled to a representative. There are in that State counties that have not thirty registered voters; yet, under this constitution, every one of those counties is entitled to a representative in the Legislature; while the populous counties are entitled to only one representative each, with an additional representative for every thousand inhabitants."

The response of Mr. Butler is particularly illuminating:

"All these arguments, all these statements, all the provisions of this constitution have been submitted to the Judiciary Com-mittee of the Senate, and they have found the constitution republican and proper. This constitution has been submitted to the Senate, and they have found it republican and proper. It has been submitted to your own Committee on Reconstruction, and they have found it republican and proper, and have reported it to this House."

The Constitutions of six of the 10 States contained provisions departing substantially from the method of apportionment now held to be required by the Amendment. And, as in the North, the departures were as real in fact as in theory. In North Carolina, 90 of the 120 representatives were apportioned among the counties without regard to population, leaving 30 seats to be distributed by numbers. Since there were seven counties with populations under 5,000 and 26 counties with populations over 15,000, the disproportions must have been widespread and substantial. In South Carolina, Charleston, with a population of 88,863, elected two Senators; each of the other counties, with populations ranging from 10,269 to 42,486 elected one Senator. In Florida, each of the 39 counties was entitled to elect one Representative; no county was entitled to more than four. These principles applied to Dade County with a population of 85 and to Alachua County and Leon County, with populations of 17,328 and 15,236, respectively.

It is incredible that Congress would have exacted ratification of the Fourteenth Amendment as the price of readmission, would have studied the State Constitutions for compliance with the Amendment, and would then have disregarded violations of it.

The facts recited above show beyond any possible doubt:

(1) that Congress, with full awareness of and attention to the possibility that the States would not afford full equality in voting rights to all their citizens, nevertheless deliberately chose not to interfere with the States' plenary power in this regard when it proposed the Fourteenth Amendment;

(2) that Congress did not include in the Fourteenth

Amendment restrictions on the States' power to control voting rights because it believed that if such restrictions were included, the Amendment would not be adopted.

(3) that at least a substantial majority, if not all, of the States which ratified the Fourteenth Amendment did not consider that in so doing, they were accepting limitations on their freedom, never before questioned, to regulate voting rights as they chose.

Even if one were to accept the majority's belief that it is proper entirely to disregard the unmistakable implications of the second section of the Amendment in construing the first section, one is confounded by its disregard of all this history. There is here none of the difficulty which may attend the application of basic principles to situations not contemplated or understood when the principles were framed. The problems which concern the Court now were problems when the Amendment was adopted. By the deliberate choice of those responsible for the Amendment, it left those problems untouched.

C. *After 1868.*

The years following 1868, far from indicating a developing awareness of the applicability of the Fourteenth Amendment to problems of apportionment, demonstrate precisely the reverse: that the States retained and exercised the power independently to apportion their legislatures. In its Constitutions of 1875 and 1901, Alabama carried forward earlier provisions guaranteeing each county at least one representative and fixing an upper limit to the number of seats in the House. Florida's Constitution of 1885 continued the guarantee of one representative for each county and reduced the maximum number of representatives per county from four to three. Georgia, in 1877, continued to favor the smaller counties. Louisiana, in 1879, guaranteed each parish at least one representative in the House. In 1890, Mississippi guaranteed each county one representative, established a maximum number of representatives, and provided that specified groups of counties should each have approximately one-third of the seats in the House, whatever the spread of population. Missouri's Constitution of 1875 gave each county one representative and otherwise favored less populous areas. Montana's original Constitution of 1889 apportioned the State Senate by counties. In 1877, New Hampshire amended its Constitution's provisions for apportionment, but continued to favor sparsely settled areas in the House and to apportion seats in the Senate according to direct taxes paid; the same was true of New Hampshire's Constitution of 1902.

In 1894, New York adopted a Constitution the peculiar apportionment provisions of which were obviously intended to prevent representation according to population: no county was allowed to have more than one-third of all the senators, no two counties which were adjoining or "separated only by public waters" could have more than one-half of all the senators, and whenever any county became entitled to more than three senators, the total number of senators was increased, thus preserving to the small counties their original number of seats. In addition, each county except Hamilton was guaranteed a seat in the Assembly. The North Carolina Constitution of 1876 gave each county at least one representative and fixed a maximum number of representatives for the whole House. Oklahoma's Constitution at the time of its admission to the Union (1907) favored small counties by the use of partial ratios and a maximum number of seats in the House; in addition, no county was permitted to "take part" in the election of more than seven representatives. Pennsylvania, in 1873, continued to guarantee each county one representative in the House. The same was true of South Carolina's Constitution of 1895, which provided also that each county should elect one and only one Senator. Utah's original Constitution of 1895 assured each county of one representative in the House.

Wyoming, when it entered the Union in 1889, guaranteed each county at least one senator and one representative.

D. *Today.*

Since the Court now invalidates the legislative apportionments in six States, and has so far upheld the apportionment in none, it is scarcely necessary to comment on the situation in the States today, which is, of course, as fully contrary to the Court's decision as is the record of every prior period in this Nation's history. As of 1961, the Constitutions of all but 11 States, roughly 20% of the total, recognized bases of apportionment other than geographic spread of population, and to some extent favored sparsely populated areas by a variety of devices, ranging from straight area representation or guaranteed minimum area representation to complicated schemes of the kind exemplified by the provisions of New York's Constitution of 1894, still in effect until struck down by the Court today in No. 20, *post*, p. ——. Since Tennessee, which was the subject of *Baker* v. *Carr,* and Virginia, scrutinized and disapproved today in No. 69, *post*, p. ——, are among the 11 States whose own Constitutions are sound from the standpoint of the Federal Constitution as construed today, it is evident that the actual practice of the States is even more uniformly than their theory opposed to the Court's view of what is constitutionally permissible.

E. *Other factors.*

In this summary of what the majority ignores, note should be taken of the Fifteenth and Nineteenth Amendments. The former prohibited the States from denying or abridging the right to vote "on account of race, color, or previous condition of servitude." The latter, certified as part of the Constitution in 1920, added sex to the prohibited classifications. In *Minor* v. *Happersett,* 21 Wall. 162, this Court considered the claim that the right of women to vote was protected by the Privileges and Immunities Clause of the Fourteenth Amendment. The Court's discussion there of the significance of the Fifteenth Amendment is fully applicable here with respect to the Nineteenth Amendment as well.

> "And still again, after the adoption of the fourteenth amendment, it was deemed necessary to adopt a fifteenth, as follows: 'The right of citizens of the United States to vote shall not be denied or abridged by the United States, or by any State, on account of race, color, or previous condition of servitude.' The fourteenth amendment had already provided that no State should make or enforce any law which should abridge the privileges or immunities of citizens of the United States. If suffrage was one of these privileges or immunities, why amend the Constitution to prevent its being denied on account of race, &c.? Nothing is more evident than that the greater must include the less, and if all were already protected why go through with the form of amending the Constitution to protect a part?" *Id.,* at 175.

In the present case, we can go still further. If constitutional amendment was the only means by which all men and, later, women, could be guaranteed the right to vote at all, even for *federal* officers, how can it be that the far less obvious right to a particular kind of apportionment of *state* legislatures—a right to which is opposed a far more plausible conflicting interest of the State than the interest which opposes the general right to vote—can be conferred by judicial construction of the Fourteenth Amendment? Yet, unless one takes the highly implausible view that the Fourteenth Amendment controls methods of apportionment but leaves the right to vote itself unprotected, the conclusion is inescapable that the Court has, for purposes of these cases, relegated the Fifteenth and Nineteenth Amendments to the same limbo of constitutional anachronisms to which the second section of the Fourteenth Amendment has been assigned.

Mention should be made finally of the decisions of this Court which are disregarded or, more accurately, silently overruled today. *Minor* v. *Happersett, supra,* in which the Court held that the Fourteenth Amendment did *not* confer the right to vote on anyone, has already been noted. Other cases are more directly in point. In *Colegrove* v. *Barrett,* 330 U.S. 804, this Court dismissed "for want of a substantial federal question" an appeal from the dismissal of a complaint alleging that the Illinois legislative apportionment resulted in "gross inequality in voting power" and "gross and arbitrary and atrocious discrimination in voting" which denied the plaintiffs equal protection of the laws. In *Remmey* v. *Smith,* 102 F. Supp. 708 (D. C. E. D. Pa.), a three-judge District Court dismissed a complaint alleging that the apportionment of the Pennsylvania Legislature deprived the plaintiffs of "constitutional rights guaranteed to them by the Fourteenth Amendment." *Id.,* at 709. The District Court stated that it was aware that the plaintiffs' allegations were "notoriously true" and that "the practical disenfranchisement of qualified electors in certain of the election districts in Philadelphia County is a matter of common knowledge." *Id.,* at 710. This Court dismissed the appeal "for the want of a substantial federal question." 342 U.S. 916.

In *Kidd* v. *McCanless,* 292 S. W. 2d 40, the Supreme Court of Tennessee dismissed an action for a declaratory judgment that the Tennessee Apportionment Act of 1901 was unconstitutional. The complaint alleged that "a minority of approximately 37% of the voting population of the State now elects and controls 20 of the 33 members of the Senate; that a minority of 40% of the voting population of the State now controls 63 of the 99 members of the House of Representatives." *Id.,* at 42. Without dissent, this Court granted the motion to dismiss the appeal. 352 U. S. 920. In *Radford* v. *Gary,* 145 F. Supp. 541 (D. C. W. D. Okla.), a three-judge District Court was convened to consider "the complaint of the plaintiff to the effect that the existing apportionment statutes of the State of Oklahoma violate the plain mandate of the Oklahoma Constitution and operate to deprive him of the equal protection of the laws guaranteed by the Fourteenth Amendment to the Constitution of the United States." *Id.*, at 542. The plaintiff alleged that he was a resident and voter in the most populous county of the State, which had about 15% of the total population of the State but only about 2% of the seats in the State Senate and less than 4% of the seats in the House. The complaint recited the unwillingness or inability of the branches of the state government to provide relief and alleged that there was no state remedy available. The District Court granted a motion to dismiss. This Court affirmed without dissent. 352 U.S. 991.

Each of these recent cases is distinguished on some ground or other in *Baker* v. *Carr.* See 369 U.S., at 235–236. Their summary dispositions prevent consideration whether these after-the-fact distinctions are real or imaginary. The fact remains, however, that between 1947 and 1957, four cases raising issues precisely the same as those decided today were presented to the Court. Three were dismissed because the issues presented were thought insubstantial and in the fourth the lower court's dismissal was affirmed.

I have tried to make the catalogue complete, yet to keep it within the manageable limits of a judicial opinion. In my judgment, today's decisions are refuted by the language of the Amendment which they construe and by the inference fairly to be drawn from subsequently enacted Amendments. They are unequivocally refuted by history and by consistent theory and practice from the time of the adoption of the Fourteenth Amendment until today.

II.

The Court's elaboration of its new "constitutional" doctrine indicates how far—and how unwisely—it has strayed from the appropriate bounds of its authority. The consequence of today's decision is that in all but the handful of States which may already satisfy the new requirements the local District Court or, it may be, the state courts, are given blanket authority and the constitutional duty to supervise apportionment of the State Legislatures. It is difficult to imagine a more intolerable and inappropriate interference by the judiciary with the independent legislatures of the States.

In the *Alabama* cases (Nos. 23, 27, 41), the District Court held invalid not only existing provisions of the State Constitution—which this Court lightly dismisses with a wave of the Supremacy Clause and the remark that "it makes no difference whether a State's apportionment scheme is embodied in its constitution or in statutory provisions," *ante,* p. 49—but also a proposed amendment to the Alabama Constitution which had never been submitted to the voters of Alabama for ratification, and "standby" legislation which was not to become effective unless the amendment was rejected (or declared unconstitutional) and in no event before 1966. *Sims* v. *Frink,* 208 F. Supp. 431. See *ante,* pp. 8–16. Both of these measures had been adopted only nine days before, at an Extraordinary Session of the Alabama Legislature, convened pursuant to what was very nearly a directive of the District Court, see *Sims* v. *Frink,* 205 F. Supp. 245, 248. The District Court formulated its own plan for the apportionment of the Alabama Legislature, by picking and choosing among the provisions of the legislative measures. 208 F. Supp., at 441–442. See *ante,* p. 17. Beyond that, the court warned the legislature that there would be still further judicial reapportionment unless the legislature, like it or not, undertook the task for itself. 208 F. Supp., at 442. This Court now states that the District Court acted in "a most proper and commendable manner," *ante,* p. 51, and approves the District Court's avowed intention of taking "some further action" unless the State Legislature acts by 1966, *ante,* p. 52.

In the *Maryland* case (No. 29, *post,* p. ——), the State Legislature was called into Special Session and enacted a temporary reapportionment of the House of Delegates, under pressure from the state courts. Thereafter, the Maryland Court of Appeals held that the Maryland Senate was constitutionally apportioned. *Maryland Committee for Fair Representation* v. *Tawes*, 229 Md. 406. This Court now holds that neither branch of the State Legislature meets constitutional requirements. *Post*, p. 17. The Court *presumes* that since "the Maryland constitutional provisions relating to legislative apportionment [are] hereby held unconstitutional, the Maryland Legislature . . . has the inherent power to enact at least temporary reapportionment legislation pending adoption of state constitutional provisions" which satisfy the Federal Constitution, *id.*, at 18. On this premise, the Court concludes that the Maryland courts need not "feel obliged to take further affirmative action" now, but that "under no circumstances should the 1966 election of members of the Maryland Legislature be permitted to be conducted pursuant to the existing or any other unconstitutional plan." *Id.*, at 19.

In the *Virginia* case (No. 69, *post*, p. ——), the State Legislature in 1962 complied with the state constitutional requirement of regular reapportionment. Two days later, a complaint was filed in the District Court. Eight months later, the legislative reapportionment was declared unconstitutional. *Mann* v. *Davis*, 213 F. Supp. 577. The District Court gave the State Legislature two months within which to reapportion itself in special session, under penalty of being reapportioned by the court. Only a stay granted by a member of this Court slowed the process; it is plain that no stay will be forthcoming in the future. The Virginia Legislature is to be given "an adequate opportunity to enact a valid plan"; but if it fails "to act promptly in remedying the constitutional defects in the State's legislative apportionment plan," the District Court is to "take further action." *Post*, p. 14.

In *Delaware* (No. 307, *post*, p. ——), the District Court entered an order on July 25, 1962, which stayed proceedings until August 7, 1962, "in the hope and expectation" that the

General Assembly would take "some appropriate action" in the intervening 13 days. *Sincock* v. *Terry*, 207 F. Supp. 205, 207. By way of prodding, presumably, the court noted that if no legislative action were taken and the court sustained the plaintiffs' claim, "the present General Assembly and any subsequent General Assembly, the members of which were elected pursuant to Section 2 of Article 2 [the challenged provisions of the Delaware Constitution], might be held not to be a *de jure* legislature and its legislative acts might be held invalid and unconstitutional." *Id.*, at 205–206. Five days later, on July 30, 1962, the General Assembly approved a proposed amendment to the State Constitution. On August 7, 1962, the District Court entered an order denying the defendants' motion to dismiss. The court said that it did not wish to substitute its judgment "for the collective wisdom of the General Assembly of Delaware," but that "in the light of all the circumstances," it had to proceed promptly. 210 F. Supp. 395, 396. On October 16, 1962, the court declined to enjoin the conduct of elections in November. 210 F. Supp. 396. The court went on to express its regret that the General Assembly had not adopted the court's suggestion, see 207 F. Supp., at 206–207, that the Delaware Constitution be amended to make apportionment a statutory rather than a constitutional matter, so as to facilitate further changes in apportionment which might be required. 210 F. Supp. 401. In January 1963, the General Assembly again approved the proposed amendments of the apportionment provisions of the Delaware Constitution, which thereby became effective on January 17, 1963. Three months later, on April 17, 1963, the District Court reached "the reluctant conclusion" that Art. II, § 2, of the Delaware Constitution was unconstitutional, with or without the 1963 amendment. *Sincock* v. *Duffy*, 215 F. Supp. 169, 189. Observing that "the State of Delaware, the General Assembly, and this court all seem to be trapped in a kind of box of time," *id.*, at 191, the court gave the General Assembly until October 1, 1963, to adopt acceptable provisions for apportionment. On May 20, 1963, the District Court enjoined the defendants from conducting any elections, including the general election scheduled for November 1964, pursuant to the old or the new constitutional provisions. This Court now approves all these proceedings, noting particularly that in allowing the 1962 elections to go forward, "the District Court acted in a wise and temperate manner." *Post*, p. 14.

Records such as these in the cases decided today are sure to be duplicated in most of the other States if they have not already. They present a jarring picture of courts threatening to take action in an area which they have no business entering, inevitably on the basis of political judgments which they are incompetent to make. They show legislatures of the States meeting in haste and deliberating and deciding in haste to avoid the threat of judicial interference. So far as I can tell, the Court's only response to this unseemly state of affairs is ponderous insistence that "a denial of constitutionally protected rights demands judicial protection," *ante*, p. 31. By thus refusing to recognize the bearing which a potential for conflict of this kind may have on the question whether the claimed rights are in fact constitutionally entitled to judicial protection, the Court assumes, rather than supports, its conclusion.

It should by now be obvious that these cases do not mark the end of reapportionment problems in the courts. Predictions once made that the courts would never have to face the problem of actually working out an apportionment have proved false. This Court, however, continues to avoid the consequences of its decisions, simply assuring us that the lower courts "can and . . . will work out more concrete and specific standards," *ante*, p. 43. Deeming it "expedient" not to spell out "precise constitutional tests," the Court contents itself with stating "only a few rather general considerations." *Ibid.*

Generalities cannot obscure the cold truth that cases of this type are not amenable to the development of judicial standards. No set of standards can guide a court which has to decide how many legislative districts a State shall have, or what the shape of the districts shall be, or where to draw a particular district line. No judicially manageable standard can determine whether a State should have single-member districts or multimember districts or some combination of both. No such standard can control the balance between keeping up with population shifts and having stable districts. In all these respects, the courts will be called upon to make particular decisions with respect to which a principle of equally populated districts will be of no assistance whatsoever. Quite obviously, there are limitless possibilities for districting consistent with such a principle. Nor can these problems be avoided by judicial reliance on legislative judgments so far as possible. Reshaping or combining one or two districts, or modifying just a few district lines, is no less a matter of choosing among many possible solutions, with varying political consequences, than reapportionment broadside.

The Court ignores all this, saying only that "what is marginally permissible in one State may be unsatisfactory in another, depending on the particular circumstances of the case," *ante,* p. 43. It is well to remember that the product of today's decisions will not be readjustment of a few districts in a few States which most glaringly depart from the principle of equally populated districts. It will be a redetermination, extensive in many cases, of legislative districts in all but a few States.

Although the Court—necessarily, as I believe—provides only generalities in elaboration of its main thesis, its opinion nevertheless fully demonstrates how far removed these problems are from fields of judicial competence. Recognizing that "indiscriminate districting" is an invitation to "partisan gerrymandering," *ante,* pp. 43–44, the Court nevertheless excludes virtually every basis for the formation of electoral districts other than "indiscriminate districting." In one or another of today's opinions, the Court declares it unconstitutional for a State to give effective consideration to any of the following in establishing legislative districts:

(1) history;

(2) "economic or other sorts of group interests";

(3) area;

(4) geographical considerations;

(5) a desire "to insure effective representation for sparsely settled areas";

(6) "availability of access of citizens to their representatives";

(7) theories of bicameralism (except those approved by the Court);

(8) occupation;

(9) "an attempt to balance urban and rural power."

(10) the preference of a majority of voters in the State.

So far as presently appears, the *only* factor which a State may consider, apart from numbers, is political subdivisions. But even "a clearly rational state policy" recognizing this factor is unconstitutional if "population is submerged as the controlling consideration. . . ."

I know of no principle of logic or practical or theoretical politics, still less any constitutional principle, which establishes all or any of these exclusions. Certain it is that the Court's opinion does not establish them. So far as the Court says anything at all on this score, it says only that "legislators represent people, not trees or acres," *ante*, p. 27; that "citizens, not history or economic interests, cast votes," *ante*, p. 45; that "people, not land or trees or pastures, vote," *ibid.* All this may be conceded. But it is surely equally obvious, and, in the context of elections, more meaningful to note that people are not ciphers and that legislators can represent their electors only by speaking for their interests—economic, social, political —many of which do reflect the place where the electors live.

The Court does not establish, or indeed even attempt to make a case for the proposition that conflicting interests within a State can only be adjusted by disregarding them when voters are grouped for purposes of representation.

CONCLUSION.

With these cases the Court approaches the end of the third round set in motion by the complaint filed in *Baker* v. *Carr*. What is done today deepens my conviction that judicial entry into this realm is profoundly ill-advised and constitutionally impermissible. As I have said before, *Wesberry* v. *Sanders, supra,* at 48, I believe that the vitality of our political system, on which in the last analysis all else depends, is weakened by reliance on the judiciary for political reform; in time a complacent body politic may result.

These decisions also cut deeply into the fabric of our federalism. What must follow from them may eventually appear to be the product of State Legislatures. Nevertheless, no thinking person can fail to recognize that the aftermath of these cases, however desirable it may be thought in itself, will have been achieved at the cost of a radical alteration in the relationship between the States and the Federal Government, more particularly the Federal Judiciary. Only one who has an overbearing impatience with the federal system and its political processes will believe that that cost was not too high or was inevitable.

Finally, these decisions give support to a current mistaken view of the Constitution and the constitutional function of this Court. This view, in a nutshell, is that every major social ill in this country can find its cure in some constitutional "principle," and that this Court should "take the lead" in promoting reform when other branches of government fail to act. The Constitution is not a panacea for every blot upon the public welfare, nor should this Court, ordained as a judicial body, he thought of as a general haven for reform movements. The Constitution is an instrument of government, fundamental to which is the premise that in a diffusion of governmental authority lies the greatest promise that this Nation will realize liberty for all its citizens. This Court, limited in function in accordance with that premise, does not serve its high purpose when it exceeds its authority, even to satisfy justified impatience with the slow workings of the political process. For when, in the name of constitutional interpretation, the Court *adds* something to the Constitution that was deliberately excluded from it, the Court in reality substitutes its view of what should be so for the amending process.

I dissent in each of these cases, believing that in none of them have the plaintiffs stated a cause of action. To the extent that *Baker* v. *Carr,* expressly or by implication, went beyond a discussion of jurisdictional doctrines independent of the substantive issues involved here, it should be limited to what it in fact was: an experiment in venturesome constitutionalism. I would reverse the judgments of the District Court in Nos. 23, 27, and 41 (Alabama), No. 69 (Virginia), and No. 307 (Delaware), and remand with directions to dismiss the complaints. I would affirm the judgments of the District Court in No. 20 (New York), and No. 508 (Colorado), and of the Court of Appeals of Maryland in No. 29.

Governor Earl Warren
on Redistricting

Some sixteen years before the *Reynolds* decision, California was considering a proposal to apportion the state senate in accordance with population. In a speech at Merced, California, on October 29, 1948, Governor Warren (then the Republican candidate for the Vice-Presidency of the United States) made the following remarks:

Many California counties are far more important in the life of the State than their population bears to the entire population of the State. It is for this reason that I have never been in favor of restricting the representation in the senate to a strictly population basis.

It is [for] the same reason that the Founding Fathers of our country gave balanced representation to the States of the Union—equal representation in one house and proportionate representation based on population in the other.

Moves have been made to upset the balanced representation in our State, even though it has served us well and is strictly in accord with American tradition and the pattern of our National Government.

There was a time when California was completely dominated by boss rule. The liberal election laws and legislative reapportionment of the system have liberated us from such domination. Any weakening of the laws would invite a return to boss rule which we are now happily rid of.

Our State has made almost unbelievable progress under our present system of legislative representation. I believe we should keep it.

WMCA, Inc. v. *Lomenzo*
and
Lucas v. *Forty-fourth General Assembly of Colorado*
84 S. Ct. 1418, 1472 (1964)

In these cases the Court found New York's and Colorado's legislative apportionment schemes not based substantially on population— and hence unconstitutional. Mr. Justice Harlan's dissent in *Sims* covers these cases.

MR. JUSTICE STEWART, whom MR. JUSTICE CLARK joins, dissenting. . . .

Simply stated, the question is to what degree, if at all, the Equal Protection Clause of the Fourteenth Amendment limits each sovereign State's freedom to establish appropriate electoral constituencies from which representatives to the State's bicameral legislative assembly are to be chosen. The Court's answer is a blunt one, and, I think, woefully wrong. The Equal Protection Clause, says the Court, "requires that the seats in both houses of a bicameral state legislature must be apportioned on a population basis."

After searching carefully through the Court's opinions in these and their companion cases, I have been able to find but two reasons offered in support of this rule. First, says the Court, it is "established that the fundamental principle of representative government in this country is one of equal representation for equal numbers of people. . . ." With all respect, I think that this is not correct, simply as a matter of fact. It has been unanswerably demonstrated before now that this "was not the colonial system, it was not the system chosen for the national government by the Constitution, it was not the system exclusively or even predominantly practiced by the States at the time of adoption of the Fourteenth Amendment, it is not predominantly practiced by the States today." Secondly, says the Court, unless legislative districts are equal in population, voters in the more populous districts will suffer a "debasement" amounting to a constitutional injury. As the Court explains it, "To the extent that a citizen's right to vote is debased, he is that much less a citizen." We are not told how or why the vote of a person in a more populated legislative district is "debased," or how or why he is less a citizen, nor is the proposition self-evident. I find it impossible to understand how or why a voter in California, for instance, either feels or is less a citizen than a voter in Nevada, simply because, despite their population disparities, each of those States is represented by two United States Senators.

To put the matter plainly, there is nothing in all the history of this Court's decisions which supports this constitutional rule. The Court's draconian pronouncement, which makes unconstitutional the legislatures of most of the 50 States, finds no support in the words of the Constitution, in any prior decision of this Court, or in the 175-year political history of our Federal Union. With all respect, I am convinced these decisions mark a long step backward into that unhappy era when a majority of the members of this Court were thought by many to have convinced themselves and each other that the demands of the Constitution were to be measured not by what it says, but by their own notions of wise political theory. The rule announced today is at odds with long-established principles of constitutional adjudication under the Equal Protection Clause, and it stifles values of local individuality and initiative vital to the character of the Federal Union which it was the genius of our Constitution to create.

I.

What the Court has done is to convert a particular political philosophy into a constitutional rule, binding upon each of the 50 States, from Maine to Hawaii, from Alaska to Texas, without regard and without respect for the many individualized and differentiated characteristics of each State, characteristics stemming from each State's distinct history, distinct geography, distinct distribution of population, and distinct political heritage. My own understanding of the various theories of representative government is that no one theory has ever commanded unanimous assent among political scientists, historians, or others who have considered the problem. But even if it were thought that the rule announced today by the Court is, as a matter of political theory, the most desirable general rule which can be devised as a basis for the make-up of the representative assembly of a typical State, I could not join in the fabrication of a constitutional mandate which imports and forever freezes one theory of political thought into our Constitution, and forever denies to every State any opportunity for enlightened and progressive innovation in the design of its democratic institutions, so as to accommodate within a system of representative government the interests and aspirations of diverse groups of people, without subjecting any group or class to absolute domination by a geographically concentrated or highly organized majority.

Representative government is a process of accommodating group interests through democratic institutional arrangements. Its function is to channel the numerous opinions, interests, and abilities of the people of a State into the making of the State's public policy. Appropriate legislative apportionment, therefore, should ideally be designed to insure effective representation in the State's legislature, in cooperation with other organs of political power, of the various groups and interests making up the electorate. In practice, of course, this ideal is approximated in the particular apportionment system of any State by a realistic accommodation of the diverse and often conflicting political forces operating within the State.

I do not pretend to any specialized knowledge of the myriad of individual characteristics of the several States, beyond the records in the cases before us today. But I do know enough to be aware that a system of legislative apportionment which might be best for South Dakota, might be unwise for Hawaii with its many islands, or Michigan with its Northern Peninsula. I do know enough to realize that Montana with its vast distances is not Rhode Island with its heavy concentrations of people. I do know enough to be aware of the great variations among the several States in their historic manner of distributing legislative power—of the Governors' Councils in New England, of the broad powers of initiative and referendum retained in some States by the people, of the legislative power which some States give to their Governors, by the right of veto or otherwise, of the widely autonomous home rule which many States give to their cities. The Court today declines to give any recognition to these considerations and countless others, tangible and intangible, in holding unconstitutional the particular systems of legislative apportionment which these States have chosen. Instead, the Court says that the requirements of the Equal Protection Clause can be met in any State only by the uncritical, simplistic, and heavy-handed application of sixth-grade arithmetic.

But legislators do not represent faceless numbers. They represent people, or, more accurately, a majority of the voters in their districts—people with identifiable needs and interests which require legislative representation, and which can often be related to the geographical areas in which these people live. The very fact of geographic districting, the constitutional validity of which the Court does not question, carries with it an acceptance of the idea of legislative representation of regional needs and interests. Yet if geographical residence is irrelevant, as the Court suggests, and the goal is solely that of equally "weighted" votes, I do not understand why the Court's constitutional rule does not require the abolition of districts and the holding of all elections at large.[1]

The fact is, of course, that population factors must often to some degree be subordinated in devising a legislative apportionment plan which is to achieve the important goal of ensuring a fair, effective, and balanced representation of the regional, social, and economic interests within a State. And the

---

[1] Even with legislative districts of exactly equal voter population, 26% of the electorate (a bare majority of the voters in a bare majority of the districts) can, as a matter of the kind of theoretical mathematics embraced by the Court, elect a majority of the legislature under our simple majority electoral system. Thus, the Court's constitutional rule permits minority rule.

Students of the mechanics of voting systems tell us that if all that matters is that votes count equally, the best vote-counting electoral system is proportional representation in state-wide elections. See, e.g., *Lakeman and Lambert, supra,* n. 10. It is just because electoral systems are intended to serve functions other than satisfying mathematical theories, however, that the system of proportional representation has not been widely adopted. *Ibid.*

further fact is that throughout our history the apportionments of State Legislatures have reflected the strongly felt American tradition that the public interest is composed of many diverse interests, and that in the long run it can better be expressed by a medley of component voices than by the majority's monolithic command. What constitutes a rational plan reasonably designed to achieve this objective will vary from State to State, since each State is unique, in terms of topography, geography, demography, history, heterogeneity and concentration of population, variety of social and economic interests, and in the operation and interrelation of its political institutions. But so long as a State's apportionment plan reasonably achieves, in the light of the State's own characteristics, effective and balanced representation of all substantial interests, without sacrificing the principle of effective majority rule, that plan cannot be considered irrational.

II.

This brings me to what I consider to be the proper constitutional standards to be applied in these cases. Quite simply, I think the cases should be decided by application of accepted principles of constitutional adjudication under the Equal Protection Clause. A recent expression by the Court of these principles will serve as a generalized compendium:

"[T]he Fourteenth Amendment permits the States a wide scope of discretion in enacting laws which affect some groups of citizens differently than others. The constitutional safeguard is offended only if the classification rests on grounds wholly irrelevant to the achievement of the State's objective. State legislatures are presumed to have acted within their constitutional power despite the fact that, in practice, their laws result in some inequality. A statutory discrimination will not be set aside if any state of facts reasonably may be conceived to justify it." *McGowan* v. *Maryland,* 366 U.S. 420, 425–426.

These principles reflect an understanding respect for the

unique values inherent in the Federal Union of States established by our Constitution. They reflect, too, a wise perception of this Court's role in that constitutional system. The point was never better made than by Mr. Justice Brandeis, dissenting in *New State Ice Co.* v. *Liebmann,* 285 U.S. 262, 280. The final paragraph of that classic dissent is worth repeating here:

"To stay experimentation in things social and economic is a grave responsibility. Denial of the right to experiment may be fraught with serious consequences to the nation. It is one of the happy incidents of the federal system that a single courageous state may, if its citizens choose, serve as a laboratory; and try novel social and economic experiments without risk to the rest of the country. This Court has the power to prevent an experiment. We may strike down the statute which embodies it on the ground that, in our opinion, the measure is arbitrary, capricious or unreasonable. . . . But, in the exercise of this high power, we must be ever on our guard, lest we erect our prejudices into legal principles. If we would guide by the light of reason we must let our minds be bold." 285 U.S., at 311.

That cases such as the ones now before us were to be decided under these accepted Equal Protection Clauses standards was the clear import of what was said on this score in *Baker* v. *Carr,* 369 U.S. 186, 226:

"Nor need the appellants, in order to succeed in this action, ask the Court to enter upon policy determinations for which judicially manageable standards are lacking. Judicial standards under the Equal Protection Clause are well developed and familiar, and it has been open to courts since the enactment of the Fourteenth Amendment to determine, if on the particular facts they must, that a discrimination reflects *no* policy, but simply arbitrary and capricious action."

It is to be remembered that the Court in *Baker* v. *Carr* did not question what had been said only a few years earlier in *MacDougall* v. *Green,* 335 U.S. 281, 284:

"It would be strange indeed, and doctrinaire, for this Court, applying such broad constitutional concepts as due process and equal protection of the laws, to deny a State the power to assure a proper diffusion of political initiative as between its thinly populated counties and those having concentrated masses, in view of the fact that the latter have practical opportunities for exerting their political weight at the polls not available to the former. The Constitution—a practical instrument of government—makes no such demands on the States."

Moving from the general to the specific, I think that the Equal Protection Clause demands but two basic attributes of any plan of state legislative apportionment. First, it demands that, in the light of the State's own characteristics and needs, the plan must be a rational one. Secondly, it demands that the plan must be such as not to permit the systematic frustration of the will of a majority of the electorate of the State. I think it is apparent that any plan of legislative apportionment which could be shown to reflect no policy, but simply arbitrary and capricious action or inaction, and that any plan which could be shown systematically to prevent ultimate effective majority rule, would be invalid under accepted Equal Protection Clause standards. But, beyond this, I think there is nothing in the Federal Constitution to prevent a State from choosing any electoral legislative structure it thinks best suited to the interests, temper, and customs of its people. In the light of these standards, I turn to the Colorado and New York plans of legislative apportionment.

III.

COLORADO

The Colorado plan creates a General Assembly composed of a Senate of 39 members and a House of 65 members. The State is divided into 65 equal population representative districts, with one representative to be elected from each district, and 39 senatorial districts, 14 of which include more than one county. In the Colorado House, the majority unquestionably rules supreme, with the population factor untempered by other considerations. In the Senate rural minorities do not have effective control, and therefore do not have even a veto power over the will of the urban majorities. It is true that, as a matter of theoretical arithmetic, a minority of 36% of the voters could elect a majority of the Senate, but this percentage has no real meaning in terms of the legislative process.[2] Under the Colorado plan, no possible combination of Colorado senators from rural districts, even assuming *arguendo* that they would vote as a bloc, could control the Senate. To arrive at the 36% figure, one must include with the rural districts a substantial number of urban districts, districts with substantially dissimilar interests. There is absolutely no reason to assume that this theoretical majority would ever vote together on any issue so as to thwart the wishes of the majority of the voters of Colorado. Indeed, when we eschew the world of numbers, and look to the real world of effective representation, the simple fact of the matter is that Colorado's three metropolitan areas, Denver, Pueblo, and Colorado Springs, elect a majority of the Senate.

The State of Colorado is not an economically or geographically homogeneous unit. The Continental Divide crosses the State in a meandering line from north to south, and Colorado's 104,247 square miles of area are almost equally divided be-

---

[2] The theoretical figure is arrived at by placing the legislative districts for each house in rank order of population, and by counting down the smallest population end of the list a sufficient distance to accumulate the minimum population which could elect a majority of the house in question. It is a meaningless abstraction as applied to a multimembered body because the factors of political party alignment and interest representation make such theoretical bloc voting a practical impossibility. For example, 31,000,000 people in the 26 least populous States representing only 17% of United States population have 52% of the Senators in the United States Senate. But no one contends that this bloc controls the Senate's legislative process.

tween high plains in the east and rugged mountains in the west. The State's population is highly concentrated in the urbanized eastern edge of the foothills, while farther to the east lies that agricultural area of Colorado which is a part of the Great Plains. The area lying to the west of the Continental Divide is largely mountainous, with two-thirds of the population living in communities of less than 2,500 inhabitants or on farms. Livestock raising, mining and tourism are the dominant occupations. This area is further subdivided by a series of mountain ranges containing some of the highest peaks in the United States, isolating communities and making transportation from point to point difficult, and in some places during the winter months almost impossible. The fourth distinct region of the State is the South Central region, in which is located the most economically depressed area in the State. A scarcity of water makes a state-wide water policy a necessity, with each region affected differently by the problem.

The District Court found that the people living in each of these four regions have interests unifying themselves and differentiating them from those in other regions. Given these underlying facts, certainly it was not irrational to conclude that effective representation of the interests of the residents of each of these regions was unlikely to be achieved if the rule of equal population districts were mechanically imposed; that planned departures from a strict per capita standard of representation were a desirable way of assuring some representation of distinct localities whose needs and problems might have passed unnoticed if districts had been drawn solely on a per capita basis; a desirable way of assuring that districts should be small enough in area, in a mountainous State like Colorado, where accessibility is affected by configuration as well as compactness of districts, to enable each senator to have firsthand knowledge of his entire district and to maintain close contact with his constituents; and a desirable way of avoiding the drawing of district lines which would submerge

the needs and wishes of a portion of the electorate by grouping them in districts with larger numbers of voters with wholly
different interests.

It is clear from the record that if per capita representation
were the rule in both houses of the Colorado Legislature, counties having small populations would have to be merged with
larger counties having totally dissimilar interests. Their representatives would not only be unfamiliar with the problems
of the smaller county, but the interests of the smaller counties
might well be totally submerged to the interests of the larger
counties with which they are joined. Since representatives
representing conflicting interests might well pay greater attention to the views of the majority, the minority interest could
be denied any effective representation at all. Its votes would
not be merely "diluted," an injury which the Court considers
of constitutional dimensions, but rendered totally nugatory.

The findings of the District Court speak for themselves:

"The heterogeneous characteristics of Colorado justify
geographic districting for the election of the members of one
chamber of the legislature. In no other way may representation
be afforded to insular minorities. Without such districting the
metropolitan areas could theoretically, and no doubt practically, dominate both chambers of the legislature. . . .

"The realities of topographic conditions with their resulting
effect on population may not be ignored. For an example, if
[the rule of equal population districts] was to be accepted,
Colorado would have one senator for approximately every
45,000 persons. Two contiguous Western Region senatorial
districts, Nos. 29 and 37, have a combined population of 51,675
persons inhabiting an area of 20,514 square miles. The division of this area into two districts does not offend any constitutional provisions. Rather, it is a wise recognition of the
practicalities of life. . . .

"We are convinced that the apportionment of the Senate by
Amendment No. 7 recognizes population as a prime, but not
controlling, factor and gives effect to such important consider-

ations as geography, compactness and contiguity of territory, accessibility, observance of natural boundaries, conformity to historical divisions such as county lines and prior representation districts, and 'a proper diffusion of political initiative as between a state's thinly populated counties and those having concentrated masses.'" 219 F. Supp., at 932.

From 1954 until the adoption of Amendment 7 in 1962, the issue of apportionment had been the subject of intense public debate. The present apportionment was proposed and supported by many of Colorado's leading citizens. The factual data underlying the apportionment were prepared by the wholly independent Denver Research Institute of the University of Denver. Finally, the apportionment was adopted by a popular referendum in which not only a 2–1 majority of all the voters in Colorado, but a majority in each county, including those urban counties allegedly discriminated against, voted for the present plan in preference to an alternative proposal providing for equal representation per capita in both legislative houses. As the District Court said:

"The contention that the voters have discriminated against themselves appalls rather than convinces. Difficult as it may be at times to understand mass behaviour of human beings, a proper recognition of the judicial function precludes a court from holding that the free choice of the voters between two conflicting theories of apportionment is irrational or the result arbitrary." Ibid.

The present apportionment, adopted overwhelmingly by the people in a 1962 popular referendum as a state constitutional amendment, is entirely rational, and the amendment by its terms provides for keeping the apportionment current.[3] Thus the majority has consciously chosen to protect the minority's interests, and under the liberal initiative provisions of

---

[3] Within the last 12 years, the people of Michigan, California, Washington, and Nebraska (unicameral legislature) have expressed their will in popular referenda in favor of apportionment plans departing from the Court's rule. See *Dixon*, 38 Notre Dame Lawyer, *supra*, at 383–385.

the Colorado Constitution, it retains the power to reverse its decision to do so. Therefore, there can be no question of frustration of the basic principle of majority rule.

IV.

NEW YORK

"Constitutional statecraft often involves a degree of protection from minorities which limits the principle of majority rule. Perfect numerical equality in voting rights would be achieved if an entire State legislature were elected at large but the danger is too great that the remote and less populated sections would be neglected or that, in the event of a conflict between two parts of the State, the more populous region would elect the entire legislature and in its councils the minority would never be heard.

"Due recognition of geographic and other minority interests is also a comprehensible reason for reducing the weight of votes in great cities. If seventy percent of a State's population lived in a single city and the remainder was scattered over wide country areas and small towns, it might be reasonable to give the city voters somewhat smaller representation than that to which they would be entitled by a strictly numerical apportionment in order to reduce the danger of total neglect of the needs and wishes of rural areas."

The above two paragraphs are from the brief which the United States filed in *Baker* v. *Carr*, 369 U.S. 186, 82 S.Ct. 691.[4] It would be difficult to find words more aptly to describe

---

[4] Brief for the United States as *amicus curiae* on reargument, No. 6, 1961 Term, pp. 29–30.

The Solicitor General, appearing as *amicus* in the present cases, declined to urge this Court to adopt the rule of per capita equality in both houses, stating that "[s]uch an interpretation would press the Equal Protection Clause to an extreme, as applied to State legislative apportionment, would require radical changes in three-quarters of the State governments, and would eliminate the opportunities for local variation." Brief for the United States as *amicus curiae*, No. 508, 1963 Term, p. 32.

the State of New York, or more clearly to justify the system of legislative apportionment which that State has chosen.

Legislative apportionment in New York follows a formula which is written into the New York Constitution and which has been a part of its fundamental law since 1894. The apportionment is not a crazy quilt; it is rational, it is applied systematically, and it is kept reasonably current. The formula reflects a policy which accords major emphasis to population, some emphasis to region and community, and a reasonable limitation upon massive over-centralization of power. In order to effectuate this policy, the apportionment formula provides that each county shall have at least one representative in the Assembly, that the smaller counties shall have somewhat greater representation in the legislature than representation based solely on numbers would accord, and that some limits be placed on the representation of the largest counties in order to prevent one megalopolis from completely dominating the legislature.

New York is not unique in considering factors other than population in its apportionment formula. Indeed, the inclusion of such other considerations is more the rule than the exception throughout the states. Two-thirds of the States have given effect to factors other than population in apportioning representation in both houses of their legislatures, and over four-fifths of the States give effect to nonpopulation factors in at least one house. The typical restrictions are those like New York's affording minimal representation to certain political subdivisions, or prohibiting districts composed of parts of two or more counties, or requiring districts to be composed of contiguous and compact territory, or fixing the membership of the legislative body. All of these factors tend to place practical limitations on apportionment according to population, even if the basic underlying system is one of equal population districts for representation in one or both houses of the legislature.

That these are rational policy considerations can be seen
from even a cursory examination of New York's political
makeup. In New York many of the interests which a citizen
may wish to assert through the legislative process are interests
which touch on his relation to the government of his county
as well as to that of the State, and consequently these interests
are often peculiar to the citizens of one county. As the District
Court found, counties have been an integral part of New
York's governmental structure since early colonial times, and
the many functions performed by the counties today reflect
both the historic gravitation toward the county as the central
unit of political activity and the realistic fact that the county
is usually the most efficient and practical unit for carrying out
many governmental programs.

A policy guaranteeing minimum representation to each
county is certainly rational, particularly in a State like New
York. It prevents less densely populated counties from being
merged into multi-county districts where they would receive
no effective representation at all. Further, it may be only by
individual county representation that the needs and interests
of all the areas of the State can be brought to the attention
of the legislative body. The rationality of individual county
representation becomes particularly apparent in States where
legislative action applicable only to one or more particular
counties is the permissible tradition.

Despite the rationality of according at least one representative to each county, it is clear that such a system of representation, coupled with a provision fixing the maximum number
of members in the legislative body—a necessity if the body
is to remain small enough for manageably effective action—
has the result of creating some population disparities among
districts. But since the disparity flows from the effectuation
of a rational state policy, the mere existence of the disparity
itself can hardly be considered an invidious discrimination.

In addition to ensuring minimum representation to each

county, the New York apportionment formula, by allocating somewhat greater representation to the smaller counties while placing limitations on the representation of the largest counties, is clearly designed to protect against overcentralization of power. To understand fully the practical importance of this consideration in New York, one must look to its unique characteristics. New York is one of the few States in which the central cities can elect a majority of representatives to the legislature. As the District Court found, the 10 most populous counties in the State control both houses of the legislature under the existing apportionment system. Each of these counties is heavily urban; each is in a metropolitan area. Together they contain 73.5% of the citizen population, and are represented by 65.5% of the seats in the Senate and 62% of the seats in the Assembly. Moreover, the nine counties comprising one metropolitan area—New York City, Nassau, Rockland, Suffolk and Westchester—contain 63.2% of the total citizen population and elect a clear majority of both houses of the legislature under the existing system which the Court today holds invalid. Obviously, therefore, the existing system of apportionment clearly guarantees effective majority representation and control in the State Legislature.

But this is not the whole story. New York City, with its seven million people and a budget larger than that of the State, has, by virtue of its concentration of population, homogeneity of interest, and political cohesiveness, acquired an institutional power and political influence of its own hardly measurable simply by counting the number of its representatives in the legislature. Elihu Root, a delegate to the New York Constitutional Convention of 1894, which formulated the basic structure of the present apportionment plan, made this very point at that time:

"The question is whether thirty separate centers of 38,606 each scattered over the country are to be compared upon the basis of absolute numerical equality with one center of thirty times 38,606 in one city, with all the multiplications of power that comes from representing a single interest, standing together on all measures against a scattered and disunited representation from the thirty widely separated single centers of 38,606. Thirty men from one place owing their allegiance to one political organization representing the interest of one community, voting together, acting together solidly; why they are worth double the scattered elements of power coming from hundreds of miles apart." 3 Revised Record of the New York State Constitutional Convention of 1894, p. 1215.

Surely it is not irrational for the State of New York to be justifiably concerned about balancing such a concentration of political power, and certainly there is nothing in our Federal Constitution which prevents a State from reasonably translating such a concern into its apportionment formula. See *Mac-Dougall* v. *Green*, 335 U.S. 281, 69 S. Ct. 1.

The State of New York is large in area and diverse in interests. The Hudson and Mohawk Valleys, the farm communities along the southern belt, the many suburban areas throughout the State, the upstate urban and industrial centers, the Thousand Islands, the Finger Lakes, the Berkshire Hills, the Adirondacks—the people of all these and many other areas, with their aspirations and their interests, just as surely belong to the State as does the giant metropolis which is New York City. What the State has done is to adopt a plan of legislative apportionment which is designed in a rational way to ensure that minority voices may be heard, but that the will of the majority shall prevail.

V.

In the allocation of representation in their State Legislatures, Colorado and New York have adopted completely rational plans which reflect an informed response to their particularized characteristics and needs. The plans are quite different, just as Colorado and New York are quite different. But each State, while clearly ensuring that in its legislative councils the will of the majority of the electorate shall rule, has sought to provide that no identifiable minority shall be completely silenced or engulfed. The Court today holds unconstitutional the considered governmental choices of these two Sovereign States. By contrast, I believe that what each State has achieved fully comports with the letter and the spirit of our constitutional traditions.

I would affirm the judgments in both cases.

MR. JUSTICE CLARK, dissenting. . . .

Bell v. *Maryland*
84 S. Ct. 1814 (1964)

A state court found Negro "sit-ins" guilty of criminal trespass. Pending appeal, the state had adopted public-accommodation laws. Here the Supreme Court remanded the case to the state courts for consideration of the effect of the new laws upon the convictions. In short, the Court again avoided the basic constitutional issue raised by the sit-in and related cases: Does the Fourteenth Amendment outlaw only *state* discrimination (the literal reading) or does it also forbid at least some forms of private discrimination? The following minority opinions suggest that the reason for the Court's repeated recent avoidance of this problem is a basic multiple disagreement among the Justices.

The case is significant, because here surprisingly Mr. Justice Black is found on the anti-activist, "illiberal" side of a constitutional issue. Indeed, his position favors "property" over "personal" interests; favors a "literal" versus a "creative" or "imaginative" interpretation of the Fourteenth Amendment; and favors the Harlan-White wing of the Court over the Warren-Douglas-Goldberg wing.

MR. JUSTICE DOUGLAS [with whom MR. JUSTICE GOLDBERG concurred, would reverse "outright" the judgments of conviction]. . . .

II.

The issue in this case, according to those who would affirm, is whether a person's "personal prejudices" may dictate the way in which he uses his property and whether he can enlist the aid of the state to enforce those "personal prejudices." With all respect, that is not the real issue. The corporation that owns this restaurant did not refuse service to these Negroes because "it" did not like Negroes. The reason "it" refused service was because "it" thought "it" could make more money by running a segregated restaurant. . . .

Here, as in most of the sit-in cases before us, the refusal of service did not reflect "personal prejudices" but business reasons. Were we today to hold that segregated restaurants, whose racial policies were enforced by a State, violated the Equal Protection Clause, all restaurants would be on an equal footing and the reasons given in this and most of the companion cases for refusing service to Negroes would evaporate. Moreover, when corporate restaurateurs are involved, whose "personal prejudices" are being protected? The stockholders'? The directors'? The officers'? The managers'? The truth is, I think, that the corporate interest is in making money, not in protecting "personal prejudices."

III.

I leave those questions to another part of this opinion and turn to an even more basic issue.

I now assume that the issue is the one stated by those who would affirm. The case in that posture deals with a relic of slavery—an institution that has cast a long shadow across the land, resulting today in a second-class citizenship in this area of public accommodations.

The Thirteenth, Fourteenth, and Fifteenth Amendments had "one pervading purpose . . . we mean the freedom of the slave race, the security and firm establishment of that freedom, and the protection of the newly-made freeman and citizen from the oppressions of those who had formerly exercised

unlimited dominion over him." Slaughter-House Cases, 16
Wall. 36, 71.

Prior to those Amendments, Negroes were segregated and
disallowed the use of public accommodations except and unless the owners chose to serve them. To affirm these judgments
would remit those Negroes to their old status and allow the
States to keep them there by the force of their police and
their judiciary.

We deal here with public accommodations—with the right
of people to eat and travel as they like and to use facilities
whose only claim to existence is serving the public. What
the President said in his State of the Union Message on January 8, 1964, states the constitutional right of all Americans,
regardless of race or color, to be treated equally by all
branches of government:

> "Today Americans of all races stand side by side in Berlin
> and Vietnam.
> "They died side by side in Korea.
> "Surely they can work and eat and travel side by side in
> America."

The Black Codes were a substitute for slavery; segregation
was a substitute for the Black Codes; the discrimination in
these sit-in cases is a relic of slavery.

The Fourteenth Amendment says "No State shall make or
enforce any law which shall abridge the privileges or immunities of citizens of the United States." The Fourteenth Amendment also makes every person who is born here a citizen; and
there is no second or third or fourth class of citizenship. See,
e. g., Schneider v. Rusk, 377 U.S. ——, 84 S.Ct. 1187.

We deal here with incidents of national citizenship. As
stated in the Slaughter-House Cases, 16 Wall. 36, 71–72, concerning the *federal rights* resting on the Thirteenth, Fourteenth, and Fifteenth Amendments:

> ". . . no one can fail to be impressed with the one pervading
> purpose found in them all, lying at the foundation of each, and

without which none of them would have been even suggested;
we mean the freedom of the slave race, the security and firm
establishment of that freedom, and the protection of the newly-
made freeman and citizen from the oppressions of those who had
formerly exercised unlimited dominion over him. It is true that
only the 15th Amendment, in terms, mentions the negro by
speaking of his color and his slavery. But it is just as true that
each of the other articles was addressed to the grievances of
that race, and designed to remedy them as the fifteenth."

When we deal with Amendments touching the liberation of
people from slavery, we deal with rights "which owe their
existence to the Federal Government, its national character,
its Constitution, or its laws." Id., 16 Wall. at 79. We are not
in the field of exclusive municipal regulation where federal
intrusion might "fetter and degrade the State governments by
subjecting them to control of Congress, in the exercise of powers heretofore universally conceded to them of the most
ordinary and fundamental character." Id., 16 Wall. at 78. . . .

IV.

The problem in this case, and in the other sit-in cases before
us, is presented as though it involved the situation of "a private
operator conducting his own business on his own premises
and exercising his own judgment" as to whom he will admit
to the premises.

The property involved is not, however, a man's home or his
yard or even his fields. Private property is involved, but it is
property that is serving the public. As my Brother GOLDBERG
says, it is a "civil" right, not a "social" right, with which we
deal. Here it is a restaurant refusing service to a Negro.
But so far as principle and law are concerned it might just as
well be a hospital refusing admission to a sick or injured Negro
(cf. Simkins v. Moses H. Cone Memorial Hospital, 4 Cir., 323
F.2d 959), or a drug store refusing antibiotics to a Negro, or
a bus denying transportation to a Negro, or a telephone company refusing to install a telephone in a Negro's home.

The problem with which we deal has no relation to opening or closing the door of one's home. The home of course is the essence of privacy, in no way dedicated to public use, in no way extending an invitation to the public. Some businesses, like the classical country store where the owner lives overhead or in the rear, make the store an extension, so to speak, of the home. But such is not this case. The facts of these sit-in cases have little resemblance to any institution of property which we customarily associate with privacy. . . .

Charles A. Beard had the theory that the Constitution was "an economic document drawn with superb skill by men whose property interests were immediately at stake." An Economic Interpretation of the Constitution of the United States (1939), p. 188. That school of thought would receive new impetus from an affirmance of these judgments. Seldom have modern cases (cf. the ill-starred Dred Scott decision, 19 How. 393) so exalted property in suppression of individual rights. We would reverse the modern trend were we to hold that property voluntarily serving the public can receive state protection when the owner refuses to serve some solely because they are colored.

There is no specific provision in the Constitution which protects rights of privacy and enables restaurant owners to refuse service to Negroes. The word "property" is, indeed, not often used in the Constitution, though as a matter of experience and practice we are committed to free enterprise. The Fifth Amendment makes it possible to take "private property" for public use only on payment of "just compensation." The ban on quartering soldiers in any home in time of peace, laid down by the Third Amendment, is one aspect of the right of privacy. The Fourth Amendment in its restrictions on searches and seizures also sets an aura of privacy around private interests. And the Due Process Clauses of the Fifth and Fourteenth Amendments lay down the command that no person shall be deprived "of life, liberty, or *property,* without the due process of law." (Italics added.) From these provisions those who would affirm find emanations that lead them to the conclusion that the private owner of a restaurant serving the public can pick and choose whom he will serve and restrict his dining room to *whites* only.

Apartheid, however, is barred by the common law as respects innkeepers and common carriers. There were, to be sure, criminal statutes that regulated the common callings. But the civil remedies were made by judges who had no written constitution. We, on the other hand, live under a constitution that proclaims equal protection under the law. Why then, even in the absence of a statute, should *apartheid* be given constitutional sanction in the restaurant field. That was the question I asked in Lombard v. Louisiana, 373 U.S. 267. I repeat it here. Constitutionally speaking, why should Hooper Food Co., Inc., or People's Drug Stores—or any other establishment that dispenses medicines or food—stand on a higher, more sanctified level than Greyhound Bus when it comes to a constitutional right to pick and choose its customers?

The debates on the Fourteenth Amendment show, as my Brother GOLDBERG points out, that one of its purposes was to grant the Negro "the rights and guarantees of the good old common law." Post, 377 U.S. at——. The duty of common carriers to carry all, regardless of race, creed, or color, was in part the product of the inventive genius of judges. See Lombard v. Louisiana, 373 U.S., at 275–277. We should make that body of law the common law of the Thirteenth and Fourteenth Amendments so to speak. Restaurants in the modern setting are as essential to travelers as inns and carriers.

Are they not as much affected with a public interest? Is the right of a person to eat less basic than his right to travel, which we protected in Edwards v. California, 314 U.S. 160? Does not a right to travel in modern times shrink in value materially when there is no accompanying right to eat in public places?

The right of any person to travel *interstate* irrespective of

race, creed, or color is protected by the Constitution. Edwards
v. California, supra. Certainly his right to travel *intrastate*
is as basic. Certainly his right to eat at public restaurants is
as important in the modern setting as the right of mobility.
In these times that right is, indeed, practically indispensable
to travel either interstate or intrastate.

V.

The requirement of Equal Protection, like the guarantee
of Privileges and Immunities of citizenship, is a constitutional
command directed to each State.

State judicial action is as clearly "state" action as state administrative action. Indeed, we held in Shelley v. Kraemer,
334 U.S. 1, 20, that "State action, as that phrase is understood
for the purposes of the Fourteenth Amendment, refers to ex-
ertions of state power in all forms.". . .

The revolutionary change effected by an affirmance in these
sit-in cases would be much more damaging to an open and
free society than what the Court did when it gave the corporation the sword and the shield of the Due Process and Equal
Protection Clauses of the Fourteenth Amendment. Affirmance
finds in the Constitution a corporate right to refuse service to
anyone "it" chooses and to get the State to put people in jail
who defy "its" will. . . .

*Affirmance would make corporate management the arbiter
of one of the deepest conflicts in our society:* corporate management could then enlist the aid of state police, state prose-
cutors, and state courts to force *apartheid* on the community
they served, if *apartheid* best suited the corporate need; or,
if its profits would be better served by lowering the barriers
of segregation, it could do so. . . .

The point is that corporate motives in the retail field relate
to corporate profits, corporate prestige, and corporate public
relations. Corporate motives have no tinge of an individual's
choice to associate only with one class of customers, to keep

members of one race from his "property," to erect a wall of privacy around a business in the manner that one is erected around the home. . . .

MR. JUSTICE GOLDBERG, with whom THE CHIEF JUSTICE joins, and with whom MR. JUSTICE DOUGLAS joins as to Parts II–V, concurring.

I.

I join in the opinion and the judgment of the Court and would therefore have no occasion under ordinary circumstances to express my views on the underlying constitutional issue. Since, however, the dissent at length discusses this constitutional issue and reaches a conclusion with which I profoundly disagree, I am impelled to state the reasons for my conviction that the Constitution guarantees to all Americans the right to be treated as equal members of the community with respect to public accommodations. . . .

V.

In my view the historical evidence demonstrates that the traditional rights of access to places of public accommodation were quite familiar to Congressmen and to the general public who naturally assumed that the Fourteenth Amendment extended these traditional rights to Negroes. But even if the historical evidence were not as convincing as I believe it to be, the logic of Brown v. Board of Education, 347 U.S. 483, based as it was on the fundamental principle of constitutional interpretation proclaimed by Chief Justice Marshall, requires that petitioners' claim be sustained.

In Brown, after stating that the available history was "inconclusive" on the specific issue of segregated public schools, the Court went on to say:

"In approaching this problem, we cannot turn the clock back to 1868 when the Amendment was adopted, or even to 1896 when Plessy v. Ferguson was written. We must consider public education in the light of its full development and its present place in American life throughout the Nation. Only in this way can it be determined if segregation in public schools deprives these plaintiffs of the equal protection of the laws." 347 U.S., at 492–493.

The dissent makes no effort to assess the status of places of public accommodation "in the light of" their "full development and . . . present place" in the life of American citizens. In failing to adhere to that approach the dissent ignores a pervasive principle of constitutional adjudication and departs from the ultimate logic of Brown. As Mr. Justice Holmes so aptly said:

"[W]hen we are dealing with words that also are a constituent act, like the Constitution of the United States, we must realize that they have called into life a being the development of which could not have been foreseen completely by the most gifted of its begetters. It was enough for them to realize or to hope that they had created an organism; it has taken a century and has cost their successors much sweat and blood to prove that they created a nation. The case before us must be considered in the light of our whole experience and not merely in that of what was said a hundred years ago." Missouri v. Holland, 252 U.S. 416, 433. . . .

Mr. Justice Black, with whom Mr. Justice Harlan and Mr. Justice White, join, dissenting. . . .

III.

Section 1 of the Fourteenth Amendment provides in part:

"No State shall . . . deprive any person of life, liberty, or property, without due process of law; nor deny to any person within its jurisdiction the equal protection of the laws."

This section of the Amendment, unlike other sections, is a prohibition against certain conduct only when done by a

State—"state action" as it has come to be known—and "erects no shield against merely private conduct, however discriminatory or wrongful." Shelley v. Kraemer, 334 U.S. 1 (1948). This well-established interpretation of section 1 of the Amendment—which all the parties here, including the petitioners and the Solicitor General, accept—means that this section of the Amendment does not of itself, standing alone, in the absence of some cooperative state action or compulsion, forbid property holders, including restaurant owners, to ban people from entering or remaining upon their premises, even if the owners act out of racial prejudice. But "the prohibitions of the amendment extend to all action of the State denying equal protection of the laws" whether "by its legislative, its executive, or its judicial authorities." Virginia v. Rives, 100 U.S. 313, 318 (1880). The Amendment thus forbids all kinds of state action, by all state agencies and officers, that discriminate against persons on account of their race. . . .

Petitioners, but not the Solicitor General, contend that their conviction for trespass under the state statute was by itself the kind of discriminatory state action forbidden by the Fourteenth Amendment. This contention, on its face, has plausibility when considered along with general statements to the effect that under the Amendment forbidden "state action" may be that of the Judicial as well as of the Legislative or Executive Branches of Government. But a mechanical application of the Fourteenth Amendment to this case cannot survive analysis. The Amendment does not forbid a State to prosecute for crimes committed against a person or his property, however prejudiced or narrow the victim's views may be. Nor can whatever prejudice and bigotry the victim of a crime may have be automatically attributed to the State that prosecutes. Such a doctrine would not only be based on a fiction; it would also severely handicap a State's efforts to maintain a peaceful and orderly society. Our society has put its trust in a system of criminal laws to punish lawless conduct. To avert personal feuds and violent brawls it has led its people to believe and expect that wrongs against them will be vindicated in the courts. Instead of attempting to take the law into their own hands people have been taught to call for police protection to protect their rights wherever possible. It would betray our whole plan for a tranquil and orderly society to say that a citizen, because of his personal prejudices, habits, attitudes, or beliefs, is cast outside the law's protection and cannot call for the aid of officers sworn to uphold the law and preserve the peace. The worst citizen no less than the best is entitled to equal protection of the laws of his State and of his Nation. None of our past cases justifies reading the Fourteenth Amendment in a way that might well penalize citizens who are law-abiding enough to call upon the law and its officers for protection instead of using their own physical strength or dangerous weapons to preserve their rights.

In contending that the State's prosecution of petitioners for trespass is state action forbidden by the Fourteenth Amendment, petitioners rely chiefly on Shelley v. Kraemer, supra. That reliance is misplaced. Shelley held that the Fourteenth Amendment was violated by a State's enforcement of restrictive covenants providing that certain pieces of real estate should not be used or occupied by Negroes, orientals, or any other non-caucasians, either as owners or tenants, and that in case of use or occupancy by such proscribed classes the title of any person so using or occupying it should be divested. . . .

It seems pretty clear that the reason judicial enforcement of the restrictive covenants in Shelley was deemed state action was, not merely the fact that a state court had acted, but rather that it had acted "to deny to petitioners, on the grounds of race or color, the enjoyment of property rights in premises which petitioners are willing and financially able to acquire and which the grantors are willing to sell." 334 U.S., at 19. In other words, this Court held that state enforcement of the covenants had the effect of denying to the parties their federally guaranteed right to own, occupy, enjoy, and use their property without regard to race or color. Thus, the line of cases from Buchanan through Shelley establishes these propositions: (1) When an owner of property is willing to sell and a would-be purchaser is willing to buy, then the Civil Rights Act of 1866, which gives all persons the same right to "inherit, lease, sell, hold, and convey" property, prohibits a State, whether through its legislature, executive, or judiciary, from preventing the sale on the grounds of the race or color of one of the parties. Shelley v. Kraemer, supra, 334 U.S., at 19. (2) Once a person has become a property owner, then he acquires all the rights that go with ownership: "the free use, enjoyment, and disposal of a person's acquisitions without control or diminution save by the law of the land." Buchanan v. Warley, supra, 245 U.S., at 74. This means that the property owner may, in the absence of a valid statute forbidding it, sell his property to whom he pleases and admit to that property whom he will; so long as *both* parties are willing parties, then the principles stated in Buchanan and Shelley protect this right. But equally, when one party is unwilling, as when the property owner chooses *not* to sell to a particular person or *not* to admit that person, then, as this Court emphasized in Buchanan, he is entitled to rely on the guarantee of due process of law, that is, "law of the land," to protect his free use and enjoyment of property and to know that only by valid legislation, passed pursuant to some constitutional grant of power, can anyone disturb this free use. But petitioners here would have us hold that, despite the absence of any valid statute restricting the use of his property, the owner of Hooper's restaurant in Baltimore must not be accorded the same federally guaranteed right to occupy, enjoy, and use property given to the parties in Buchanan and Shelley; instead, petitioners would have us say that Hooper's federal right must be cut down and he be compelled—though no statute said he must—to allow people to force their way into his restaurant and remain there over his protest. We cannot subscribe to such a mutilating, one-sided interpretation of federal guarantees the very heart of which is equal treatment under law to all. We must never forget that the Fourteenth Amendment protects "life, liberty, or property" of all people generally, not just some people's "life," some people's "liberty," and some kinds of "property.". . . We, like the Solicitor General, reject the argument that the State's protection of Hooper's desire to choose customers on the basis of race by prosecuting trespassers is enough, standing alone, to deprive Hooper of his right to operate the property in his own way. But we disagree with the contention that there are other circumstances which, added to the State's prosecution for trespass, justify a finding of state action. There is no Maryland law, no municipal ordinance, and no official proclamation or action of any kind that shows the slightest state coercion of, or encouragement to, Hooper to bar Negroes from his restaurant. Neither the State, the city, nor any of their agencies has leased publicly owned property to Hooper. It is true that the State and city regulate the restaurants—but not by compelling restaurants to deny service to customers because of their race. License fees are collected, but this licensing has no relationship to race. Under such circumstances, to hold that a State must be held to have participated in prejudicial conduct of its licensees is too big a jump for us to take. Businesses owned by private persons do not become agencies of the State because they are licensed; to hold that they do would be completely to negate all our private ownership concepts and practices.

Neither the parties nor the Solicitor General, at least with respect to Maryland, has been able to find the present existence of any state law or local ordinance, any state court or administrative ruling, or any other official state conduct which could possibly have had any coercive influence on Hooper's racial practices. Yet despite a complete absence of any sort of proof or even respectable speculation that Maryland in any way instigated or encouraged Hooper's refusal to serve Negroes, it is argued at length that Hooper's practice should be classified as "state action." This contention rests on a long narrative of historical events, both before and since the Civil War, to show that in Maryland, and indeed in the whole South, state laws and state actions have been a part of a pattern of racial segregation in the conduct of business, social, religious, and other activities. This pattern of segregation hardly needs historical references to prove it. The argument is made that the trespass conviction should be labeled "state action" because the "momentum" of Maryland's "past legislation" is still substantial in the realm of public accommodations. To that extent, the Solicitor General argues, "a State which has drawn a color line may not suddenly assert that it is color blind." We cannot accept such an *ex post facto* argument to hold the application here of Maryland's trespass law unconstitutional. Nor can we appreciate the fairness or justice of holding the present generation of Marylanders responsible for what their ancestors did in other days—even if we had the right to substitute our own ideas of what the Fourteenth Amendment ought to be for what it was written and adopted to achieve.

There is another objection to accepting this argument. If it were accepted, we would have one Fourteenth Amendment for the South and quite a different and more lenient one for the other parts of the country. Present "state action" in this area of constitutional rights would be governed by past history in the South—by present conduct in the North and West. Our Constitution was not written to be read that way, and we will not do it.

IV.

Our Brother GOLDBERG in his opinion argues that the Fourteenth Amendment, of its own force and without the need of congressional legislation, prohibits privately owned restaurants to discriminate on account of color or race. His argument runs something like this: (1) Congress understood the "Anglo-American" common law, as it then existed in the several States, to prohibit owners of inns and other establishments open to the public from discriminating on account of race; (2) in passing the Civil Rights Act of 1866 and other civil rights legislation, Congress meant access to such establishments to be among the "civil rights" protected; (3) finally, those who framed and passed the Fourteenth Amendment intended it, of its own force, to assure persons of all races equal access to privately owned inns and other accommodations. In making this argument, the opinion refers us to three state supreme court cases and to congressional debates on various post-Civil War civil rights bills. However, not only does the very material cited furnish scant, and often contradictory, support for the first two propositions (about the common law and the Reconstruction era statutes), but, even more important, the material furnishes absolutely none for the third proposition, which is the issue in the case. . . .

[An examination of Mr. Justice Goldberg's historical materials is here omitted.]

We are admonished that in deciding this case we should remember that "it is *a constitution* we are expounding." We conclude as we do because we remember that it *is* a Constitution and that it is our duty "to bow with respectful submission to its provisions." And in recalling that it is a Constitution "intended to endure for ages to come," we also remember that the Founders wisely provided the means for that endurance: changes in the Constitution, when thought necessary, are to be proposed by Congress or conventions and ratified by the States. The Founders gave no such amending power to this Court. Cf. Ex parte Virginia, 100 U.S. 339, 345–346 (1880). Our duty is simply to interpret the Constitution, and in doing so the test of constitutionality is not whether a law is offensive to our conscience or to the "good old common law," but whether it is offensive to the Constitution. Confining ourselves to our constitutional duty to construe, not to rewrite or amend, the Constitution, we believe that section 1 of the Fourteenth Amendment does not bar Maryland from enforcing its trespass laws so long as it does so with impartiality.

This Court has done much in carrying out its solemn duty to protect people from unlawful discrimination. And it will, of course, continue to carry out this duty in the future as it has in the past. But the Fourteenth Amendment of itself does not compel either a black man or a white man running his own private business to trade with anyone else against his will. We do not believe that section 1 of the Fourteenth Amendment was written or designed to interfere with a store-keeper's right to choose his customers or with a property owner's right to choose his social or business associates, so long as he does not run counter to valid state or federal regulation. The case before us does not involve the power of the Congress to pass a law compelling privately owned businesses to refrain from discrimination on the basis of race and to trade with all if they trade with any. We express no views as to the power of Congress, acting under one or another provision of the Constitution, to prevent racial discrimination in the operation of privately owned businesses, nor upon any particular form of legislation to that end. Our sole conclusion is that section 1 of the Fourteenth Amendment, standing alone, does not prohibit privately owned restaurants from choosing their own customers. It does not destroy what has until very recently been universally recognized in this country as the unchallenged right of a man who owns a business to run the business in his own way so long as some valid regulatory statute does not tell him to do otherwise. . . .

[*Quaere:* Do you find Mr. Justice Black's strictures in *Bell* against judicial "amending" of the Constitution compatible with his contemporaneous position in *Sims*, which outlaws geographic representation in both houses of the state legislature? Do you find it compatible with his recent view that laws against libel and slander are unconstitutional?

Do you find his concern for property in *Bell* compatible with his position in *Polk* v. *Glover,* above, and his related efforts to read substantive protection for property out of the Fourteenth Amendment?]

[Note: The impasse caused by the deep differences among the Justices (as revealed in *Bell*) seems to have been largely "solved" in *Hamm* v. *City of Rockhill,* 85 S. Ct. 384 (1964). Hamm and others had been prosecuted for trespass in *peaceful,* lunch-counter "sit-ins." The Court held that no such prosecutions were permissible with respect to places of "public accommodation" covered by the federal Civil Rights Act of 1964—for Congress had, in effect, prohibited application of state trespass laws that would deprive any person of the rights granted under the new federal act. Moreover, the Court held that prosecutions (as in Hamm's case) begun before, but not concluded at, the time of the passage of the 1964 Civil Rights Act were abated. Such abatement was derived from the old principle that Congress must be presumed to have intended there should be no punishment when punishment could no longer further any legislative policy (the original policy having been repealed or invalidated by later legislation).

Justices Black, Stewart, Harlan, and White, in separate dissenting opinions, found, *inter alia*, that the abatement principle was not relevant to these cases.]

Griswold v. *Connecticut*
85 S. Ct. 1678 (1965)

Was Mr. Justice Black's dissent in *Bell* merely a sport—a rare exception in his customary libertarian activism? A few months later, in *Hamm* v. *City of Rock Hill,* above, and *Cox* v. *Louisiana,* 85 S.

Ct. 453 (1965), the Justice again found himself aligned in dissent with the anti-activists. Then came his unequivocal stand in the present case.

MR. JUSTICE DOUGLAS delivered the opinion of the Court.

Appellant Griswold is Executive Director of the Planned Parenthood League of Connecticut. Appellant Buxton is a licensed physician and a professor at the Yale Medical School who served as Medical Director for the League at its Center in New Haven—a center open and operating from November 1 to November 10, 1961, when appellants were arrested.

They gave information, instruction, and medical advice to *married persons* as to the means of preventing conception. They examined the wife and prescribed the best contraceptive device or material for her use. Fees were usually charged, although some couples were serviced free.

The statutes whose constitutionality is involved in this appeal are §§ 53-32 and 54-196 of the General Statutes of Connecticut (1938). The former provides:

"Any person who uses any drug, medicinal article or instrument for the purpose of preventing conception shall be fined not less than fifty dollars or imprisoned not less than sixty days nor more than one year or be both fined and imprisoned."

Section 54-196 provides:

"Any person who assists, abets, counsels, causes, hires or commands another to commit any offense may be prosecuted and punished as if he were the principal offender."

The appellants were found guilty as accessories and fined $100 each, against the claim that the accessory statute as so applied violated the Fourteenth Amendment. The Appellate Division of the Circuit Court affirmed. The Court of Errors affirmed that judgment. 151 Conn. 544, 200 A.2d 479. We noted probable jurisdiction. 379 U.S. 962. . . .

Coming to the merits, we are met with a wide range of questions that implicate the Due Process Clause of the Fourteenth Amendment. Overtones of some arguments suggest that Lochner v. State of New York, 198 U.S. 45, should be our guide. But we decline that invitation as we did in West Coast Hotel Co. v. Parrish, 300 U.S. 379; Olsen v. State of Nebraska, 313 U.S. 236; Lincoln Federal Labor Union v. Northwestern Co., 335 U.S. 525; Williamson v. Lee Optical Co., 348 U.S. 483; Giboney v. Empire Storage Co., 336 U.S. 490. We do not sit as a super-legislature to determine the wisdom, need, and propriety of laws that touch economic problems, business affairs, or social conditions. This law, however, operates directly on an intimate relation of husband and wife and their physician's role in one aspect of that relation.

The association of people is not mentioned in the Constitution nor in the Bill of Rights. The right to educate a child in a school of the parents' choice—whether public or private or parochial—is also not mentioned. Nor is the right to study any particular subject or any foreign language. Yet the First Amendment has been construed to include certain of those rights.

By Pierce v. Society of Sisters [268 U.S. 510] the right to educate one's children as one chooses is made applicable to the States by the force of the First and Fourteenth Amendments. By Meyer v. State of Nebraska, supra, the same dignity is given the right to study the German language in a private school. In other words, the State may not, consistently with the spirit of the First Amendment, contract the spectrum of available knowledge. The right of freedom of speech and press includes not only the right to utter or to print, but the right to distribute, the right to receive, the right to read (Martin v. City of Struthers, 319 U.S. 141, 143) and freedom of inquiry, freedom of thought, and freedom to teach (see Wieman v. Updegraff, 344 U.S. 183, 195)—indeed the freedom of the entire university community. Sweezy v. State of New Hampshire, 354 U.S. 234, 249–250, 261–263; Barenblatt v. United

States, 360 U.S. 109, 112; Baggett v. Bullitt, 377 U.S. 360, 369. Without those peripheral rights the specific rights would be less secure.   And so we reaffirm the principle of the Pierce and the Meyer cases.

In NAACP v. State of Alabama, 357 U.S. 449, 462, we protected the "freedom to associate and privacy in one's associations," noting that freedom of association was a peripheral First Amendment right.   Disclosure of membership lists of a constitutionally valid association, we held, was invalid "as entailing the likelihood of a substantial restraint upon the exercise by petitioner's members of their right to freedom of association."   Ibid.   In other words, the First Amendment has a penumbra where privacy is protected from governmental intrusion.   In like context, we have protected forms of "association" that are not political in the customary sense but pertain to the social, legal, and economic benefit of the members.   NAACP v. Button, 371 U.S. 415, 430–431.   In Schware v. Board of Bar Examiners, 353 U.S. 232, we held it not permissible to bar a lawyer from practice, because he had once been a member of the Communist Party.   The man's "association with that Party" was not shown to be "anything more than a political faith in a political party" (id., at 244,) and not action of a kind proving bad moral character. Id., at 245–246.

Those cases involved more than the "right of assembly"— a right that extends to all irrespective of their race or ideology. DeJonge v. State of Oregon, 299 U.S. 353.   The right of "association," like the right of belief (West Virginia State Board of Education v. Barnette, 319 U.S. 624), is more than the right to attend a meeting; it includes the right to express one's attitudes or philosophies by membership in a group or by affiliation with it or by other lawful means.   Association in that context is a form of expression of opinion; and while it is not expressly included in the First Amendment its existence is necessary in making the express guarantees fully meaningful.

The foregoing cases suggest that specific guarantees in the Bill of Rights have penumbras, formed by emanations from those guarantees that help give them life and substance. See Poe v. Ullman, 367 U.S. 497, 516–522 (dissenting opinion). Various guarantees create zones of privacy. The right of association contained in the penumbra of the First Amendment is one, as we have seen. The Third Amendment in its prohibition against the quartering of soldiers "in any house" in time of peace without the consent of the owner is another facet of that privacy. The Fourth Amendment explicitly affirms the "right of the people to be secure in their persons, houses, papers, and effects, against unreasonable searches and seizures." The Fifth Amendment in its Self-Incrimination Clause enables the citizen to create a zone of privacy which government may not force him to surrender to his detriment. The Ninth Amendment provides: "The enumeration in the Constitution, of certain rights, shall not be construed to deny or disparage others retained by the people."

The Fourth and Fifth Amendments were described in Boyd v. United States, 116 U.S. 616, 630, as protection against all governmental invasions "of the sanctity of a man's home and the privacies of life." We recently referred in Mapp v. Ohio, 367 U.S. 643, 656, to the Fourth Amendment as creating a "right to privacy, no less important than any other right carefully and particularly reserved to the people." See Beaney, The Constitutional Right to Privacy, 1962 Sup.Ct.Rev. 212; Griswold, The Right to be Let Alone, 55 N.W.U.L.Rev. 216 (1960).

We have had many controversies over these penumbral rights of "privacy and repose." . . . These cases bear witness that the right of privacy which presses for recognition here is a legitimate one.

The present case, then, concerns a relationship lying within the zone of privacy created by several fundamental constitutional guarantees. And it concerns a law which, in forbidding the *use* of contraceptives rather than regulating their manufacture or sale, seeks to achieve its goals by means having a maximum destructive impact upon that relationship. Such a law cannot stand in light of the familiar principle, so often applied by this Court, that a "governmental purpose to control or prevent activities constitutionally subject to state regulation may not be achieved by means which sweep unnecessarily broadly and thereby invade the area of protected freedoms." NAACP v. Alabama, 377 U.S. 288, 307. Would we allow the police to search the sacred precincts of marital bedrooms for telltale signs of the use of contraceptives? The very idea is repulsive to the notions of privacy surrounding the marriage relationship.

We deal with a right of privacy older than the Bill of Rights—older than our political parties, older than our school system. Marriage is a coming together for better or for worse, hopefully enduring, and intimate to the degree of being sacred. It is an association that promotes a way of life, not causes; a harmony in living, not political faiths; a bilateral loyalty, not commercial or social projects. Yet it is an association for as noble a purpose as any involved in our prior decisions.

Reversed.

MR. JUSTICE GOLDBERG, whom THE CHIEF JUSTICE and MR. JUSTICE BRENNAN join, concurring.

I agree with the Court that Connecticut's birth control law unconstitutionally intrudes upon the right of marital privacy, and I join in its opinion and judgment. Although I have not accepted the view that " 'due process' as used in the Four-teenth Amendment includes all of the first eight Amendments," id., 367 U.S. at 516 (see my concurring opinion in Pointer v. Texas, 380 U.S. 400, 410, and the dissenting opinion of Mr. Justice Brennan in Cohen v. Hurley, 366 U.S. 117), I do agree that the concept of liberty protects those personal rights that are fundamental, and is not confined to the specific terms of the Bill of Rights. My conclusion that the concept of liberty is not so restricted and that it embraces the right of marital privacy though that right is not mentioned explicitly in the Constitution is supported both by numerous decisions of this Court, referred to in the Court's opinion, and by the language and history of the Ninth Amendment. In reaching the conclusion that the right of marital privacy is protected, as being within the protected penumbra of specific guarantees of the Bill of Rights, the Court refers to the Ninth Amendment, ante, at 1681. I add these words to emphasize the relevance of that Amendment to the Court's holding.

The Court stated many years ago that the Due Process Clause protects those liberties that are "so rooted in the traditions and conscience of our people as to be ranked as fundamental." Snyder v. Com. of Massachusetts, 291 U.S. 97, 105. . . .

This Court, in a series of decisions, has held that the Fourteenth Amendment absorbs and applies to the States those specifics of the first eight amendments which express fundamental personal rights. The language and history of the Ninth Amendment reveal that the Framers of the Constitution believed that there are additional fundamental rights, protected from governmental infringement, which exist alongside those fundamental rights specifically mentioned in the first eight constitutional amendments.

The Ninth Amendment reads, "The enumeration in the Constitution, of certain rights, shall not be construed to deny or disparage others retained by the people." The Amendment is almost entirely the work of James Madison. It was introduced in Congress by him and passed the House and Senate with little or no debate and virtually no change in language. It was proffered to quiet expressed fears that a bill of specifically enumerated rights could not be sufficiently broad to cover all essential rights and that the specific mention of certain rights would be interpreted as a denial that others were protected.

In presenting the proposed Amendment, Madison said:

"It has been objected also against a bill of rights, that, by enumerating particular exceptions to the grant of power, it would disparage those rights which were not placed in that enumeration; and it might follow by implication, that those rights which were not signaled out, were intended to be assigned into the hands of the General Government, and were consequently insecure. This is one of the most plausible arguments I have ever heard urged against the admission of a bill of rights into this system; but, I conceive, that it may be guarded against. I have attempted it, as gentlemen may see by turning to the last clause of the fourth resolution [the Ninth Amendment]." I Annals of Congress 440 (Gales and Seaton ed. 1834).

Mr. Justice Story wrote of this argument against a bill of rights and the meaning of the Ninth Amendment:

"In regard to . . . [a] suggestion, that the affirmance of certain rights might disparage others, or might lead to argumentative implications in favor of other powers, it might be sufficient to say that such a course of reasoning could never be sustained upon any solid basis. . . . But a conclusive answer is, that such an attempt may be interdicted (as it has been) by a positive declaration in such a bill of rights that the enumeration of certain rights shall not be construed to deny or disparage other rights retained by the people." II Story on the Constitution 626–627 (5th ed. 1891). . . .

These statements of Madison and Story make clear that the Framers did not intend that the first eight amendments be construed to exhaust the basic and fundamental rights which the Constitution guaranteed to the people.

While this Court has had little occasion to interpret the Ninth Amendment, "[i]t cannot be presumed that any clause in the constitution is intended to be without effect." Marbury v. Madison, 1 Cranch 137, 174. In interpreting the Constitution, "real effect should be given to all the words it uses."

Myers v. United States, 272 U.S. 52, 151. The Ninth Amendment to the Constitution may be regarded by some as a recent discovery but since 1791 it has been a basic part of the Constitution which we are sworn to uphold. To hold that a right so basic and fundamental and so deep-rooted in our society as the right of privacy in marriage may be infringed because that right is not guaranteed in so many words by the first eight amendments to the Constitution is to ignore the Ninth Amendment and to give it no effect whatsoever. Moreover, a judicial construction that this fundamental right is not protected by the Constitution because it is not mentioned in explicit terms by one of the first eight amendments or elsewhere in the Constitution would violate the Ninth Amendment, which specifically states that "[t]he enumeration in the Constitution, of certain rights shall not be *construed* to deny or disparage others retained by the people." (Emphasis added.)

A dissenting opinion suggests that my interpretation of the Ninth Amendment somehow "broaden[s] the powers of this Court." Post at 1701. With all due respect, I believe that it misses the import of what I am saying. I do not take the position of my Brother Black in his dissent in Adamson v. People of State of California, 332 U.S. 46, 68, that the entire Bill of Rights is incorporated in the Fourteenth Amendment, and I do not mean to imply that the Ninth Amendment is applied against the States by the Fourteenth. Nor do I mean to state that the Ninth Amendment constitutes an independent source of rights protected from infringement by either the States or Federal Government. Rather, the Ninth Amendment shows a belief of the Constitution's authors that fundamental rights exist that are not expressly enumerated in the first eight amendments and an intent that the list of rights included there not be exhaustive. As any student of this Court's opinions knows, this Court has held, often unanimously, that the Fifth and Fourteenth Amendments protect certain fundamental personal liberties from abridgement by the Federal Government or the States. . . . The Ninth Amendment simply shows the intent of the Constitution's authors that other fundamental personal rights should not be denied such protection or disparaged in any other way simply because they are not specifically listed in the first eight constitutional amendments. I do not see how this broadens the authority of the court; rather it serves to support what this Court has been doing in protecting fundamental rights.

Nor am I turning somersaults with history in arguing that the Ninth Amendment is relevant in a case dealing with a *State's* infringement of a fundamental right. While the Ninth Amendment—and indeed the entire Bill of Rights—originally concerned restrictions upon *federal* power, the subsequently enacted Fourteenth Amendment prohibits the States as well from abridging fundamental personal liberties. And, the Ninth Amendment, in indicating that not all such liberties are specifically mentioned in the first eight amendments, is surely relevant in showing the existence of other fundamental personal rights, now protected from state, as well as federal, infringement. In sum, the Ninth Amendment simply lends strong support to the view that the "liberty" protected by the Fifth and Fourteenth Amendments from infringement by the Federal Government or the States is not restricted to rights specifically mentioned in the first eight amendments. Cf. United Public Workers v. Mitchell, 330 U.S. 75, 94–95.

In determining which rights are fundamental, judges are not left at large to decide cases in light of their personal and private notions. Rather, they must look to the "traditions and [collective] conscience of our people" to determine whether a principle is "so rooted [there] . . . as to be ranked as fundamental." Snyder v. Com. of Massachusetts, 291 U.S. 97, 105. . . .

The entire fabric of the Constitution and the purposes that clearly underlie its specific guarantees demonstrate that the rights to marital privacy and to marry and raise a family are of similar order and magnitude as the fundamental rights specifically protected.

Although the Constitution does not speak in so many words of the right of privacy in marriage, I cannot believe that it offers these fundamental rights no protection. The fact that no particular provision of the Constitution explicitly forbids the State from disrupting the traditional relation of the family—a relation as old and as fundamental as our entire civilization—surely does not show that the Government was meant to have the power to do so. Rather, as the Ninth Amendment expressly recognizes, there are fundamental personal rights such as this one, which are protected from abridgement by the Government though not specifically mentioned in the Constitution.

My Brother STEWART, while characterizing the Connecticut birth control law as "an uncommonly silly law," post, at 1705, would nevertheless let it stand on the ground that it is not for the courts to " 'substitute their social and economic beliefs for the judgment of legislative bodies, who are elected to pass laws.' " Post, at 1705. Elsewhere, I have stated that "[w]hile I quite agree with Mr. Justice Brandeis that . . . 'a . . . state may . . . serve as a laboratory; and try novel social and economic experiments,' New State Ice Co. v. Liebmann, 285 U.S. 262, 280, 311 (dissenting opinion), I do not believe that this includes the power to experiment with the fundamental liberties of citizens. . . ." The vice of the dissenters' views is that it would permit such experimentation by the States in the area of the fundamental personal rights of its citizens. I cannot agree that the Constitution grants such power either to the States or to the Federal Government.

The logic of the dissents would sanction federal or state legislation that seems to me even more plainly unconstitutional than the statute before us. Surely the Government, absent a showing of a compelling subordinate state interest, could not decree that all husbands and wives must be sterilized after two children have been born to them. Yet by their reasoning such an invasion of marital privacy would not be subject to constitutional challenge because, while it might be "silly," no provision of the Constitution specifically prevents the Government from curtailing the marital right to bear children and raise a family. While it may shock some of my Brethren that the Court today holds that the Constitution protects the right of marital privacy, in my view it is far more shocking to believe that the personal liberty guaranteed by the Constitution does not include protection against such totalitarian limitation of family size, which is at complete variance with our constitutional concepts. Yet, if upon a showing of a slender basis of rationality, a law outlawing voluntary birth control by married persons is valid, then, by the same reasoning, a law requiring compulsory birth control also would seem to be valid. In my view, however, both types of law would unjustifiably intrude upon rights of marital privacy which are constitutionally protected. . . .

In sum, I believe that the right of privacy in the marital relation is fundamental and basic—a personal right "retained by the people" within the meaning of the Ninth Amendment. Connecticut cannot constitutionally abridge this fundamental right, which is protected by the Fourteenth Amendment from infringement by the States. I agree with the Court that petitioners' convictions must therefore be reversed.

MR. JUSTICE HARLAN, concurring in the judgment.

I fully agree with the judgment of reversal, but find myself unable to join the Court's opinion. The reason is that it seems to me to evince an approach to this case very much like that taken by my Brothers BLACK and STEWART in dissent, namely: the Due Process Clause of the Fourteenth Amendment does not touch this Connecticut statute unless the enactment is found to violate some right assured by the letter or penumbra of the Bill of Rights.

In other words, what I find implicit in the Court's opinion is that the "incorporation" doctrine may be used to *restrict* the reach of Fourteenth Amendment Due Process. For me this is just as unacceptable constitutional doctrine as is the use of the "incorporation" approach to *impose* upon the States all the requirements of the Bill of Rights as found in the provisions of the first eight amendments and in the decisions of this Court interpreting them. . . .

In my view, the proper constitutional inquiry in this case is whether this Connecticut statute infringes the Due Process Clause of the Fourteenth Amendment because the enactment violates basic values "implicit in the concept of ordered liberty," Palko v. State of Connecticut, 302 U.S. 319, 325. For reasons stated at length in my dissenting opinion in Poe v. Ullman, supra, I believe that it does. While the relevant inquiry may be aided by resort to one or more of the provisions of the Bill of Rights, it is not dependent on them or any of their radiations. The Due Process Clause of the Fourteenth Amendment stands, in my opinion, on its own bottom.

A further observation seems in order respecting the justification of my Brothers BLACK and STEWART for their "incorporation" approach to this case. Their approach does not rest on historical reasons, which are of course wholly lacking (see Fairman, Does the Fourteenth Amendment Incorporate the Bill of Rights? The Original Understanding, 2 Stan.L.Rev. 5 [1949]), but on the thesis that by limiting the content of the Due Process Clause of the Fourteenth Amendment to the protection of rights which can be found elsewhere in the Constitution, in this instance in the Bill of Rights, judges will thus be confined to "interpretation" of specific constitutional provisions, and will thereby be restrained from introducing their own notions of constitutional right and wrong into the "vague contours of the Due Process Clause." Rochin v. People of State of California, 342 U.S. 165, 170.

While I could not more heartily agree that judicial "self restraint" is an indispensable ingredient of sound constitutional adjudication, I do submit that the formula suggested for achieving it is more hollow than real. "Specific" provisions of the Constitution, no less than "due process," lend themselves as readily to "personal" interpretations by judges whose constitutional outlook is simply to keep the Constitution in supposed "tune with the times" (post, p. 1702). Need one go further than to call up last Term's reapportionment cases, Wesberry v. Sanders, 376 U.S. 1, and Reynolds v. Sims, 377 U.S. 533, where a majority of the Court "interpreted" "by the People" (Art. I, § 2) and "equal protection" (Amd. 14) to command "one person, one vote," an interpretation that was made in the face of irrefutable and still unanswered history to the contrary? See my dissenting opinions in those cases, 376 U.S., at 20; 377 U.S., at 589.

Judicial self-restraint will not, I suggest, be brought about in the "due process" area by the historically unfounded incorporation formula long advanced by my Brother BLACK, and now in part espoused by my Brother STEWART. It will be achieved in this area, as in other constitutional areas, only by continual insistence upon respect for the teachings of history, solid recognition of the basic values that underlie our society, and wise appreciation of the great roles that the doctrines of federalism and separation of powers have played in establishing and preserving American freedoms. See Adamson v. People of State of California, 332 U.S. 46, 59 (Mr. Justice Frankfurter, concurring). Adherence to these principles will not, of course, obviate all constitutional differences of opinion among judges, nor should it. Their continued recognition will, however, go farther toward keeping most judges from roaming at large in the constitutional field than will the interpolation into the Constitution of an artificial and largely illusory restriction on the content of the Due Process Clause.

MR. JUSTICE WHITE, concurring in the judgment.
In my view this Connecticut law as applied to married cou-

ples deprives them of "liberty" without due process of law, as that concept is used in the Fourteenth Amendment. I therefore concur in the judgment of the Court reversing these convictions under Connecticut's aiding and abetting statute. . . .

Mr. Justice Black, with whom Mr. Justice Stewart joins, dissenting.

I agree with my Brother Stewart's dissenting opinion. And like him I do not to any extent whatever base my view that this Connecticut law is constitutional on a belief that the law is wise or that its policy is a good one. In order that there may be no room at all to doubt why I vote as I do, I feel constrained to add that the law is every bit as offensive to me as it is [to] my Brethren of the majority and my Brothers Harlan, White and Goldberg who, reciting reasons why it is offensive to them, hold it unconstitutional. There is no single one of the graphic and eloquent strictures and criticisms fired at the policy of this Connecticut law either by the Court's opinion or by those of my concurring Brethren to which I cannot subscribe—except their conclusion that the evil qualities they see in the law make it unconstitutional.

Had the doctor defendant here, or even the nondoctor defendant, been convicted for doing nothing more than expressing opinions to persons coming to the clinic that certain contraceptive devices, medicines or practices would do them good and would be desirable, or for telling people how devices could be used, I can think of no reasons at this time why their expressions of views would not be protected by the First and Fourteenth Amendments, which guarantee freedom of speech. Cf. Brotherhood of Railroad Trainmen v. Virginia ex rel. Virginia State Bar, 377 U.S. 1; NAACP v. Button, 371 U.S. 415. But speech is one thing; conduct and physical activities are quite another. See, e.g., Cox v. State of Louisiana, 379 U.S. 536, 554–555; Cox v. State of Louisiana, 379 U.S. 559, 563–564; id., 575–584 (concurring opinion); Giboney v. Empire Storage

& Ice Co., 336 U.S. 490; cf. Reynolds v. United States, 98 U.S. 145, 163–164. The two defendants here were active participants in an organization which gave physical examinations to women, advised them what kind of contraceptive devices or medicines would most likely be satisfactory for them, and then supplied the devices themselves, all for a graduated scale of fees, based on the family income. Thus these defendants admittedly engaged with others in a planned course of conduct to help people violate the Connecticut law. Merely because some speech was used in carrying on the conduct—just as in ordinary life some speech accompanies most kinds of conduct —we are not in my view any more justified in holding that the First Amendment forbids the State to punish their conduct. Strongly as I desire to protect all First Amendment freedoms, I am unable to stretch the Amendment so as to afford protection to the conduct of these defendants in violating the Connecticut law. What would be the constitutional fate of the law if hereafter applied to punish nothing but speech is, as I have said, quite another matter.

The Court talks about a constitutional "right of privacy" as though there is some constitutional provision or provisions forbidding any law ever to be passed which might abridge the "privacy" of individuals. But there is not. There are, of course, guarantees in certain specific constitutional provisions which are designed in part to protect privacy at certain times and places with respect to certain activities. Such, for example, is the Fourth Amendment's guarantee against "unreasonable searches and seizures." But I think it belittles that Amendment to talk about it as though it protects nothing but "privacy." To treat it that way is to give it a niggardly interpretation, not the kind of liberal reading I think any Bill of Rights provision should be given. The average man would very likely not have his feelings soothed any more by having his property seized openly than by having it seized privately and by stealth. He simply wants his property left alone. And a person can be just as much, if not more, irritated, annoyed and injured by an unceremonious public arrest by a policeman as he is by a seizure in the privacy of his office or home.

One of the most effective ways of diluting or expanding a constitutionally guaranteed right is to substitute for the crucial word or words of a constitutional guarantee another word, more or less flexible and more or less restricted in its meaning. This fact is well illustrated by the use of the term "right of privacy" as a comprehensive substitute for the Fourth Amendment's guarantee against "unreasonable searches and seizures." "Privacy" is a broad, abstract and ambiguous concept which can easily be shrunken in meaning but which can also, on the other hand, easily be interpreted as a constitutional ban against many things other than searches and seizures. I have expressed the view many times that First Amendment freedoms, for example, have suffered from a failure of the courts to stick to the simple language of the First Amendment in construing it, instead of invoking multitudes of words substituted for those the Framers used. . . . For these reasons I get nowhere in this case by talk about a constitutional "right of privacy" as an emanation from one or more constitutional provisions. I like my privacy as well as the next one, but I am nevertheless compelled to admit that government has a right to invade it unless prohibited by some specific constitutional provision. For these reasons I cannot agree with the Court's judgment and the reasons it gives for holding this Connecticut law unconstitutional.

This brings me to the arguments made by my Brothers HARLAN, WHITE and GOLDBERG for invalidating the Connecticut law. Brothers HARLAN and WHITE would invalidate it by reliance on the Due Process Clause of the Fourteenth Amendment, but Brother GOLDBERG, while agreeing with Brother HARLAN, relies also on the Ninth Amendment. I have no doubt that the Connecticut law could be applied in such a way as to abridge freedom of speech and press and therefore violate the

First and Fourteenth Amendments. My disagreement with the Court's opinion holding that there is such a violation here is a narrow one, relating to the application of the First Amendment to the facts and circumstances of this particular case. But my disagreement with Brothers HARLAN, WHITE and GOLDBERG is more basic. I think that if properly construed neither the Due Process Clause nor the Ninth Amendment, nor both together, could under any circumstances be a proper basis for invalidating the Connecticut law. I discuss the due process and Ninth Amendment arguments together because on analysis they turn out to be the same thing—merely using different words to claim for this Court and the federal judiciary power to invalidate any legislative act which the judges find irrational, unreasonable or offensive.

The due process argument which my Brothers HARLAN and WHITE adopt here is based, as their opinions indicate, on the premise that this Court is vested with power to invalidate all state laws that it considers to be arbitrary, capricious, unreasonable, or oppressive, or because of this Court's belief, that a particular state law under scrutiny has no "rational or justifying purpose," or is offensive to a "sense of fairness and justice." If these formulas based on "natural justice," or others which mean the same thing, are to prevail, they require judges to determine what is or is not constitutional on the basis of their own appraisal of what laws are unwise or unnecessary. The power to make such decisions is of course that of a legislative body. Surely it has to be admitted that no provision of the Constitution specifically gives such blanket power to courts to exercise such a supervisory veto over the wisdom and value of legislative policies and to hold unconstitutional those laws which they believe unwise or dangerous. I readily admit that no legislative body, state or national, should pass laws that can justly be given any of the invidious labels invoked as constitutional excuses to strike down state laws. But perhaps it is not too much to say that no legislative body ever does pass laws without believing that they will accomplish a sane, rational, wise and justifiable purpose. While I completely subscribe to the holding of Marbury v. Madison, 1 Cranch 137, 2 L.Ed. 60, and subsequent cases, that our Court has constitutional power to strike down statutes, state or federal, that violate commands of the Federal Constitution, I do not believe that we are granted power by the Due Process Clause or any other constitutional provision or provisions to measure constitutionality by our belief that legislation is arbitrary, capricious or unreasonable, or accomplishes no justifiable purpose, or is offensive to our own notions of "civilized standards of conduct." Such an appraisal of the wisdom of legislation is an attribute of the power to make laws, not of the power to interpret them. The use by federal courts of such a formula or doctrine or what not to veto federal state laws simply takes away from Congress and States the power to make laws based on their own judgment of fairness and wisdom and transfers that power to this Court for ultimate determination—a power which was specifically denied to federal courts by the convention that framed the Constitution. . . .

My Brother GOLDBERG has adopted the recent discovery that the Ninth Amendment as well as the Due Process Clause can be used by this Court as authority to strike down all state legislation which this Court thinks violates "fundamental principles of liberty and justice," or is contrary to the "traditions and collective conscience of our people." He also states, without proof satisfactory to me, that in making decisions on this basis judges will not consider "their personal and private notions." One may ask how they can avoid considering them. Our Court certainly has no machinery with which to take a Gallup Poll. And the scientific miracles of this age have not yet produced a gadget which the Court can use to determine what traditions are rooted in the "collective conscience of our people." Moreover, one would certainly have to look far beyond the language of the Ninth Amendment to find that the Framers vested in this Court any such awesome veto powers over law-making, either by the States or by the Congress. Nor does anything in the history of the Amendment offer any support for such a shocking doctrine. The whole history of the adoption of the Constitution and Bill of Rights points the other way, and the very material quoted by my Brother GOLDBERG shows that the Ninth Amendment was intended to protect against the idea that "by enumerating particular exceptions to the grant of power" to the Federal Government, "those rights which were not singled out, were intended to be assigned into the hands of the General Government [the United States], and were consequently insecure." That Amendment was passed, not to broaden the powers of this Court or any other department of "the General Government," but, as every student of history knows, to assure the people that the Constitution in all its provisions was intended to limit the Federal Government to the powers granted expressly or by necessary implication. If any broad, unlimited power to hold laws unconstitutional because they offend what this Court conceives to be "the collective conscience of our people" is vested in this Court by the Ninth Amendment, the Fourteenth Amendment, or any other provision of the Constitution, it was not given by the Framers, but rather has been bestowed on the Court by the Court. This fact is perhaps responsible for the peculiar phenomenon that for a period of a century and a half no serious suggestion was ever made that the Ninth Amendment, enacted to protect State powers against federal invasion, could be used as a weapon of federal power to prevent state legislatures from passing laws they consider appropriate to govern local affairs. Use of any such broad, unbounded judicial authority would make of this Court's members a day-to-day constitutional convention.

I repeat so as not to be misunderstood that this Court does have power, which it should exercise, to hold laws unconstitutional where they are forbidden by the Federal Constitution. My point is that there is no provision of the Constitution which either expressly or impliedly vests power in this Court to sit as a supervisory agency over acts of duly constituted legislative body and set aside their laws because of the Court's belief that the legislative policies adopted are unreasonable, unwise, arbitrary, capricious or irrational. The adoption of such a loose, flexible, uncontrolled standard for holding laws unconstitutional, if ever it is finally achieved, will amount to a great unconstitutional shift of power to the courts which I believe and am constrained to say will be bad for the courts and worse for the country. Subjecting federal and state laws to such an unrestrained and unrestrainable judicial control as to the wisdom of legislative enactments would, I fear, jeopardize the separation of governmental powers that the Framers set up and at the same time threaten to take away much of the power of States to govern themselves which the Constitution plainly intended them to have.

I realize that many good and able men have eloquently spoken and written, sometimes in rhapsodical strains, about the duty of this Court to keep the Constitution in tune with the times. The idea is that the Constitution must be changed from time to time and that this Court is charged with a duty to make those changes. For myself, I must with all deference reject that philosophy. The Constitution makers knew the need for change and provided for it. Amendments suggested by the people's elected representatives can be submitted to the people or their selected agents for ratification. That method of change was good for our Fathers, and being somewhat old-fashioned I must add it is good enough for me. And so, I cannot rely on the Due Process Clause or the Ninth Amendment or any mysterious and uncertain natural law concept as a reason for striking down this state law. The Due Process Clause with an "arbitrary and capricious" or "shocking to the conscience" formula was liberally used by this Court to strike down economic legislation in the early decades of this century, threatening, many people thought, the tranquility and stability of the Nation. See, e.g., Lochner v. State of New York, 198, U.S. 45. That formula, based on subjective considerations of "natural justice," is no less dangerous when used to enforce this Court's views about personal rights than those about economic rights. I had thought that we had laid that formula, as a means for striking down state legislation, to rest once and for all in cases like West Coast Hotel Co. v. Parrish, 300 U.S. 379; Olsen v. State of Nebraska ex rel. Western Reference & Bond Assn., 313 U.S. 236, and many other opinions. . . . And only six weeks ago, without even bothering to hear argument, this Court overruled Tyson & Brother v. Banton, 273 U.S. 418, which had held state laws regulating ticket brokers to be a denial of due process of law. Gold v. DiCarlo, 380 U.S. 520. I find April's holding hard to square with what my concurring Brethren urge today. They would reinstate the Lochner, Coppage, Adkins, Burns line of cases, cases from which this Court recoiled after the 1930's, and which had been I thought totally discredited until now. Apparently my Brethren have less quarrel with state economic regulations than former Justices of their persuasion had. But any limitation upon their using the natural law due process philosophy to strike down any state law, dealing with any activity whatever, will obviously be only self-imposed. . . .

The late Judge Learned Hand, after emphasizing his view that judges should not use the due process formula suggested in the concurring opinions today or any other formula like it to invalidate legislation offensive to their "personal preferences,"[1] made the statements, with which I fully agree, that:

"For myself it would be most irksome to be ruled by a bevy of Platonic Guardians, even if I knew how to choose them,

---

[1] Hand, The Bill of Rights (1958) 70. . . .

which I assuredly do not."[2] So far as I am concerned, Connecticut's law as applied here is not forbidden by any provision of the Federal Constitution as that Constitution was written, and I am therefore to affirm.

MR. JUSTICE STEWART, whom MR. JUSTICE BLACK joins, dissenting.

Since 1879 Connecticut has had on its books a law which forbids the use of contraceptives by anyone. I think this is an uncommonly silly law. As a practical matter, the law is obviously unenforceable, except in the oblique context of the present case. As a philosophical matter, I believe the use of contraceptives in the relationship of marriage should be left to personal and private choice, based upon each individual's moral, ethical, and religious beliefs. As a matter of social policy, I think professional counsel about methods of birth control should be available to all, so that each individual's choice can be meaningfully made. But we are not asked in this case to say whether we think this law is unwise, or even asinine. We are asked to hold that it violates the United States Constitution. And that I cannot do.

In the course of its opinion the Court refers to no less than six Amendments to the Constitution: the First, the Third, the Fourth, the Fifth, the Ninth, and the Fourteenth. But the Court does not say which of these Amendments, if any, it thinks is infringed by this Connecticut law.

We *are* told that the Due Process Clause of the Fourteenth Amendment is not, as such, the "guide" in this case. With that much I agree. There is no claim that this law, duly enacted

---

[2] Id., at 73. While Judge Hand condemned as unjustified the invalidation of state laws under the natural law due process formula, . . . he also expressed the view that this Court in a number of cases had gone too far in holding legislation to be in violation of specific guarantees of the Bill of Rights. Although I agree with this criticism of use of the due process formula, I do not agree with all the views he expressed about construing the specific guarantees of the Bill of Rights.

by the Connecticut Legislature, is unconstitutionally vague. There is no claim that the appellants were denied any of the elements of procedural due process at their trial, so as to make their convictions constitutionally invalid. And, as the Court says, the day has long passed since the Due Process Clause was regarded as a proper instrument for determining "the wisdom, need, and propriety" of state laws. Compare Lochner v. State of New York, 198 U.S. 45, with Ferguson v. Skrupa, 372 U.S. 726. My Brothers Harlan and White to the contrary, "[w]e have returned to the original constitutional proposition that courts do not substitute their social and economic beliefs for the judgment of legislative bodies, who are elected to pass laws." Ferguson v. Skrupa, supra, 372 U.S. at 730.

As to the First, Third, Fourth, and Fifth Amendments, I can find nothing in any of them to invalidate this Connecticut law, even assuming that all those Amendments are fully applicable against the States. It has not even been argued that this is a law "respecting an establishment of religion, or prohibiting the free exercise thereof." And surely, unless the solemn process of constitutional adjudication is to descend to the level of a play on words, there is not involved here any abridgment of "the freedom of speech, or of the press; or the right of the people peaceably to assemble, and to petition the Government for a redress of grievances." No soldier has been quartered in any house. There has been no search, and no seizure. Nobody has been compelled to be a witness against himself.

The Court also quotes the Ninth Amendment, and my Brother Goldberg's concurring opinion relies heavily upon it. But to say that the Ninth Amendment has anything to do with this case is to turn somersaults with history. The Ninth Amendment, like its companion the Tenth, which this Court held "states but a truism that all is retained which has not been surrendered," United States v. Darby, 312 U.S. 100, 124, was framed by James Madison and adopted by the State simply to make clear that the adoption of the Bill of Rights did not alter the plan that the *Federal* Government was to be a government of express and limited powers, and that all rights and powers not delegated to it were retained by the people and the individual States. Until today no member of this Court has ever suggested that the Ninth Amendment meant anything else, and the idea that a federal court could ever use the Ninth Amendment to annul a law passed by the elected representatives of the people of the State of Connecticut would have caused James Madison no little wonder.

What provision of the Constitution, then, does make this state law invalid? The Court says it is the right of privacy "created by several fundamental constitutional guarantees." With all deference, I can find no such general right of privacy in the Bill of Rights, in any other part of the Constitution, or in any case ever before decided by this Court.

At the oral argument in this case we were told that the Connecticut law does not "conform to current community standards." But it is not the function of this Court to decide cases on the basis of community standards. We are here to decide cases "agreeably to the Constitution and laws of the United States." It is the essence of judicial duty to subordinate our own personal views, our own ideas of what legislation is wise and what is not. If, as I should surely hope, the law before us does not reflect the standards of the people of Connecticut, the people of Connecticut can freely exercise their true Ninth and Tenth Amendment rights to persuade their elected representatives to repeal it. That is the constitutional way to take this law off the books.

[*Quaere:* Plainly in *Griswold* Mr. Justice Black repudiates judicial activism in favor of judicial restraint. Does this constitute a reversal of his position, or does the Justice believe that he has always been an anti-activist?

Would Messrs. Frank and Reich (the judge's admiring former

law clerks) agree that Mr. Justice Black has been an anti-activist, or indeed that anti-activism is admirable? Their above-quoted comments were of course written before the *Griswold* case.]

THE NEW ECONOMIC ACTIVISM

(1937-?)

As we have seen, the Supreme Court long ago abandoned Field's laissez-faire activism. Mr. Justice Black apparently would go even further, outlawing all substantive business claims under the Fourteenth Amendment.[82] But "substantive due process" was not the only vehicle of laissez-faire. The Commerce Clause (Constitution, Art. 1, Sec. 8) served almost as effectively to frustrate state regulation of business; e.g., *Di Santo's* case, above. Indeed, in the first important use of the clause for this purpose Mr. Justice Field was with the majority; Chief Justice Waite dissented. (See *Wabash, St. Louis & Pacific Ry.* v. *Illinois*, 118 U.S. 557 [1886].) And so it is hardly surprising that, parallel with his veto of "substantive due process," Mr. Justice Black has rejected the Commerce Clause as a restraint upon state regulatory power. (See *Southern Pacific Co.* v. *Arizona*, below.) In his view, even what seems to have been a thinly disguised effort to promote local, at the expense of interstate, trade was permissible in the *Dean Milk* case, below. Surely his opinion there is a triumph of doctrine over reality. Yet the strain can get too great, particularly when libertarian interests are involved—and

---

[82] See his unique position in *Polk* v. *Glover*, reproduced below; and in *Phillips Petroleum Co.* v. *Oklahoma*, 340 U.S. 190, 192 (1950); and *International Shoe Co.* v. *Washington*, 326 U.S. 310, 322 (1945).

then doctrine gives way, with due apology. (See *Morgan v. Virginia,* below.) As in the Fourteenth Amendment cases, here too the Court's more flexible position saves it from Black's recurring dilemma: inconsistency, or unresponsiveness to stubborn reality.

Court-imposed laissez-faire is now plainly gone, but there is evidence of a new economic activism, particularly in the interpretation of statutes involving claims *against* business. Thus, Mr. Justice Black's voting record seems peculiarly pro-consumer in Sherman Act cases, and pro-labor in FLSA, FELA, NLRB and other cases. Of course this pattern—if such it be—is more obvious in the over-all view than in any particular item. One stone does not reveal a mosaic's design. Of the scores of relevant cases included in the statistical data (see pp. 33-39), those presented here (*Callus, Moore,* and *Oregon Medical*) were chosen for their relative simplicity, and to give some notion of the problem as it arises under three different statutes (in that marginal area where Mr. Justice Black is more "liberal" than the Court). None of these cases alone is of major significance. Each is important only as a small item that combines with many others to form the mosaic of neo-economic-activism.

Southern Pacific Co. v. Arizona

325 U.S. 761 (1945)

An Arizona statute of 1912 prohibited trains in excess of seventy freight, or fourteen passenger, cars within that state. The Southern Pacific was prosecuted for violating this limitation.

MR. CHIEF JUSTICE STONE delivered the opinion of the Court:

Although the commerce clause conferred on the national government power to regulate commerce, its possession of the power does not exclude all state power of regulation. Ever since *Willson* v. *Black-Bird Creek Marsh Co.,* 2 Pet. 245, and *Cooley* v. *Board of Wardens,* 12 How. 299, it has been recognized that, in the absence of conflicting legislation by Congress, there is a residuum of power in the state to make laws governing matters of local concern which nevertheless in some measure affect interstate commerce or even, to some extent, regulate it. . . .

But ever since *Gibbons* v. *Ogden,* 9 Wheat. 1, the states have not been deemed to have authority to impede substantially the free flow of commerce from state to state, or to regulate those phases of the national commerce which, because of the need of national uniformity, demand that their regulation, if any, be prescribed by a single authority.

In the application of these principles some enactments may be found to be plainly within and others plainly without state power. But between these extremes lies the infinite variety of cases, in which regulation of local matters may also operate as a regulation of commerce, in which reconcilation of the conflicting claims of state and national power is to be attained only by some appraisal and accommodation of the competing demands of the state and national interests involved. . . .

For a hundred years it has been accepted constitutional doctrine that the commerce clause, without the aid of Congressional legislation, thus affords some protection from state legislation inimical to the national commerce, and that in such cases, where Congress has not acted, this Court, and not the state legislature, is under the commerce clause the final arbiter of the competing demands of state and national interest. . . .

Congress has undoubted power to redefine the distribution of power over interstate commerce. It may either permit the states to regulate the commerce in a manner which would otherwise not be permissible, . . . or exclude state regulation even of matters of peculiarly local concern which nevertheless affect interstate commerce. . . .

But in general Congress has left it to the courts to formulate the rules thus interpreting the commerce clause in its application, doubtless because it has appreciated the destructive consequences to the commerce of the nation if their protection were withdrawn, *Gwin, White & Prince* v. *Henneford, supra,* 441, and has been aware that in their application state laws will not be invalidated without the support of relevant factual material which will "afford a sure basis" for an informed judgment. *Terminal Railroad Assn.* v. *Brotherhood, supra,* 8; *Southern R. Co.* v. *King,* 217 U.S. 524. Meanwhile, Congress has accommodated its legislation, as have the states, to these rules as an established feature of our constitutional system. There has thus been left to the states wide scope for the regulation of matters of local state concern, even though it in some measure affects the commerce, provided it does not materially restrict the free flow of commerce across state line, or interfere with it in matters with respect to which uniformity of regulation is of predominant national concern.

Hence the matters for ultimate determination here are the nature and extent of the burden which the state regulation of interstate trains, adopted as a safety measure, imposes on interstate commerce, and whether the relative weights of the state and national interests involved are such as to make inapplicable the rule, generally observed, that the free flow of interstate commerce and its freedom from local restraints in matters requiring uniformity of regulation are interests safeguarded by the commerce clause from state interference.

While this Court is not bound by the findings of the state court, and may determine for itself the facts of a case upon which an asserted federal right depends, . . . the facts found by the state trial court showing the nature of the interstate commerce involved, and the effect upon it of the train limit law, are not seriously questioned. Its findings with respect to the need for and effect of the statute as a safety measure, although challenged in some particulars which we do not regard as material to our decision, are likewise supported by evidence. Taken together the findings supply an adequate basis for decision of the constitutional issue.

The findings show that the operation of long trains, that is trains of more than fourteen passenger and more than seventy freight cars, is standard practice over the main lines of the railroads of the United States, and that, if the length of trains is to be regulated at all, national uniformity in the regulation adopted, such as only Congress can prescribe, is practically indispensable to the operation of an efficient and economical national railway system. On many railroads passenger trains of more than fourteen cars and freight trains of more than seventy cars are operated, and on some systems freight trains are run ranging from one hundred and twenty-five to one hundred and sixty cars in length. Outside of Arizona, where the length of trains is not restricted, appellant runs a substantial proportion of long trains. In 1939 on its comparable route for through traffic through Utah and Nevada from 66 to 85% of its freight trains were over seventy cars in length and over 43% of its passenger trains included more than fourteen passenger cars.

In Arizona, approximately 93% of the freight traffic and 95% of the passenger traffic is interstate. Because of the Train Limit Law appellant is required to haul over 30% more trains in Arizona than would otherwise have been necessary. The record shows a definite relationship between operating costs and the length of trains, the increase in length resulting in a reduction of operating costs per car. The additional cost of operation of trains complying with the Train Limit Law in Arizona amounts for the two railroads traversing that state to about $1,000,000 a year. The reduction in train lengths also impedes efficient operation. More locomotives and more manpower are required; the necessary conversion and reconversion of train lengths at terminals and the delay caused by breaking up and remaking long trains upon entering and leaving the state in order to comply with the law, delays the traffic and diminishes its volume moved in a given time, especially when traffic is heavy.

To relieve the railroads of these burdens, during the war emergency only, the Interstate Commerce Commission, acting under § 1 of the Interstate Commerce Act, suspended the operation of the state law for the duration of the war by its order of September 15, 1942, to which we have referred. In support of the order the Commission declared: "It was designed to save manpower, motive power, engine-miles and train-miles; to avoid delay in the movement of trains; to increase the efficient use of locomotives and cars and to augment the available supply thereof; and to relieve congestion at terminals caused by setting out and picking up cars on each side of the train-limit law States." *In the Matter of Service Order No. 85,* 256 I.C.C. 523, 524. Appellant, because of its past compliance with the Arizona Train Limit Law, has been unable to avail itself fully of the benefits of the suspension order because some of its equipment and the length of its sidings in Arizona are not suitable for the operation of long trains. Engines capable of hauling long trains were not in service. It can engage in long train operations to the best advantage only by rebuilding its road to some extent and by changing or adding to its motive power equipment, which it desires to do in order to secure more efficient and economical operation of its trains.

The unchallenged findings leave no doubt that the Arizona Train Limit Law imposes a serious burden on the interstate commerce conducted by appellant. It materially impedes the movement of appellant's interstate trains through that state and interposes a substantial obstruction to the national policy proclaimed by Congress to promote adequate, economical and efficient railway transportation service. Interstate Commerce Act, preceding § 1, 54 Stat. 899. Enforcement of the law in Arizona, while train lengths remain unregulated or are regulated by varying standards in other states, must inevitably result in an impairment of uniformity of efficient railroad operation because the railroads are subjected to regulation which is not uniform in its application. Compliance with a state statute limiting train lengths requires interstate trains of a length lawful in other states to be broken up and reconstituted as they enter each state according as it may impose varying limitations upon train lengths. The alternative is for the carrier to conform to the lowest train limit restriction of any of the states through which its trains pass, whose laws thus control the carriers' operations both within and without the regulating state.

Although the seventy car maximum for freight trains is the limitation which has been most commonly proposed, various bills introduced in the state legislatures provided for maximum freight train lengths of from fifty to one hundred and twenty-five cars, and maximum passenger train lengths of from ten to eighteen cars. With such laws in force in states which are interspersed with those having no limit on train lengths, the confusion and difficulty with which interstate operations would be burdened under the varied system of state regulation and the unsatisfied need for uniformity in such regulation, if any, are evident.

At present the seventy freight car laws are enforced only in Arizona and Oklahoma, with a fourteen car passenger car limit in Arizona. The record here shows that the enforcement of the Arizona statute results in freight trains being broken up and reformed at the California border and in New Mexico, some distance from the Arizona line. Frequently it is not feasible to operate a newly assembled train from the New Mexico yard nearest to Arizona, with the result that the Arizona limitation governs the flow of traffic as far east as El Paso, Texas.

For similar reasons the Arizona law often controls the length of passenger trains all the way from Los Angeles to El Paso.

If one state may regulate train lengths, so may all the others, and they need not prescribe the same maximum limitation. The practical effect of such regulation is to control train operations beyond the boundaries of the state exacting it because of the necessity of breaking up and reassembling long trains at the nearest terminal points before entering and after leaving the regulating state. The serious impediment to the free flow of commerce by the local regulation of train lengths and the practical necessity that such regulation, if any, must be prescribed by a single body having a nation-wide authority are apparent.

The trial court found that the Arizona law had no reasonable relation to safety, and made train operation more dangerous. Examination of the evidence and the detailed findings makes it clear that this conclusion was rested on facts found which indicate that such increased danger of accident and personal injury as may result from the greater length of trains is more than offset by the increase in the number of accidents resulting from the larger number of trains when train lengths are reduced. In considering the effect of the statute as a safety measure, therefore, the factor of controlling significance for present purposes is not whether there is basis for the conclusion of the Arizona Supreme Court that the increase in length of trains beyond the statutory maximum has an adverse effect upon safety of operation. The decisive question is whether in the circumstances the total effect of the law as a safety measure in reducing accidents and casualties is so slight or problematical as not to outweigh the national interest in keeping interstate commerce free from interferences which seriously impede it and subject it to local regulation which does not have a uniform effect on the interstate train journey which it interrupts.

The principal source of danger of accident from increased

length of trains is the resulting increase of "slack action" of the train. Slack action is the amount of free movement of one car before it transmits its motion to an adjoining coupled car. This free movement results from the fact that in railroad practice cars are loosely coupled and the coupling is often combined with a shock-absorbing device, a "draft-gear," which, under stress, substantially increases the free movement as the train is started or stopped. Loose coupling is necessary to enable the train to proceed freely around curves and is an aid in starting heavy trains, since the application of the locomotive power to the train operates on each car in a train successively and the power is thus utilized to start only one car at a time.

The slack action between cars due to loose couplings varies from seven-eighths of an inch to one and one-eighth inches and, with the added free movement due to the use of draft gears, may be as high as six or seven inches between cars. The length of the train increases the slack since the slack action of a train is the total of the free movement between its several cars. The amount of slack action has some effect on the severity of the shock of train movements, and on freight trains sometimes results in injuries to operatives, which most frequently occur to occupants of the caboose. The amount and severity of slack action, however, are not wholly dependent upon the length of train, as they may be affected by the mode and conditions of operation as to grades, speed, and load. And accidents due to slack action also occur in the operation of short trains. On comparison of the number of slack action accidents in Arizona with those in Nevada, where the length of trains is now unregulated, the trial court found that with substantially the same amount of traffic in each state the number of accidents was relatively the same in long as in short train operations. While accidents from slack action do occur in the operation of passenger trains, it does not appear that they are more frequent or the resulting shocks more severe on long than on short passenger trains. Nor does it appear that slack action accidents occurring on passenger trains, whatever their length, are of sufficient severity to cause serious injury or damage.

As the trial court found, reduction of the length of trains also tends to increase the number of accidents because of the increase in the number of trains. The application of the Arizona law compelled appellant to operate 30.08%, or 4,304, more freight trains in 1938 than would otherwise have been necessary. And the record amply supports the trial court's conclusion that the frequency of accidents is closely related to the number of trains run. The number of accidents due to grade crossing collisions between trains and motor vehicles and pedestrians, and to collisions between trains, which are usually far more serious than those due to slack action, and accidents due to locomotive failures, in general vary with the number of trains. Increase in the number of trains results in more starts and stops, more "meets" and "passes," and more switching movements, all tending to increase the number of accidents not only to train operatives and other railroad employees, but to passengers and members of the public exposed to danger by train operations.

Railroad statistics introduced into the record tend to show that this is the result of the application of the Arizona Train Limit Law to appellant, both with respect to all railroad casualties within the state and those affecting only trainmen whom the train limit law is supposed to protect. The accident rate in Arizona is much higher than on comparable lines elsewhere, where there is no regulation of length of trains. The record lends support to the trial court's conclusion that the train length limitation increased rather than diminished the number of accidents. This is shown by comparison of appellant's operations in Arizona with those in Nevada, and by comparison of operations of appellant and of the Sante Fe Railroad in Arizona with those of the same roads in New Mexico, and by like comparison between appellant's operations in Arizona and operations throughout the country.

Upon an examination of the whole case the trial court found that "if short-train operation may or should result in any decrease in the number of severity of the 'slack' or 'slack-surge' type of accidents or casualties, such decrease is substantially more than offset by the increased number of accidents and casualties from other causes that follow the arbitrary limitation of freight trains to 70 cars . . . and passenger trains to 14 cars."

We think, as the trial court found that the Arizona Train Limit Law, viewed as a safety measure, affords at most slight and dubious advantage, if any, over unregulated train lengths, because it results in an increase in the number of trains and train operations and the consequent increase in train accidents of a character generally more severe than those due to slack action. Its undoubted effect on the commerce is the regulation, without securing uniformity, of the length of trains operated in interstate commerce, which lack is itself a primary cause of preventing the free flow of commerce by delaying it and by substantially increasing its cost and impairing its efficiency. In these respects the case differs from those where a state, by regulatory measures affecting the commerce, has removed or reduced safety hazards without substantial interference with the interstate movement of trains. Such are measures abolishing the car stove, *New York, N. H. & H. R. Co.* v. *New York*, 165 U.S. 628; requiring locomotives to be supplied with electric headlights, *Atlantic Coast Line R. Co.* v. *Georgia*, 234 U.S. 280; providing for full train crews, *Chicago, R. I. & P. R. Co.* v. *Arkansas*, 219 U.S. 453; *St. Louis & I. M. R. Co.* v. *Arkansas*, 240 U.S. 518; *Missouri Pacific R. Co.* v. *Norwood*, 283 U.S. 249; and for the equipment of freight trains with cabooses, *Terminal Railroad Assn.* v. *Brotherhood, supra.*

The principle that, without controlling Congressional action, a state may not regulate interstate commerce so as to substantially to affect its flow or deprive it of needed uniformity in its regulation is not to be avoided by "simply invoking the convenient apologetics of the police power," *Kansas City Southern R. Co.* v. *Kaw Valley District, supra,* 79; *Buck* v. *Kuykendall,* 267 U.S. 307, 315. In the *Kaw Valley* case the Court held that the state was without constitutional power to order a railroad to remove a railroad bridge over which its interstate trains passed, as a means of preventing floods in the district and of improving its drainage, because it was "not pretended that local welfare needs the removal of the defendants' bridges at the expense of the dominant requirements of commerce with other States, but merely that it would be helped by raising them." And in *Seaboard Air Line R. Co.* v. *Blackwell,* 244 U.S. 310, it was held that the interference with interstate rail transportation resulting from a state statute requiring as a safety measure that trains come almost to a stop at grade crossings, outweigh[ed] the local interest in safety, when it appeared that compliance increased the scheduled running time more than six hours in a distance of one hundred and twenty-three miles. *Cf. Southern R. Co.* v. *King, supra,* where the crossings were less numerous and the burden to interstate commerce was not shown to be heavy; and see *Erb* v. *Morasch,* 177 U.S. 584.

Similarly the commerce clause has been held to invalidate local "police power" enactments fixing the number of cars in an interstate train and the number of passengers to be carried in each car, *South Covington R. Co.* v. *Covington, supra,* 547; regulating the segregation of colored passengers in interstate trains, *Hall* v. *DeCuir, supra,* 488–9; requiring burdensome intrastate stops of interstate trains, *Illinois Central R. Co.* v. *Illinois,* 163 U.S. 142; *Cleveland, C., C. & St. L. R. Co.* v. *Illinois,* 177 U.S. 514; *Mississippi Railroad Comm'n* v. *Illinois Central R. Co.,* 203 U.S. 335; *Herndon* v. *Chicago, R. I. & P. R. Co.,* 218 U.S. 135; *St. Louis & S. F. R. Co.* v. *Public Service Comm'n,* 261 U.S. 369; requiring an interstate railroad to detour its through passenger trains for the benefit of a small city,

St. Louis & S. F. R. Co. v. *Public Service Comm'n, supra;* interfering with interstate commerce by requiring interstate trains to leave on time, *Missouri, K. & T. R. Co.* v. *Texas,* 245 U.S. 484; regulating car distribution to interstate shippers, *St. Louis S. W. R. Co.* v. *Arkansas,* 217 U.S. 136; or establishing venue provisions requiring railroads to defend accident suits at points distant from the place of injury and the residence and activities of the parties, *Davis* v. *Farmers Co-operative Co.,* 262 U.S. 312; *Michigan Central R. Co.* v. *Mix,* 278 U.S. 492; *cf. Denver & R. G. W. R. Co.* v. *Terte,* 284 U.S. 284; see also *Buck* v. *Kuykendall, supra; Foster-Fountain Packing Co.* v. *Haydel, supra; Baldwin* v. *Selig, supra,* 524; *South Carolina Highway Dept.* v. *Barnwell Bros., supra,* 184–5 n., and cases cited. . . .

Here we conclude that the state does go too far. Its regulation of train lengths, admittedly obstructive to interstate train operation, and having a seriously adverse effect on transportation efficiency and economy, passes beyond what is plainly essential for safety since it does not appear that it will lessen rather than increase the danger of accident. Its attempted regulation of the operation of interstate trains cannot establish nation-wide control such as is essential to the maintenance of an efficient transportation system, which Congress alone can prescribe. The state interest cannot be preserved at the expense of the national interest by an enactment which regulates interstate train lengths without securing such control, which is a matter of national concern. To this the interest of the state here asserted is subordinate.

Appellees especially rely on the full train crew cases, *Chicago, R. I. & P. R. Co.* v. *Arkansas, supra; St. Louis & I. M. R. Co.* v. *Arkansas, supra; Missouri Pacific R. Co.* v. *Norwood, supra,* and also on *South Carolina Highway Dept.* v. *Barnwell Bros., supra,* as supporting the state's authority to regulate the length of interstate trains. While the full train crew laws undoubtedly placed an added financial burden on the railroads in order to serve a local interest, they did not obstruct interstate transportation or seriously impede it. They had no effects outside the state beyond those of picking up and setting down the extra employees at the state boundaries; they involved no wasted use of facilities or serious impairment of transportation efficiency, which are among the factors of controlling weight here. In sustaining those laws the Court considered the restriction a minimal burden on commerce comparable to the law requiring the licensing of engineers as a safeguard against those of reckless and intemperate habits, sustained in *Smith* v. *Alabama*, 124 U.S. 465, or those afflicted with color blindness, upheld in *Nashville, C. & St. L. R. Co.* v. *Alabama*, 128 U.S. 96, and other similar regulations. *New York, N. H. & H. R. Co.* v. *New York, supra; Atlantic Coast Line R. Co.* v. *Georgia, supra; cf. County of Mobile* v. *Kimball*, 102 U.S. 691.

South Carolina Highway Dept. v. *Barnwell Bros., supra*, was concerned with the power of the state to regulate the weight and width of motor cars passing interstate over its highways, a legislative field over which the state has a far more extensive control than over interstate railroads. In that case, and in *Maurer* v. *Hamilton, supra*, we were at pains to point out that there are few subjects of state regulation affecting interstate commerce which are so peculiarly of local concern as is the use of the state's highways. Unlike the railroads local highways are built, owned and maintained by the state or its municipal subdivisions. The state is responsible for their safe and economical administration. Regulations affecting the safety of their use must be applied alike to intrastate and interstate traffic. The fact that they affect alike shippers in interstate and intrastate commerce in great numbers, within as well as without the state, is a safeguard against regulatory abuses. Their regulation is akin to quarantine measures, game laws, and like local regulations of rivers, harbors, piers, and docks, with respect to which the state has exceptional scope for the exercise of its regulatory power, and which, Congress not acting, have been sustained even though they materially interfere with interstate commerce (303 U.S. 187–188 and cases cited).

The contrast between the present regulation and the full train crew laws in point of their effects on the commerce, and the like contrast with the highway safety regulations, in point of the nature of the subject of regulation and the state's interest in it, illustrate and emphasize the considerations which enter into a determination of the relative weights of state and national interests where state regulation affecting interstate commerce is attempted. Here examination of all the relevant factors makes it plain that the state interest is outweighed by the interest of the nation in an adequate, economical and efficient railway transportation service, which must prevail.

Reversed.

MR. JUSTICE RUTLEDGE concurs in the result.

MR. JUSTICE BLACK, *dissenting.*

In *Hennington* v. *Georgia,* 163 U.S. 299, 304, a case which involved the power of a state to regulate interstate traffic, this Court said, "The whole theory of our government, federal and state, is hostile to the idea that questions of legislative authority may depend . . . upon opinions of judges as to the wisdom or want of wisdom in the enactment of laws under powers clearly conferred upon the legislature." What the Court decides today is that it is unwise governmental policy to regulate the length of trains. I am therefore constrained to note my dissent.

For more than a quarter of a century, railroads and their employees have engaged in controversies over the relative virtues and dangers of long trains. Railroads have argued that they could carry goods and passengers cheaper in long trains than in short trains. They have also argued that while the danger of personal injury to their employees might in some respects be greater on account of the operation of long trains, this danger was more than offset by an increased number of accidents from other causes brought about by the operation of a much larger number of short trains. These arguments have been, and are now, vigorously denied. While there are others, the chief causes assigned for the belief that long trains unnecessarily jeopardize the lives and limbs of railroad employees relate to "slack action." Cars coupled together retain a certain free play of movement, ranging between 1½ inches and 1 foot, and this is called "slack action." Train brakes do not ordinarily apply or release simultaneously on all cars. This frequently results in a severe shock or jar to cars, particularly those in the rear of a train. It has always been the position of the employees that the dangers from "slack action" correspond to and are proportionate with the length of the train. The argument that "slack movements" are more dangerous in long trains than in short trains seems never to have been denied. The railroads have answered it by what is in effect a plea of confession and avoidance. They say that the added cost of running short trains places an unconstitutional burden on interstate commerce. Their second answer is that the operation of short trains requires the use of more separate train units; that a certain number of accidents resulting in injury are inherent in the operation of each unit, injuries which may be inflicted either on employees or on the public; consequently, they have asserted that it is not in the public interest to prohibit the operation of long trains.

In 1912, the year Arizona became a state, its legislature adopted and referred to the people several safety measures concerning the operation of railroads. One of these required railroads to install electric headlights, a power which the state had under this Court's opinion in *Atlantic Coast Line R. Co.* v. *Georgia*, 234 U.S. 280. Another Arizona safety statute submitted at the same time required certain tests and service before a person could act as an engineer or train conductor, and thereby exercised a state power similar to that which this Court upheld in *Nashville, C. & St. L. R. Co.* v. *Alabama*, 128

U.S. 96. The third safety statute which the Arizona legislature submitted to the electorate, and which was adopted by it, is the train limitation statute now under consideration. By its enactment the legislature and the people adopted the viewpoint that long trains were more dangerous than short trains, and limited the operation of train units to 14 cars for passenger and 70 cars for freight. This same question was considered in other states, and some of them, over the vigorous protests of railroads, adopted laws similar to the Arizona statute.

This controversy between the railroads and their employees, which was nationwide, was carried to Congress. Extensive hearings took place. The employees' position was urged by members of the various Brotherhoods. The railroads' viewpoint was presented through representatives of their National Association. In 1937, the Senate Interstate Commerce Committee after its own exhaustive hearings unanimously recommended that trains be limited to 70 cars as a safety measure. The Committee in its Report reviewed the evidence and specifically referred to the large and increasing number of injuries and deaths suffered by railroad employees; it concluded that the admitted danger from slack movement was greatly intensified by the operation of long trains; that short trains reduce this danger; that the added cost of short trains to the railroad was no justification for jeopardizing the safety of railroad employees; and that the legislation would provide a greater degree of safety for persons and property, increase protection for railway employees and the public, and improve transportation services for shippers and consumers. The Senate passed the bill but the House Committee failed to report it out.

During the hearings on that measure, frequent references were made to the Arizona statute. It is significant, however, that American railroads never once asked Congress to exercise its unquestioned power to enact uniform legislation on that subject, and thereby invalidate the Arizona law. That which for some unexplained reason they did not ask Congress to do when it had the very subject of train length limitations under consideration, they shortly thereafter asked an Arizona state court to do.

In the state court a rather extraordinary "trial" took place. Charged with violating the law, the railroad admitted the charge. It alleged that the law was unconstitutional, however, and sought a trial of facts on that issue. The essence of its charge of unconstitutionality rested on one of these two grounds: (1) the legislature and people of Arizona erred in 1912 in determining that the running of long trains was dangerous; or (2) railroad conditions had so improved since 1912 that previous dangers did not exist to the same extent, and that the statute should be stricken down either because it cast an undue burden on interstate commerce by reason of the added cost, or because the changed conditions had rendered the Act "arbitrary and unreasonable." Thus, the issue which the court "tried" was not whether the railroad was guilty of violating the law, but whether the law was unconstitutional either because the legislature had been guilty of misjudging the facts concerning the degree of the danger of long trains, or because the 1912 conditions of danger no longer existed.

Before the state trial court finally determined that the dangers found by the legislature in 1912 no longer existed, it heard evidence over a period of 5½ months which appears in about 3,000 pages of the printed record before us. It then adopted findings of fact submitted to it by the railroad, which cover 148 printed pages, and conclusions of law which cover 5 pages. We can best understand the nature of this "trial" by analogizing the same procedure to a defendant charged with violating a state or national safety appliance act, where the defendant comes into court and admits violation of the act. In such cases, the ordinary procedure would be for the court to pass upon the constitutionality of the act, and either discharge or convict the defendants. The procedure here, however, would justify quite a different trial method. Under it, a defendant is permitted to offer voluminous evidence to show that a legislative body has erroneously resolved disputed facts in finding a danger great enough to justify the passage of the law.   This new pattern of trial procedure makes it necessary for a judge to hear all the evidence offered as to why a legislature passed a law and to make findings of fact as to the validity of those reasons. If under today's ruling a court does make findings, as to a danger contrary to the findings of the legislature, and the evidence heard "lends support" to those findings, a court can then invalidate the law.   In this respect, the Arizona County Court acted, and this Court today is acting, as a "super-legislature."

Even if this method of invalidating legislative acts is a correct one, I still think that the "findings" of the state court do not authorize today's decision. That court did not find that there is no unusual danger from slack movements in long trains.   It did decide on disputed evidence that the long train "slack movement" dangers were more than offset by prospective dangers as a result of running a larger number of short trains, since many people might be hurt at grade crossings. There was undoubtedly some evidence before the state court from which it could have reached such a conclusion.   There was undoubtedly as much evidence before it which would have justified a different conclusion.

Under those circumstances, the determination of whether it is in the interest of society for the length of trains to be governmentally regulated is a matter of public policy.   Someone must fix that policy—either the Congress, or the state, or the courts. A century and a half of constitutional history and government admonishes this Court to leave that choice to the elected legislative representatives of the people themselves, where it properly belongs both on democratic principles and the requirements of efficient government.

I think that legislatures, to the exclusion of courts, have the constitutional power to enact laws limiting train lengths, for

the purpose of reducing injuries brought about by "slack movements." Their power is not less because a requirement of short
trains might increase grade crossing accidents. This latter
fact raises an entirely different element of danger which is
itself subject to legislative regulation. For legislatures may,
if necessary, require railroads to take appropriate steps to
reduce the likelihood of injuries at grade crossings. *Denver &
R. G. R. Co.* v. *Denver*, 250 U.S. 241. And the fact that grade-
crossing improvements may be expensive is no sufficient reason
to say that an unconstitutional "burden" is put upon a railroad
even though it be an interstate road. *Erie R. Co.* v. *Public
Utility Commissioners*, 254 U.S. 394, 408–411.

The Supreme Court of Arizona did not discuss the County
Court's so-called findings of fact. It properly designated the
Arizona statute as a safety measure, and finding that it bore
a reasonable relation to its purpose declined to review the
judgment of the legislature as to the necessity for the passage
of the act. In so doing it was well fortified by a long line of
decisions of this Court. Today's decision marks an abrupt
departure from that line of cases.

There have been many sharp divisions of this Court concerning its authority, in the absence of congressional enactment, to invalidate state laws as violating the Commerce
Clause. See *e.g.*, *Adams Manufacturing Co.* v. *Storen*, 304
U.S. 307; *Gwin, White & Prince* v. *Henneford*, 305 U.S. 434;
McCarroll v. *Dixie Greyhound Lines*, 309 U.S. 176. That
discussion need not be renewed here, because even the broadest exponents of judicial power in this field have not heretofore expressed doubt as to a state's power, absent a paramount
congressional declaration, to regulate interstate trains in the
interest of safety. For as early as 1913, this Court, speaking
through Mr. Justice Hughes, later Chief Justice, referred to
"the settled principle that, in the absence of legislation by
Congress, the states are not denied the exercise of their power
to secure safety in the physical operation of railroad trains

within their territory, even though such trains are used in interstate commerce. That has been the law since the beginning of railroad transportation." *Atlantic Coast Line R. Co.* v. *Georgia,* 234 U.S. 280, 291. Until today, the oft-repeated principles of that case have never been repudiated in whole or in part. . . .

When we finally get down to the gist of what the Court today actually decides, it is this: Even though more railroad employees will be injured by "slack action" movements on long trains than on short trains, there must be no regulation of this danger in the absence of "uniform regulations." That means that no one can legislate against this danger except the Congress; and even though the Congress is perfectly content to leave the matter to the different state legislatures, this Court, on the ground of "lack of uniformity," will require it to make an express avowal of that fact before it will permit a state to guard against that admitted danger.

We are not left in doubt as to why, as against the potential peril of injuries to employees, the Court tips the scales on the side of "uniformity." For the evil it finds in a lack of uniformity is that it (1) delays interstate commerce, (2) increases its cost and (3) impairs its efficiency. All three of these boil down to the same thing, and that is that running shorter trains would increase the cost of railroad operations. The "burden" on commerce reduces itself to mere cost because there was no finding, and no evidence to support a finding, that by the expenditure of sufficient sums of money, the railroads could not enable themselves to carry goods and passengers just as quickly and efficiently with short trains as with long trains. Thus the conclusion that a requirement for long trains will "burden interstate commerce" is a mere euphemism for the statement that a requirement for long trains will increase the cost of railroad operations. . . .

This record in its entirety leaves me with no doubt whatever that many employees have been seriously injured and killed in the past, and that many more are likely to be so in the future, because of "slack movement" in trains. Everyday knowledge as well as direct evidence presented at the various hearings, substantiates the report of the Senate Committee that the danger from slack movement is greater in long trains than in short trains. It may be that offsetting dangers are possible in the operation of short trains. The balancing of these probabilities, however, is not in my judgment a matter for judicial determination, but one which calls for legislative consideration. Representatives elected by the people to make their laws, rather than judges appointed to interpret those laws, can best determine the policies which govern the people. That at least is the basic principle on which our democratic society rests. I would affirm the judgment of the Supreme Court of Arizona.

Mr. Justice Douglas, *dissenting.*

I have expressed my doubts whether the courts should intervene in situations like the present and strike down state legislation on the grounds that it burdens interstate commerce. *McCarroll* v. *Dixie Greyhound Lines,* 309 U.S. 176, 183–189. My view has been that the courts should intervene only where the state legislation discriminated against interstate commerce or was out of harmony with laws which Congress had enacted, p. 184. It seems to me particularly appropriate that that course be followed here. For Congress has given the Interstate Commerce Commission broad powers of regulation over interstate carriers. The Commission is the national agency which has been entrusted with the task of promoting a safe, adequate, efficient, and economical transportation service. It is the expert on this subject. It is in a position to police the field. And if its powers prove inadequate for the task, Congress, which has paramount authority in this field, can implement them.

But the Court has not taken that view. As a result the

question presented is whether the total effect of Arizona's train-limit as a safety measure is so slight as not to outweigh the national interest in keeping interstate commerce free from interferences which seriously impede or burden it.   The voluminous evidence has been reviewed in the opinion of the Court and in the dissenting opinion of MR. JUSTICE BLACK.   If I sat as a member of the Interstate Commerce Commission or of a legislative committee to decide whether Arizona's train-limit law should be superseded by a federal regulation, the question would not be free from doubt for me.   If we had before us the ruling of the Interstate Commerce Commission (*In the Matter of Service Order No. 85,* 256 I.C.C. 523, 534) that Arizona's train-limit law infringes "the national interest in maintaining the free flow of commerce under the present emergency war conditions," I would accept its expert appraisal of the facts, assuming it had the authority to act.   But that order is not before us.   And the present case deals with a period of time which antedates the war emergency. Moreover, we are dealing here with state legislation in the field of safety where the propriety of local regulation has long been recognized. See *Atlantic Coast Line R. Co.* v. *Georgia,* 234 U.S. 280, 291, and cases collected in *California* v. *Thompson,* 313 U.S. 109, 113–114.   Whether the question arises under the Commerce Clause or the Fourteenth Amendment, I think the legislation is entitled to a presumption of validity. If a State passed a law prohibiting the hauling of more than one freight car at a time, we would have a situation comparable in effect to a state law requiring all railroads within its borders to operate on narrow gauge tracks.   The question is one of degree and calls for a close appraisal of the facts.   I am not persuaded that the evidence adduced by the railroads overcomes the presumption of validity to which this train-limit law is entitled. For the reasons stated by MR. JUSTICE BLACK, Arizona's train-limit law should stand as an allowable regulation enacted to protect the lives and limbs of the men who operate the trains.

[*Quaere:* Do you think the Arizona Train Limit Law was in fact adopted as a safety measure, or do you think the safety language was merely a "sugar coating" for a "featherbedding" measure to provide more jobs for Arizona workmen? Note how the Court— surely with tongue in cheek—respects the state's characterization of the act as safety legislation.

There is obviously a vast difference between the Court's conceptual approach in *Di Santo*, see above, and its pragmatic approach in *Southern Pacific*. Is the activist judge inevitably a conceptualist, and is his counterpart necessarily a pragmatist?]

Dean Milk Co. v. City of Madison

340 U.S. 349 (1951)

Mr. Justice Clark delivered the opinion of the Court.

This appeal challenges the constitutional validity of two sections of an ordinance of the City of Madison, Wisconsin, regulating the sale of milk and milk products within the municipality's jurisdiction. One section in issue makes it unlawful to sell any milk as pasteurized unless it has been processed and bottled at an approved pasteurization plant within a radius of five miles from the central square of Madison. Another section, which prohibits the sale of milk, or the importation, receipt or storage of milk for sale, in Madison unless from a source of supply possessing a permit issued after inspection by Madison officials, is attacked insofar as it expressly relieves municipal authorities from any duty to inspect farms located beyond twenty-five miles from the center of the city.

Appellant is an Illinois corporation engaged in distributing milk and milk products in Illinois and Wisconsin. It contended below as it does here that both the five-mile limit on pasteurization plants and the twenty-five-mile limit on sources of milk violate the Commerce Clause and the Fourteenth Amendment to the Federal Constitution. The Supreme Court of

Wisconsin upheld the five-mile limit on pasteurization. As to the twenty-five-mile limitation the court ordered the complaint dismissed for want of a justiciable controversy. 257 Wis. 308, 43 N.W.2d 480 (1950). This appeal, contesting both rulings, invokes the jurisdiction of this Court under 28 U.S.C. § 1257 (2).

The City of Madison is the county seat of Dane County. Within the county are some 5,600 dairy farms with total raw milk production in excess of 600,000,000 pounds annually and more than ten times the requirements of Madison. Aside from the milk supplied to Madison, fluid milk produced in the county moves in large quantities to Chicago and more distant consuming areas, and the remainder is used in making cheese, butter and other products. At the time of trial the Madison milkshed was not of "Grade A" quality by the standards recommended by the United States Public Health Service, and no milk labeled "Grade A" was distributed in Madison.

The area defined by the ordinance with respect to milk sources encompasses practically all of Dane County and includes some 500 farms which supply milk for Madison. Within the five-mile area for pasteurization are plants of five processors, only three of which are engaged in the general wholesale and retail trade in Madison. Inspection of these farms and plants is scheduled once every thirty days and is performed by two municipal inspectors, one of whom is full-time. The courts below found that the ordinance in question promotes convenient, economical and efficient plant inspection.

Appellant purchases and gathers milk from approximately 950 farms in northern Illinois and southern Wisconsin, none being within twenty-five miles of Madison. Its pasteurization plants are located at Chemung and Huntley, Illinois, about 65 and 85 miles respectively from Madison. Appellant was denied a license to sell its products within Madison solely because its pasteurization plants were more than five miles away.

It is conceded that the milk which appellant seeks to sell in Madison is supplied from farms and processed in plants licensed and inspected by public health authorities of Chicago, and is labeled "Grade A" under the Chicago ordinance which adopts the rating standards recommended by the United States Public Health Service. Both the Chicago and Madison ordinances, though not the sections of the latter here in issue, are largely patterned after the Model Milk Ordinance of the Public Health Service. However, Madison contends and we assume that in some particulars its ordinance is more rigorous than that of Chicago.

Upon these facts we find it necessary to determine only the issue raised under the Commerce Clause, for we agree with appellant that the ordinance imposes an undue burden on interstate commerce.

This is not an instance in which an enactment falls because of federal legislation which, as a proper exercise of paramount national power over commerce, excludes measures which might otherwise be within the police power of the states. See *Currin* v. *Wallace,* 306 U.S. 1, 12–13 (1939). There is no pertinent national regulation by the Congress, and statutes enacted for the District of Columbia indicate that Congress has recognized the appropriateness of local regulation of the sale of fluid milk. D. C. Code, 1940, §§ 33-301 *et seq.* It is not contended, however, that Congress has authorized the regulation before us.

Nor can there be objection to the avowed purpose of this enactment. We assume that difficulties in sanitary regulation of milk and milk products originating in remote areas may present a situation in which "upon a consideration of all the relevant facts and circumstances it appears that the matter is one which may appropriately be regulated in the interest of the safety, health and well-being of local communities. . . ."

Parker v. *Brown,* 317 U.S. 341, 362–363 (1943); see *H. P. Hood & Sons* v. *DuMond,* 336 U.S. 525, 531–532 (1949). We also assume that since Congress has not spoken to the contrary, the subject matter of the ordinance lies within the sphere of state regulation even though interstate commerce may be affected. *Milk Control Board* v. *Eisenberg Farm Products,* 306 U.S. 346 (1939); see *Baldwin* v. *Seelig, Inc.,* 294 U.S. 511, 524 (1935).

But this regulation, like the provision invalidated in *Baldwin* v. *Seelig, Inc., supra,* in practical effect excludes from distribution in Madison wholesome milk produced and pasteurized in Illinois. "The importer . . . may keep his milk or drink it, but sell it he may not." *Id.,* at 521. In thus erecting an economic barrier protecting a major local industry against competition from without the State, Madison plainly discriminates against interstate commerce. This it cannot do, even in the exercise of its unquestioned power to protect the health and safety of its people, if reasonable nondiscriminatory alternatives, adequate to conserve legitimate local interests, are available. *Cf. Baldwin* v. *Seelig, Inc., supra,* at 524; *Minnesota* v. *Barber,* 136 U.S. 313, 328 (1890). A different view, that the ordinance is valid simply because it professes to be a health measure, would mean that the Commerce Clause of itself imposes no limitations on state action other than those laid down by the Due Process Clause, save for the rare instance where a state artlessly discloses an avowed purpose to discriminate against interstate goods. *Cf. H. P. Hood & Sons* v. *DuMond, supra.* Our issue then is whether the discrimination inherent in the Madison ordinance can be justified in view of the character of the local interests and the available methods of protecting them. *Cf. Union Brokerage Co.* v. *Jensen,* 322 U.S. 202, 211 (1944).

It appears that reasonable and adequate alternatives are available. If the City of Madison prefers to rely upon its own officials for inspection of distant milk sources, such inspection is readily open to it without hardship for it could charge the actual and reasonable cost of such inspection to the importing producers and processors. *Cf. Sprout* v. *City of South Bend,* 277 U.S. 163, 169 (1928); see *Miller* v. *Williams,* 12 F. Supp. 236, 242, 244 (D. C. Md. 1935). Moreover, appellee Health Commissioner of Madison testified that as proponent of the local milk ordinance he had submitted the provisions here in controversy and an alternative proposal based on § 11 of the Model Milk Ordinance recommended by the United States Public Health Service. The model provision imposes no geographical limitation on location of milk sources and processing plants but excludes from the municipality milk not produced and pasteurized conformably to standards as high as those enforced by the receiving city. In implementing such an ordinance, the importing city obtains milk ratings based on uniform standards and established by health authorities in the jurisdiction where production and processing occur. The receiving city may determine the extent of enforcement of sanitary standards in the exporting area by verifying the accuracy of safety ratings of specific plants or of the milkshed in the distant jurisdiction through the United States Public Health Service, which routinely and on request spot checks the local ratings. The Commissioner testified that Madison consumers "would be safeguarded adequately" under either proposal and that he had expressed no preference. The milk sanitarian of the Wisconsin State Board of Health testified that the State Health Department recommends the adoption of a provision based on the Model Ordinance. Both officials agreed that a local health officer would be justified in relying upon the evaluation by the Public Health Service of enforcement conditions in remote producing areas.

To permit Madison to adopt a regulation not essential for the protection of local health interests and placing a discriminatory burden on interstate commerce would invite a multiplication of preferential trade areas destructive of the very purpose of the Commerce Clause. Under the circumstances here presented, the regulation must yield to the principle that "one state in its dealings with another may not place itself in a position of economic isolation." *Baldwin* v. *Seelig, Inc., supra,* at 527.

For these reasons we conclude that the judgment below sustaining the five-mile provision as to pasteurization must be reversed.

The Supreme Court of Wisconsin thought it unnecessary to pass upon the validity of the twenty-five-mile limitation, apparently in part for the reason that this issue was made academic by its decision upholding the five-mile section. In view of our conclusion as to the latter provision, a determination of appellant's contention as to the other section is now necessary. As to this issue, therefore, we vacate the judgment below and remand for further proceedings not inconsistent with principles announced in this opinion.

It is so ordered.

MR. JUSTICE BLACK, with whom MR. JUSTICE DOUGLAS and MR. JUSTICE MINTON concur, *dissenting.*

Today's holding invalidates § 7.21 of the Madison, Wisconsin, ordinance on the following reasoning: (1) the section excludes wholesome milk coming from Illinois; (2) this imposes a discriminatory burden on interstate commerce; (3) such a burden cannot be imposed where, as here, there are reasonable, nondiscriminatory and adequate alternatives available. I disagree with the Court's premises, reasoning, and judgment.

(1) This ordinance does not exclude wholesome milk coming from Illinois or anywhere else. It does require that all milk sold in Madison must be pasteurized within five miles of the center of the city. But there was no finding in the state courts, nor evidence to justify a finding there or here, that appellant, Dean Milk Company, is unable to have its milk

pasteurized within the defined geographical area. As a practical matter, so far as the record shows, Dean can easily comply with the ordinance whenever it wants to. Therefore, Dean's personal preference to pasteurize in Illinois, not the ordinance, keeps Dean's milk out of Madison.

(2) Characterization of § 7.21 as a "discriminatory burden" on interstate commerce is merely a statement of the Court's result, which I think incorrect. The section does prohibit the sale of milk in Madison by interstate and intrastate producers who prefer to pasteurize over five miles distant from the city. But both state courts below found that § 7.21 represents a good-faith attempt to safeguard public health by making adequate sanitation inspections possible. While we are not bound by these findings I do not understand the Court to overturn them. Therefore, the fact that § 7.21, like all health regulations, imposes some burden on trade, does not mean that it "discriminates" against interstate commerce.

(3) This health regulation should not be invalidated merely because the Court believes that alternative milk-inspection methods might insure the cleanliness and healthfulness of Dean's Illinois milk. I find it difficult to explain why the Court uses the "reasonable alternative" concept to protect trade when today it refuses to apply the same principle to protect freedom of speech. *Feiner* v. *New York*, 340 U.S. 315. For while the "reasonable alternative" concept has been invoked to protect First Amendment rights, *e.g., Schneider* v. *State*, 308 U.S. 147, 162, it has not heretofore been considered an appropriate weapon for striking down local health laws. Since the days of Chief Justice Marshall, federal courts have left states and municipalities free to pass bona fide health regulations subject only "to the paramount authority of Congress if it decides to assume control. . . ." *The Minnesota Rate Cases*, 230 U.S. 352, 406; *Gibbons* v. *Ogden*, 9 Wheat. 1, 203, 204; *Mintz* v. *Baldwin*, 289 U.S. 346, 349–350; and see *Baldwin* v. *Seelig*, 294 U.S. 511, 524. This established judicial policy

of refusing to invalidate genuine local health laws under the Commerce Clause has been approvingly noted even in our recent opinions measuring state regulation by stringent standards. See, *e.g., Hood & Sons* v. *DuMond,* 336 U.S. 525, 531–532. No case is cited, and I have found none, in which a bona fide health law was struck down on the ground that some other method of safeguarding health would be as good as, or better than, the one the Court was called on to review. In my view, to use this ground now elevates the right to traffic in commerce for profit above the power of the people to guard the purity of their daily diet of milk.

If, however, the principle announced today is to be followed, the Court should not strike down local health regulations unless satisfied beyond a reasonable doubt that the substitutes it proposes would not lower health standards. I do not think that the Court can so satisfy itself on the basis of its judicial knowledge. And the evidence in the record leads me to the conclusion that the substitute health measures suggested by the Court do not insure milk as safe as the Madison ordinance requires.

One of the Court's proposals is that Madison require milk processors to pay reasonable inspection fees at the milk supply "sources." Experience shows, however, that the fee method gives rise to prolonged litigation over the calculation and collection of the charges. *E.g., Sprout* v. *South Bend,* 277 U.S. 163; *Capitol Greyhound Lines* v. *Brice,* 339 U.S. 542. To throw local milk regulation into such a quagmire of uncertainty jeopardizes the admirable milk-inspection systems in force in many municipalities. Moreover, nothing in the record before us indicates that the fee system might not be as costly to Dean as having its milk pasteurized in Madison. Surely the Court is not resolving this question by drawing on its "judicial knowledge" to supply information as to comparative costs, convenience, or effectiveness.

The Court's second proposal is that Madison adopt § 11 of

the "Model Milk Ordinance." The state courts made no findings as to the relative merits of this inspection ordinance and
the one chosen by Madison. The evidence indicates to me that
enforcement of the Madison law would assure a more health-
ful quality of milk than that which is entitled to use the label
of "Grade A" under the Model Ordinance. Indeed, the United
States Board of Public Health, which drafted the Model Ordinance, suggests that the provisions are "minimum" standards
only. The Model Ordinance does not provide for continuous
investigation of all pasteurization plants as does § 7.21 of the
Madison ordinance. Under § 11, moreover, Madison would be
required to depend on the Chicago inspection system since
Dean's plants, and the farms supplying them with raw milk,
are located in the Chicago milkshed. But there is direct and
positive evidence in the record that milk produced under
Chicago standards did not meet the Madison requirements.

From what, the Model Ordinance would force the Madison
health authorities to rely on "spot checks" by the United States
Public Health Service to determine whether Chicago enforced
its milk regulations. The evidence shows that these "spot
checks" are based on random inspection of farms and pasteurization plants: the United States Public Health Service
rates the ten thousand or more dairy farms in the Chicago
milkshed by a sampling of no more than two hundred farms.
The same sampling technique is employed to inspect pasteurization plants. There was evidence that neither the farms
supplying Dean with milk nor Dean's pasteurization plants
were necessarily inspected in the last "spot check" of the
Chicago milkshed made two years before the present case was
tried.

From what this record shows, and from what it fails to show,
I do not think that either of the alternatives suggested by the
Court would assure the people of Madison as pure a supply
of milk as they receive under their own ordinance. On this
record I would uphold the Madison law. At the very least,

however, I would not invalidate it without giving the parties a chance to present evidence and get findings on the ultimate issues the Court thinks crucial—namely, the relative merits of the Madison ordinance and the alternatives suggested by the Court today.

[*Quaere:* Do you think the Madison ordinance was in fact adopted primarily as a health measure, or do you think it was an effort to promote a local industry?

Mr. Justice Black assumes that the Dean Milk Company "can easily" have its milk pasteurized within five miles of Madison: "Therefore, Dean's personal preference to pasteurize in Illinois, not the ordinance, keeps Dean's milk out of Madison." The company had pasteurizing plants in northern Illinois but not in Wisconsin. That being the case, do you suppose it was caprice or business reality that dictated its "personal preference" to process in Illinois? Even if the company could "easily" pasteurize within five miles of Madison, would it not run afoul of the prohibition against sale of milk that had not come from approved sources within twenty-five miles of the city?

Do you find Black's absolutist position on the Commerce Clause comparable to his absolutist position on free speech?]

Morgan v. *Virginia*

328 U.S. 373 (1946)

Mr. Justice Reed delivered the opinion of the Court.

This appeal brings to this Court the question of the constitutionality of an act of Virginia, which requires all passenger motor vehicle carriers, both interstate and intrastate, to separate without discrimination the white and colored passengers in their motor buses so that contiguous seats will not be occupied by persons of different races at the same time. A violation of the requirement of separation by the carrier is a misdemeanor. The driver or other person in charge is directed and required to increase or decrease the space allotted to the respective races as may be necessary or proper and may require passengers to change their seats to comply with the allocation. The operator's failure to enforce the provisions is made a misdemeanor.

These regulations were applied to an interstate passenger, this appellant, on a motor vehicle then making an interstate run or trip. According to the statement of fact by the Supreme Court of Appeals of Virginia, appellant, who is a Negro, was traveling on a motor common carrier, operating under the above-mentioned statute, from Gloucester County, Virginia, through the District of Columbia, to Baltimore, Maryland, the destination of the bus. There were other passengers, both white and colored. On her refusal to accede to a request of the driver to move to a back seat, which was partly occupied by other colored passengers, so as to permit the seat that she vacated to be used by white passengers, a warrant was obtained and appellant was arrested, tried and convicted of a violation of §4097dd of the Virginia Code. [This section makes a passenger's refusal to obey lawful directions of the driver a misdemeanor.] On a writ of error the conviction was affirmed by the Supreme Court of Appeals of Virginia. 184 Va. 24, 34 S.E.2d 491. . . .

The errors of the Court of Appeals that are assigned and relied upon by appellant are in form only two. The first is that the decision is repugnant to Clause 3, §8, Article 1 of the Constitution of the United States, and the second the holding that powers reserved to the states by the Tenth Amendment include the power to require an interstate motor passenger to occupy a seat restricted for the use of his race. Actually, the first question alone needs consideration for if the statute unlawfully burdens interstate commerce, the reserved powers of the state will not validate it.

We think, as the Court of Appeals apparently did, that the appellant is a proper person to challenge the validity of this statute as a burden on commerce. If it is an invalid burden, the conviction under it would fail. The statute affects appellant as well as the transportation company. Constitutional protection against burdens on commerce is for her benefit on a criminal trial for violation of the challenged statute. New York ex rel. Hatch v. Reardon, 204 U.S. 152, 160; Alabama State Federation of Labor v. McAdory, 325 U.S. 450, 463.

This court frequently must determine the validity of state statutes that are attacked as unconstitutional interferences with the national power over interstate commerce. This appeal presents that question as to a statute that compels racial segregation of interstate passengers in vehicles moving interstate.

The precise degree of a permissible restriction on state power cannot be fixed generally or indeed not even for one kind of state legislation, such as taxation or health or safety. There is a recognized abstract principle, however, that may be taken as a postulate for testing whether particular state legislation in the absence of action by Congress is beyond state power. This is that the state legislation is invalid if it unduly burdens that commerce in matters where uniformity is necessary—necessary in the constitutional sense of useful in accomplishing a permitted purpose. Where uniformity is essential for the functioning of commerce, a state may not interpose its local regulation. Too true it is that the principle lacks in precision. Although the quality of such a principle is abstract, its application to the facts of a situation created by the attempted enforcement of a statute brings about a specific determination as to whether or not the statute in question is a burden on commerce. Within the broad limits of the principle, the cases turn on their own facts.

In the field of transportation, there have been a series of decisions which hold that where Congress has not acted and although the state statute affects interstate commerce, a state may validly enact legislation which has predominantly only a local influence on the course of commerce. . . . It is equally well settled that, even where Congress has not acted, state legislation or a final court order is invalid which materially affects interstate commerce. . . .

Because the Constitution puts the ultimate power to regulate commerce in Congress, rather than the states, the degree of state legislation's interference with that commerce may be weighed by federal courts to determine whether the burden makes the statute unconstitutional. The courts could not invalidate federal legislation for the same reason because Congress, within the limits of the Fifth Amendment, has authority to burden commerce if that seems to it a desirable means of accomplishing a permitted end.

This statute is attacked on the ground that it imposes undue burdens on interstate commerce. It is said by the Court of Appeals to have been passed in the exercise of the state's police power to avoid friction between the races. But this Court pointed out years ago "that a State cannot avoid the operation of this rule by simply invoking the convenient apologetics of the police power." Burdens upon commerce are those actions of a state which directly "impair the usefulness of its facilities for such traffic." That impairment, we think, may arise from other causes than costs or long delays. A burden may arise from a state statute which requires interstate passengers to order their movements on the vehicle in accordance with local rather than national requirements.

On appellant's journey, this statute required that she sit in designated seats in Virginia. Changes in seat designation might be made "at any time" during the journey when "necessary or proper for the comfort and convenience of passengers." This occurred in this instance. Upon such change of designation, the statute authorizes the operator of the vehicle to require, as he did here, "any passenger to change his or her seat as it may be necessary or proper." An interstate passenger must if necessary repeatedly shift seats while moving in Virginia to meet the seating requirements of the changing passenger group. On arrival at the District of Columbia line, the appellant would have had freedom to occupy any available seat and so to the end of her journey.

Interstate passengers traveling via motors between the north and south or the east and west may pass through Virginia on through lines in the day or in the night. The large buses approach the comfort of pullmans and have seats convenient for rest. On such interstate journeys the enforcement of the requirements for reseating would be disturbing.

Appellant's argument, properly we think, includes facts bearing on interstate motor transportation beyond those immediately involved in this journey under the Virginia statutory regulations. To appraise the weight of the burden of the Virginia statute on interstate commerce, related statutes of other states are important to show whether there are cumulative effects which may make local regulation impracticable. Eighteen states, it appears, prohibit racial separation on public carriers. Ten require separation on motor carriers. . . . Of these Alabama applies specifically to interstate passengers with an exception for interstate passengers with through tickets from states without laws on separation of passengers. . . .

In states where separation of races is required in motor vehicles, a method of identification as white or colored must be employed. This may be done by definition. Any ascertainable Negro blood identifies a person as colored for purposes of separation in some states. [Citation of state statutes omitted.] In the other states which require the separation of the races in motor carriers, apparently no definition generally applicable or made for the purposes of the statute is given. Court definition or further legislative enactments would be required to clarify the line between the races. Obviously there may be changes by legislation in the definition.

The interferences to interstate commerce which arise from state regulation of racial association on interstate vehicles has long been recognized. Such regulation hampers freedom of choice in selecting accommodations. The recent changes in transportation brought about by the coming of automobiles does not seem of great significance in the problem. People of all races travel today more extensively than in 1878 when this Court first passed upon state regulation of racial segregation in commerce. The factual situation set out in preceding paragraphs emphasizes the soundness of this Court's early conclusion in Hall v. De Cuir, 95 U.S. 485. . . .

In weighing the factors that enter into our conclusion as to whether this statute so burdens interstate commerce or so infringes the requirements of national uniformity as to be invalid, we are mindful of the fact that conditions vary between northern or western states such as Maine or Montana, with practically no colored population; industrial states such as Illinois, Ohio, New Jersey and Pennsylvania with a small, although appreciable, percentage of colored citizens; and the states of the deep south with percentages of from twenty-five to nearly fifty per cent colored, all with varying densities of the white and colored races in certain localities. Local efforts to promote amicable relations in difficult areas by legislative segregation in interstate transportation emerge from the latter racial distribution. As no state law can reach beyond its own border nor bar transportation of passengers across its boundaries, diverse seating requirements for the races in interstate journeys result. As there is no federal act dealing with the separation of races in interstate transportation, we must decide the validity of this Virginia statute on the challenge that it interferes with commerce, as a matter of balance between the exercise of the local police power and the need for national uniformity in the regulations for interstate travel. It seems clear to us that seating arrangements for the different races in interstate motor travel require a single, uniform rule to promote and protect national travel. Consequently, we hold the Virginia statute in controversy invalid.

Reversed.

MR. JUSTICE RUTLEDGE concurs in the result.

MR. JUSTICE BLACK concurring.

The Commerce Clause of the Constitution provides that "Congress shall have power . . . to regulate commerce . . . among the several States." I have believed, and still believe that this provision means that Congress can regulate commerce and that the courts cannot. But in a series of cases decided in recent years this Court over my protest has held that the Commerce Clause justifies this Court in nullifying state legislation which this Court concludes imposes an "undue burden" on interstate commerce. I think that whether state legislation imposes an "undue burden" on interstate commerce raises pure questions of policy, which the Constitution intended should be resolved by the Congress.

. . . I . . . still believe, that in these cases the Court was assuming the role of a "super-legislature" in determining matters of governmental policy.

But the Court, at least for the present, seems committed to this interpretation of the Commerce Clause. . . .

So long as the Court remains committed to the "undue burden on commerce formula," I must make decisions under it. . . . [That formula] requires the majority's decision. In view of the Court's present disposition to apply that formula, I acquiesce.

MR. JUSTICE FRANKFURTER, concurring.

My brother BURTON has stated with great force reasons for not invalidating the Virginia statute. But for me Hall v. De Cuir, 95 U.S. 485, is controlling. Since it was decided nearly seventy years ago, that case on several occasions has been approvingly cited and has never been questioned. Chiefly for this reason I concur in the opinion of the Court. . . .

MR. JUSTICE BURTON, dissenting.

On the application of the interstate commerce clause of the Federal Constitution to this case, I find myself obliged to differ from the majority of the Court. I would sustain the Virginia statute against that clause. The issue is neither the desirability of the statute nor the constitutionality of racial segregation as such. The opinion of the Court does not claim that the Virginia statute, regulating seating arrangements for interstate passengers in motor vehicles, violates the Fourteenth Amendment or is in conflict with a federal statute. The Court holds this statute unconstitutional for but one reason. It holds that the burden imposed by the statute upon the nation's interest in interstate commerce so greatly outweighs the contribution made by the statute to the state's interest in its public welfare as to make it unconstitutional.

The undue burden upon interstate commerce thus relied upon by the Court is not complained of by the Federal Government, by any state, or by any carrier. This statute has been in effect since 1930. The carrier concerned is operating under regulations of its own which conform to the statute. The statute conforms to the policy adopted by Virginia as to steamboats (1900), electric or street cars and railroads (1902–1904). . . .

If the mere diversity between the Virginia statute and comparable statutes of other states is so serious as to render the Virginia statute invalid, it probably means that the comparable statutes of those other states, being diverse from it and from each other, are equally invalid. . . . In the absence of federal law, this may eliminate state regulation of racial separation in the seating of interstate passengers on motor vehicles and leave the regulation of the subject to the respective carriers.

The present decision will lead to the questioning of the validity of statutory regulation of the seating of intrastate passengers in the same motor vehicles with interstate passengers. . . .

The basic weakness in the appellant's case is the lack of facts and findings essential to demonstrate the existence of such a serious and major burden upon the national interest in interstate commerce as to outweigh whatever state or local benefits are attributable to the statute and which would be lost by its invalidation. . . . In weighing these competing demands, if this Court is to justify the invalidation of this statute, it must, first of all, be satisfied that the many years of experience of the state and the carrier that are reflected in this state law should be set aside. It represents the tested public policy of Virginia regularly enacted, long maintained and currently observed. The officially declared state interests, even when affecting interstate commerce, should not be laid aside summarily by this Court in the absence of Congressional action. It is only Congress that can supply affirmative national uniformity of action. . . .

The Court makes its own further assumption that the question of racial separation of interstate passengers in motor vehicle carriers requires national uniformity of treatment rather than diversity of treatment at this time. The inaction of Congress is an important indication that, in the opinion of Congress, this issue is better met without nationally uniform affirmative regulation than with it. Legislation raising the issue long has been, and is now, pending before Congress but has not reached the floor of either House. The fact that 18 states have prohibited in some degree racial separation in public carriers is important progress in the direction of uniformity. The fact, however, that 10 contiguous states in some degree require, by state law, some racial separation of passengers on motor carriers indicates a different appraisal by them of the needs and conditions in those areas than in others. The remaining 20 states have not gone equally far in either direction. This recital of existing legislative diversity is evidence against the validity of the assumption by this Court that there exists today a requirement of a single uniform national rule on the subject.

It is a fundamental concept of our Constitution that where conditions are diverse the solution of problems arising out of them may well come through the application of diversified treatment matching the diversified needs as determined by our local governments. Uniformity of treatment is appropriate where a substantial uniformity of conditions exists.

10 East 40th Street Bldg. Inc. v. Callus

325 U.S. 578 (1945)

As introduced in the Senate in 1937, the embryo of the Fair Labor Standards Act invoked the full scope of national power to regulate wages "affecting" interstate commerce. After running the gauntlet of opposition from business and other interests, it emerged from Congress in much-compromised form. Full use of the commerce power had been abandoned in favor of coverage only for workers "engaged in [interstate] commerce," or "in the production of goods for [interstate] commerce," with the gloss that a worker "shall be deemed to have been engaged in the production of goods if . . . employed . . . in any process or occupation necessary to the production thereof, in any state."

How much had Congress meant to include in the latter provision? Which jobs are, and which are not, "necessary" to the production of goods for interstate trade? How far back in the chain of causation do these words carry? Surely there is no one-and-only "correct" answer to such questions. Even Congressmen who had voted for FLSA could well disagree on its meaning and application in a concrete case. Pro-business sympathy could yield one response, pro-labor sympathy another—and neither would be demonstrably "wrong" in a close case. Pressured from both sides, Congress obviously had struck a compromise between maximum and minimum use of its regulatory power. Surely a conscientious judge would try to honor that compromise.

In *Kirschbaum* v. *Walling*, 316 U.S. 517 (1942), the Court was all but unanimous in holding that maintenance employees of a loft building leased out for the manufacturing of goods for interstate trade were protected by FLSA. In *Borden Co.* v. *Borella*, 325 U.S.

679 (1945), even maintenance workers in what was primarily the executive-office building of a producer for interstate commerce were held to be covered. But what of maintenance men for a general-office building leased to a great variety of enterprises, including some executive and sales offices of "interstate" manufacturing and mining concerns? Such is the present case.

MR. JUSTICE FRANKFURTER delivered the opinion of the Court.

The Fair Labor Standards Act of 1938 regulates wages and hours not only of employees who are "engaged in commerce" but also those engaged "in the production of goods for commerce." Sections 6, 7, 52 Stat. 1060, 1062–63, 29 U.S.C. §§ 206, 207. For the purposes of that Act "an employee shall be deemed to have been engaged in the production of goods if such employee was employed . . . in any process or occupation necessary to the production thereof, in any State." § 3 (j). When these provisions first came here we made it abundantly clear that their enforcement would involve the courts in the empiric process of drawing lines from case to case, and inevitably nice lines. *Kirschbaum Co.* v. *Walling*, 316 U.S. 517. And this for two reasons. In enacting this statute Congress did not see fit, as it did in other regulatory measures, *e.g.,* the Interstate Commerce Act and the National Labor Relations Act, to exhaust its constitutional power over commerce. And "Unlike the Interstate Commerce Act and the National Labor Relations Act and other legislation, the Fair Labor Standards Act puts upon the courts the independent responsibility of applying *ad hoc* the general terms of the statute to an infinite variety of complicated industrial situations." *Kirschbaum Co.* v. *Walling, supra,* at 523. Thus, Congress withheld from the courts the aid of constitutional criteria, compare, *e. g., Currin* v. *Wallace,* 306 U.S. 1; *Wickard* v. *Filburn,* 317 U.S. 111; *Polish Alliance* v. *Labor Board,* 322 U.S. 643, as well as the benefit of a prior judgment, on vexing and ambiguous facts, by an expert administrative agency. Compare, *e. g., Labor Board* v. *Fruehauf Co.,* 301 U.S. 49; *Gray* v. *Powell,* 314 U.S. 402, 412.

The Act has produced a considerable volume of litigation and has inevitably given rise to judicial conflicts and divisions. The lower courts, and only in a lesser measure this Court, have been plagued with problems in connection with employees of buildings occupied by those having at least some relation to goods that eventually find their way into interstate commerce.

In *Kirschbaum Co.* v. *Walling, supra,* we were concerned with maintenance employees of buildings concededly devoted to manufacture for commerce. In *Borden Co.* v. *Borella, post,* p. 679, the Fair Labor Standards Act was invoked on behalf of maintenance employees of a building owned by an interstate producer and predominantly occupied for its offices. Recognizing that the question in every case is "whether the particular situation is within the regulated area," we concluded that the employees of the buildings in the *Kirschbaum* case "had such a close and immediate tie with the process of production" carried on by the lessees as to come within the Act. The *Borden* case involved Borden employees who, if they had been under the same roof where the physical handling of the goods took place, could hardly, without drawing gossamer and not merely nice lines, be deemed not to be engaged in an "occupation necessary to the production of goods" as described by § 3 (j). To differentiate, in the incidence of the Fair Labor Standards Act, between maintenance employees who worked in the building where the business of the manufacture of milk products goes on and employees pursuing the same occupation for the Borden enterprise in an office separate from the manufacturing building, is to make too much turn on the accident of the division of the whole industrial process. The case immediately before us presents still a third situation differing both from *Kirschbaum* and *Borden.*

The facts are these. Petitioner owns and manages a 48-story New York office building. The offices are leased to more than a hundred tenants pursuing a great variety of enterprises including executive and sales offices of manufacturing and mining concerns, sales agencies representing such concerns, engineering and construction firms, advertising and publicity agencies, law firms, investment and credit organizations and the United States Employment Service. The distribution of occupancy in relation to the ultimate enterprises of the different groups of tenants was the subject of conflicting testimony and interpretation, but in our view does not call for particularization. Indisputably, the building is devoted exclusively to offices, and no manufacturing is carried on within it. The respondents are maintenance employees of the building, elevator starters and operators, window cleaners, watchmen and the like. They brought this suit under § 16 (b) of the Fair Labor Standards Act for claims of overtime payment to which they are entitled if their occupations be deemed "necessary to the production" of goods for commerce. Obviously they are not "engaged in commerce." The District Court dismissed the suit. 51 F. Supp. 528. The Circuit Court of Appeals reversed. 146 F. 2d 438. By a meticulous calculation, it found that the executive offices of manufacturing and mining concerns, sales agencies representing such concerns, and publicity concerns were engaged in the production of goods for interstate commerce, and, since the offices of these concerns occupied 42% of the rentable area and 48% of the rented area, the maintenance employees of the owners of the building are engaged in occupations "necessary to the production" of goods for commerce. Conflict between this result and that reached by other circuits led us to bring the case here. 324 U.S. 833.

The series of cases in which we have had to decide when employees are engaged in an "occupation necessary to the production" of goods for commerce has settled at least some matters. Merely because an occupation involves a function not indispensable to the production of goods, in the sense that it can be done without, does not exclude it from the scope of the Fair Labor Standards Act. Conversely, merely because an occupation is indispensable, in the sense of being included in the long chain of causation which brings about so complicated a result as finished goods, does not bring it within the scope of the Fair Labor Standards Act. See *Walling* v. *Jacksonville Paper Co.*, 317 U.S. 564; *Walton* v. *Southern Package Corp.*, 320 U.S. 540; *Armour & Co.* v. *Wantock*, 323 U.S. 126; *Skidmore* v. *Swift & Co.*, 323 U.S. 134. In giving a fair application to § 3 (j), courts must remember that the "necessary" in the phrase "necessary to the production" of goods for commerce "is colored by the context not only of the terms of this legislation but of its implications in the relation between state and national authority." *Kirschbaum Co.* v. *Walling, supra,* at 525. For as was pointed out in *Walling* v. *Jacksonville Paper Co., supra,* at 570, we cannot "be unmindful that Congress in enacting this statute plainly indicated its purpose to leave local business to the protection of the states." We must be alert, therefore, not to absorb by adjudication essentially local activities that Congress did not see fit to take over by legislation.

Renting office space in a building exclusively set aside for an unrestricted variety of office work spontaneously satisfies the common understanding of what is local business and makes the employees of such a building engaged in local business. Mere separation of an occupation from the physical process of production does not preclude application of the Fair Labor Standards Act. But remoteness of a particular occupation from the physical process is a relevant factor in drawing the line. Running an office building as an entirely independent enterprise is too many steps removed from the physical process of the production of goods. Such remoteness is insulated from the Fair Labor Standards Act by those considerations pertinent to the federal system which led Congress not to sweep predominantly local situations within the confines of the Act. To assign the maintenance men of such an office building to the productive process because some proportion of the offices in the building may, for the time being, be offices of manufacturing enterprises is to indulge in an analysis too attenuated for appropriate regard to the regulatory power of the States which Congress saw fit to reserve to them. Dialectic inconsistencies do not weaken the validity of practical adjustments, as between the State and federal authority, when Congress has cast the duty of making them upon the courts. Our problem is not an exercise in scholastic logic.

The differences between employees of a building owned by occupants producing therein goods for commerce, and the employees of a building intended for tenants who produce such goods therein, and the employees of the office building of a large interstate producer, are too thin for the practicalities of adjudication. But an office building exclusively devoted to the purpose of housing all the usual miscellany of offices has many differences in the practical affairs of life from a manufacturing building, or the office building of a manufacturer. And the differences are too important in the setting of the Fair Labor Standards Act not to be recognized by the courts.

We have heretofore tried to indicate the nature of the nexus between employees who, though not themselves engaged in commerce, are engaged in occupations necessary for the production of goods for commerce by describing the necessary work that brings the occupation within the scope of the Act as work that had "a close and immediate tie with the process of production." *Kirschbaum Co.* v. *Walling, supra,* at 525. Doubtless more felicitous adjectives could be chosen, but the attempt to achieve a form of words that could avoid an exercise of judgment that a particular occupation is more in the nature of local business than not, is merely to be content with formulas of illusory certainty.

On the terms in which Congress drew the legislation we

cannot escape the duty of drawing lines. And when lines have to be drawn they are bound to appear arbitrary when judged solely by bordering cases. To speak of drawing lines in adjudication is to express figuratively the task of keeping in mind the considerations relevant to a problem and the duty of coming down on the side of the considerations having controlling weight. Lines are not the worse for being narrow if they are drawn on rational considerations. It is a distinction appropriate to the subject matter to hold that where occupations form part of a distinctive enterprise, such as the enterprise of running an office building, they are properly to be treated as distinct from those necessary parts of a commercial process which alone, with due regard to local regulations, Congress dealt with in the Fair Labor Standards Act. Of course an argument can be made on the other side. That is what is meant by a question of degree, as is the question before us. But for drawing the figurative line the basis must be something practically relevant to the problem in hand. We believe that is true of the line drawn in this case.

Judgment reversed.

MR. CHIEF JUSTICE STONE.

The views I expressed in my dissent in *Borden Co.* v. *Borella, post,* p. 679, would, if accepted, control the decision in this case. As those views have been rejected by the Court, I join in the Court's opinion in this case.

MR. JUSTICE MURPHY, dissenting.

A proper understanding of the nature of the activities carried on in petitioner's 48-story office building in New York City leads to the inevitable conclusion that the respondent maintenance employees, like those in *Kirschbaum Co.* v. *Walling,* 316 U.S. 517, and in *Borden Co.* v. *Borella, post,* p. 679, are engaged in occupations "necessary to the production of goods for commerce" and hence are entitled to the benefits of the Fair Labor Standards Act of 1938.

(1) Approximately 26% of the rentable area of the building is occupied by the executive offices of manufacturing and mining concerns which are concededly engaged in the production of goods for commerce. Corporate policies are formed and directed from these offices. Most of them purchase raw materials for use in the physical processes of manufacturing. They keep in constant and close contact with the factories, supervising all of the manufacturing activities. Some of these offices draft designs and specifications for the articles produced in the factories. Business and sales departments located in these offices do work in connection with the distribution of these products. One office even handles parts for the machines manufactured by the company, doing repair work on the parts and packing and shipping them to out-of-state customers.

The case in this respect is indistinguishable from the facts in the *Borden* case. Here, as in the *Borden* case, the officers and employees working in these offices are part of the coordinated productive pattern of modern industry. The fact that none of the physical processes of manufacturing occurs in the same building is immaterial. Production requires central planning, control, supervision, purchase of raw materials, designing of products, sales promotion and the like as well as the physical, manual processes of manufacturing. These various central offices, then, are "part of an integrated effort for the production of goods," *Armour & Co.* v. *Wantock*, 323 U.S. 126, 130. And since the maintenance employees stand in the same relation to this productive process as did the employees in the *Kirschbaum* case, it follows that they are engaged in occupations "necessary to the production of goods for commerce."

The *Kirschbaum* case also made it clear that the provisions of the Act "expressly make its application dependent upon the character of the employees' activities." 316 U.S. at 524. Hence it is immaterial that the owner of the building which employs the respondent maintenance employees is not shown to have been engaged in the production of goods for commerce. As in the *Kirschbaum* case, it is enough if the employees are necessary to the production of goods by tenants occupying the building in which they work.

(2) Approximately 6.5% of the rentable area of the building is occupied by concerns engaged in writing and preparing mimeographed, photographic and printed matter which is shipped in interstate commerce. One company produces between 15,000 and 20,000 pages of mimeographed materials per week, 90% of which is sent outside the state. Another tenant produces 60 magazines having national circulations. Other concerns produce large quantities of pamphlets, photographs, magazines and advertising matter for interstate shipment.

Since telegraphic messages are "goods" within the meaning of the Act, *Western Union Co.* v. *Lenroot*, 323 U.S. 490, 502–503, it would seem clear that these magazines, pamphlets, etc. which are prepared in petitioner's office building are likewise "goods." And since the term "produced" includes "every kind of incidental operation preparatory to putting goods into the stream of commerce," *ibid.*, 503, the writing and preparation of these materials constitutes "production of goods" for interstate commerce. Here again the respondent maintenance employees are related to production in the same way as were the employees in the *Kirschbaum* case, thus making it clear that they are covered by the Act from this standpoint.

It is unnecessary to describe the activities of the other tenants, although it is conceded that about 58% of the total rentable area is occupied by concerns not engaged in the production of goods for commerce. It is sufficient that approximately 32.5% of the rentable area is devoted to production. The Administrator of the Wage and Hour Division of the Department of Labor has stated that he will take no enforcement action "with respect to maintenance employees in buildings in which less than 20 percent of the space is occupied by firms engaged there or elsewhere in the production of goods for commerce." Wage and Hour Division Release, November 19, 1943, P. R.–19 (rev.). Whether 20% occupancy by such firms is a reasonable minimum is not in issue here. Clearly a 32.5% occupancy is so substantial as to remove any doubt that the maintenance employees devote a large part of their time to activities necessary to the production of goods for commerce. Hence they are covered by the Act.

The starting point in cases of this nature is not to decide whether the activities carried on in the office building in question satisfy some nebulous "common understanding of what is local business." The crucial problem, rather, is to determine whether such activities constitute an integral part of the productive process. Once it is clear that the activities are part of the process of production of goods for interstate commerce the interstate character of the activities becomes obvious; and it follows that occupations necessary to those activities partake of their interstate flavor. Neither attenuated analysis nor scholastic logic is necessary to understand the scope and coordination of the modern productive pattern and the integral part played by those who manage and direct the physical processes of production. To apply the Act in light of elementary economic facts is not beyond the ability of judges or beyond the intention of Congress.

Congress plainly intended "to leave local business to the protection of the states," *Walling* v. *Jacksonville Paper Co.*, 317 U.S. 564, 570, when it enacted this statute. But there is no indication that it intended to divide the process of producing goods for interstate commerce into interstate and local segments, applying the statute only to the former. And when Congress said that employees "necessary to the production" of goods for commerce were to be included within the Act, it meant just that, without limitation to those who were necessary only to the physical manufacturing aspects of production. Under such circumstances it is our duty to recognize economic reality in interpreting and applying the mandate of the people.

MR. JUSTICE BLACK, MR. JUSTICE REED and MR. JUSTICE RUTLEDGE join in this dissent.

[Note: In 1949 Congress apparently approved the Court's position, and repudiated the dissent, when it deleted the "necessary . . . to production" clause and substituted "directly essential to . . . production."]

Moore v. Chesapeake & Ohio Ry. Co.

340 U.S. 573 (1951)

The Federal Employers' Liability Act gives workmen (or their heirs) a somewhat liberalized right to "compensation" for injuries resulting from employer negligence. (For example, FELA abolishes the old common-law defenses of contributory negligence, assumption of risk, and the fellow-servant rule.) But, unlike some state workmen's-compensation laws, it still retains employer negligence as the basis for a worker's claim. Thus an injured workman (or his heirs) must prove employer negligence in order to win an FELA judgment.

In the present case, the Missouri Supreme Court had rejected a jury finding of negligence as beyond the realm of reason. For years, state and federal judges have exercised such authority when, in their views, the evidence in a case plainly points in only one direction. The thought is that a jury's function is to decide between competing claims *when the evidence is in substantial conflict.* But when a court is satisfied that there is no real conflict in the evidence, that one side has simply failed to make a case, the matter may be taken from the jury. This is a safeguard against runaway verdicts, for experience teaches that in contests between unfortunate plaintiffs and "rich" corporate defendants juries tend to follow their sympathies rather than the evidence. (It costs a jury nothing to give away someone else's money.) The present case went to the

Supreme Court on the claim that the negligence issue had been improperly taken from the jury.

It may be that industry (ultimately, the consumer) should bear the cost of all industrial accidents regardless of fault, but Congress (unlike some state legislatures) has provided otherwise. By watering down the concept of negligence, a court can of course impose something close to the principle of industrial liability without fault. Is that, in effect, what the dissenters are trying to do in the present case?

Mr. Justice Minton delivered the opinion of the Court. . . .

On September 25, 1948, petitioner's decedent was employed by respondent as a brakeman in respondent's switching yards at Richmond, Virginia. The day was fair. At about 3:50 p. m., the crew with which decedent was working undertook its first car movement of the day. An engine and tender were headed into Track 12 and the front end of the engine was coupled onto 33 loaded freight cars which were to be moved out initially upon the straight track referred to as the ladder track. The switch at the junction of Track 12 and the ladder track was properly aligned for the train to pass onto the ladder track. Who aligned the switch does not appear.

Decedent gave the signal for the engine to back out of Track 12 with the cars. It moved out in a westerly direction, with the rear of the tender as the front of the moving train. Decedent was standing on a footboard at the rear of the tender, his back to the tender; the outer edge of the footboard was about ten inches in from the outer edge of the tender and about a foot above the rail. The engineer was in his seat on the same side of the train as the footboard on which decedent was standing. The engineer was turned in the seat and leaning out the side cab window, looking in the direction in which the train was moving. Decedent's duty as he rode on the footboard was to give signals to the engineer, who testified that he could at all times see the edge of the arm and shoulder of decedent. To be thus seen and in a position to give signals, decedent had to extend outward beyond the edge of the tender, supporting himself partly by a handrail, otherwise the tender, the top of which was eight feet seven inches above the footboard, would have obstructed the engineer's view of him altogether.

The engineer testified that as the train approached Switch 12 at about five miles an hour, having moved ten or twelve car lengths, he saw decedent slump as if his knees had given way, then right himself, then tumble forward in a somersault toward the outside of the track. The engineer testified that he then made an emergency stop in an unsuccessful effort to avoid injuring decedent. The train ran the length of the tender and engine and about a car length and a half before it stopped at a point about an engine or car length past the switch on the ladder track. Decedent died immediately of the injuries received.

To recover under the Act, it was incumbent upon petitioner to prove negligence of respondent which caused the fatal accident. *Tennant* v. *Peoria & P.U.R. Co.*, 321 U.S. 29, 32. The negligence she alleged was that respondent's engineer made a sudden and unexpected stop without warning, "thereby causing decedent to be thrown from a position of safety on the rear of the tender" into the path of the train.

It is undisputed that only one stop of the train was made and that a sudden stop without warning. The engineer was the only witness to the accident and was called to testify by petitioner. He testified that he saw decedent fall from the tender and that he made an emergency stop in an attempt to avoid injuring him. He testified that he received no signal to stop and had no reason to stop until he saw decedent fall. When his attention was directed to the point, the engineer never wavered in his testimony that decedent was continuously in his view and in a position to give signals up to the time he was seen to fall and the emergency stop was made.

Petitioner attempts to avoid the effect of this by pointing to statements of the engineer which allegedly contradict his testimony that decedent was continuously in his view. Petitioner relies on testimony and measurements of an expert witness, and upon the fact that the jury was permitted to view the engine and tender, to support the alleged contradiction. As a consequence, it is asserted, the jury was entitled to disbelieve the engineer's version of the accident and to accept petitioner's.

True, it is the jury's function to credit or discredit all or part of the testimony. But disbelief of the engineer's testimony would not supply a want of proof. *Bunt* v. *Sierra Butte Gold Mng. Co.*, 138 U.S. 483, 485. Nor would the possibility alone that the jury might disbelieve the engineer's version make the case submissible to it.

The burden was upon petitioner to prove that decedent fell after the train stopped without warning, which was the act of negligence she charged. Her evidence showed he fell before the train stopped. The only evidence which petitioner can glean from this record to support her charge is the engineer's testimony that there was no one around the switch as the train approached it, and that he did not know whether "they" intended to take all of the 33 cars out of the switch at one time, or to stop and cut off some of them.[1] From this it is said a jury might reasonably infer that the engineer decided to make and did make an emergency stop which threw decedent from the tender. However, the engineer's testimony, appearing at the very same page of the transcript as the statement relied on, was that he worked by signals; that he had received no signal to stop or do anything; that in the event he did not receive a signal he would "[k]eep pulling the cars on back" until he received a signal, until he "cleared the switch"—"[p]robably

---

[1] "Q. Were you going to take all of those thirty-eight [*sic*] cars out at one time through that switch?

"A. I don't know about that. I work by signals. I don't know whether they intended to put them all out and switch them or to stop and cut part of them off." R. 30.

beyond."[2] We do not think that the isolated portion of the engineer's testimony relied on by petitioner permits an inference of negligence when placed in its setting of uncontradicted and unequivocal testimony totally at variance with such an inference.

Hence, all the evidence shows is that decedent fell before the train stopped. If one does not believe the engineer's testimony that he stopped after—indeed, because of—the fall, then there is no evidence as to when decedent fell. There would still be a failure of proof.

To sustain petitioner, one would have to infer from no evidence at all that the train stopped where and when it did for no purpose at all, contrary to all good railroading practice, prior to the time decedent fell, and then infer that decedent fell because the train stopped. This would be speculation run riot. Speculation cannot supply the place of proof. *Galloway* v. *United States*, 319 U.S. 372, 395.

Since there was no evidence of negligence, the court properly sustained the motion for judgment notwithstanding the verdict. The judgment is

Affirmed.

MR. JUSTICE FRANKFURTER would dismiss this writ as improvidently granted, for reasons set forth by him in *Carter* v. *Atlanta & St. Andrews Bay R. Co.*, 338 U.S. 430, 437. See

---

[2] *Supra*, n. 2;

"Q. Had you received any signal at that time to stop or to do anything—cut off any of the cars?

"A. No, sir, I had not.

"Q. What were you going to do in the event you didn't receive any further signals either from the conductor or from Mr. Moore or from anybody else?

"A. Keep pulling the cars on back until I received a signal.

"Q. And until you cleared the switch, until you cleared No. 12 switch?

"A. Yes, sir.

"Q. You keep——

"A. Probably beyond.

"Q. You keep on going?

"A. Yes." R. 30.

Affolder v. *N. Y., C. & St. L. R. Co.*, 339 U.S. 96, 101.

MR. JUSTICE REED took no part in the consideration or decision of this case.

MR. JUSTICE BLACK, with whom MR. JUSTICE DOUGLAS concurs, dissenting.

The complaint in this case alleged that petitioner's husband, while performing his duties as a railroad brakeman, was thrown from a footboard at the back of a tender and killed as a result of a sudden and unexpected stop made by the engineer. That these allegations, if proved, supported the jury's finding of negligence is not and could not be denied. I have no doubt but that the following evidence was sufficient to justify such a finding and the verdict for petitioner:

Decedent was an experienced brakeman with respondent railroad, having served in that capacity for about seven years. On the day of the accident, his duty required him to ride the footboard on the rear of a tender which was being moved backwards by an engine coupled to 33 loaded freight cars. The engineer testified that he suddenly threw the engine into reverse and made an emergency stop without warning. Decedent's badly broken and mutilated body was found lying beside the track. He had died as a result of his injuries.

Unless we are to require the element of proximate cause to be proved by eye-witness testimony, a reasonable jury certainly could infer from the foregoing facts that the sudden stopping of the engine threw the decedent to his death. Yet the Court apparently ignores this strong circumstantial evidence by relying upon the engineer's testimony that he made the sudden stop after he saw the decedent "somersault" off the tender. Of course, had the jury believed both that the engineer stopped the train abruptly and that he did so at the time he said he did, it would have found for respondent. But as the Court concedes, the jury was not compelled wholly to accept or wholly to reject the engineer's version. It was entitled to credit part of his testimony and discredit the balance, especially since there were noticeable inconsistencies, improbabilities and self-interest in the engineer's story as to how and when the fall occurred. If the jury rejected the statement that decedent fell before the engine stopped, it could find for petitioner on the basis of the circumstantial evidence previously set out.

The technique used today in depriving petitioner of her verdict is to frame the issue in terms of "When did the decedent fall?" and then to hold that petitioner failed to sustain the burden of proof because she introduced no eye-witness evidence on this point.[3] Such a myopic view loses sight of all the circumstances from which the time and cause of the fall can be inferred. What the record shows is that petitioner tried the case on a theory that decedent's fall resulted from a sudden stopping of the engine, while respondent asserted the theory that the fall was due to a heart attack. Although there was some showing that decedent had been afflicted with heart trouble in the past, respondent failed to produce any evidence that the body when found gave indications of heart disease. The jury therefore quite reasonably rejected respondent's theory for lack of proof. Just as reasonably, it accepted the petitioner's evidence as proving the allegations of her complaint. In my opinion, the taking of this verdict from petitioner is a totally unwarranted substitution of a court's view of the evidence for that of a jury.

I would reverse.

United States v. *Oregon Medical Society*
343 U.S. 326 (1952)

The Department of Justice thought that certain medical associations in Oregon had engaged in practices outlawed by the Sherman Anti-

---

[3] The Court also appears to believe that petitioner should have proved the engineer's purpose in stopping the train so suddenly. But whatever was the engineer's purpose, petitioner was entitled to recover in this case if her husband's death was caused by the sudden, unexpected stop.

trust Act. In this case the government sought to injoin such conduct in the future. The case was dismissed at the trial level.

MR. JUSTICE JACKSON delivered the opinion of the Court.

This is a direct appeal by the United States from dismissal by the District Court of its complaint seeking an injunction to prevent and restrain violations of §§ 1 and 2 of the Sherman Act. 26 Stat. 209, as amended, 15 U.S.C. §§ 1, 2.

Appellees are the Oregon State Medical Society, eight county medical societies, Oregon Physicians' Service (an Oregon corporation engaged in the sale of prepaid medical care), and eight doctors who are or have been at some time responsible officers in those organizations.

This controversy centers about two forms of "contract practice" of medicine. In one, private corporations organized for profit sell what amounts to a policy of insurance by which small periodic payments purchase the right to certain hospital facilities and medical attention. In the other, railroad and large industrial employers of labor contract with one or more doctors to treat their ailing or injured employees. Both forms of "contract practice," for rendering the promised medical and surgical service, depend upon doctors or panels of doctors who cooperate on a fee basis or who associate themselves with the plan on a full- or part-time employment basis.

Objections of the organized medical profession to contract practice are both monetary and ethical. Such practice diverts patients from independent practioners to contract doctors. It tends to standardize fees. The ethical objection has been that intervention by employer or insurance company makes a tripartite matter of the doctor-patient relation. Since the contract doctor owes his employment and looks for his pay to the employer or the insurance company rather than to the patient, he serves two masters with conflicting interests. In many cases companies assumed liability for medical or surgical service only if they approved the treatment in advance. There was evidence of instances where promptly needed treatment was delayed while obtaining company approval, and where a lay insurance official disapproved treatment advised by a doctor.

In 1936, five private associations were selling prepaid medical certificates in Oregon, and doctors of that State, alarmed at the extent to which private practice was being invaded and superseded by contract practice, commenced a crusade to stamp it out. A tooth-and-claw struggle ensued between the organized medical profession, on the one hand, and the organizations employing contract doctors on the other. The campaign was bitter on both sides. State and county medical societies adopted resolutions and policy statements condemning contract practice and physicians who engaged in it. They brought pressure on individual doctors to decline or abandon it. They threatened expulsion from medical societies, and one society did expel several doctors for refusal to terminate contract practices.

However, in 1941, seven years before this action was commenced, there was an abrupt about-face on the part of the organized medical profession in Oregon. It was apparently convinced that the public demanded and was entitled to purchase protection against unexpected costs of disease and accident, which are catastrophic to persons without reserves. The organized doctors completely reversed their strategy, and, instead of trying to discourage prepaid medical service, decided to render it on a nonprofit basis themselves.

In that year, Oregon Physicians' Service, one of the defendants in this action, was formed. It is a nonprofit Oregon corporation, furnishing prepaid medical, surgical, and hospital care on a contract basis. As charged in the complaint, "It is sponsored and approved by the Oregon State Medical Society and is controlled and operated by members of that society. It sponsors, approves, and cooperates with component county societies and organizations controlled by the latter which offer prepaid medical plans." 95 F. Supp., at 121. After seven years of successful operation, the Government brought this suit against the doctors, their professional organizations and their prepaid medical care company, asserting two basic charges: first, that they conspired to restrain and monopolize the business of providing prepaid medical care in the State of Oregon, and, second, that they conspired to restrain competition between doctor-sponsored prepaid medical plans within the State of Oregon in that Oregon Physicians' Service would not furnish prepaid medical care in an area serviced by a local society plan.

The District Judge, after a long trial, dismissed the complaint on the ground that the Government had proved none of its charges by a preponderance of evidence. The direct appeal procedure does not give us the benefit of review by a Court of Appeals of findings of fact.

The appeal brings to us no important questions of law or unsettled problems of statutory construction. It is much like *United States* v. *Yellow Cab Co.*, 338 U.S. 338. Its issues are solely ones of fact. The record is long, replete with conflicts in testimony, and includes quantities of documentary material taken from the appellees' files and letters written by doctors, employers, and employees. The Government and the appellees each put more than two score of witnesses on the stand. At the close of the trial the judge stated that his work "does not permit the preparation of a formal opinion in so complex a case. I will state my conclusions on the main issues and then will append some notes made at various stages throughout the trial. These may be of aid to counsel in the preparation of Findings of Fact and Conclusions of Law to be submitted as a basis for final judgment." 95 F. Supp., at 104. These notes indicated his disposition of the issues, but the Government predicates a suggestion of bias on irrelevant soliloquies on socialized medicine, socialized law, and the like, which they contained. Admitting that these do not add strength or persuasiveness to his opinion, they do not becloud his clear disposition of the main issues of the case, in all of which he ruled against the Government. Counsel for the doctors submitted detailed findings in accordance therewith. The Government did not submit requests to find, but by letter raised objections to various proposals of the appellees.

The trial judge found that appellees did not conspire to restrain or attempt to monopolize prepaid medical care in Oregon in the period 1936–1941, and that, even if such conspiracy during that time was proved, it was abandoned in 1941 with the formation of Oregon Physicians' Service marking the entry of appellees into the prepaid medical care business. He ruled that what restraints were proved could be justified as reasonable to maintain proper standards of medical ethics. He found that supplying prepaid medical care within the State of Oregon by doctor-sponsored organizations does not constitute trade or commerce within the meaning of the Sherman Act, but he declined to rule on the question whether supplying prepaid medical care by the private associations is interstate commerce.

The Government asks us to overrule each of these findings as contrary to the evidence, and to find that the business of providing prepaid medical care is interstate commerce. We are asked to review the facts and reverse and remand the case "for entry of a decree granting appropriate relief." We are asked in substance to try the case *de novo* on the record, make findings and determine the nature and form of relief. We have heretofore declined to give such scope to our review. *United States* v. *Yellow Cab Co., supra.*

While Congress has provided direct appeal to this Court, it also has provided that where an action is tried by a court without a jury "Findings of fact shall not be set aside unless clearly erroneous, and due regard shall be given to the opportunity of the trial court to judge of the credibility of the witnesses." Rule 52 (a), Fed. Rules Civ. Proc. There is no case more appropriate for adherence to this rule than one in which the complaining party creates a vast record of cumulative evidence as to long-past transactions, motives, and purposes, the effect of which depends largely on credibility of witnesses.

The trial court rejected a grouping by the Government of its evidentiary facts into four periods, 1930–1936, the year 1936, 1936–1941, and 1941 to trial. That proposal projected the inquiry over an eighteen-year period before the action was instituted. The court accepted only the period since the organization of Oregon Physicians' Service as significant and rejected the earlier years as "ancient history" of a time "when the Doctors were trying to find themselves. . . . It was a period of groping for the correct position to take to accord with changing times." 95 F. Supp., at 105. Of course, present events have roots in the past, and it is quite proper to trace currently questioned conduct backwards to illuminate its connections and meanings. But we think the trial judge was quite right in rejecting pre-1941 events as establishing the cause of action the Government was trying to maintain, and adopt his division of the time involved into two periods, 1936–1941, and 1941 to trial.

It will simplify consideration of such cases as this to keep in sight the target at which relief is aimed. The sole function of an action for injunction is to forestall future violations. It is so unrelated to punishment or reparations for those past that its pendency or decision does not prevent concurrent or later remedy for past violations by indictment or action for damages by those injured. All it takes to make the cause of action for relief by injunction is a real threat of future violation or a contemporary violation of a nature likely to continue or recur. This established, it adds nothing that the calendar of years gone by might have been filled with transgressions. Even where relief is mandatory in form, it is to undo existing conditions, because otherwise they are likely to continue. In a forward-looking action such as this, an examination of "a great amount of archeology" is justified only when it illuminates or explains the present and predicts the shape of things to come.

When defendants are shown to have settled into a continuing practice or entered into a conspiracy violative of antitrust laws, courts will not assume that it has been abandoned without clear proof. *Local 167* v. *United States*, 291 U.S. 293, 298. It is the duty of the courts to beware of efforts to defeat injunctive relief by protestations of repentance and reform, especially when abandonment seems timed to anticipate suit, and there is probability of resumption. Cf. *United States* v. *United States Steel Corp.*, 251 U.S. 417, 445.

But we find not the slightest reason to doubt the genuineness, good faith or permanence of the changed attitude and strategy of these defendant-appellees which took place in 1941. It occurred seven years before this suit was commenced and, so far as we are informed, before it was predictable. It did not consist merely of pretensions or promises but was an overt and visible reversal of policy, carried out by extensive operations which have every appearance of being permanent because wise and advantageous for the doctors. The record discloses no threat or probability of resumption of the abandoned warfare against prepaid medical service and the contract practice it entails. We agree with the trial court that conduct discontinued in 1941 does not warrant the issuance of an injunction in 1949. *Industrial Assn.* v. *United States*, 268 U.S. 64, 84.

Appellees, in providing prepaid medical care, may engage in activities which violate the antitrust laws. They are now competitors in the field and restraints, if any are to be expected, will be in their methods of promotion and operation of their own prepaid plan. Our duty is to inquire whether any restraints have been proved of a character likely to continue if not enjoined.

Striking the events prior to 1941 out of the Government's case, except for purposes of illustration or background information, little of substance is left. The case derived its coloration and support almost entirely from the abandoned practices. It would prolong this opinion beyond useful length, to review evidentiary details peculiar to this case. We mention what appear to be some highlights.

Only the Multnomah County Medical Society resorted to expulsions of doctors because of contract-practice activities, and there have been no expulsions for such cause since 1941. There were hints in the testimony that Multnomah was reviving the expulsion threat a short time before this action was commenced, but nothing came of it, and what that Society might do within the limits of its own membership does not necessarily indicate a joint venture or conspiracy with other appellees.

Some emphasis is placed on a report of a meeting of the House of Delegates of the State Society at which it was voted that the "private patient status" policy theretofore applied to private commercial hospital association contracts be extended to the industrial and railroad type of contracts. Any significance of this provision seems neutralized by another paragraph in the same report, which reads: "A receipt should be furnished each patient at the time of each visit, as it is understood the [industrial and railroad plan] companies concerned will probably establish a program of reimbursement to the affected employees." That does not strike us as a threat to restrict the practice of industrial and railroad companies of reimbursing employees for medical expenses and we cannot say that any ambiguity was not properly resolved in appellees' favor by the trial court.

The record contains a number of letters from doctors to private associations refusing to accept checks directly from them. Some base refusal on a policy of their local medical society, others are silent as to reasons. Some may be attributed to the writers' personal resistance to dealing directly with the private health associations, for it is clear that many doctors objected to filling out the company forms and supplying details required by the associations, and preferred to confine themselves to direct dealing with the patient and leaving the patient to deal with the associations. Some writers may have mistaken or misunderstood the policy of local associations. Others may have avoided disclosure of personal opposition by the handy and impersonal excuse of association "policy." The letters have some evidentiary value, but it is not compelling and, weighed against the other post-1941 evidence, does not satisfy us that the trial court's findings are "clearly erroneous."

Since no concerted refusal to deal with private health associations has been proved, we need not decide whether it would violate the antitrust laws. We might observe in passing, however, that there are ethical considerations where the historic direct relationship between patient and physician is involved which are quite different than the usual considerations prevailing in ordinary commercial matters. This Court has recognized that forms of competition usual in the business world may be demoralizing to the ethical standards of a profession. *Semler* v. *Oregon State Board of Dental Examiners*, 294 U.S. 608.

Appellees' evidence to disprove conspiracy is not conclusive, is necessarily largely negative, but is too persuasive for us to say it was clear error to accept it. In 1948, 1,210 of the 1,660 licensed physicians in Oregon were members of the Oregon State Medical Society, and between January 1, 1947, and June 30, 1948, 1,085 Oregon doctors billed and received payment directly from the Industrial Hospital Association, only one of the several private plans operating in the State. Surely there was no effective boycott, and ineffectiveness, in view of the power over its members which the Government attributes to the Society, strongly suggests the lack of an attempt to boycott these private associations. A parade of local medical society members from all parts of the State, apparently reputable, credible, and informed professional men, testified that their societies now have no policy of discrimination against private health associations, and that no attempts are made to prevent

individual doctors from cooperating with them. Members of
the governing councils of the State and Multnomah County
Societies testified that since 1940 there have been no suggestions in their meetings of attempts to prevent individual doctors from serving private associations. The manager of Oregon
Physicians' Service testified that at none of the many meetings
and conferences of local societies attended by him did he hear
any proposal to prevent doctors from cooperation with private
plans.

If the testimony of these many responsible witnesses is given
credit, no finding of conspiracy to restrain or monopolize this
business could be sustained. Certainly we cannot say that the
trial court's refusal to find such a conspiracy was clearly
erroneous.

The other charge is that appellees conspired to restrain competition between the several doctor-sponsored organizations
within the State of Oregon. The charge here, as we understand
it from paragraph 33 (i) of the complaint, 95 F. Supp., at
124, is that Oregon Physicians' Service, the state-wide organization, and the county-medical-society-sponsored plans agreed
not to compete with one another. Apparently if a county was
provided with prepaid medical care by a local society, the
state society would stay out, or if the county society wanted
to inaugurate a local plan, the state society would withdraw
from the area.

This is not a situation where suppliers of commercial com-
modities divide territories and make reciprocal agreements to
exploit only the allotted market, thereby depriving allocated
communities of competition. This prepaid plan does not supply to, and its allocation does not withhold from, any community medical service or facilities of any description. No
matter what organization issues the certificate, it will be performed, in the main, by the local doctors. The certificate
serves only to prepay their fees. The result, if the state association should enter into local competition with the county

association, would be that the inhabitants could prepay medical services through either one of two medical society channels. There is not the least proof that duplicating sources of the prepaid certificates would make them cheaper, more available or would result in an improved service or have any beneficial effect on anybody. Through these nonprofit organizations the doctors of each locality, in practical effect, offer their services and hospitalization on a prepaid basis instead of on the usual cash fee or credit basis. To hold it illegal because they do not offer their services simultaneously and in the same locality through both a state and a county organization would be to require them to compete with themselves in sale of certificates. Under the circumstances proved here, we cannot regard the agreement by these nonprofit organizations not to compete as an unreasonable restraint of trade in violation of the Sherman Act.

With regard to this charge, the court found, "The sale of medical services, by Doctor Sponsored Organizations, as conducted within the State of Oregon, is not trade or commerce within the meaning of Section 1 of the Sherman Anti-Trust Law, nor is it commerce within the meaning of the constitutional grant of power to Congress 'To regulate Commerce . . . among the several States.'" 95 F. Supp., at 118. If that finding in both aspects is not to be overturned as clearly erroneous, it, of course, disposes of this charge, for if there was no restraint of interstate commerce, the conduct charged does not fall within the prohibitions of the Sherman Act.

Almost everything pointed to in the record by the Government as evidence that interstate commerce is involved in this case relates to across-state-line activities of the private associations. It is not proven, however, to be adversely affected by any allocation of territories by doctor-sponsored plans. So far as any evidence brought to our attention discloses, the activities of the latter are wholly intrastate. The Government did show that Oregon Physicians' Service made a number of payments to out-of-state doctors and hospitals, presumably for treatment of policyholders who happened to remove or temporarily to be away from Oregon when need for service arose. These were, however, few, sporadic and incidental. Cf. *Industrial Assn.* v. *United States, supra,* at 84.

American Medical Assn. v. *United States,* 317 U.S. 519, does not stand for the proposition that furnishing of prepaid medical care on a local plane is interstate commerce. That was a prosecution under § 3 of the Sherman Act of a conspiracy to restrain trade or commerce in the District of Columbia. Interstate commerce was not necessary to the operation of the statute there.

We conclude that the Government has not clearly proved its charges. Certainly the court's findings are not clearly erroneous. "A finding is 'clearly erroneous' when, although there is evidence to support it, the reviewing court on the entire evidence is left with the definite and firm conviction that a mistake has been committed." *United States* v. *United States Gypsum Co.,* 333 U.S. 364, 395. The Government's contentions have been plausibly and earnestly argued but the record does not leave us with any "definite and firm conviction that a mistake has been committed."

As was aptly stated by the New York Court of Appeals, although in a case of a rather different substantive nature: "Face to face with living witnesses the original trier of the facts holds a position of advantage from which appellate judges are excluded. In doubtful cases the exercise of his power of observation often proves the most accurate method of ascertaining the truth. . . . How can we say the judge is wrong? We never saw the witnesses. . . . To the sophistication and sagacity of the trial judge the law confides the duty of appraisal." *Boyd* v. *Boyd,* 252 N. Y. 422, 429, 169 N. E. 632, 634.

Affirmance is, of course, without prejudice to future suit if practices in conduct of the Oregon Physicians' Service or the county services, whether or not involved in the present action, shall threaten or constitute violation of the antitrust laws. Cf. *United States* v. *Reading Co.*, 226 U. S. 324, 373.

Judgment affirmed.

MR. JUSTICE BLACK is of opinion that the judgment below is clearly erroneous and should be reversed.

MR. JUSTICE CLARK took no part in the consideration or decision of this case.

OFF-THE-BENCH VIEWS

In the two off-the-bench statements that follow, Justices Black and Frankfurter—the leading modern exponents of, respectively, activism[83] and anti-activism—reveal their quite different views and assumptions as to the role of judges in a democratic society. The first statement is the printed version of a public interview of Mr. Justice Black by Professor Edmond Cahn. It is followed by the comments of a distinguished philosopher and anti-activist, Professor Sidney Hook.

The printed version of Mr. Justice Frankfurter's address to the American Philosophical Society is followed by the (earlier) comments of Walter Hamilton, a distinguished, pro-activist professor of law.

Mr. Justice Black
"The Judicial Process and the Bill of Rights"[84]

CAHN: Let me start by explaining the purpose of this interview. Two years ago, when you delivered your James Madison

---

[83] This, of course, and all of the material that follows was written before Mr. Justice Black's opinion in *Griswold,* above.

[84] This is the transcript of an interview on April 14, 1962, at the American Jewish Congress banquet in honor of Mr. Justice Black. It was published under the title, "Mr. Justice Black and First Amendment Absolutes: A Public Interview," in *New York University Law Review,* 37 (1962), 549, and is reproduced here with the permission of New York University, as copyright owner.

470 The Supreme Court: Law and Discretion

Lecture at New York University, you declared your basic attitude toward our Bill of Rights. This was the positive side of
your constitutional philosophy. Tonight I propose we bring
out the other side, that is, your answers to the people who
disagree with and criticize your principles. The questions I
will ask, most of them at least, will be based on the criticism.
As you know, I consider your answers so convincing that I
want the public to have them.

Suppose we start with one of the key sentences in your
James Madison Lecture where you said, "It is my belief that
there *are* 'absolutes' in our Bill of Rights, and that they were
put there on purpose by men who knew what words meant
and meant their prohibitions to be 'absolutes.'" Will you
please explain your reasons for this?

JUSTICE BLACK: My first reason is that I believe the words
do mean what they say. I have no reason to challenge the
intelligence, integrity or honesty of the men who wrote the
First Amendment. Among those I call the great men of the
world are Thomas Jefferson, James Madison, and various
others who participated in formulating the ideas behind the
First Amendment for this country and in writing it.

I learned a long time ago that there are affirmative and
negative words. The beginning of the First Amendment is that
"Congress shall make no law." I understand that it is rather
old-fashioned and shows a slight naïveté to say that "no law"
means no law. It is one of the most amazing things about the
ingeniousness of the times that strong arguments are made,
which *almost* convince me, that it is very foolish of me to think
"no law" means no law. But what it *says* is "Congress shall
make no law respecting an establishment of religion," and
so on.

I have to be honest about it. I confess not only that I think
the Amendment means what it says but also that I may be
slightly influenced by the fact that I do not think Congress
should make any law with respect to these subjects. That has

become a rather bad confession to make in these days, the confession that one is actually for something because he believes in it.

Then we move on, and it says "or prohibiting the free exercise thereof." I have not always exercised myself in regard to religion as much as I should, or perhaps as much as all of you have. Nevertheless, I want to be able to do it when I want to do it. I do not want anybody who is my servant, who is my agent, elected by me and others like me, to tell me that I can or cannot do it. Of course, some will remark that that is too simple on my part. To them, all this discussion of mine is too simple, because I come back to saying that these few plain words actually mean what they say, and I know of no college professor or law school professor, outside of my friend, Professor Cahn here, and a few others, who could not write one hundred pages to show that the Amendment does not mean what it says.

Then I move on to the words "abridging the freedom of speech or of the press." It *says* Congress shall make no law doing that. What it *means*—according to a current philosophy that I do not share—is that Congress shall be able to make just such a law unless we judges object too strongly. One of the statements of that philosophy is that if it shocks us too much, then they cannot do it. But when I get down to the really basic reason why I believe that "no law" means no law, I presume it could come to this, that I took an obligation to support and defend the Constitution as I understand it. And being a rather backward country fellow, I understand it to mean what the words say. Gesticulations apart, I know of no way in the world to communicate ideas except by words. And if I were to talk at great length on the subject, I would still be saying—although I understand that some people say that I just say it and do not believe it—that I believe when our Founding Fathers, with their wisdom and patriotism, wrote this Amendment, they knew what they were talking about.

They knew what history was behind them and they wanted to ordain in this country that Congress, elected by the people, should not tell the people what religion they should have or what they should believe or say or publish, and that is about it. It says "no law," and that is what I believe it means.

CAHN: Some of your colleagues would say that it is better to interpret the Bill of Rights so as to permit Congress to take what it considers reasonable steps to preserve the security of the nation even at some sacrifice of freedom of speech and association. Otherwise what will happen to the nation and the Bill of Rights as well? What is your view of this?

JUSTICE BLACK: I fully agree with them that the country should protect itself. It should protect itself in peace and in war. It should do whatever is necessary to preserve itself. But the question is: Preserve what? And how?

It is not very much trouble for a dictator to know how it is best to preserve his government. He wants to stay in power, and the best way to stay in power is to have plenty of force behind him. He cannot stay in power without force. He is afraid of too much talk; it is dangerous for him. And he should be afraid, because dictators do not have a way of contributing very greatly to the happiness, joy, contentment, and prosperity of the plain, everyday citizen. Their business is to protect themselves. Therefore, they need an army; they need to be able to stop people from talking; they need to have one religion, and that is the religion they promulgate. Frequently in the past it has been the worship of the dictator himself. To preserve a dictatorship, you must be able to stifle thought, imprison the human mind and intellect.

I want this Government to protect itself. If there is any man in the United States who owes a great deal to this Government, I am that man. Seventy years ago, when I was a boy, perhaps no one who knew me thought I would ever get beyond the confines of the small country county in which I was born. There was no reason for them to suspect that I would. But we had a free country and the way was open for me. The Government and the people of the United States have been good to me. Of course, I want this country to do what will preserve it. I want it to be preserved as the kind of Government it was intended to be. I would not desire to live at any place where my thoughts were under the suspicion of government and where my words could be censored by government, and where worship, whatever it was or wasn't, had to be determined by an officer of the government. That is not the kind of government I want preserved.

I agree with those who wrote our Constitution, that too much power in the hands of officials is a dangerous thing. What was government created for except to serve the people? Why was a Constitution written for the first time in this country except to limit the power of government and those who were selected to exercise it at the moment?

My answer to the statement that this Government should preserve itself is yes. The method I would adopt is different, however, from that of some other people. I think it can be preserved only by leaving people with the utmost freedom to think and to hope and to talk and to dream if they want to dream. I do not think this Government must look to force, stifling the minds and aspirations of the people. Yes, I believe in self-preservation, but I would preserve it as the Founders said, by leaving people free. I think here, as in another time, it cannot live half slave and half free.

CAHN: . . . In order to preserve the guaranteed freedom of the press, are you willing to allow sensational newspaper reports about a crime and about police investigation of the crime to go so far that they prejudice and inflame a whole state and thus deprive the accused of his right to a fair jury?

JUSTICE BLACK: The question assumes in the first place that a whole state can be inflamed so that a fair trial is not possible. On most of these assumptions that are made with reference to the dangers of the spread of information, I perhaps diverge at a point from many of those who disagree with my views. I have again a kind of old-fashioned trust in human beings. I learned it as a boy and have never wholly lost that faith.

I believe in trial by jury. Here again perhaps I am a literalist. I do not think that trial by jury is a perfect way of determining facts, of adjudicating guilt, or of adjudicating controversies. But I do not know of a better way. That is where I stand on that.

I do not think myself that anyone can say that there can be enough publicity completely to destroy the ideas of fairness in the minds of people, including the judges. One of the great things about trials by jury in criminal cases that have developed in this country—I refer to criminal cases because there is where most of the persecutions are found in connection with bringing charges against unpopular people or people in unpopular causes—we should not forget that if the jury happens to go wrong, the judge has a solemn duty in a criminal case not to let an unfair verdict stand. Also, in this country, an appellate court can hear the case.

I realize that we do not have cases now like the ones they had when William Penn was tried for preaching on the streets of London. The jury which was called in to send him off quickly to jail refused to do so, and suffered punishment from the judge because they would not convict a man for preaching on the streets. But that is a part of history, and it is but one of thousands of cases of the kind. Those people had publicity; that is why they would not convict William Penn. They knew, because the people had been talking, despite the fact that there was so much censorship then, that William Penn was being prosecuted largely because he was a dissenter from the orthodox views. So they stood up like men and would not convict. They lost their property, some of them their liberty. But they stood up like men.

I do not myself think that it is necessary to stifle the press in order to reach fair verdicts. Of course, we do not want juries to be influenced wrongfully. But with our system of education we should be in better condition than they were in those days in England, when they found that the jury was one of the greatest steps on their way to freedom. As a matter of fact, Madison placed trial by jury along with freedom of the press and freedom of conscience as the three most highly cherished liberties of the American people in his time.

I do not withdraw my loyalty to the First Amendment or say that the press should be censored on the theory that in order to preserve fair trials it is necessary to try the people of the press in summary contempt proceedings and send them to jail for what they have published. I want both fair trials and freedom of the press. I grant that you cannot get everything you want perfectly, and you never will. But you won't do any good in this country, which aspires to freedom, by saying just give the courts a little more power, just a little more power to suppress the people and the press, and things will be all right. You just take a little chunk off here and a little bit there. I would not take it off anywhere. I believe that they meant what they said about freedom of the press just as they meant what they said about establishment of religion, and I would answer this question as I have answered the other one.

CAHN: Do you make an exception in freedom of speech and press for the law of defamation? That is, are you willing to allow people to sue for damages when they are subjected to libel or slander?

JUSTICE BLACK: My view of the First Amendment, as originally ratified, is that it said Congress should pass none of these kinds of laws. As written at that time, the Amendment applied only to Congress. I have no doubt myself that the provision, as written and adopted, intended that there should be no libel or defamation law in the United States under the United States Government, just absolutely none so far as I am concerned.

That is, no federal law. At that time—I will have to state this in order to let you know what I think about libel and defamation—people were afraid of the new Federal Government. I hope that they have not wholly lost that fear up to this time because, while government is a wonderful and an essential thing in order to have any kind of liberty, order or peace, it has such power that people must always remember to check them here and balance them there and limit them here in order to see that you do not lose too much liberty in exchange for government. So I have no doubt about what the Amendment intended. As a matter of fact, shortly after the Constitution was written, a man named St. George Tucker, a great friend of Madison's, who served as one of the commissioners at the Annapolis Convention of 1786 which first attempted to fill the need for a national constitution, put out a revised edition of Blackstone. In it he explained what our Constitution meant with reference to freedom of speech and press. He said there was no doubt in his mind, as one of the earliest participants in the development of the Constitution, that it was intended that there should be no libel under the laws of the United States. Lawyers might profit from consulting Tucker's edition of Blackstone on that subject.

As far as public libel is concerned, or seditious libel, I have been very much disturbed sometimes to see that there is present an idea that because we have had the practice of suing individuals for libel, seditious libel still remains for the use of government in this country. Seditious libel, as it has been put into practice throughout the centuries, is nothing in the world except the prosecution of people who are on the wrong side politically; they have said something and their group has lost and they are prosecuted. Those of you who read the newspaper see that this is happening all over the world now, every week somewhere. Somebody gets out, somebody else gets in, they call a military court or a special commission, and they try him. When he gets through sometimes he is not living.

My belief is that the First Amendment was made applicable to the states by the Fourteenth. I do not hesitate, so far as my own view is concerned, as to what should be and what I hope will sometime be the constitutional doctrine that just as it was not intended to authorize damage suits for mere words as distinguished from conduct as far as the Federal Government is concerned, the same rule should apply to the states.

I realize that sometimes you have a libel suit that accomplishes some good. I practiced law twenty years. I was a pretty active trial lawyer. The biggest judgment I ever got for a libel was $300. I never took a case for political libel because I found out that Alabama juries, at least, do not believe in political libel suits and they just do not give verdicts. I knew of one verdict given against a big newspaper down there for $25,000, and the Supreme Court of Alabama reversed it. So even that one did not pan out very well.

I believe with Jefferson that it is time enough for government to step in to regulate people when they *do* something, not when they *say* something, and I do not believe myself that there is *any* halfway ground if you enforce the protections of the First Amendment.

CAHN: Would it be constitutional to prosecute someone who falsely shouted "fire" in a theater?

JUSTICE BLACK: I went to a theater last night with you. I have an idea if you and I had gotten up and marched around that theater, whether we said anything or not, we would have been arrested. Nobody has ever said that the First Amendment gives people a right to go anywhere in the world they want to go or say anything in the world they want to say. Buying the theater tickets did not buy the opportunity to make a speech there. We have a system of property in this country which is also protected by the Constitution. We have a system of property, which means that a man does not have a right to do anything he wants anywhere he wants to do it. For instance, I would feel a little badly if somebody were to try to come into my house and tell me that he had a constitutional right to come in there because he wanted to make a speech against the Supreme Court. I realize the freedom of people to make a speech against the Supreme Court, but I do not want him to make it in my house.

That is a wonderful aphorism about shouting "fire" in a crowded theater. But you do not have to shout "fire" to get arrested. If a person creates a disorder in a theater, they would get him there not because of *what* he hollered but because he *hollered*. They would get him not because of any views he had but because they thought he did not have any views that they wanted to hear there. That is the way I would answer: not because of what he shouted but because he shouted.

CAHN: Is there any kind of obscene material, whether defined as hard-core pornography or otherwise, the distribution and sale of which can be constitutionally restricted in any manner whatever, in your opinion?

JUSTICE BLACK: I will say it can in this country, because the courts have held that it can.

CAHN: Yes, but you won't get off so easily. I want to know what you think.

JUSTICE BLACK: My view is, without deviation, without exception, without any ifs, buts, or whereases, that freedom of speech means that you shall not do something to people either for the views they have or the views they express or the words they speak or write.

There is strong argument for the position taken by a man whom I admire very greatly, Dr. Meiklejohn, that the First Amendment really was intended to protect *political* speech, and I do think that was the basic purpose; that plus the fact that they wanted to protect *religious* speech. Those were the two main things they had in mind.

It is the law that there can be an arrest made for obscenity. It was the law in Rome that they could arrest people for obscenity after Augustus became Caesar. Tacitus says that then it became obscene to criticize the Emperor. It is not any trouble to establish a classification so that whatever it is that you do not want said is within that classification. So far as I am concerned, I do not believe there is any halfway ground for protecting freedom of speech and press. If you say it is half free, you can rest assured that it will not remain as much as half free. Madison explained that in his great Remonstrance when he said in effect, "If you make laws to force people to speak the words of Christianity, it won't be long until the same power will narrow the sole religion to the most powerful sect in it." I realize that there are dangers in freedom of speech, but I do not believe there are any halfway marks.

CAHN: Do you subscribe to the idea involved in the clear and present danger rule?

JUSTICE BLACK: I do not.

CAHN: By way of conclusion, Justice Black, would you kindly summarize what you consider the judge's role in cases arising under the First Amendment and the Bill of Rights?

JUSTICE BLACK: The Bill of Rights to me constitutes the difference between this country and many others. I will not attempt to say most others or nearly all others or all others. But I will say it constitutes the difference to me between a free country and a country that is not free.

My idea of the whole thing is this: There has been a lot of trouble in the world between people and government. The people were afraid of government; they had a right to be afraid. All over the world men had been destroyed—and when I say "government" I mean the individuals who actually happened to be in control of it at the moment, whether they were elected, whether they were appointed, whether they got there with the sword, however they got there—the people always had a lot of trouble because power is a heady thing, a dangerous thing. There have been very few individuals in the history of the world who could be trusted with complete, unadulterated, omnipotent power over their fellowmen.

Millions of people have died throughout the world because of the evils of their governments. Those days had not wholly passed when the Pilgrims came over to this country. Many of them had suffered personally. Some of them had their ears cut off. Many of them had been mutilated. Many of their ancestors had. Some of your ancestors came here to get away from persecution. Certainly, mine did.

There had been struggles throughout the ages to curb the dangerous power of governors. Rome had a sound government at one time. Those who study it carefully will find that, except for the slave class, they had, so far as most of the people were concerned, a good form of government. But it turned, and then they had Augustus and the other Caesars, and the Neros and Caligulas and Tiberiuses.

One of the interesting things about Tiberius is that in all the history I have read he is about the only man of great prominence who ever defended informers. He made the statement that the informers were the guardians of Rome. Recently I have heard that said here once or twice.

When our ancestors came over here and started this country, they had some more persecutions of their own. It was not limited to any one religion. A lot of my Baptist brethren got into trouble; a lot of the Methodist brethren got into trouble; a lot of the Episcopal Church got in trouble, the Congregational Church—each of them in turn. A lot of the Catholics got in trouble. Whichever sect was in control in a state for a time, they would say that the others could not hold office, which is an easy way of getting rid of your adversaries if you can put it over. Even for half a century after the Constitution was adopted, some of the states barred the members of certain faiths from holding office.

Throughout all of this—as the Jewish people know as well as any people on earth—persecutions were abroad everywhere in the world. A man never knew, when he got home, whether his family would be there, and the family at home never knew whether the head of the family would get back. There was nothing strange about that when Hitler did it. It was simply a repetition of the course of history when people get too much power.

I like what the Jewish people did when they took what amounted to a written constitution. Some of the states did it before the time of the Federal Constitution; they adopted written constitutions. Why? Because they wanted to mark boundaries beyond which government could not go, stripping people of their liberty to think, to talk, to write, to work, to be happy.

So we have a written Constitution. What good is it? What good is it if, as some judges say, all it means is: "Government, you can still do this unless it is so bad that it shocks the conscience of the judges." It does not say that to me. We have certain provisions in the Constitution which say, "Thou shalt not." They do not say, "You can do this unless it offends the sense of decency of the English-speaking world." They do not say that. They do not say, "You can go ahead and do this unless it is offensive to the universal sense of decency." If they did, they would say virtually nothing. There would be no definite, binding place, no specific prohibition, if that were all it said.

I believe with Locke in the system of checks and balances. I do not think that the Constitution leaves any one department of government free without there being a check on it somewhere. Of course, things are different in England; they do have unchecked powers, and they also have a very impressive history. But it was *not* the kind of history that suited the people that formed our Constitution. Madison said that explicitly when he offered the Bill of Rights to the Congress. Jefferson repeated it time and time again. Why was it not? Because it left Parliament with power to pass such laws as it saw fit to pass. It was not the kind of government they wanted. So we have a Bill of Rights. It is intended to see that a man cannot be jerked by the back of the neck by any government official; he cannot have his home invaded; he cannot be picked up legally and carried away because his views are not satisfactory to the majority, even if they are terrible views, however bad they may be. Our system of justice is based on the assumption that men can best work out their own opinions, and that they are not under the control of government. Of course, this is particularly true in the field of religion, because a man's religion is between himself and his Creator, not between himself and his government.

I am not going to say any more except this: I was asked a question about preserving this country. I confess I am a complete chauvinist. I think it is the greatest country in the world. I think it is the greatest because it has a Bill of Rights. I think it could be the worst if it did not have one. It does not take a nation long to degenerate. We saw, only a short time ago, a neighboring country where people were walking the streets in reasonable peace one day and within a month we saw them marched to the back of a wall to meet a firing squad without a trial.

I am a chauvinist because this country offers the greatest opportunities of any country in the world to people of every kind, of every type, of every race, of every origin, of every religion—without regard to wealth, without regard to poverty. It offers an opportunity to the child born today to be reared among his people by his people, to worship his God, whatever his God may be, or to refuse to worship anybody's God if that is his wish. It is a free country; it will remain free only, however, if we recognize that the boundaries of freedom are not so flexible; they are not made of mush. They say, "Thou shalt not," and I think that is what they mean.

Now, I have read that every sophisticated person knows that you cannot have any absolute "thou shalt nots." But you know when I drive my car against a red light, I do not expect them to turn me loose if I can prove that though I was going across that red light, it was not offensive to the so-called "universal sense of decency." I have an idea there are some absolutes. I do not think I am far in that respect from the Holy Scriptures.

The Jewish people have had a glorious history. It is wonderful to think about the contributions that were made to the world from a small, remote area in the East. I have to admit that most of my ideas stem basically from there.

It is largely because of these same contributions that I am here tonight as a member of what I consider the greatest Court in the world. It is great because it is independent. If it were not independent, it would not be great. If all nine of those men came out each Monday morning like a phonograph speaking one voice, you could rest assured it would not be independent. But it does not come that way. I want to assure you that the fact that it does not come that way does not mean that there is not a good, sound, wholesome respect on the part of every justice for every other justice.

I do hope that this occasion may cause you to think a little more and study a little more about the Constitution, which is the source of your liberty; no, not the source—I will take that back—but a protection of your liberty. Yesterday a man sent me a copy of a recent speech entitled "Is the First Amendment Obsolete?" The conclusion of the writer, who is a distinguished law school dean, was that the Amendment no longer fits the times and that it needs to be modified to get away from its rigidity. The author contends that the thing to do is to take the term "due process of law" and measure everything by that standard, "due process of law"meaning that unless a law is so bad that it shocks the conscience of the Court, it cannot be unconstitutional. I do not wish to have to pass on the laws of this country according to the degree of shock I receive! Some people get shocked more readily than others at certain things. I get shocked pretty quickly, I confess, when I see—and this I say with trepidation because it is considered bad to admit it—but I do get shocked now and then when I see some gross injustice has been done, although I am solemnly informed that we do not sit to administer justice, we sit to administer law in the abstract.

I am for the First Amendment from the first word to the last. I believe it means what it says, and it says to me, "Government shall keep its hands off religion. Government shall not attempt to control the ideas a man has. Government shall not attempt to establish a religion of any kind. Government shall not abridge freedom of the press or speech. It shall let anybody talk in this country." I have never been shaken in the faith that the American people are the kind of people and have the kind of loyalty to their government that we need not fear the talk of Communists or of anybody else. Let them talk! In the American way, we will answer them.

Sidney Hook

Commentary on Mr. Justice Black[85]

. . . Since Black insists upon his words being taken in the same literal sense with which he believes he interprets the words of the Constitution, readers whose minds have not been drugged by rhetoric will find his views startling both for their intellectual simplicity and practical extremism. . . . For Justice Black would strip American citizens of any legal protection against every form of slander, libel and defamation, no matter how grave and irreparable the consequent damage to life, limb, property and reputation. The very foundations of civil society —and not merely of democratic society, whose viability depends more than any other on certain standards of public virtue—would collapse if speech which falsely charged citizens with murder, theft, rape, arson and treason was regarded as

---

[85] Sidney Hook, " 'Lord Monboddo' and the Supreme Court," *The New Leader* (May 13, 1963), 11–15. Reprinted by permission.

public discussion and hence privileged under the law.

It may be instructive to examine the assumptions from which Justice Black derives his position. Most jurists are very sensitive to the charge of absolutism, for an absolutist, like a fanatic, is one who refuses to test his principles in the light of reason and experience, and explore alternatives to what may be no more than arbitrary prejudices tricked out as self-evident axioms or convictions. Justice Black, however, is proud of his absolutism with respect to the Bill of Rights. The starting point of his public colloquy is the emphatic reassertion that there are 'absolutes' in our Bill of Rights and that they were put there on purpose by men who knew what words meant and meant their prohibitions to be 'absolutes.' "

Now there are obvious and elementary difficulties with the notion of rights being so absolute that they can never be legitimately abridged. The first difficulty is that it makes intellectually incoherent the acceptance of certain laws whose justice is acknowledged even by alleged believers in absolute rights. For example, the First Amendment forbids the making of any law "prohibiting the free exercise" of religion. As everyone knows, some religions involve morally objectionable practices ranging from polygamy to human sacrifice, all of which are forbidden by law. Simple consistency would require absolutists to deny to Congress or any other legislative body the right to proscribe the exercise of such religions. But as far as I know all absolutists, on the bench or off, approve of these laws.

This difficulty in the absolutists' position, although formidable, is not insuperable. For theoretically the absolutist of religious freedom can always abandon his rejection of inhuman or morally objectionable religious practices and in principle declare for the toleration of any religious practice. Cicero somewhere asserts that there is no absurdity to which some human beings will not resort to defend another absurdity. Those who make an absolute of the free exercise of religion or any other right will not necessarily be brought up short by the realization of the absurdity of their position if they are prepared to swallow all its consequences.

The second elementary difficulty with the doctrine of absolute rights, however, *is* insuperable. One of the commonest experiences in life is the conflict of rights. But if rights are absolute how can there be more than one of them? In this respect, rights are like the obligation to keep a promise. If promises conflict, how can we believe that *all* promises must be kept? Suppose the right to speak interferes, as it very well might, with the free exercise of someone else's religion—which one must be abridged? Or suppose, to relate the discussion to Justice Black's own text, that freedom of speech or press conflicts with a man's right to a fair trial?

Justice Black explicitly states that he wants "both fair trials and freedom of the press." He agrees with Madison that "trial by jury along with freedom of the press and freedom of conscience [are] the three most highly cherished liberties of the American people." Very well. What happens when a newspaper publishes, or a station broadcasts, so highly inflammatory an account of a crime and of an arrested suspect that it prejudices the latter's right to a fair trial by a jury? Black's reply to the question is that this *never* occurs. He does not believe it possible for a state to be so inflamed by press or radio as to prejudice a man's right to a fair trial. I think his reply is irrelevant because it avoids giving a direct answer to the hypothetical question. Even if we did not know of a situation in which a conflict like this has arisen, we could easily conceive of one. Which right should yield?

But we do not have to conceive of such a situation as if it were merely a fancied possibility. Very often motions for a change of venue are granted, among other reasons, on the ground that press reports have been prejudicial to the defendant. A newspaper often has state-wide circulation, and a radio station frequently reaches an audience in every village and hamlet in a state. Black's reply seems blithe as well as irrelevant because it substitutes his subjective impression for an entire encyclopedia of authenticated facts in legal history.

"I do not think myself," he says, "that anyone can say there can be enough publicity completely to destroy the ideas of fairness in the minds of people, including judges." Note the use of the word "completely." What can be established "completely" in law or life? If only one man remains unprejudiced by an incendiary editorial urging that a defendant be legally lynched, does that mean that a fair trial is possible? One or more persons may be unprejudiced and yet every person on the jury as well as the judge may have been profoundly influenced by tendentious press or radio reports.

A trial is unfair even if only some member or members of a jury have been prejudiced by what they have read. The wisdom of the law has no place for complete or final or absolute proof in matters of this sort. It recognizes that even when a man's very life is at stake we cannot forego reaching a verdict merely because the conclusion is less than certain. It is sufficient to reach conclusions that are beyond reasonable doubt. There are many cases in which there can be no reasonable doubt that the press treatment of a crime and of a suspect has prejudiced the defendant's right to a fair trial. When that happens, which of the two freedoms in conflict should be abridged?

An idea becomes a dogma when it blinds one to the facts of experience. The more important the recognition of these facts is to the intelligent defense of human liberty, the more dangerous these dogmas become. Were Black's position to become the dominant view of the United States Supreme Court, its effects on the already irresponsible practices of the sensationalist press in reporting criminal cases would be fearful to contemplate. The English public is far freer from racial, religious and sectional prejudice than the American public. Yet everyone knows how jealously the rights of a defendant in a criminal case are safeguarded in England. Neither the press nor the radio feels muzzled because its freedom to comment on a criminal case before the verdict is rendered is not absolute.

Justice Black refuses to admit the possibility that freedom of speech may conflict with the right to a fair trial. Nonetheless, his altogether unconvincing attempt to explain away the conflict reveals that despite what he says, he does *not* believe in the absolute right to a fair trial. In cases of actual conflict he would rule, apparently on purely *a priori* grounds, that the right to speech or press must be upheld whatever its consequences for other rights, especially the right of an individual not to be prejudged by his judges.

This creates another difficulty for him even more obvious and formidable than the ones we have considered. In developing their doctrine of "clear and present danger" as a rule which governs limitations on speech and press, Justice Holmes and Brandeis were wont to use some specific illustrations which have until now seemed very plausible to common sense. Black has no use for the doctrine of "clear and present danger," but he recognizes one of Holmes' illustrations as a challenge to his position. In his famous opinion in *Schenck* v. *U.S.*, Holmes wrote: "The most stringent protection of free speech would not protect a man in falsely shouting 'fire' in a theatre, and causing a panic." The illustration has become a paradigm case of the kind of speech which is not legally protected and morally should not be.

Justice Black's friendly questioner, Professor Edmond Cahn, with this paradigm case in mind, asked him: "Would it be constitutional to prosecute someone who falsely shouted 'fire' in a theatre?" To which Justice Black replied affirmatively but *not* for the reasons Holmes gives. Such a man would be prosecuted, he asserts, "not because of what he shouted but because he shouted." Black explains:

"Nobody has ever said that the First Amendment gives people a right to go anywhere in the world they want to go or say anything in the world they want to say. Buying theatre tickets did not buy the opportunity to make a speech there. We have a system of property in this country which is also protected by the Constitution. . . .

"That is a wonderful aphorism about shouting 'fire' in a crowded theatre. But you do not have to shout 'fire' to get arrested. If a person creates a disorder in a theatre, they would get him there not because of *what* he hollered but because he *hollered*." (Italics in original.)

. . . [Mr. Justice Black] seems unaware of the fact that he has breached the absoluteness of the right to speak when its exercise interferes with the right to property which, as he reminds us, is also protected by the Constitution. Holmes' rule limits freedom of speech when it incites to illegal violence or when it threatens life, as does the false cry of "fire" in the theater. Justice Black apparently would limit freedom of speech only when its expression is a trespass on private property. It is a fair inference from his dissenting opinion in *Yates vs. United States* that he would not penalize speech about a public issue which incites to an illegal action like lynching. ("I believe," he wrote, "that the First Amendment forbids Congress to punish people for talking about public affairs, whether or not such discussion incites to action legal or illegal.") But is not the right to life more precious than the right to property and the right to speech?

Mr. Justice Frankfurter
"The Judicial Process and the Supreme Court"[86]

Those who know tell me that the most illuminating light on painting has been furnished by painters, and that the deepest

---

[86] This paper appeared under a different title in *Proceedings of the American Philosophical Society*, 98 (1954), 233. It is reproduced here with the permission of the American Philosophical Society, as copyright holder.

revelations on the writing of poetry have come from poets. It is not so with the business of judging. The power of searching analysis of what it is that they are doing seems rarely to be possessed by judges, either because they are lacking in the art of critical exposition or because they are inhibited from practicing it. The fact is that pitifully little of significance has been contributed by judges regarding the nature of their endeavor, and, I might add, that which is written by those who are not judges is too often a confident caricature rather than a seer's vision of the judicial process of the Supreme Court.

We have, of course, one brave and felicitous attempt—Mr. Justice Cardozo's little classic. I have read and reread, and reread very recently, that charming book and yield to no one in my esteem for it. And yet you must not account it as immodesty or fractiousness if I say that the book would give me very little help in deciding any of the difficult cases that come before the Court. Why should a book about the judicial process by one of the great judges of our time shed relatively little light on the actual adjudicatory process of the Supreme Court? For the simple reason that *The Nature of the Judicial Process* derived from Cardozo's reflections while in Albany, before he came to Washington. The judicial business out of which Cardozo's experience came when he wrote the book was the business of the New York Court of Appeals, and that is very different business from the most important aspects of the litigation on which the Supreme Court must pass.

Let me indulge in one of the rare opportunities for the valid use of statistics in connection with the work of the Supreme Court. The reports of the New York decisions for the year during which Judge Cardozo delivered the lectures which comprise his book show that only about one out of a hundred cases before the New York Court of Appeals raised questions comparable to those that gave him most trouble in Washington. The year that he left Albany for Washington, 1932, only two opinions out of a hundred in the New York Reports raise the kind of questions that are the greatest concern for the Supreme Court. Cardozo wrote something like five hundred opinions on the New York Court of Appeals. In them he was concerned with matters that would not have been foreign, say, to Lord Mansfield or Lord Ellenborough, and would have been quite familiar to Cardozo's contemporaries on the English Supreme Court of Judicature.

After Cardozo came to Washington, he wrote 128 opinions for the Court during the tragically short period that fate allowed him there. He wrote twenty-one dissents. Of these 149 opinions only ten dealt with matters comparable to those which came before him while on the New York Court of Appeals. No one was more keenly aware than he of the differences between the two streams of litigation; no one more keenly alive than he to the resulting differences in the nature of the judicial process in which the two courts were engaged. Let me quickly add that such were the genius and the learning and, perhaps most important of all, the priestlike disinterestedness of his mind, that, even during his few brief years as a Justice, Cardozo became an outstanding contributor to the history of Supreme Court adjudication. What is relevant to our immediate purpose is realization of the important fact that the problems dealt with in Cardozo's illuminating little book, and in two other little books which played on the same theme, derive from an experience in the raw materials of the adjudicatory process very different from those that are the most anxious concern of the Supreme Court of the United States.

It is time for me to be explicit. I am advised by an arithmetically minded scholar that the Constitution of the United States is composed of some 6,000 words. Not every provision of that document that becomes controversial can come before the Supreme Court for adjudication. The questions that are not meet for judicial determination have elicited their own body of literature. A hint of the nature of such questions is given by their fair characterization as an exercise of judicial self-limitation. This area constitutes one very important and very troublesome aspect of the Court's functioning—its duty not to decide.

Putting to one side instances of this judicial self-restraint, De Tocqueville showed his characteristic discernment when he wrote: "Scarcely any political question arises in the United States that is not resolved sooner or later into a judicial question." (1 *Democracy in America* [Bradley ed., 1948], p. 280.) Those provisions of the Constitution that do raise justiciable issues vary in their incidence from time to time. The construction of all of them, however, is related to the circumambient condition of our Constitution—that our nation is a federalism. The most exacting problems that in recent years have come before the Court have invoked two provisions expressed in a few undefined words—the clause giving Congress power to regulate commerce among the States and the Due Process Clauses of the Fifth and Fourteenth Amendments.

A federalism presupposes the distribution of governmental powers between national and local authority. Between these two authorities there is shared the power entirely possessed by a unitary state. In addition to the provisions of our Constitution making this distribution of authority between the two governments, there is also in the United States Constitution a withdrawal of power from both governments, or, at least, the exercise of governmental power is subject to limitations protective of the rights of the individual. Of the two types of constitutional provision calling for construction from case to case, the limitation in the interest of the individual presents the most delicate and most pervasive of all issues to come before the Court, for these cases involve no less a task than the accommodation by a court of the interest of an individual over against the interest of society.

Human society keeps changing. Needs emerge, first vaguely felt and unexpressed, imperceptibly gathering strength, steadily becoming more and more exigent, generating a force which, if left unheeded and denied response so as to satisfy the impulse behind it at least in part, may burst forth with an intensity that exacts more than reasonable satisfaction. Law as the response to these needs is not merely a system of logical deduction, though considerations of logic are far from irrelevant. Law presupposes sociological wisdom as well as logical unfolding. The nature of the interplay of the two has been admirably conveyed, if I may say so, by Professor Alfred North Whitehead:

> "It is the first step in sociological wisdom, to recognize that the major advances in civilization are processes which all but wreck the societies in which they occur:—like unto an arrow in the hand of a child. The art of free society consists first in the maintenance of the symbolic code; and secondly in fearlessness of revision, to secure that the code serves those purposes which satisfy an enlightened reason. Those societies which cannot combine reverence to their symbols with freedom of revision, must ultimately decay either from anarchy, or from the slow atrophy of a life stifled by useless shadows." (Whitehead, *Symbolism* [1927], p. 88.)

The Due Process Clauses of our Constitution are the vehicles for giving response by law to this felt need by allowing accommodations or modifications in the rules and standards that govern the conduct of men. Obviously, therefore, due process as a concept is neither fixed nor finished.

The judgment of history on the inherently living and therefore changing applicability of due process was thus pronounced by Mr. Justice Sutherland, one of the most traditionally minded of judges:

> "Regulations, the wisdom, necessity and validity of which, as applied to existing conditions, are so apparent that they are now uniformly sustained, a century ago, or even half a century ago,

probably would have been rejected as arbitrary and oppressive."
(*Village of Euclid* v. *Ambler Realty Co.*, 272 U.S. 365, 387.)

A more expansive attempt at indicating the viable function
of the guarantee of due process was made in a recent opinion:

> "The requirement of 'due process' is not a fair-weather or
> timid assurance. It must be respected in periods of calm and in
> times of trouble; it protects aliens as well as citizens. But 'due
> process,' unlike some legal rules, is not a technical conception
> with a fixed content unrelated to time, place and circumstances.
> Expressing as it does in its ultimate analysis respect enforced by
> law for that feeling of just treatment which has been evolved
> through centuries of Anglo-American constitutional history and
> civilization, 'due process' cannot be imprisoned within the
> treacherous limits of any formula. Representing a profound atti-
> tude of fairness between man and man, and more particularly
> between the individual and government, 'due process' is com-
> pounded of history, reason, the past course of decisions, and
> stout confidence in the strength of the democratic faith which
> we profess. Due process is not a mechanical instrument. It is not
> a yardstick. It is a process. It is a delicate process of adjustment
> inescapably involving the exercise of judgment by those whom
> the Constitution entrusted with the unfolding of the process."
> (*Joint Anti-Fascist Refugee Committee* v. *McGrath*, 341 U.S. 123,
> 162–163, concurring opinion.)

This conception of due process meets resistance from what
has been called our pigeonholing minds, which seek to rest un-
inquiringly on formulas—phrases which, as Holmes pointed
out long ago, "by their very felicity delay further analysis,"
and often do so for a long time. This is, of course, a form of
intellectual indulgence, sometimes called the law of imitation.
"[T]raditions which no longer meet their original end" must
be subjected to the critique of history whereby we are enabled
"to make up our minds dispassionately whether the survival
which we are enforcing answers any new purpose when it

has ceased to answer the old." (Holmes, *Collected Legal Papers* [1920], p. 225.)

But a merely private judgment that the time has come for a shift of opinion regarding law does not justify such a shift. Departure from an old view, particularly one that has held unquestioned sway, "must be duly mindful of the necessary demands of continuity in a civilized society. A reversal of a long current of decisions can be justified only if rooted in the Constitution itself as an historic document designed for a developing nation." (*Graves* v. *N. Y. ex rel. O'Keefe*, 306 U.S. 466, 487–488, concurring opinion.) It makes an important difference, of course, if the validity of an old doctrine on which decisions were based was always in controversy and so did not embed deeply and widely in men's feelings justifiable reliance on the doctrine as part of the accepted outlook of society. What is most important, however, is that the Constitution of the United States, except in what might be called the skeleton or framework of our society—the anatomical as against the physiological aspects,—"was designed for a developing nation." As to those features of our Constitution which raise the most frequent perplexities for decision by the Court, they were drawn in many particulars with purposeful vagueness so as to leave room for the unfolding but undisclosed future.

At this point one wishes there were time to document these generalizations with concrete instances which would help to define the problem and illustrate generalities from which the Court starts and differences of opinion which naturally enough arise in their application. Such documentation would expose divergencies by which common starting points lead to different destinations because of differences in emphasis and valuation in the process of reasoning. They would also shed some light on the interplay between language and thought. Differences in style eventually may embody differences of content, just as a sonnet may sometimes focus thought more trenchantly than a diffuse essay.

The other major source of puzzling problems is the Commerce Clause. With us the Commerce Clause is perhaps the most fruitful and important means for asserting national authority against the particularism of state policy. The role of the Court in striking the balance between the respective spheres of federal and state power was thus adumbrated by the Court:

> "The interpenetrations of modern society have not wiped out state lines. It is not for us to make inroads upon our federal system either by indifference to its maintenance or excessive regard for the unifying forces of modern technology. Scholastic reasoning may prove that no activity is isolated within the boundaries of a single State, but that cannot justify absorption of legislative power by the United States over every activity. On the other hand, the old admonition never becomes stale that this Court is concerned with the bounds of legal power and not with the bounds of wisdom in its exercise by Congress. When the conduct of an enterprise affects commerce among the States is a matter of practical judgment, not to be determined by abstract notions. The exercise of this practical judgment the Constitution entrusts primarily and very largely to the Congress, subject to the latter's control by the electorate. Great power was thus given to the Congress: the power of legislation and thereby the power of passing judgment upon the needs of a complex society. Strictly confined though far-reaching power was given to this Court: that of determining whether the Congress has exceeded limits allowable in reason for the judgment which it has exercised. To hold that Congress could not deem the activities here in question to affect what men of practical affairs would call commerce, and to deem them related to such commerce merely by gossamer threads and not by solid ties, would be to disrespect the judgment that is open to men who have the constitutional power and responsibility to legislate for the Nation." (*Polish National Alliance* v. *Labor Board*, 322 U.S. 643, 650–651.)

The problems which the Commerce Clause raises as a result of the diffusion of power between a national government and its constituent parts are shared in variant forms by Canada, Australia, and India. While the distribution of powers between each national government and its parts varies, leading at times to different legal results, the problems faced by the United States Supreme Court under the Commerce Clause are not different in kind, as are the problems of judicial review under the Due Process Clause, from those which come before the Supreme Court of Canada and the High Court of Australia.

Judicial judgment in these two classes of the most difficult cases must take deep account, if I may paraphrase Maitland, of the day before yesterday in order that yesterday may not paralyze today, and it must take account of what it decrees for today in order that today may not paralyze tomorrow.

A judge whose preoccupation is with such matters should be compounded of the faculties that are demanded of the historian and the philosopher and the prophet. The last demand upon him—to make some forecast of the consequences of his action—is perhaps the heaviest. To pierce the curtain of the future, to give shape and visage to mysteries still in the womb of time, is the gift of imagination. It requires poetic sensibilities with which judges are rarely endowed and which their education does not normally develop. These judges, you will infer, must have something of the creative artist in them; they must have antennae registering feeling and judgment beyond logical, let alone quantitative, proof.

The decisions in the cases that really give trouble rest on judgment, and judgment derives from the totality of a man's nature and experience. Such judgment will be exercised by two types of men, broadly speaking, but of course with varying emphasis—those who express their private views or revelations, deeming them, if not *vox dei*, at least *vox populi;* or those who feel strongly that they have no authority to promulgate law by their merely personal view and whose whole training and proved performance substantially insure that their conclusions reflect understanding of, and due regard for, law as the expression of the views and feelings that may fairly be deemed representative of the community as a continuing society.

Judges are men, not disembodied spirits. Of course a judge is not free from preferences or, if you will, biases. But he may deprive a bias of its meretricious authority by stripping it of the uncritical assumption that it is founded on compelling reason or the coercive power of a syllogism. He will be alert to detect that though a conclusion has a logical form it in fact represents a choice of competing considerations of policy, one of which for the time has won the day.

An acute historian recently concluded that those "who have any share of political power . . . usually obtain it because they are exceptionally able to emancipate their purposes from the control of their unformulated wishes and impressions." (Richard Pares, "Human Nature in Politics—III," *The Listener*, Dec. 17, 1953, p. 1037.) For judges, it is not merely a desirable capacity "to emancipate their purposes" from their private desires; it is their duty. It is a cynical belief in too many quarters, though I believe this cult of cynicism is receding, that it is at best a self-delusion for judges to profess to pursue disinterestedness. It is asked with sophomoric brightness, does a man cease to be himself when he becomes a Justice? Does he change his character by putting on a gown? No, he does not change his character. He brings his whole experience, his training, his outlook, his social, intellectual, and moral environment with him when he takes a seat on the supreme bench. But a judge worth his salt is in the grip of his function. The intellectual habits of self-discipline which govern his mind are as much a part of him as the influence of the interest he may have represented at the bar, often much more so. For example, Mr. Justice Bradley was a "corporation lawyer" par excellence when he went on the Court. But his decisions on matters affecting corporate control in the years following the Civil War were strikingly free of bias in favor of corporate power.

To assume that a lawyer who becomes a judge takes on

the bench merely his views on social or economic questions leaves out of account his rooted notions regarding the scope and limits of a judge's authority. The outlook of a lawyer fit to be a Justice regarding the role of a judge cuts across all his personal preferences for this or that social arrangement. The conviction behind what John Adams wrote in the provision of the Massachusetts Declaration of Rights regarding the place of the judiciary in our governmental scheme, and the considerations which led the framers of the Constitution to give federal judges life tenure and other safeguards for their independence, have, I believe, dominated the outlook and therefore the action of the generality of men who have sat on the Supreme Court. Let me recall the Massachusetts Declaration:

> "It is essential to the preservation of the rights of every individual, his life, liberty, property, and character, that there be an impartial interpretation of the laws, and administration of justice. It is the right of every citizen to be tried by judges as free, impartial, and independent as the lot of humanity will admit. . . ." (Article XXIX.)

Need it be stated that true humility and its offspring, disinterestedness, are more indispensable for the work of the Supreme Court than for a judge's function on any other bench? These qualities alone will not assure another indispensable requisite. This is the capacity for self-searching. What Jacques Maritain said in another connection applies peculiarly to members of the Supreme Court. A Justice of that Court cannot adequately discharge his function "without passing through the door of the knowing, obscure as it may be, of his own subjective." (Maritain, *Creative Intuition in Art and Poetry* [1953], p. 114.)

This is not to say that the application of this view of the judge's function—that he is there not to impose his private views upon society, that he is not to enforce personalized justice—assures unanimity of judgments. Inevitably there are bound to be fair differences of opinion. And it would be pretense to deny that in the self-righteous exercise of this role obscurantist and even unjustifiable decisions are sometimes rendered. Why should anyone be surprised at this? The very nature of the task makes some differences of view well-nigh inevitable. The answers that the Supreme Court is required to give are based on questions and on data that preclude automatic or even undoubting answers. If the materials on which judicial judgments must be based could be fed into a machine so as to produce ineluctable answers, if such were the nature of the problems that come before the Supreme Court and such were the answers expected, we would have IBM machines doing the work instead of judges.

"How amazing it is that, in the midst of controversies on every conceivable subject, one should expect unanimity of opinion upon difficult legal questions! In the highest ranges of thought, in theology, philosophy and science, we find differences of view on the part of the most distinguished experts,—theologians, philosophers and scientists. The history of scholarship is a record of disagreements. And when we deal with questions relating to principles of law and their application, we do not suddenly rise into a stratosphere of icy certainty." (Address by Mr. Chief Justice Hughes, 13 *American Law Institute Proceedings* [1936], pp. 61, 64.)

The core of the difficulty is that there is hardly a question of any real difficulty before the Court that does not entail more than one so-called principle. Anybody can decide a question if only a single principle is in controversy. Partisans and advocates often cast a question in that form, but the form is deceptive. In a famous passage Mr. Justice Holmes has exposed this misconception:

"All rights tend to declare themselves absolute to their logical extreme. Yet all in fact are limited by the neighborhood of principles of policy which are other than those on which the particular right is founded, and which become strong enough to hold their own when a certain point is reached. . . . The boundary at which the conflicting interests balance cannot be determined by any general formula in advance, but points in the line, or helping to establish it, are fixed by decisions that this or that concrete case falls on the nearer or father side." (*Hudson County Water Co.* v. *McCarter*, 209 U.S. 349, 355.)

This contest between conflicting principles is not limited to law. In a recent discussion of two books on the conflict between the claims of literary individualism and dogma, I came across this profound observation: "But when, in any field of human observation, two truths appear in conflict it is wiser to assume that neither is exclusive, and that their contradiction, though it may be hard to bear, is part of the mystery of things." ("Literature and Dogma," *Times Literary Supplement* [London], Jan. 22, 1954, p. 51.) But judges cannot leave such contradiction between two conflicting "truths" as "part of the mystery of things." They have to adjudicate. If the conflict cannot be resolved, the task of the Court is to arrive at an accommodation of the contending claims. This is the core of the difficulties and misunderstandings about the judicial process. This, for any conscientious judge, is the agony of his duty.[87]

Walton Hamilton
Commentary on Mr. Justice Frankfurter[88]

A mythology has been created in defense of the lapse of the Court from the great tradition of the law. It is that the two

---

[87] For a more direct "response" by the Court and Mr. Justice Frankfurter to Mr. Justice Black's "absolutist" view of the First Amendment, see the excerpt from the *Beauharnais* case and related text, above (pp. 26–29).

[88] Walton Hamilton, book review, *Yale Law Journal*, 56 (September 1947), 1459–1460. Reprinted with permission. The premise of Mr. Hamilton's observations may be found in his view that "As procedure is the instrument, not the master of law; so law is the instrument, not the master of justice."

wings of the present Court represent an "activist" and a "legal" attack upon the cases. Thus Black, Douglas, Murphy and Rutledge, JJ., play their economic preferences, while Vinson, Frankfurter, Jackson and Burton, JJ., are content to sit back and refer the cases to "the law." . . . It does have a bit of oblique truth; for Douglas, Black, *et al.* have competence in the discussion of substantive questions, while Frankfurter chooses to operate in the procedural field where he has confidence in his own footing. . . . If a shift is made from the rhetoric in which they are cast to the rationale of decision, the difference in motivation between the two groups fades. Frankfurter affects a lack of concern for the "end product"; yet his votes are to be predicted in terms of the end product. You can almost always tell where he is coming out; yet not even the faithful can tell in advance how his stand is to be legalized. Frankfurter spurns "policy" and professes to lay the law down on the line. Yet he usually gets to the same place as Jackson whose law is not unspotted by the world. . . .

. . . It was the law journals, reversing the decisions of the Supreme Court, which led the fight on the Old Court. The nine young men have been subjected to no such critical and disinterested bombardment. A host of truths, quite ugly truths, need to be spoken. It does no good to impute personal blame. Mr. Justice Frankfurter has no feel for the dominant issues; he operates best when weaving crochet patches of legalism on the fingers of the case. He does the best he can, often very well indeed, with the techniques in which he is proficient; it is a calamity that his skills happen to be petty skills. He is the victim of a bad legal education; but the Court has no business allowing him to select, from all the issues the case holds, the question upon which it must turn. . . .

EPILOGUE

Thurman Arnold
The Rule of Law[89]

Without a constant and sincere pursuit of the shining but never completely attainable ideal of the rule of law above men, of "reason" above "personal preference," we would not have a civilized government. If that ideal be an illusion, to dispel it would cause men to lose themselves in an even greater illusion: the illusion that personal power can be benevolently exercised. Unattainable ideals have far more influence in moulding human institutions toward what we want them to be than any practical plan for the distribution of goods and services by executive [or judicial] fiat.

Mr. Justice Jackson
The Court as a Political Institution[90]

Of course, it would be nice if there were some authority to make everybody do the things we ought to have done and leave undone the things we ought not to have done. But are the courts the appropriate catch-all into which every such problem should be tossed?

---

[89] Thurman Arnold, "Professor Harts' Theology," *Harvard Law Review*, 73 (1960), 1311.

[90] Robert H. Jackson, *The Court in the American System of Government* (Cambridge, Mass.: Harvard University Press, 1955), p. 53.

SELECTED BIBLIOGRAPHY

BICKEL, A. M. *The Least Dangerous Branch.* Indianapolis: The Bobbs-Merrill Company, Inc., 1962.

BLACK, C. *The People and the Court.* New York: Macmillan Company, 1960.

CARDOZO, B. N. *The Nature of the Judicial Process.* New Haven: Yale University Press, 1921.

CHAFEE, Z. "Do Judges Make or Discover Law?", *Proceedings of the American Philosophical Society,* 91 (1947), 405–420.

CURTIS, C. P. *Law As Large As Life.* New York: Simon and Schuster, 1959.

FRANK, J. P. *Marble Palace: The Supreme Court in American Life.* New York: Alfred A. Knopf, 1958.

FRANK, J. P. *Mr. Justice Black: The Man and His Opinions.* New York: Alfred A. Knopf, 1948.

FREUND, P. A. *The Supreme Court of the United States.* Cleveland: The World Publishing Company, 1961.

HAND, L. *The Bill of Rights.* Cambridge: Harvard University Press, 1958.

HENKIN, L. "Some Reflections on Current Constitutional Controversy," *University of Pennsylvania Law Review,* 109 (1961), 637–662.

JAFFE, L. L. "The Judicial Universe of Mr. Justice Frankfurter," *Harvard Law Review,* 62 (1949), 357–412.

McCLOSKEY, R. G. *The American Supreme Court.* Chicago: The University of Chicago Press, 1960.

505

MENDELSON, W. *Justices Black and Frankfurter: Conflict in the Court.* 2nd ed. Chicago: The University of Chicago Press, 1966.

MILLER, A. S. and HOWELL, R. F. "The Myth of Neutrality in Constitutional Adjudication," University of Chicago Law Review, 27 (1960), 661–695.

PRITCHETT, C. H. *The American Constitution.* New York: Mc-Graw-Hill Book Company, 1959.

REICH, C. A. "Mr. Justice Black and the Living Constitution," *Harvard Law Review,* 76 (1963), 673–754.

ROSTOW, E. V. *The Sovereign Prerogative.* New Haven: Yale University Press, 1962.

SCIGLIANO, R. *The Courts: A Reader in the Judicial Process.* Boston: Little, Brown and Company, 1962.

SWISHER, C. B. *The Supreme Court in Modern Role.* New York: New York University Press, 1958.

THOMAS, H. S. *Felix Frankfurter: Scholar on the Bench.* Baltimore: The Johns Hopkins Press, 1960.

WECHSLER, H. "Toward Neutral Principles of Constitutional Law," Harvard Law Review, 73 (1959), 1–35.

INDEX

°Indicates references appearing in both original and documental material.